WAYS OF KNOWING

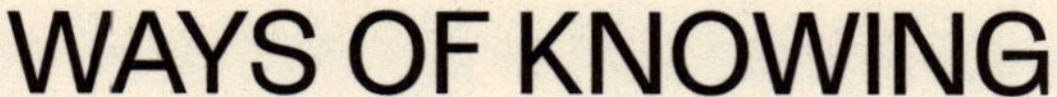
WAYS OF KNOWING

# WAYS OF KNOWING

WAYS OF KNOWING Edited by Rosario Güiraldes. Walker Art Center, Minneapolis

The artists' entries are written by Brandon Eng (BE) and Laurel Rand-Lewis (LRL).

FOREWORD As a contemporary arts institution dedicated to showcasing the art and ideas of our time, the Walker Art Center has made group exhibitions of living artists one of the central threads of its exhibition program. These presentations serve as platforms to introduce our audiences to a diverse assortment of talented artists and to offer a perspective on how artists of today are thinking and working. *Ways of Knowing*, a group exhibition featuring eleven artists working across various mediums, aligns with this mandate. It joins a rich history of exhibitions such as *No Place Like Home* (1997), *Painting at the Edge of the World* (2001), *How Latitudes Become Form* (2003), *Brave New Worlds* (2007), and *The Quick and the Dead* (2009).

Presenting artworks by a multigenerational group of artists hailing from various parts of the world, *Ways of Knowing* spans mediums, including drawing, photography, video, and large-scale installation. The exhibition examines the narratives and possibilities that artists infuse into cultural artifacts and histories, thus arguing for art's potential as a vehicle for knowing. Curator Rosario Güiraldes has meticulously curated a selection of artworks that is both focused and expansive, drawing on her previous work and on the art historian Claire Bishop's recent essay "Information Overload," published in the April 2023 issue of *Artforum*. Bishop suggests that the knowledge that artists produce is derived not from objective, scientifically proven facts but through their embodiment and unique way of assimilating information.

Contemporary group exhibitions, with their complex nature as well as their significant logistical demands, present unique challenges to curators and institutions. In her first major exhibition since joining the Walker Art Center, Güiraldes, with the support of curatorial assistant Brandon Eng, has organized a show that not only addresses important themes in contemporary art discourse but also brings to our community a compelling group of artworks, many of which are being shown in the United States for the first time. We are grateful for the participation of the institutional and private lenders who have generously contributed works to this presentation: Leopold Oetker; Forge Project Collection, traditional lands of the Moh-He-Con-Nuck; Gwangju National Museum, Korea; Michael Hershaft; Kutxa Fundazioa Bilduma, Donostia/San Sebastián, Spain; and several lenders who wish to remain anonymous. The realization of this exhibition is made possible with funding from several Walker patrons. I extend my gratitude to Kevin, Rosemary, and Hannah Rose McNeely for their significant support of this exhibition through the KHR McNeely Family Fund. I also thank the Martin and Brown Foundation and Walker trustee Jennifer Martin for generously supporting this exhibition and many other Walker projects. It is my pleasure to thank Lewis Baskerville for his commitment to this exhibition and to thank Rosina Lee Yue for her underwriting of this catalogue. In addition, I want to acknowledge the Andrew W. Mellon Foundation's grant in support of Walker publications.

I thank the Walker's Board of Trustees, who are central in supporting the vision of our institution. I am also grateful for the dedication and collaboration of the Walker's senior leadership team, whose contributions have been indispensable in bringing *Ways of Knowing* to fruition at the Walker. Special acknowledgment goes to Aslı Altay, head of content and communications; Felice Clark, director of business development; Amanda Hunt, head of public engagement, learning, and impact; Henriette Huldisch, chief curator and director of curatorial affairs; Jaidyn Martin, director of human resources; Keith Parker, director of operations; Christopher Stevens, chief of advancement; and Kim Taylor, chief financial officer. While I name these institutional leaders, am grateful to the entirety of the Walker's talented staff, whose unwavering commitment to realizing our institution's artistic program at the highest level is truly commendable.

Finally, I would like to convey our profound admiration and heartfelt thanks to the artists represented in the exhibition. *Ways of Knowing* arrives amid far-reaching technological transformations and shifts in ideology that are necessitating a reevaluation of our relationship to knowledge. In today's landscape we are constantly bombarded by information and often find ourselves navigating social media platforms that both obscure truths and reinforce existing beliefs. The artworks on view in *Ways of Knowing* resonate deeply with the current moment by being rooted in personal and idiosyncratic subject matter, thus highlighting the validity of the subjective lens in approaching the unknown. The exhibition encourages us to reflect on what art can teach us about our relationship to knowledge and the ways in which we come to know what we know.

Mary Ceruti
Executive Director
Walker Art Center

## ACKNOWLEDGMENTS

*Ways of Knowing* emerged from a convergence of my personal interests and a commitment to the immediacy and dynamism that exhibitions focusing on diverse, multigenerational groups of artists have historically brought to the Walker Art Center. The project not only engages with the institution's rich history of presenting experimental and thought-provoking exhibitions but also seeks to push those boundaries by striving to examine relevant ideas within contemporary art discourse. In line with past exhibitions such as *The Quick and the Dead* (2009), *9 Artists* (2014), *The Body Electric* (2019), and *The Paradox of Stillness: Art, Object, and Performance* (2021), *Ways of Knowing* delves into themes that have long been central to my work. It grapples with the evolving role of research as a method within artistic practices, its aesthetics and display mechanisms, art's elusiveness of meaning notwithstanding, and the deeply personal spaces that artists carve out within their practices.

My own expectations for this project were fueled by the efforts of numerous individuals within and beyond the Walker Art Center who contributed to envisioning this exhibition and publication and bringing them to fruition. Foremost among them are the artists themselves—Iosu Aramburu, Sammy Baloji, Anna Boghiguian, Cabello/Carceller, Chang Yuchen, Petrit Halilaj, Sky Hopinka, Christine Howard Sandoval, Eduardo Navarro, Gala Porras-Kim, and Rose Salane—whose creative insights and contributions profoundly influenced my perspective. My conversations with many of them early in the process were instrumental in shaping the direction of the project. Additionally, I am indebted to Nicolás Guagnini for serving as an ongoing interlocutor, providing me with sharp insight and advice at numerous junctures in the development of this project, and for agreeing to comoderate the roundtable discussion included in this volume. I also thank Claire Bishop, whose essay in the April 2023 issue of *Artforum* ignited a spark that got me thinking, and Cuauhtémoc Medina, who almost a decade ago gave me the opportunity to organize an exhibition that is undoubtedly related to this one. I thank both of them, too, for sharing their various perspectives on the ideas underpinning this show in the roundtable discussion, which further informed the conception of this exhibition.

I am deeply grateful to Leopold Oetker; Forge Project Collection, traditional lands of the Moh-He-Con-Nuck; Leeum Museum of Art, Seoul; Michael Hershaft; Kutxa Fundazioa Bilduma, Donostia/San Sebastian, Spain; and several lenders who wish to remain anonymous, who generously shared works from their collections for this exhibition. Among the many who helped facilitate *Ways of Knowing*, special thanks go to Livia Benavides of 80m2 Livia Benavides, Lima, Peru; Vanessa Carlos, Taber Colletti, and Robert Hodge of Carlos/Ishikawa, London; Jennifer Chert and Florian Lüdde of ChertLüdde, Berlin; Young Chung and Kibum Kim of Commonwealth and Council, Los Angeles; Carolina Repetto of Cosmic (Eduardo Navarro) Studio; Galerie Imane Farès; José Kuri, Mónica Manzutto, and Alexander Ferrando of kurimanzutto, New York and Mexico City; Gena Lee, Jinyoung Oh, and Jaeyeol Kim of the Leeum Museum of Art, Seoul; Emma-Charlotte Gobry-Laurencin and Alexandra Khazina of Mennour, Paris; Josh Milani and Georgia Boe of Milani Gallery, Brisbane, Australia; Mu.ZEE, Ostend, Belgium; Adelina Vlas, Noor Alé, and Julie Anne of the Power Plant, Toronto; Serena Rota, Martina Pelacchi, Sholem Krishtalka, Christina Stathakopoulou, Ferdinand Pechmann, and Vanina Saracino of Studio Petrit Halilaj; Minne De Meyer Engelbeen and Marek Szponik of Twenty Nine Studio & Production; Amber Rose Brown; and Jaime Skolfield. I join our director, Mary Ceruti, in thanking the generous funders, acknowledged on page 10, who helped make this exhibition possible. Their commitment and support are tremendously appreciated.

Over the years the Walker Art Center has earned a reputation for serving as a petri dish for artists and curators alike, an endeavor made possible by a dedicated team of individuals who infuse their passion and skills into every single project the institution undertakes. Spearheaded by the visionary leadership of executive director Mary Ceruti, the Walker continues to champion boundary-pushing exhibitions that are brought into existence with extreme care, thoughtfulness, and professionalism. I extend my sincere gratitude to Mary Ceruti and to Henriette Huldisch, chief curator and director of curatorial affairs, for encouraging me to embark on an exhibition of this kind upon my arrival in Minneapolis. They were unwavering in their support and trust in my vision from the early stages of this project, even before the exhibition's concept had fully crystallized. I must especially thank curatorial assistant, visual arts, Brandon Eng, who in addition to lending the whole gamut of his skills to this project, was a generous thought partner and infused our daily work with a sense of curiosity, excitement, and rigor. Brandon and curatorial fellow, visual arts, Laurel Rand-Lewis wrote the artists' entries for this catalogue, and I'm grateful to both of them for the care and enthusiasm they brought into that task. Additionally, I would like to acknowledge senior curator and director of visual arts Siri Engberg, whose expertise and wealth of institutional knowledge proved invaluable throughout the exhibition's development, and to Pablo de Ocampo, director and curator of moving image, and Janine DeFeo, manager of interpretation, whose insightful perspectives and artist recommendations expanded the exhibition's scope and helped me approach my ideas differently.

The Walker's design department is renowned for creating some of the best exhibition publications, and it was a pleasure to collaborate with Mark Owens, design director, and designer Brian Huddleston for the first time. Mark provided invaluable counsel, and Brian lent his extensive experience in and passion for book design and typography, creating a typeface for this project and designing a catalogue that skillfully expresses the concept of this exhibition. I extend my sincerest gratitude to Jake Yuzna, content producer, for guiding this publication and ensuring that the project stayed on track. Enormous thanks also to our editor, Karen Jacobson, for her thoughtful and meticulous work on the texts featured in this book. Karen's contributions went beyond her role; she generously engaged in a dialogue as I developed my thinking and ideas.

Having significant and complex artworks shipped from multiple locations as far afield as Seoul and Vancouver would not have been possible without the efforts of registrar Jessica Rolland. Her experience and organizational acumen were critical in ensuring the successful outcome of this project, and her baked goods provided much-needed sustenance and motivation through various stages of the exhibition's development. The exhibition also involved one major commissioned work realized in the Twin Cities, which was made possible under the guidance of Doc Czypinski, associate director, exhibition installation, and Peter Hannah, the exhibition's lead preparator, with the Walker's legendary crew: Kirk McCall, Peter Murphy, David Dick, Joel Schwarz, and many more. In addition to fulfilling all our production needs, the crew took on the heroic task of bringing this exhibition to life on a miraculous timeline, demonstrating that their reputation is well deserved. I extend my sincere gratitude to Joe King, director of collections and exhibitions management; Sarah Lampen, associate director of learning and accessibility; and Janine DeFeo, manager of interpretation, for their guidance in ensuring that this exhibition, too, was safe, accessible, meaningful, and clear to all our visitors. Sarah Lampen; Amanda Hunt, head of public engagement, learning, and impact (PELI); Megan Leafblad, associate director, PELI; La'Kayla Williams, manager of school and gallery programs, PELI; Leia Wambach, manager of youth programs, PELI; Hannah Novillo, manager of lifelong learning and accessibility, PELI; Sierra Ikwe Edwards, community engagement coordinator, PELI; and Elizabeth MacNally, associate director of event productions, were extraordinary collaborators in the realization and activation of Eduardo Navarro's commissioned work through the partnership with local stakeholders.

For her exceptional handling of all budget and contract-related matters as well as for her meticulous planning and tracking of our exhibition milestones, I thank Erin McNeil, manager of curatorial affairs. Lena Menefee-Cook, department coordinator, visual arts, coordinated artist travel plans and many other exhibition-related matters with efficiency and expertise and, together with Jessica Hakala, department coordinator for PELI; Hania Imdad, department coordinator for curatorial affairs; and Hannah Goldfarb, marketing and PR coordinator, provided invaluable support in managing countless other details.

Mounting a group exhibition of this kind requires significant resources, and I am deeply grateful for the tireless and out-of-the-box fundraising efforts of Christopher Stevens, chief of advancement; Marla Stack, director of major giving and institutional relations; and Megan Dunn, Kevin Curran, and Michelle Poss, gift officers. Their diligence, commitment, and creative fundraising strategies played a pivotal role in securing the necessary funding to realize this exhibition.

Our exhibitions and programs are able to reach diverse local, national, and international audiences thanks to the stalwart efforts of our communications and content team. I gratefully acknowledge Aslı Altay, head of content and public relations; Nathan Gould, director of marketing and public relations; Rachel Joyce, associate director of public relations; and Alina Sumajin, PAVE Communications and Consulting. Their hard work and dedication ensured that this exhibition resonated with a wide variety of audiences worldwide.

I would like to express my heartfelt gratitude to my family—María, Pedro, and Isabel and María, Fernando, and Amalia—for their unwavering support and encouragement as I continue to pursue my dreams and passions. Their love and constant presence have been a source of strength since I left Buenos Aires more than a decade ago, most recently as I embarked on this new journey in the Midwest. Lastly, I owe the deepest of thanks to Michael Rashkow, my most generous and patient interlocutor, a conscientious sounding board for all my ideas, and a constant source of joy in my life.

Rosario Güiraldes
Curator of Visual Arts
Walker Art Center

IOSU ARAMBURU *Atlas of Andean Modernism*, 2022–, printed paper, taped to the wall; number of pages variable, 8½ × 11 in. (21.6 × 27.9 cm) each sheet; wall: 93 in. (236.2 cm) high, courtesy the artist and 80m2 Livia Benavides Gallery, Lima, Peru

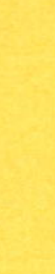

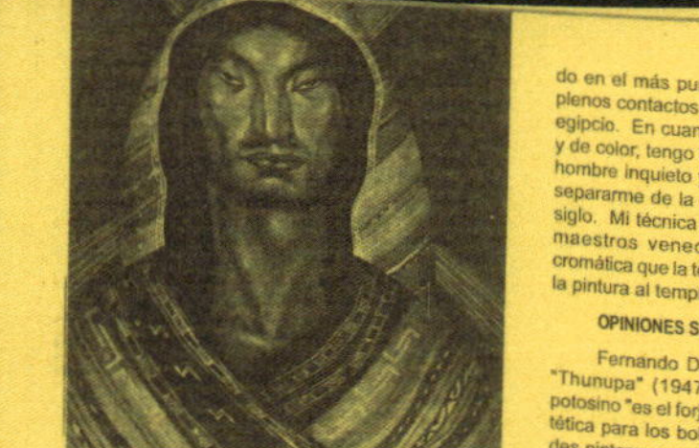



1.1



1.2

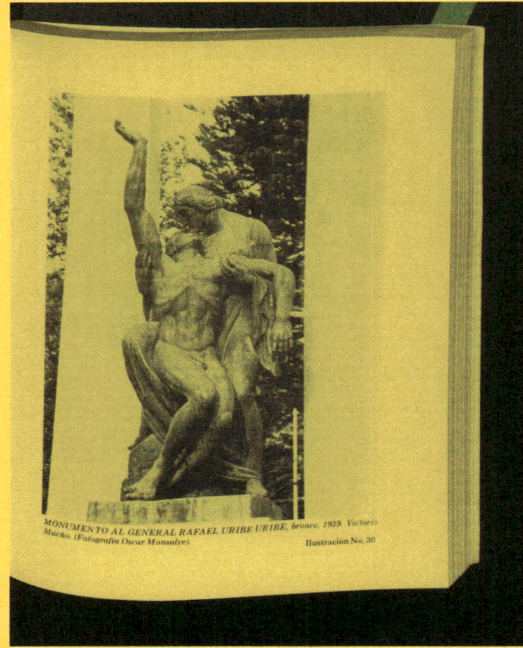



1.3

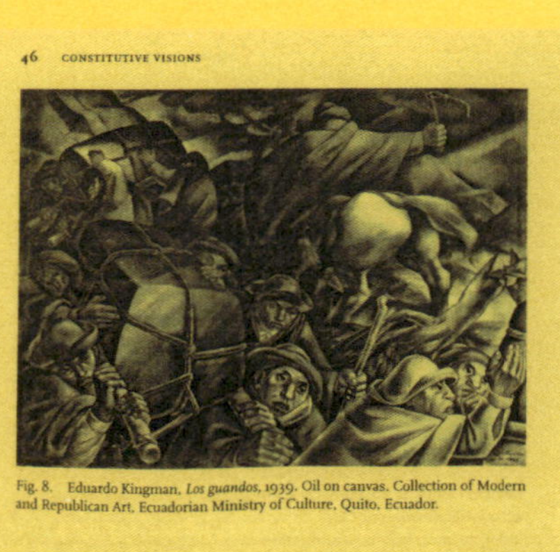



1.4

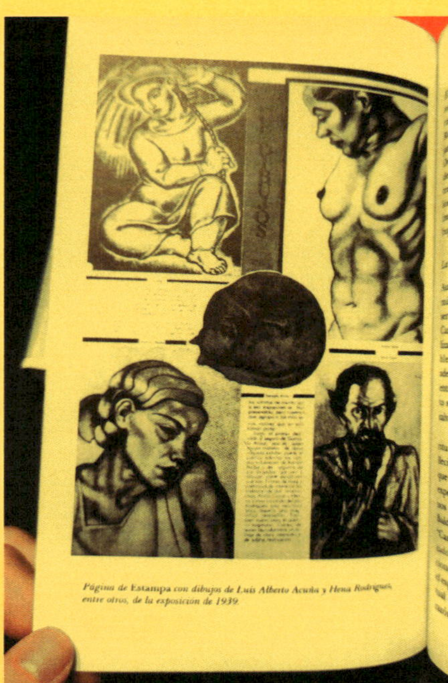



1.5

# Iosu Aramburu

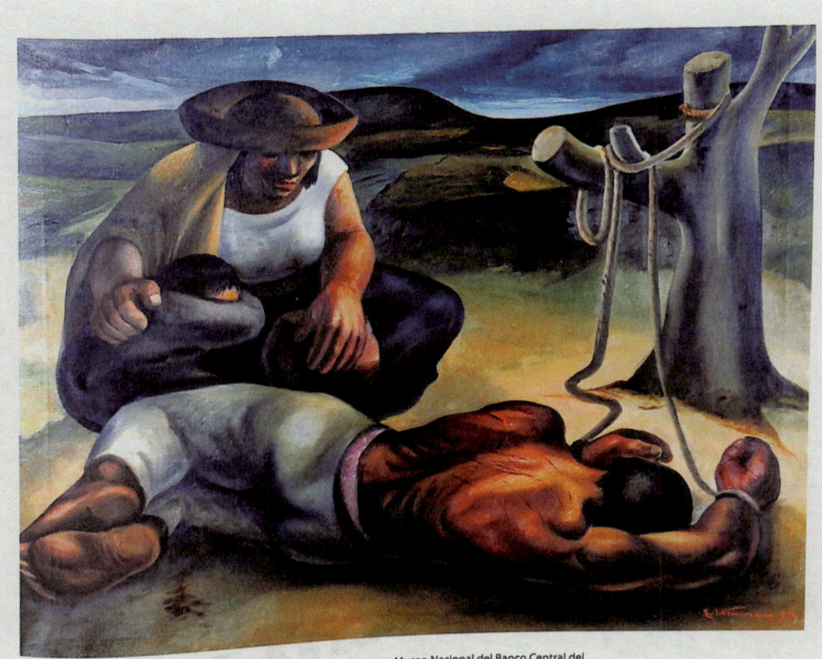

Figure 64 / Eduardo Kingman, *Flagelo* (The Whipping), oil on canvas, 1939. Museo Nacional del Banco Central del Ecuador.

was inspired by seventeenth-century paintings of the Flagellation of Christ (fig. 65), like the one at the Convento de San Francisco. The stormy sky, desolate landscape, and symbolic dead tree to which the flagellated indigenous figure is bound with heavy rope all recall viceregal images of Christ's torment. The figure lies prone, close to the picture plane, exposing his wounds to the viewer. Kneeling at his feet, the bat-

To New York and Back Again 147

1.6

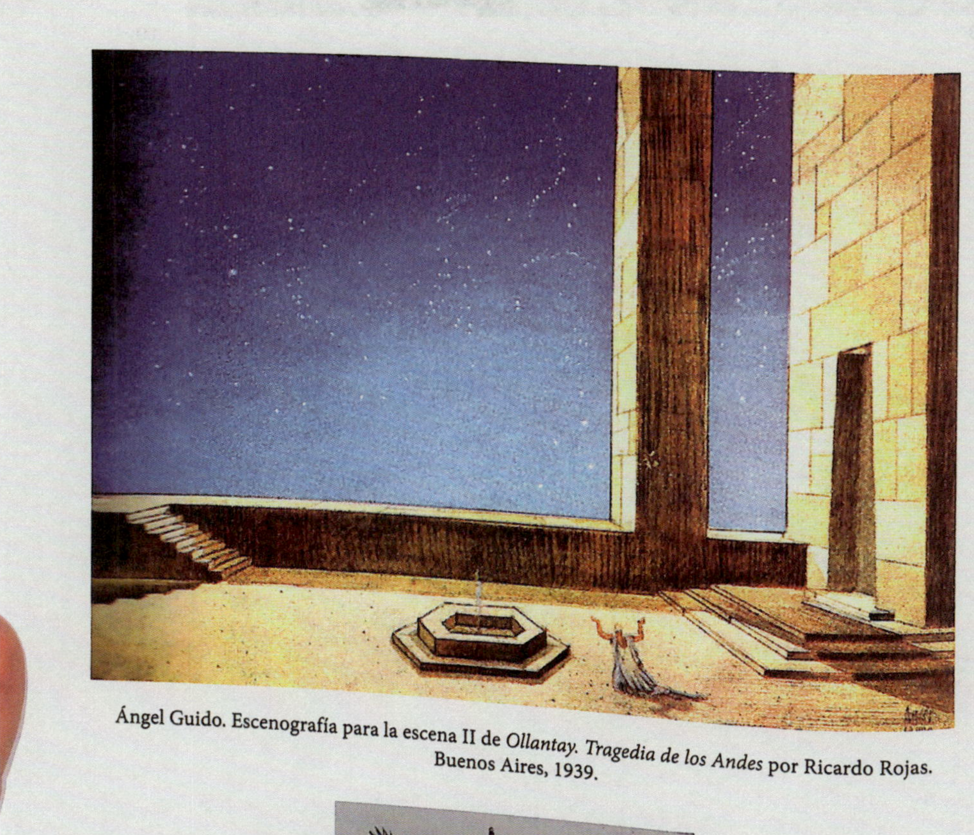

Ángel Guido. Escenografía para la escena II de *Ollantay. Tragedia de los Andes* por Ricardo Rojas. Buenos Aires, 1939.

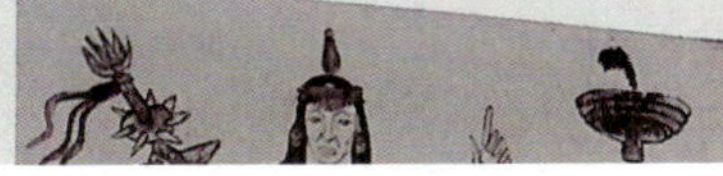

1.7

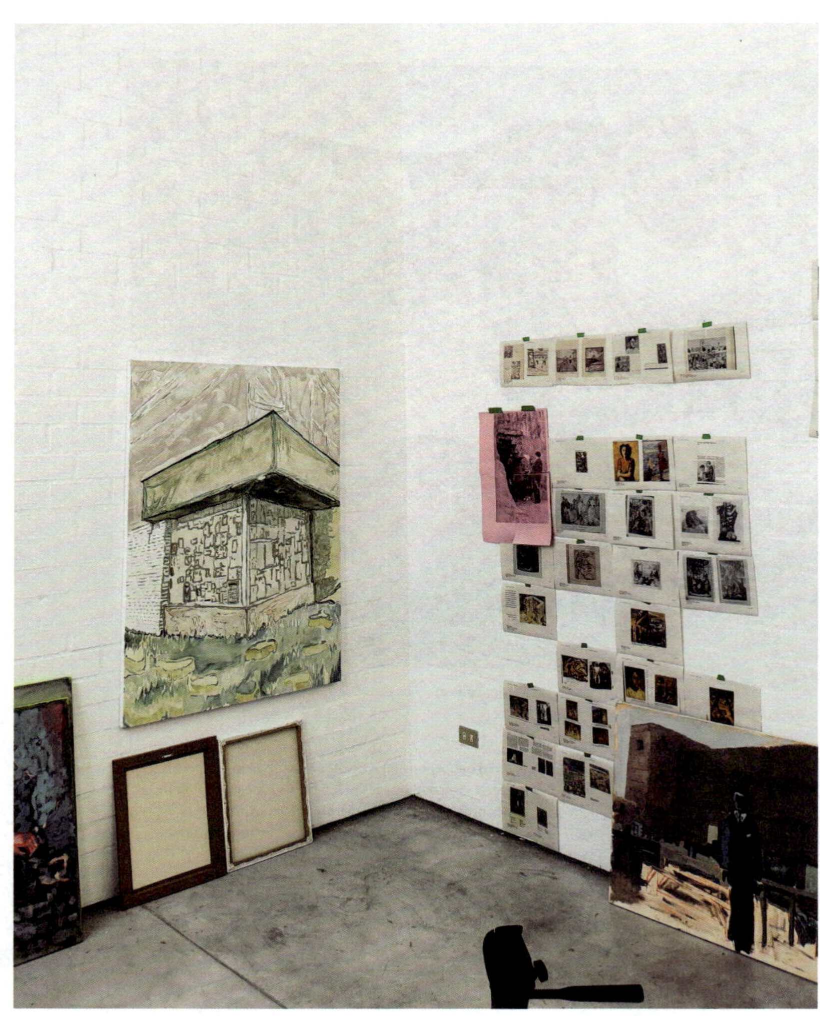

1.8

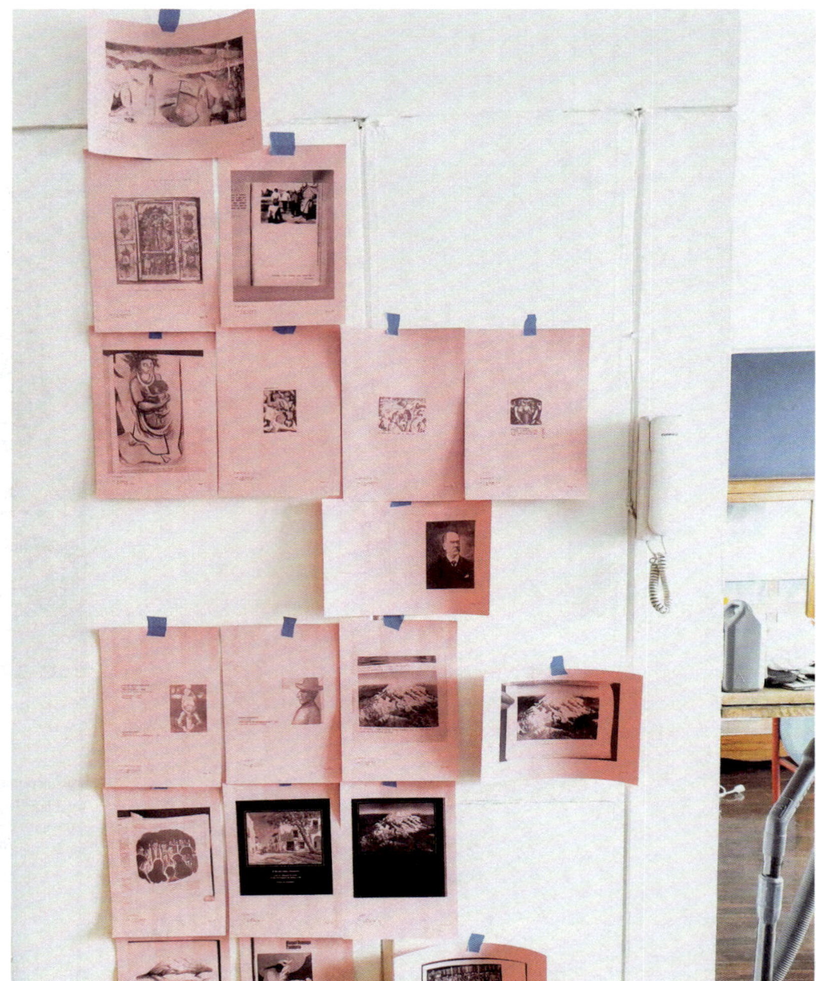

1.9

Installation tests for *Atlas of Andean Modernism*, 2022–

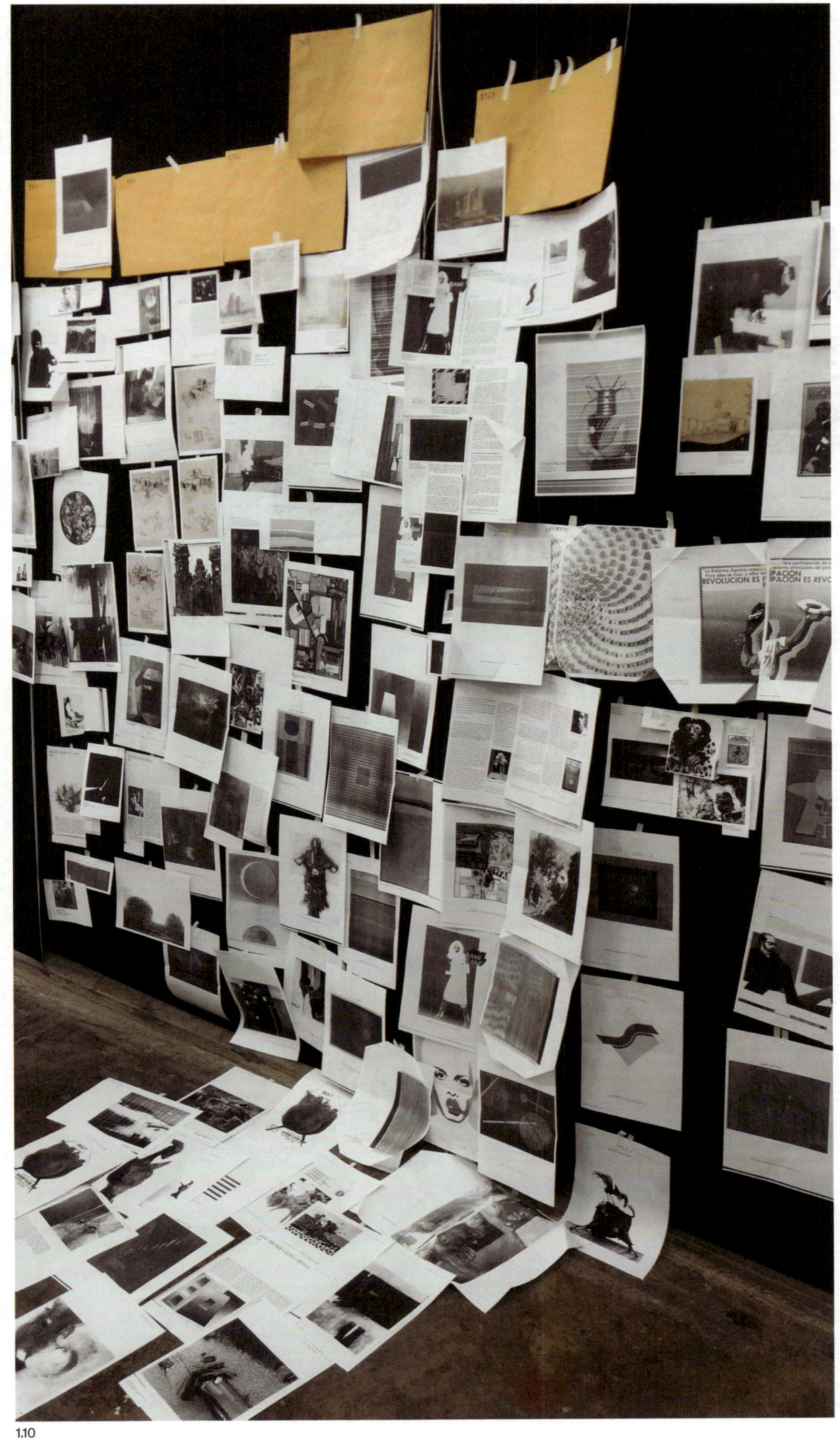

1.10

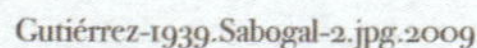



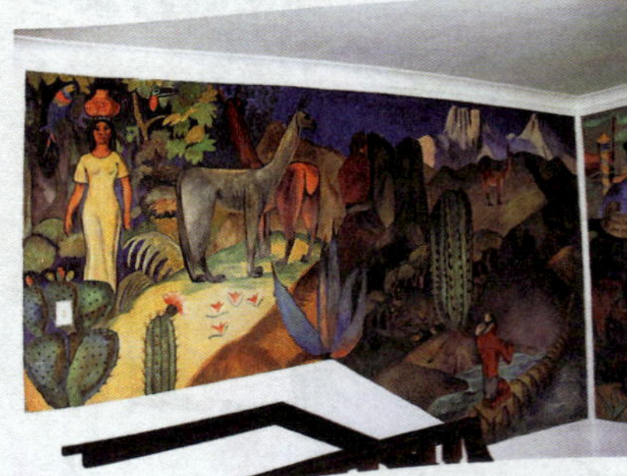

José Sabogal. *Escena andina*. Fresco. Residencia Kuroki Riva, Lima, febrero de 1939 (Foto: Gentileza Rosanna Kuon).

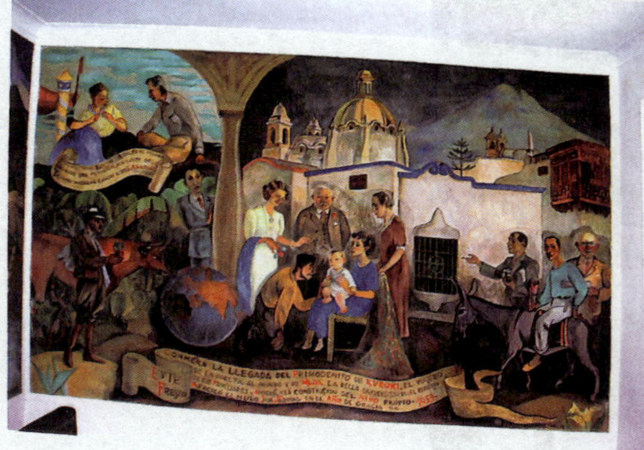

José Sabogal. Fresco conmemorativo del nacimiento del hijo del sr. Kuroki. Residencia Kuroki Riva, Lima, marzo de 1939 (Foto: Gentileza Rosanna Kuon).

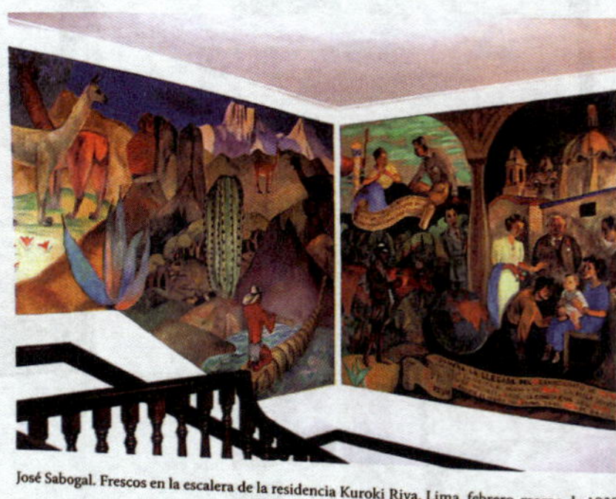

José Sabogal. Frescos en la escalera de la residencia Kuroki Riva, Lima, febrero-marzo de 1939 (Foto: Gentileza Rosanna Kuon).

⇨E. KUON A., R. GUTIERREZ V., R. GUTIERREZ & G. M. VIÑUALES CUZCO - BUENOS AIRES LIMA, 2009

1939-A 8

1.11



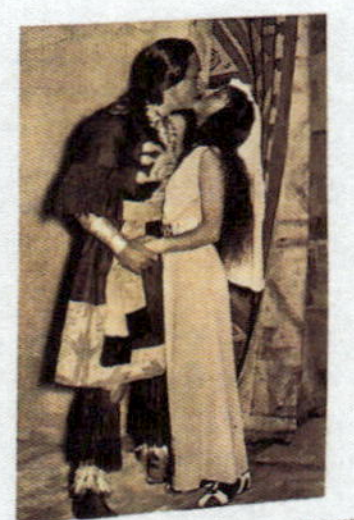

Los actores Miguel Faust Rocha y Luisa Vehil en una escena del acto III de *Ollantay*. Teatro Nacional de Comedia, Buenos Aires, 1939. (*La Prensa*, Buenos Aires, 3 de agosto de 1939).

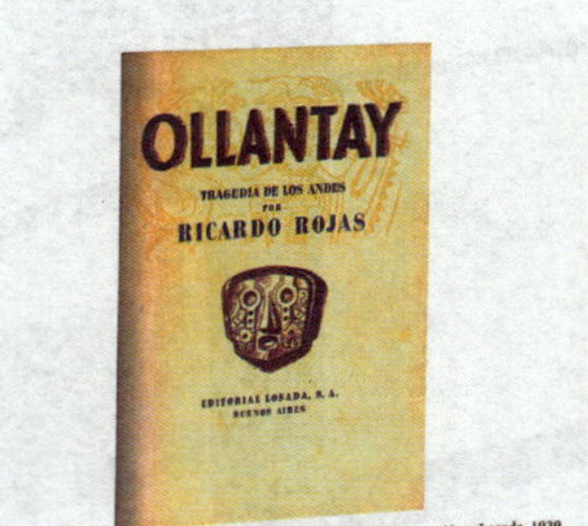


Portada del libro *Ollantay. Tragedia de los Andes* por Ricardo Rojas. Buenos Aires, Losada, 1939. (Colección CEDODAL).

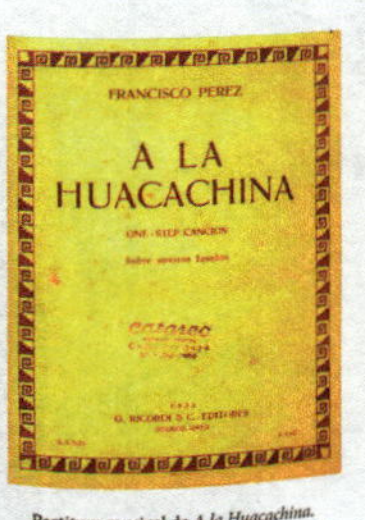


Partitura musical de *A la Huacachina. One step-canción. Sobre motivos iqueños*, de Francisco Pérez. Buenos Aires, Ricordi, 1939. (Colección CEDODAL).

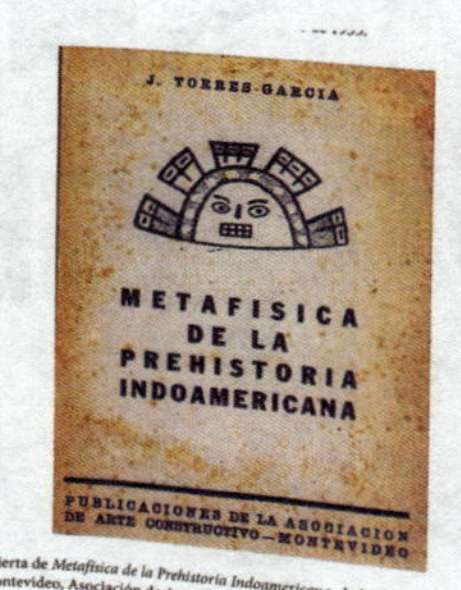


Cubierta de *Metafísica de la Prehistoria Indoamericana*, de Joaquín Torres García. Montevideo, Asociación de Arte Constructivo, 1939. (Colección CEDODAL).

⇨E. KUON A., R. GUTIERREZ V., R. GUTIERREZ & G. M. VIÑUALES CUZCO - BUENOS AIRES LIMA, 2009

1939-A 9

1.12

Greet-1939.Skidmore,Owings.jpg.2009 Greet-1939.Tejada.jpg.2009 Greet-1939.jpg.2009 26

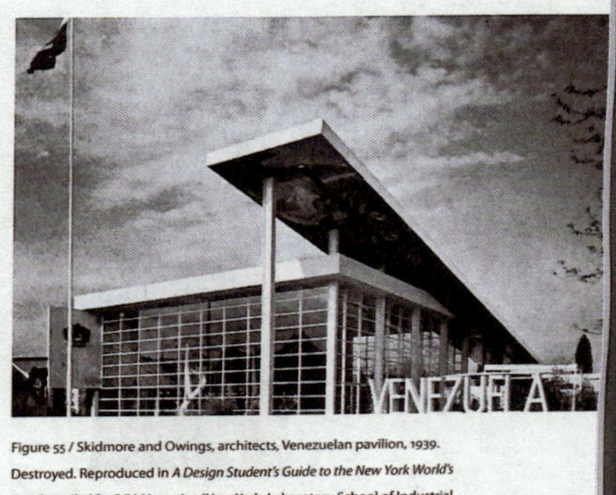


Figure 55 / Skidmore and Owings, architects, Venezuelan pavilion, 1939. Destroyed. Reproduced in *A Design Student's Guide to the New York World's Fair Compiled for P/M Magazine* (New York: Laboratory School of Industrial Design, 1939).

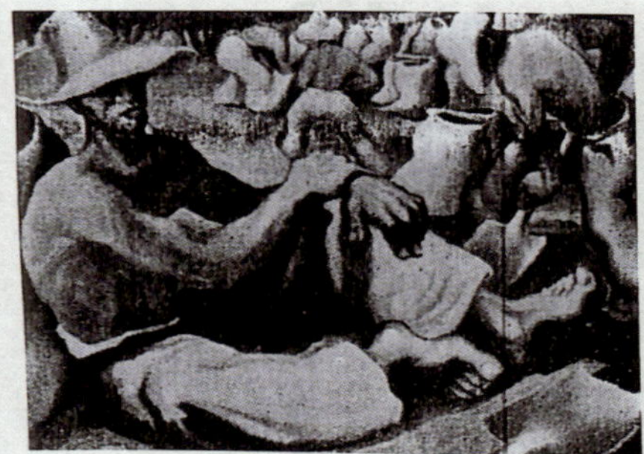

Figure 59 / Leonardo Tejada (Ecuadorian, 1908–2005), *Reposo* (Repose), ca. 1939. Reproduced in *Revista mensual del Sindicato de Escritores y Artistas del Ecuador* 5 (October 1939).

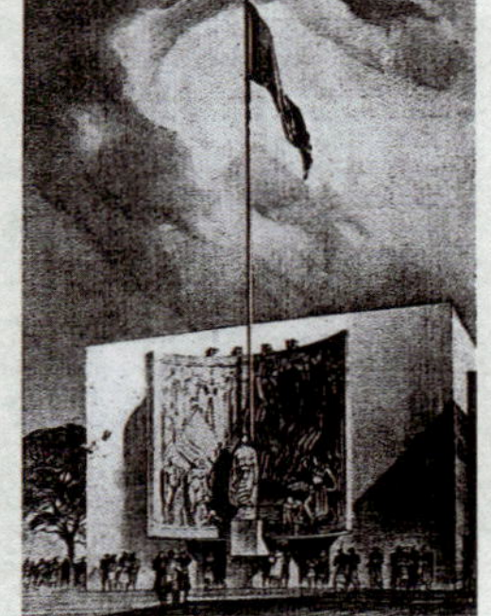

Figure 57 / Peruvian pavilion, 1939. Destroyed.

MICHELE GREET
BEYOND NATIONAL IDENTITY
PENNSYLVANIA, 2009

1939-B 8

1.13

Gutiérrez-1939.CaminoBrent.jpg.2009 Gutiérrez-1939.DeCarman.jpg.2009 Gutiérrez-1939.jpg.2009 Gutiérrez-1939.Pardo.jpg.2009 28

Catálogo de la exposición de Fortunato ... (Archivo Fundación Espigas, Buenos Aires).

... de Ollantay. *Tragedia de los Andes* por Ricardo Rojas. Buenos Aires, 1939.

... Sabogal. Cubierta de ... 1937. (Colección CEDODAL).

ENRIQUE CAMINO BRENT 39
GALERIAS WITCOMB
760-FLORIDA-760
24 D JULIO 5 D AGOSTO
BUENOS AIRES 1939

Catálogo de la exposición de Enrique Camino Brent en el Salón Witcomb, julio-agosto de 1939. (Archivo Fundación Espigas, Buenos Aires).

Mecha N. de Carman. "El inca". Reproducido en *Ollantay. Tragedia de los Andes* de Ricardo Rojas. Buenos Aires, Losada, 1939.

CUENTOS Y LEYENDAS INKAS
VALCARCEL

Cubierta de *Cuentos y leyendas inkas*, de Luis E. Valcárcel. Lima, Ediciones de la Imprenta del Museo Nacional, 1939. (Colección CEDODAL).

Cubierta de *Las tres fundaciones del Cuzco*, por Luis A. Pardo. Lima, 1939. (Colección CEDODAL).

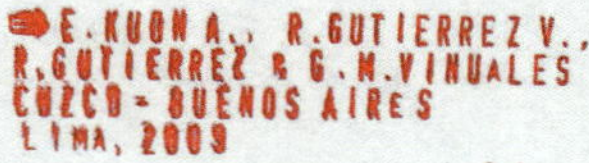


1939-B 9

1.14

Amigo-1939.Spilimbergo.jpg.2014 Amigo-1939.Perlotti.jpg.2014 36

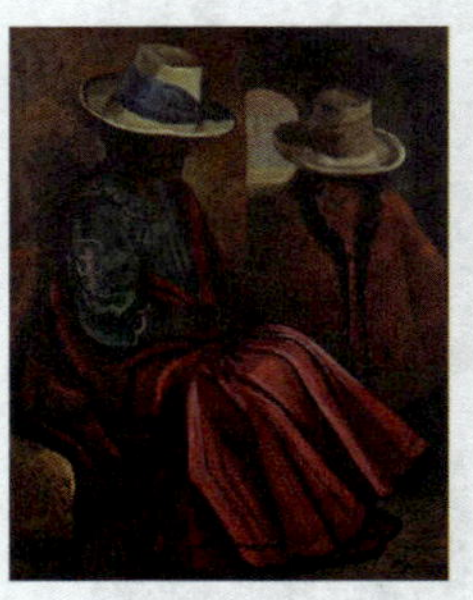

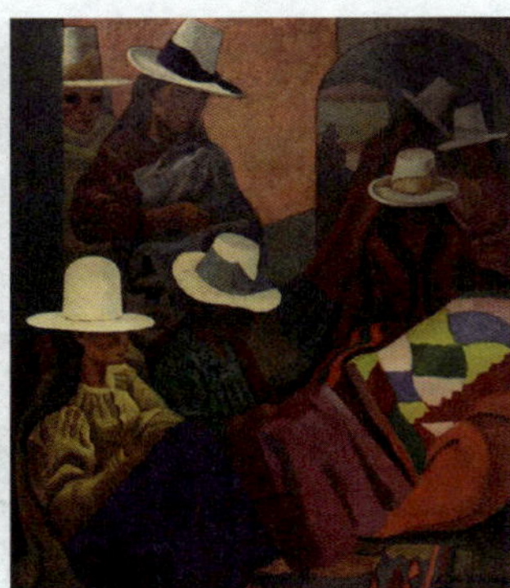

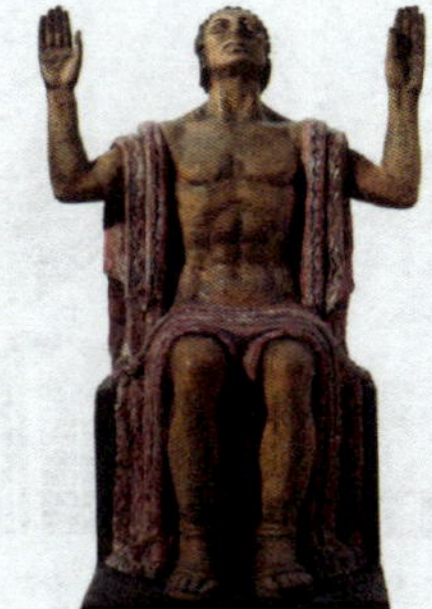

⇨ROBERTO AMIGO
LA HORA AMERICANA. 1910-1950
BUENOS AIRES, 2014

1939-C10

1.15

Gutiérrez V._1939.jpg.2019 39

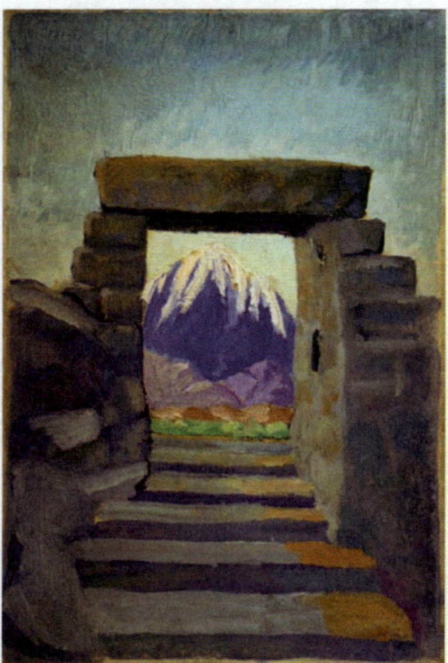

Figura 3. Gregorio López Naguil: *Paisaje incaico* (1939). Óleo sobre cuero, 24,5 x 16,5 cm. Pintado sobre la encuadernación de un ejemplar especial de: Ricardo Rojas. *Ollantay. Tragedia de los Andes.* Buenos Aires, Editorial Losada, 1939. Ejemplar dedicado por Rojas y todos los actores de la obra. Colección MLR.

⇨RODRIGO GUTIERREZ VIÑUALES
MODERNOS Y AMERICANOS
LA PAZ, 2019

1939-C11

1.16

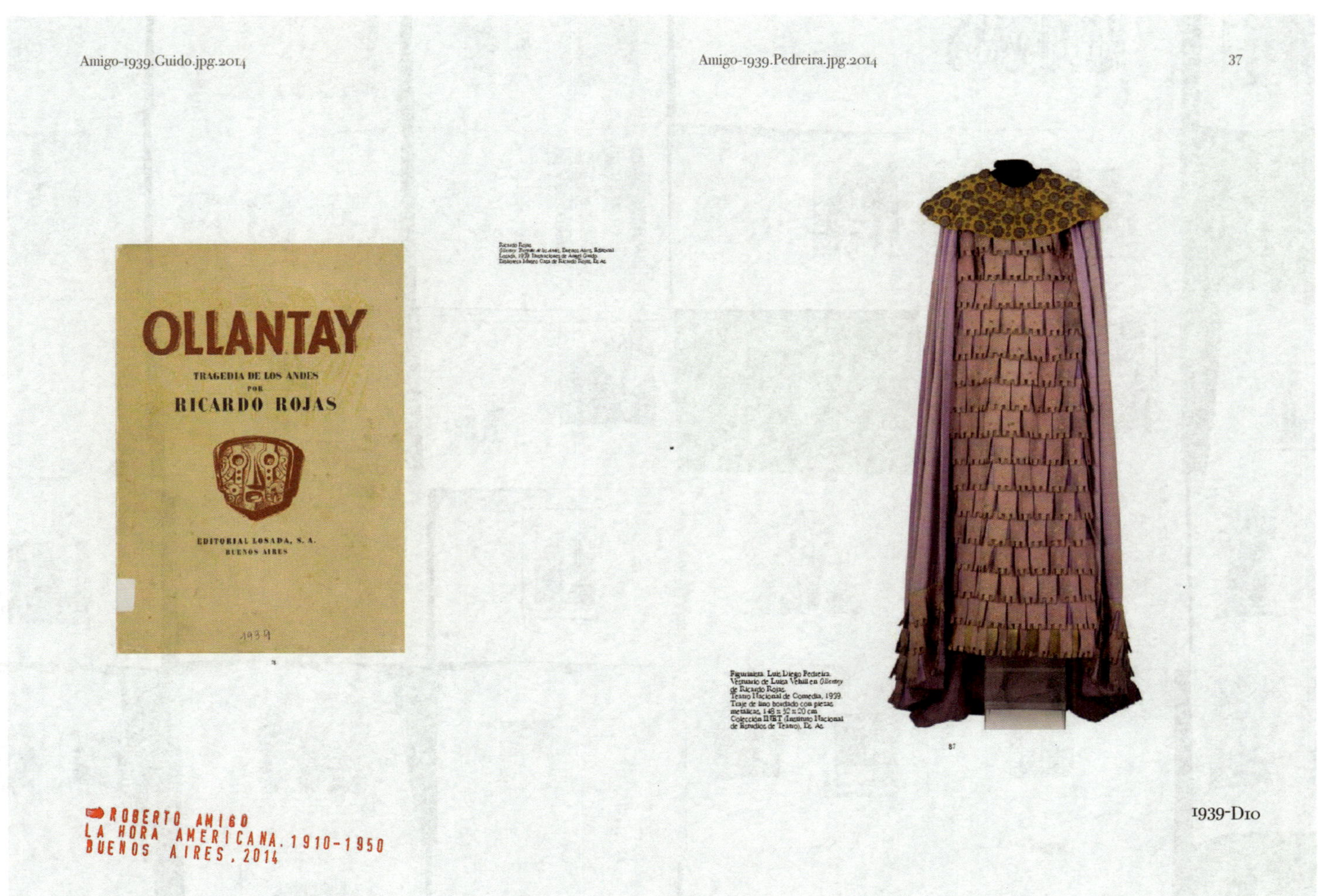


1.17

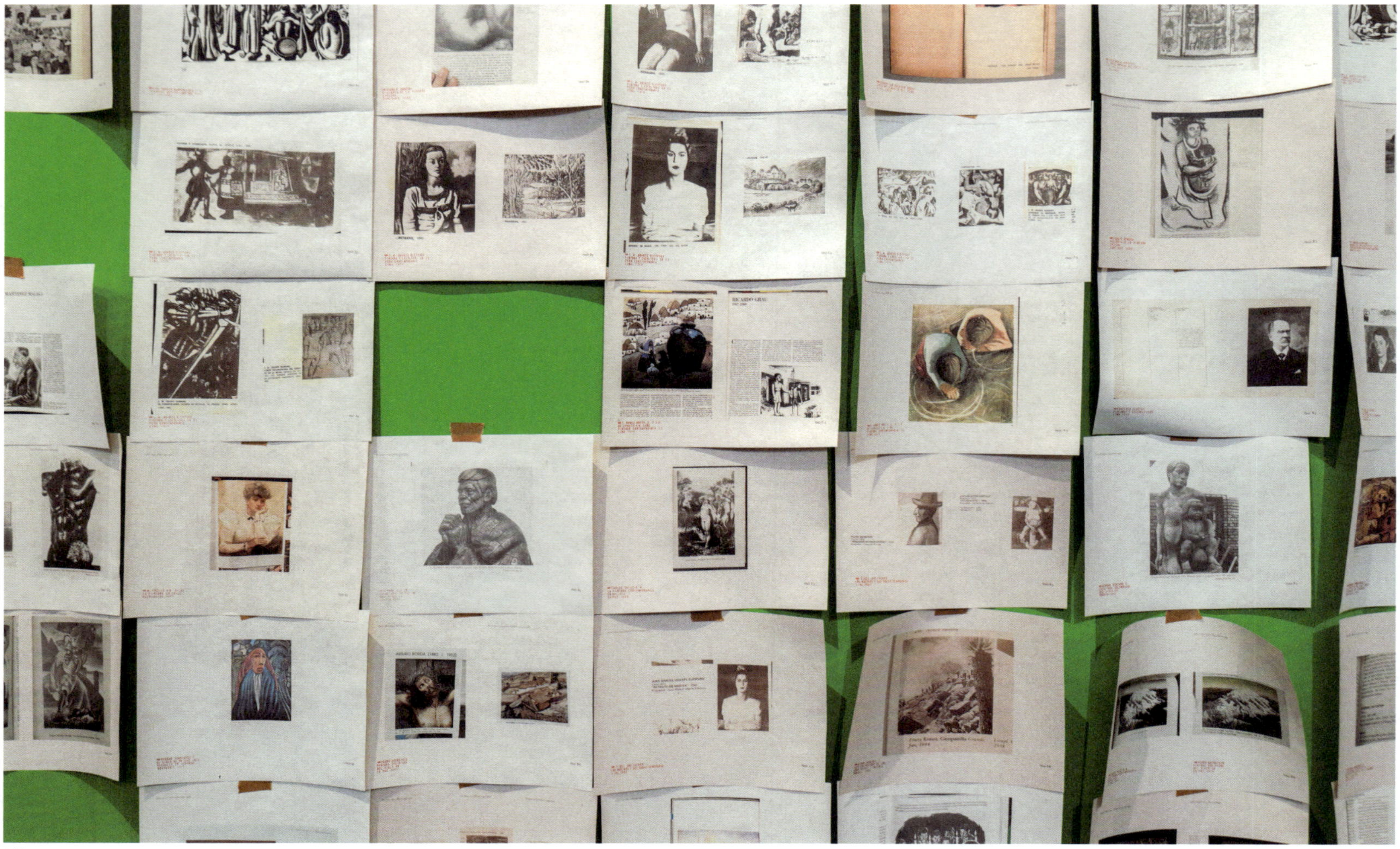

1.18

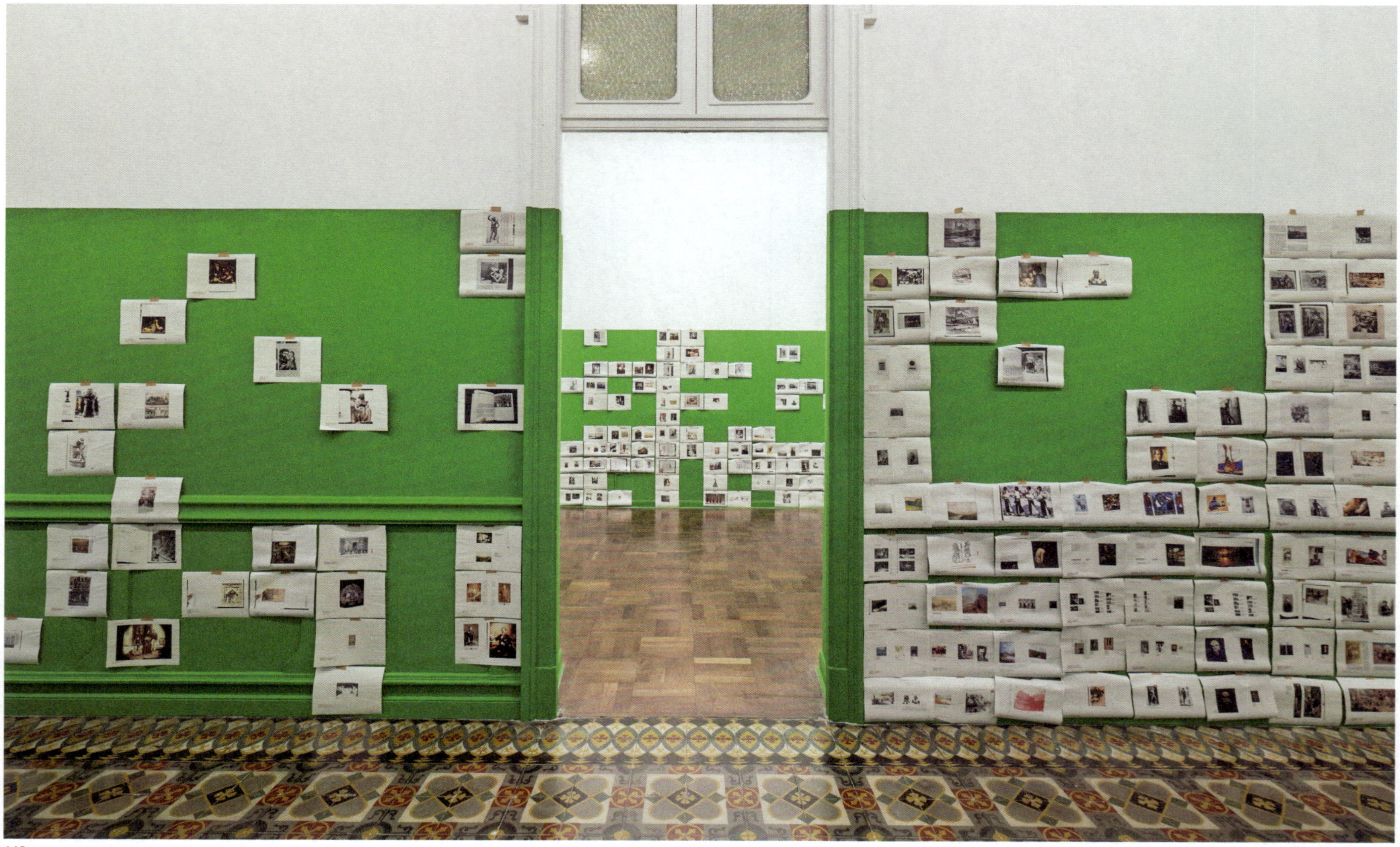

1.19

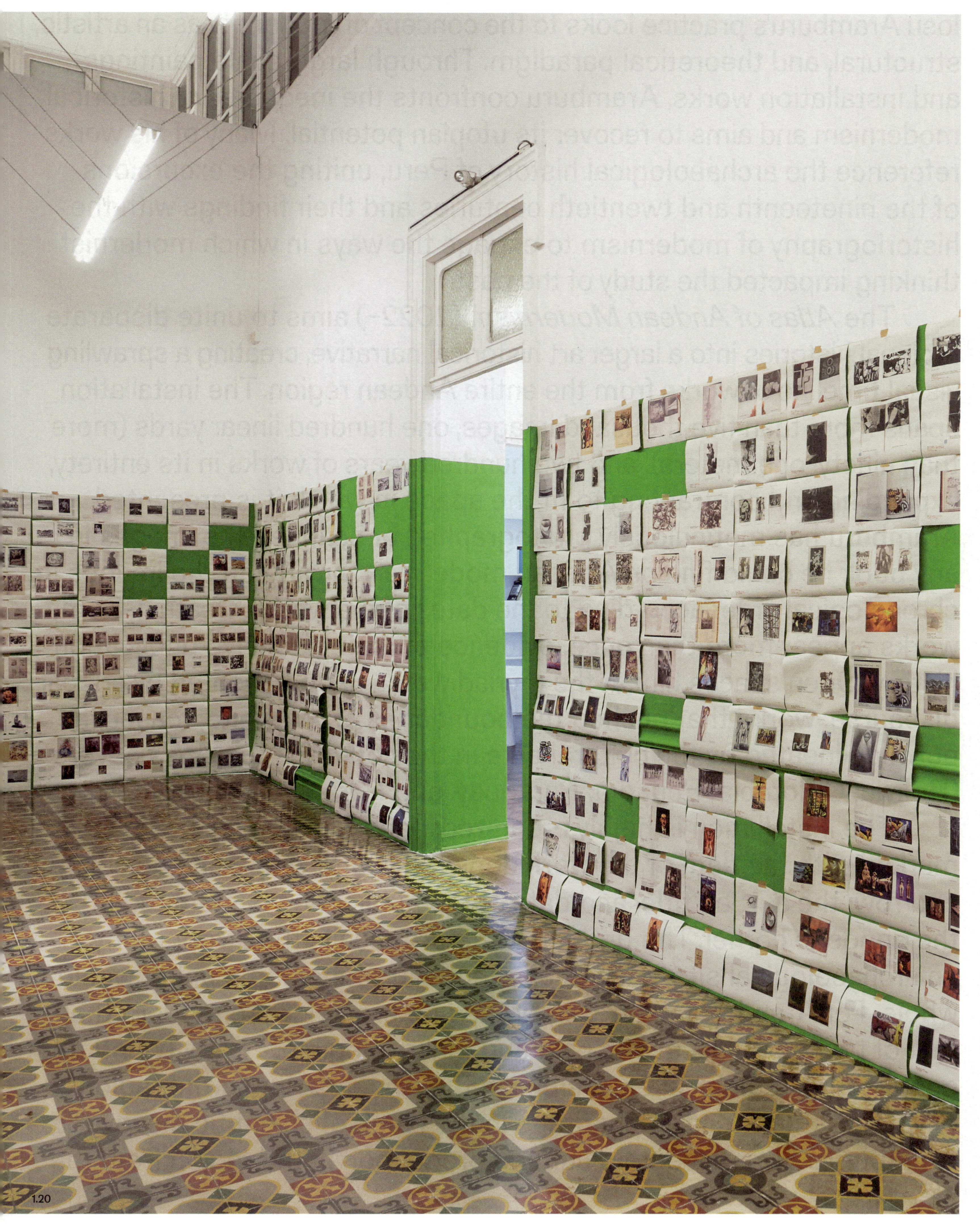

1.20

Iosu Aramburu's practice looks to the concept of modernity as an artistic, structural, and theoretical paradigm. Through large-scale paintings and installation works, Aramburu confronts the inequities of historical modernism and aims to recover its utopian potential. Many of his works reference the archaeological history of Peru, uniting the excursions of the nineteenth and twentieth centuries and their findings with the historiography of modernism to engage the ways in which modernist thinking impacted the study of the past.

The *Atlas of Andean Modernism* (2022–) aims to unite disparate regional histories into a larger art historical narrative, creating a sprawling visual timeline of works from the entire Andean region. The installation spans more than five thousand images, one hundred linear yards (more than ninety-one meters), and two hundred years of works in its entirety, expanding and contracting to fit the space in which it is presented. Aramburu has meticulously photographed or scanned the images in any book he could find on Andean modern art, arranging the images in chronological order according to the dates of the works' creation. Some works appear more than once, evidence of their extensive publication history. Open spaces hint at the myriad works undocumented by critical discourse, works that pushed the boundaries of the white, masculine norm delineated by the cultural elite in the countries the *Atlas* covers (Bolivia, Colombia, Ecuador, Paraguay, and Peru).[1]

The installation is highly organized: each sheet of A4 paper is marked with the date of the work depicted, along with a unique column and row; the author, title, and date of the publication is stamped in the opposite corner. The gridded structure recalls the stratigraphy of an archaeological site, each image reconstructing some unknowable whole. For Aramburu, "there is perhaps no project more modern than that of trying to classify the past and make it legible."[2] Early twentieth-century archaeological excursions in the Andes stripped the region of vast swaths of cultural heritage in the name of scientific discovery. Aramburu's *Atlas* recenters cultural production in the region from the same period, creating a parallel narrative to the historically reductive pursuit of knowledge.

Seen en masse, the works in the *Atlas* create an uneasy narrative. Aramburu's collection of images was dictated not only by which works were deemed worthy of publication but also by the publications he could access.[3] The selection of histories that surpassed their local boundaries and were collected into libraries and archives is just as subjective as the selection of images. The mass of the *Atlas* gives shape to bias that is most often intangible and overlooked, allowing a rich multiplicity of interpretations to rise through extended engagement with the work. (LRL)

1 Iosu Aramburu, "Atlas of Andean Modernism," Artist Research Fellowships, Cisneros Institute, Museum of Modern Art, https://www.moma.org/research/cisneros/artists-fellowships#2022-artist-fellow.

2 Elise Chagas, "On the B-Side of Modernity: An Interview with Iosu Aramburu," *MoMA Magazine*, December 28, 2022, https://www.moma.org/magazine/articles/822.

3 Luisa Fernanda Lindo, "Iosu Aramburu: Atlas Subterráneo [1933 [1810–1983] 2020]," *Artishock*, August 16, 2022, https://artishockrevista.com/2022/08/16/iosu-aramburu-atlas-subterraneo.

GALA PORRAS-KIM *530*

*National Treasures*, 2023, colored pencil and Flashe on paper, 4 panels: 71¼ × 118 in. (181 × 300 cm) each, Leeum Museum of Art, Seoul

National Treasures

1 Namdaemun, Jung District, Seoul

1. Pyongyang Castle, Pyongchon-guyok, Pyongyang

2. Wongaksa Pagoda, Tapgol Park, Jongno District, Seoul

2. Anhak Palace, Taesong-guyok, Pyongyang

3. Bukhansan Monument, National Museum of Korea, Seoul

3. Potongmun, Chung-guyok, Pyongyang

4. Stupa of Godalsa site, Yeoju County

4. Taedongmun, Chung-guyok, Pyongyang

5. Ssangsajaseokdeung, twin lion stone lantern of Beopjusa, Boeun County

5. Sungin Hall, Chung-guyok, Pyongyang

6. Seven storied stone pagoda in Tap-pyeong-ri, Chungju

6. Sungryong Hall, Jongro-dong, Chung-guyok, Pyongyang

7. Stele of Bongseon Honggyeongsa, Cheonan

7. Tabo Pagoda of Pohyonsa Budhist temple, Hyangam-ri, Hyangsan-gun

8. Stele accompanying pagoda of Budhist priest Nanghyehwasang, Seongjusa, Boryeong

8. Taesong Fortress, Taesong-guyok, Pyongyang

9. Five storied stone pagoda of Jeongnimsa Temple site, Buyeo County

9. Chongam-ri Earthen Castle, Chongam-ri, Taesong-guyok, Pyongyang

10. Three storied stone pagoda in front of Baekjangam Hermitage, Silsangsa, Namwon

10. South Gate of Taesong Fortress, Taesong-guyok, Pyongyang

11. Stone pagoda of Mireuksa, Iksan

11. Lotus-ponds of Mt. Taesong, Taesong-dong, Taesong-guyok, Pyongyang

12. Stone lantern in front of Gakhwangjeon Hall of Hwaeomsa, Gurye County

12. Group of Koguryo tombs of Mt. Taesong, Taesong-guyok, Pyongyang

13. Geungnakjeon Hall of Muwisa, Gangjin County

13. Pobun Hermitage of Yongmyongsa, Buddhist temple, Mangyongdae-guyok

14. Yeongsanjeon Hall of Geojoam Hermitage, Eunhaesa, Yeongcheon

14. Ryonggok Academy, Mangyongdae-guyok, Pyongyang

15. Geungnakjeon Hall of Bongjeongsa temple, Andong.

15. Ryongsan-ri Koguryo Tombs, Ryongsan-ri, Chunghwa-gun, Pyongyang

16. Seven storied brick pagoda in Sinse-dong, Andong.

16. Ryongwang Pavilion, Taedongmun-dong, Chung-guyok, Pyongyang

17. Stone lantern in front of Muryangsujeon Hall of Buseoksa, Yeongju

17. Pubyok Pavilion, Moranbong Park, Pyongyang

18. Muryangsujeon Hall of Buseoksa, Yeongju

18. Chilsongmun, Moranbong Park, Pyongyang.

19. Josadang Hall of Buseoksa, Yeongju

19. Ulmil Pavilion, Moranbong Park, Pyongyang

20. Dabotap (Many Treasure Pagoda) at Bulguksa, Gyeongju

20. Chongryu Pavilion, Moranbong Pavilion, Pyongyang

21. Seokgatap (Sakyamuni Pagoda), the three-storied pagoda at Bulguksa, Gyeongju

21. Choesung Pavilion, Moranbong Park, Pyongyang

22. Yeonhwagyo and Chilbogyo bridges of Bulguksa, Gyeongju

22. Jongum Gate, Moranbong Park, Pyongyang

23. Cheongungyo and Baegungyo bridges, entrance of Bulguksa, Gyeongju.

23. Bell Pavilion & Pyongyang Bell, Taedongmun-dong, Pyongyang

24. Seokguram grotto and Buddha statue, Gyeongju

24. 7-storied octagonal pagoda of Hongboksa Buddhist temple, Pyongyang



*National Treasures*, 2015 (detail)

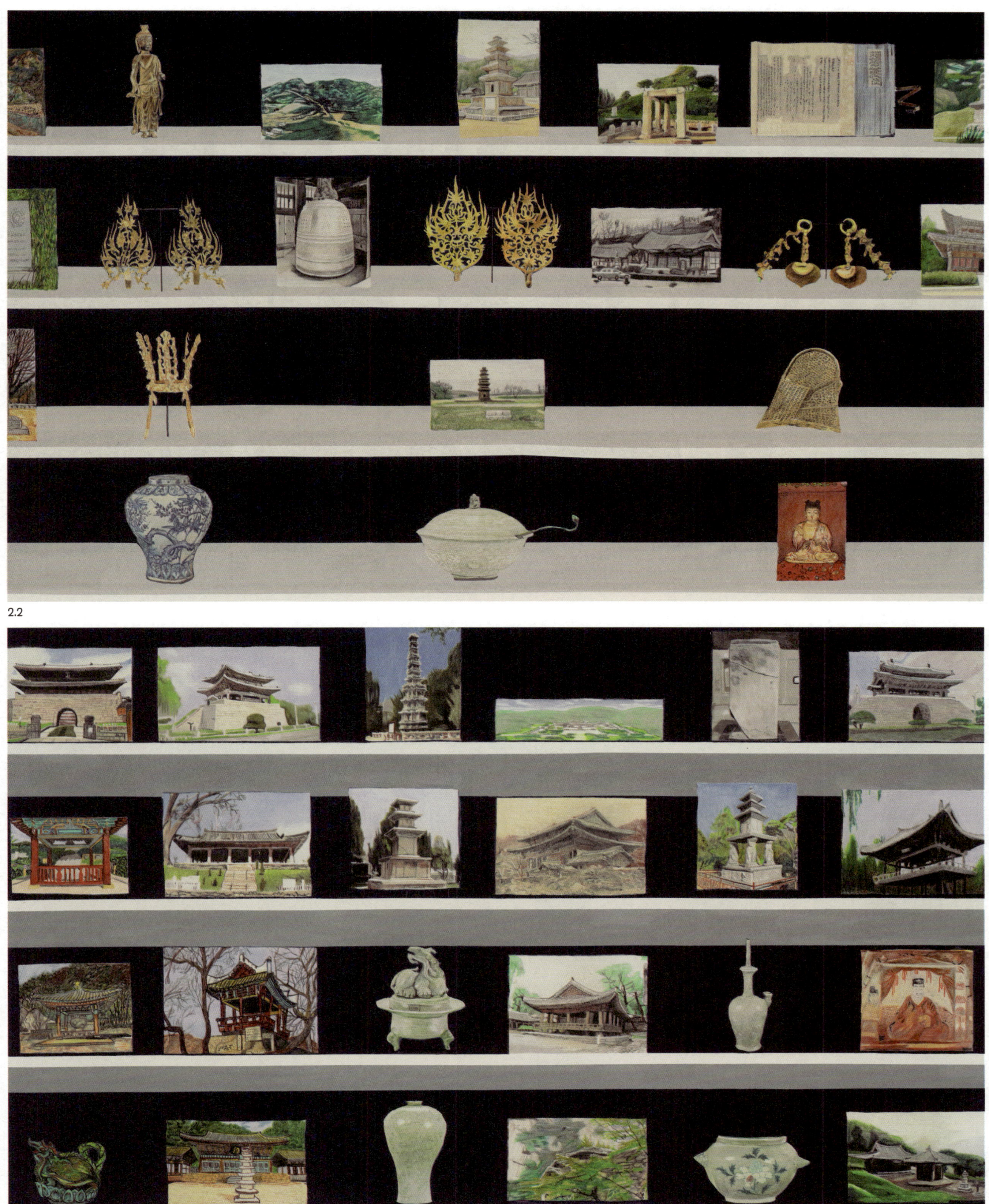

2.2

2.3

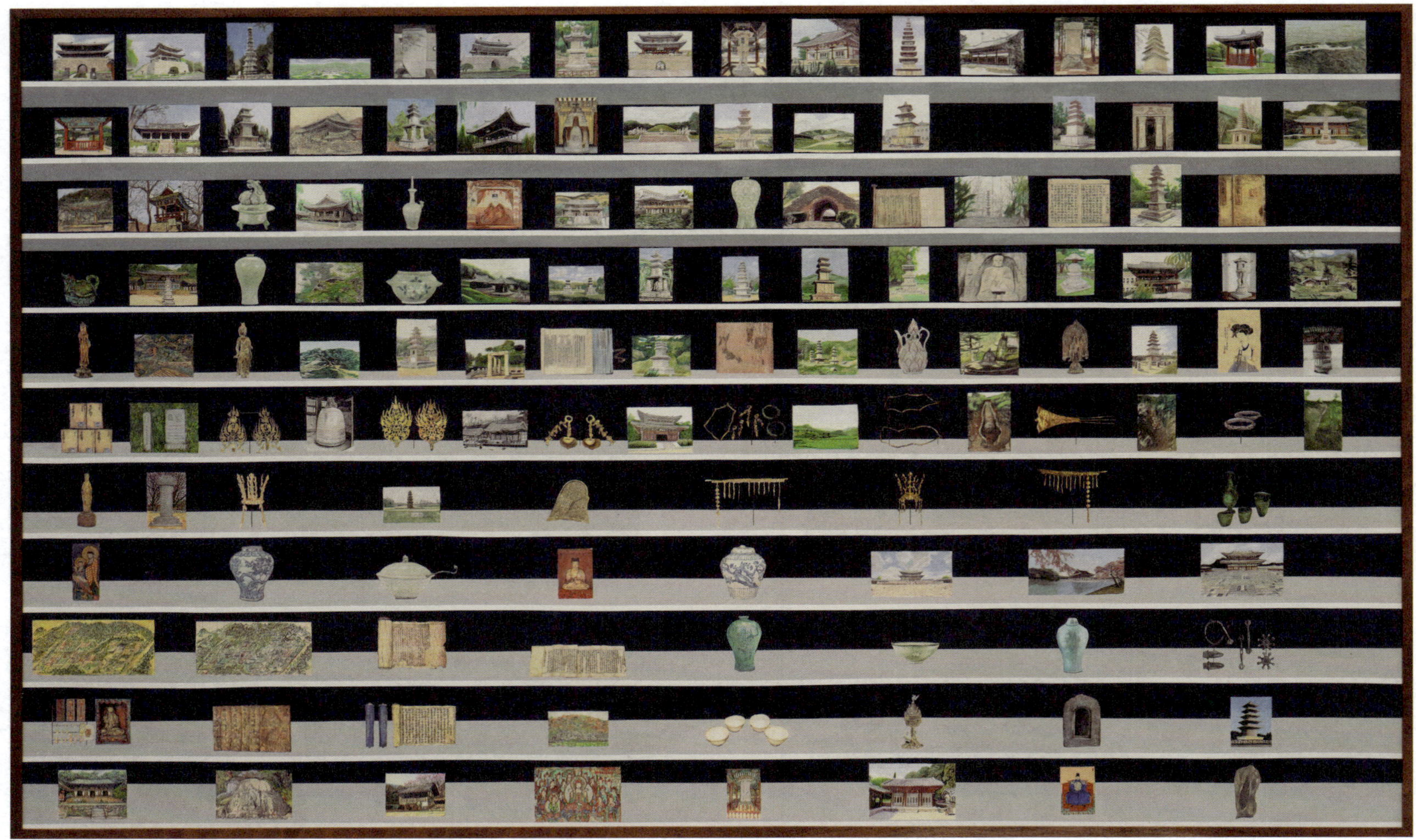

2.4

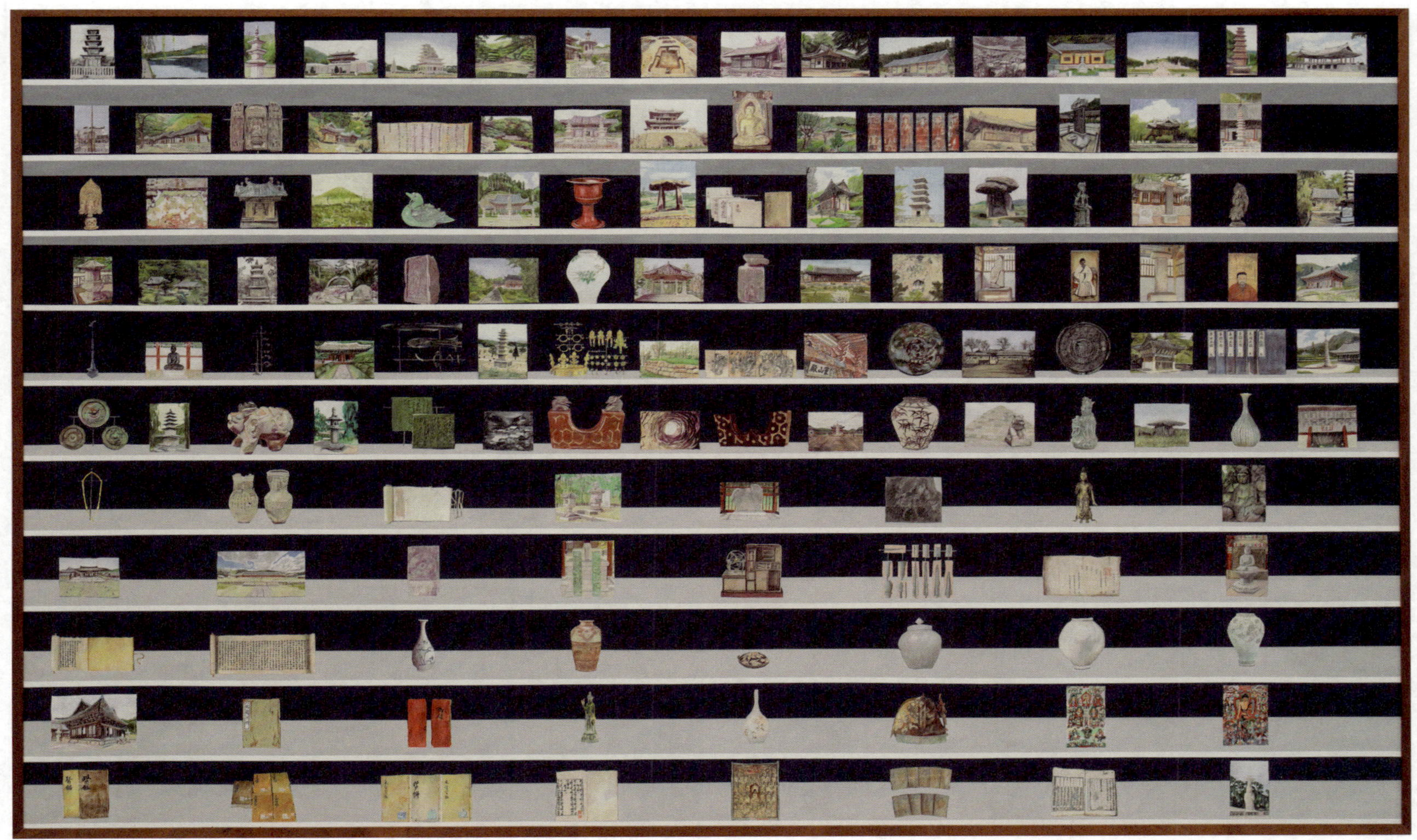

2.5

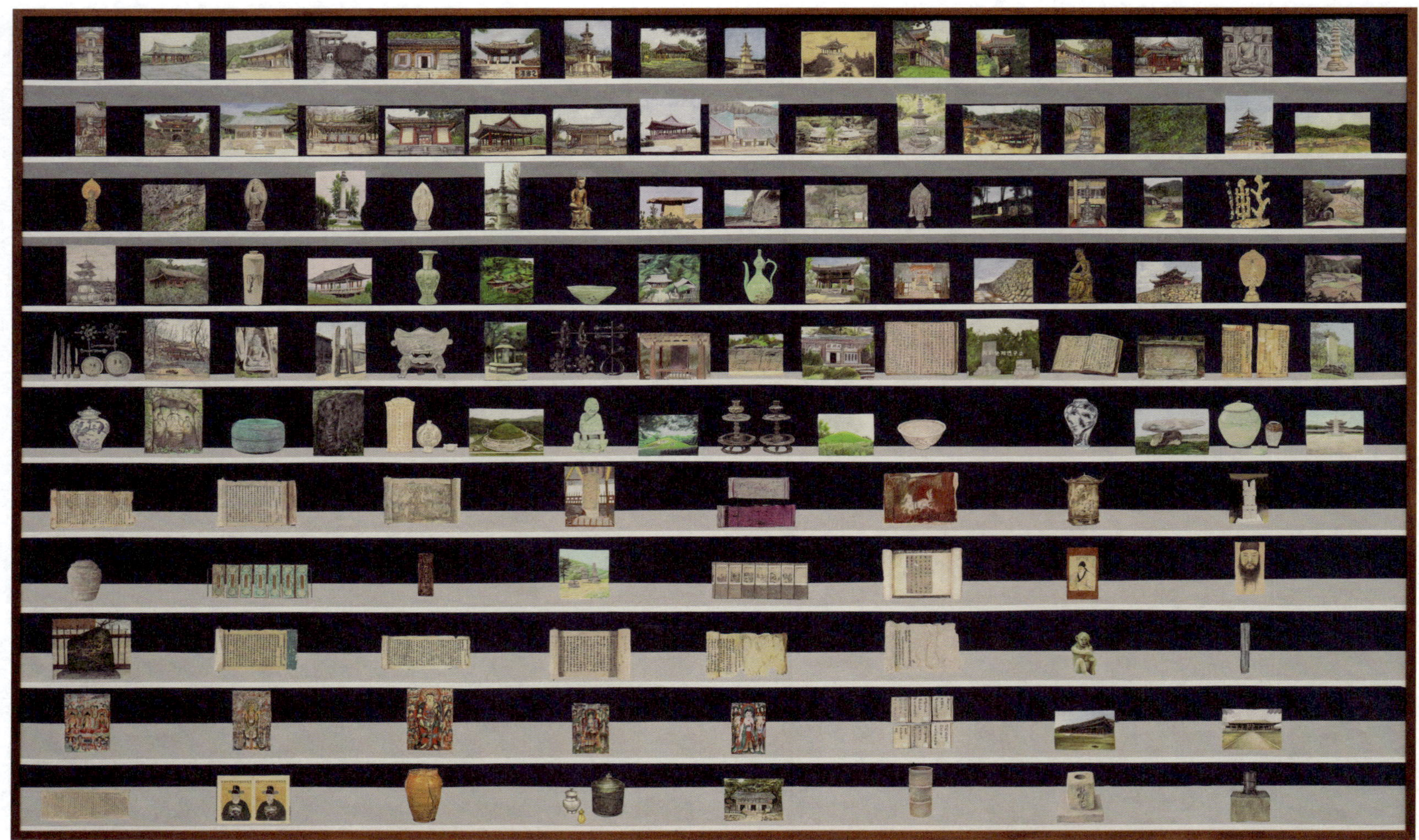
2.6

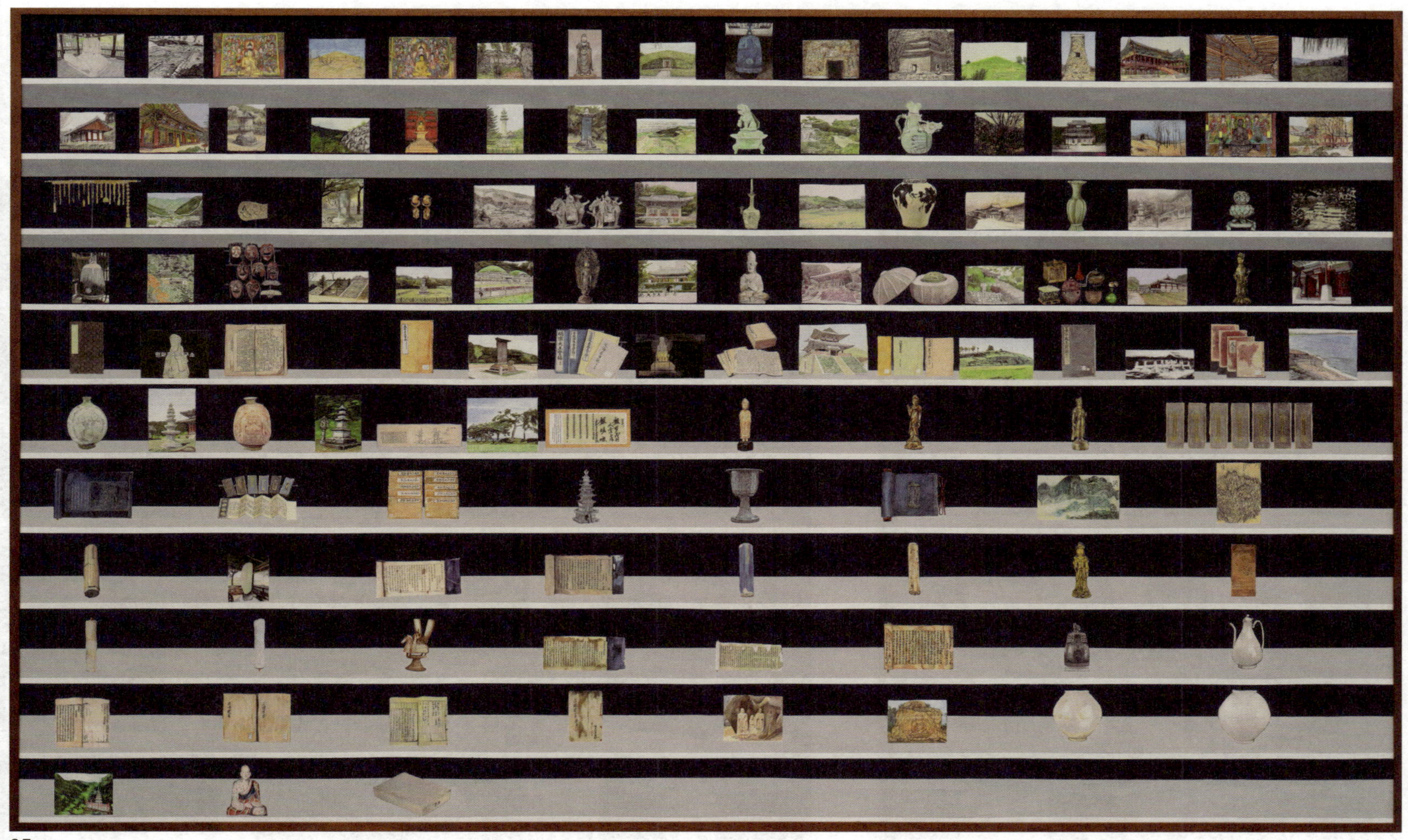

2.7

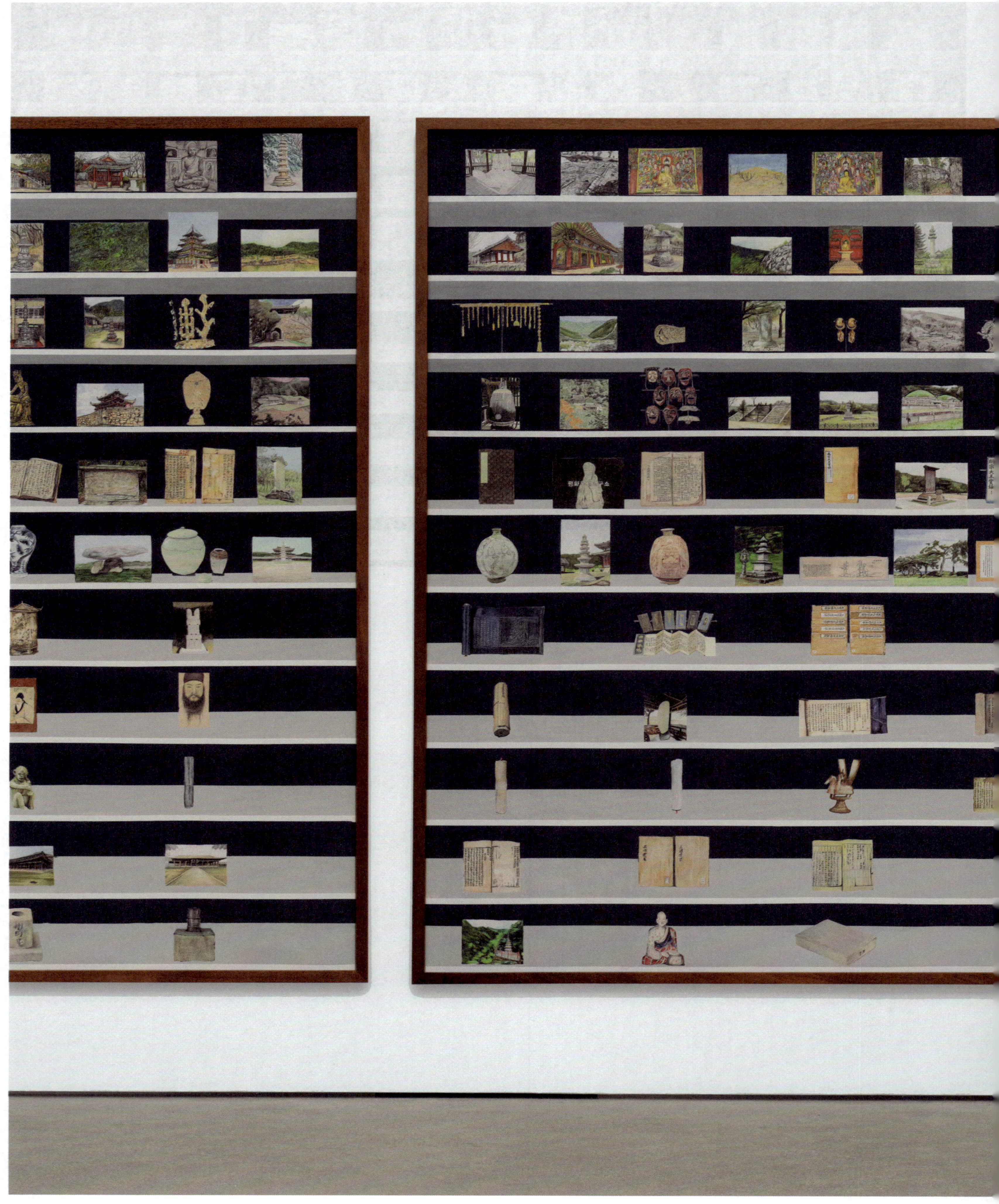

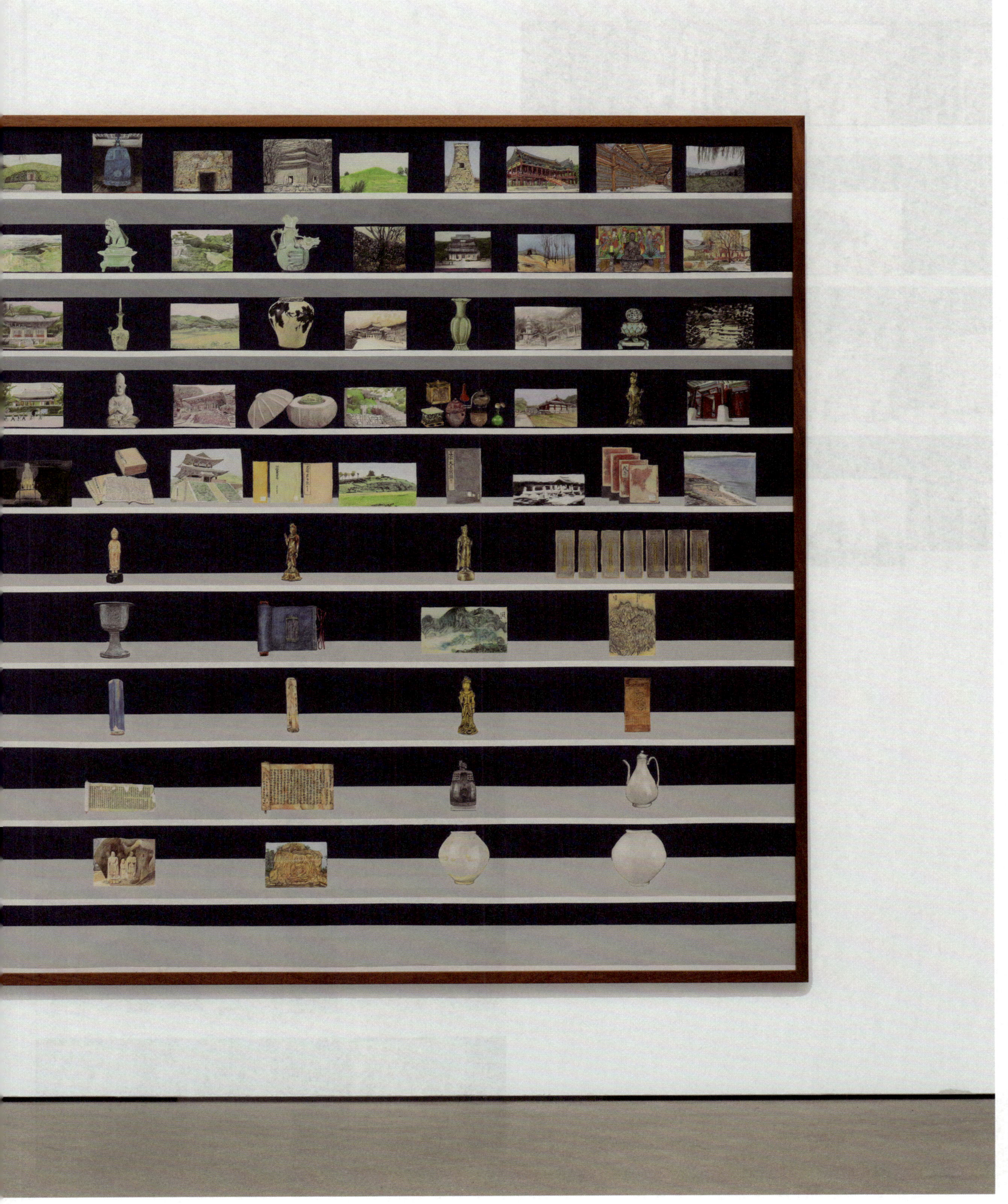

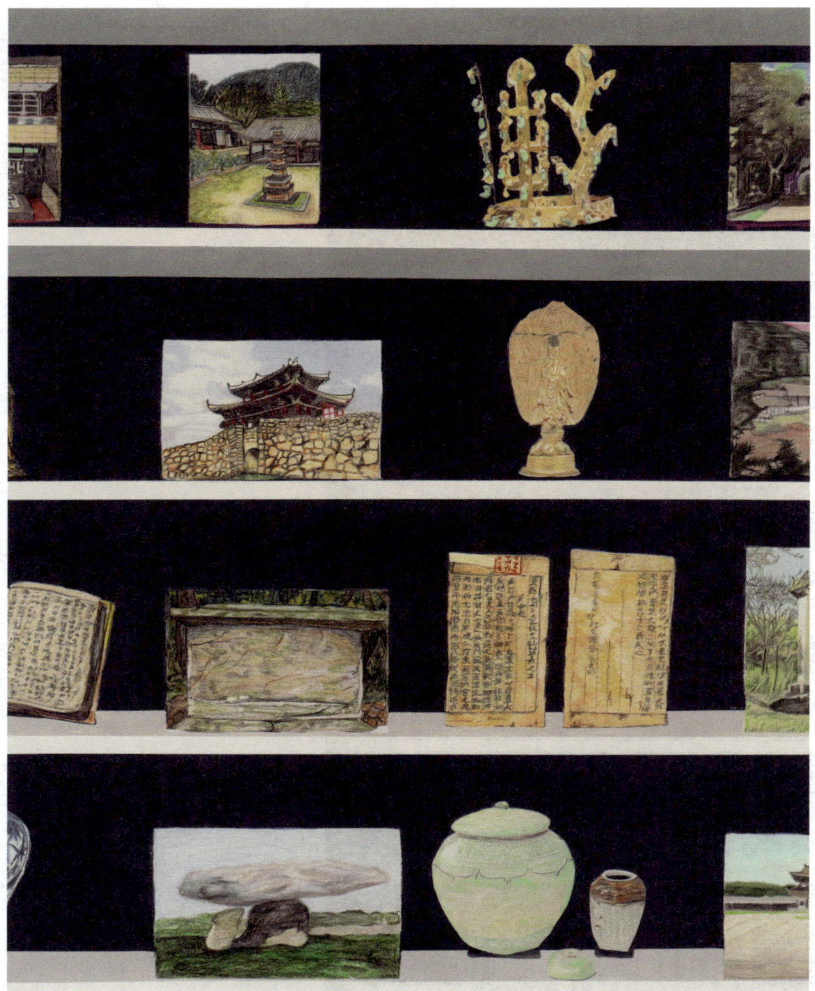

2.9

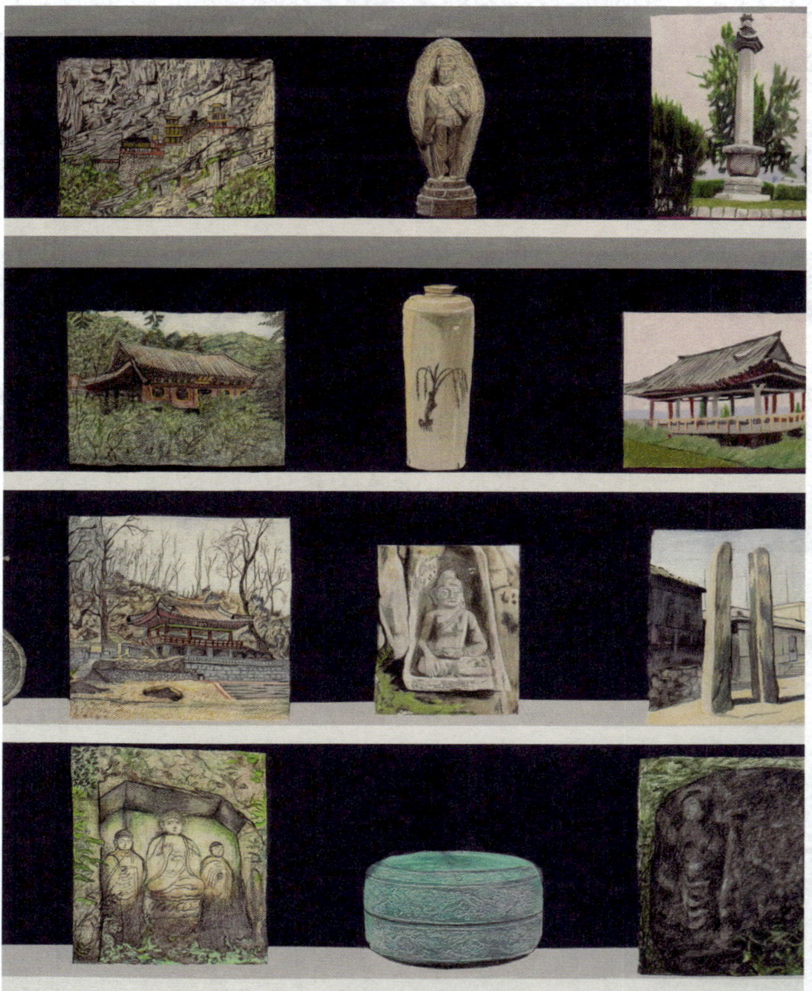
2.10

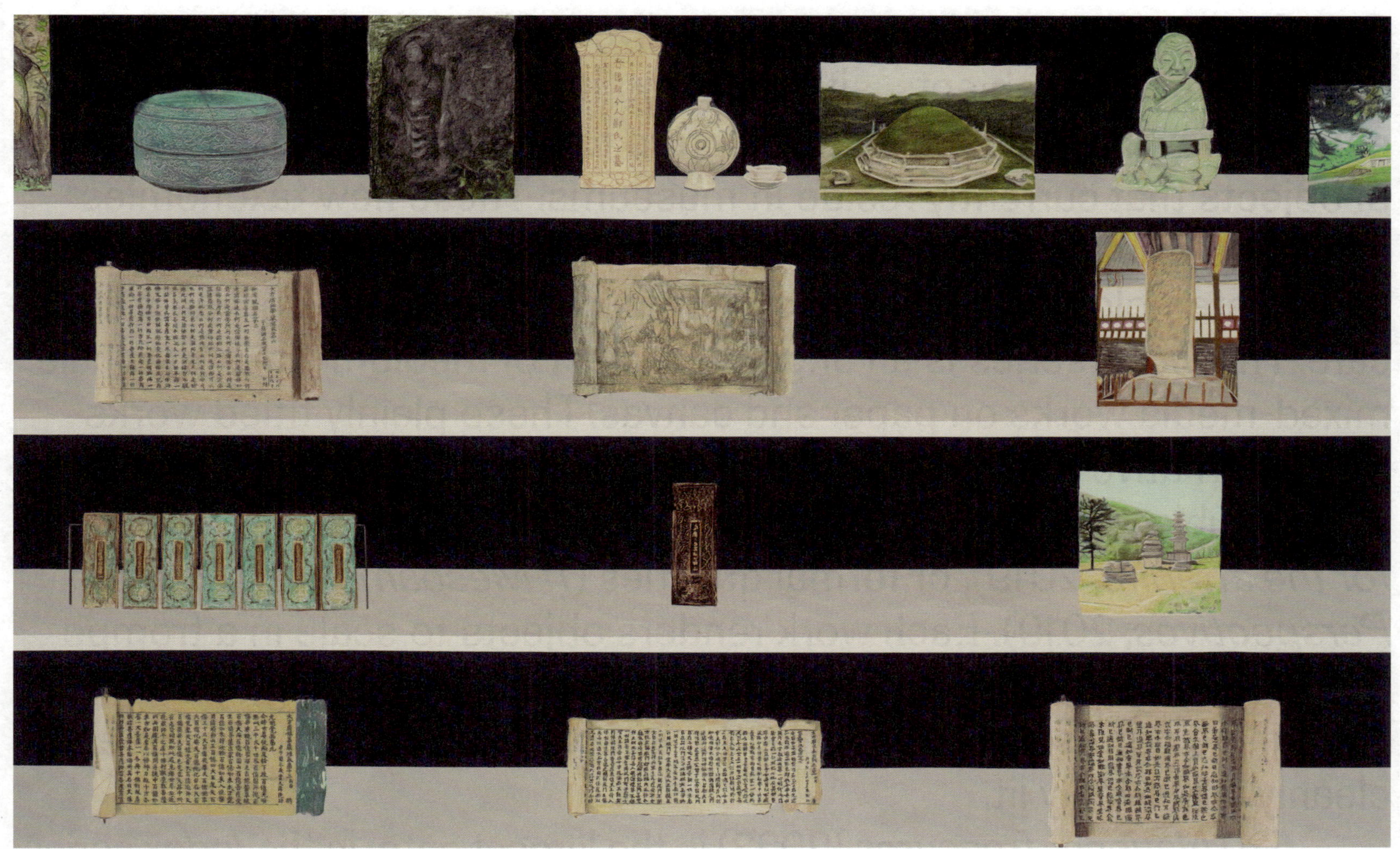

2.11

Gala Porras-Kim's work considers the lives of historical, archaeological, and ethnographic objects, sites, and institutions. Many of her projects employ drawing, painting, and sculpture to present novel arrangements of objects that currently reside in museums. These new taxonomies challenge existing organizational systems and question the historical and epistemological origins of contemporary hierarchies of value and care. The *Index* series is an ongoing project of medium- to large-scale mixed-media works on paper and canvas. These plainly titled works offer alternative arrangements of diverse objects, reorganized according to their subject matter (*13 International Dogs*, 2019), use value (*18 artifacts for the afterlife*, 2019), or formal qualities (*11 Mesoamerican Multiple Perspectives*, 2019). Each work renders objects to scale in a trompe l'oeil cabinet structure with a zigzagging irregular shelving system. Though no light source is visible, the imagined arrangements appear cleanly and evenly lit.

*530 National Treasures* (2023) is the largest entry in the *Index* series to date. Across four nearly ten-foot-wide (three-meter-wide) panels rendered in colored pencil and Flashe on paper, the artist depicts 530 sites and objects that have been designated "National Treasures" across the now-divided Korean Peninsula. Porras-Kim first conceived of the work in 2015, when she began researching the system of National Treasures. She became interested in the origins of the system, which lie in late nineteenth- and early twentieth-century Japanese colonial surveys of Korean cultural heritage that sought to portray the great works of Korean art and architecture as the products of Japanese influence.[1]

As with other works in this series, the artist drew and painted the National Treasures in the hyperprecise style of archaeological illustration. This technical aesthetic emphasizes the act of manual reproduction as an embodied tool for study. *530 National Treasures* also includes several important departures from the earlier *Index* drawings. The free-form shelving systems of the *Index* drawings offered a formal expression of Porras-Kim's idiosyncratic arrangements. Here the nearly forty-foot-long (twelve-meter-long) span of drawings is structured as an evenly spaced grid, a form that reflects the strictly state-controlled system of classification that the artist has chosen to reproduce. The objects and sites listed as National Treasures are highly diverse and too varied to be depicted at scale. Among them are prehistoric shell mounds, bronze burial goods, golden crowns, Buddhist shrines, palaces, fortresses, and ancient rock reliefs.[2] Many of the National Treasures are represented as drawings of photographic documentation of sites, which sit alongside depictions of objects of ambiguous scale. Starting in the upper left corner of the work hung to the far left, Porras-Kim depicted Sungnyemun, the first National Treasure of South Korea, followed by Pyongyangseong, the first National Treasure of North Korea. The list continues apace from left to right and crosses horizontally from one panel to the next before moving to the next row. Midway down, the grid loses density. While South Korea has an active cultural preservation program and regularly designates new National Treasures, North Korea has named significantly fewer treasures. Many of those that have been selected are not well documented. The artist's research turned up only images of what appear to be landscapes that apparently hold imperceptible treasures.[3] Despite these distinctions, the work visually suggests the enormity of the shared history between the two Koreas. *530 National Treasures* emphasizes visual and historical continuities that stretch across the contemporary border of the two Koreas, foregrounding a shared experience of Japanese colonial rule. (BE)

1 Hyung Il Pai, "The Creation of National Treasures and Monuments: The 1916 Japanese Laws on the Preservation of Korean Remains and Relics and Their Colonial Legacies," *Korean Studies* 25, no. 1 (2001): 84.

2 Pai, "Creation of National Treasures," 73.

3 "Mediation between the Past and the Present: A Conversation with Gala Porras-Kim," *Eazel Magazine*, January 24, 2024, https://www.eazel.net/magazine/206.

ROSE SALANE Selections from *Confessions*, 2023, chromogenic prints, 12 photographs, 30⅝ × 42¾ × 1⅞ in. (77.8 × 108.6 × 4.8 cm) each framed, Walker Art Center, Minneapolis, and private collections

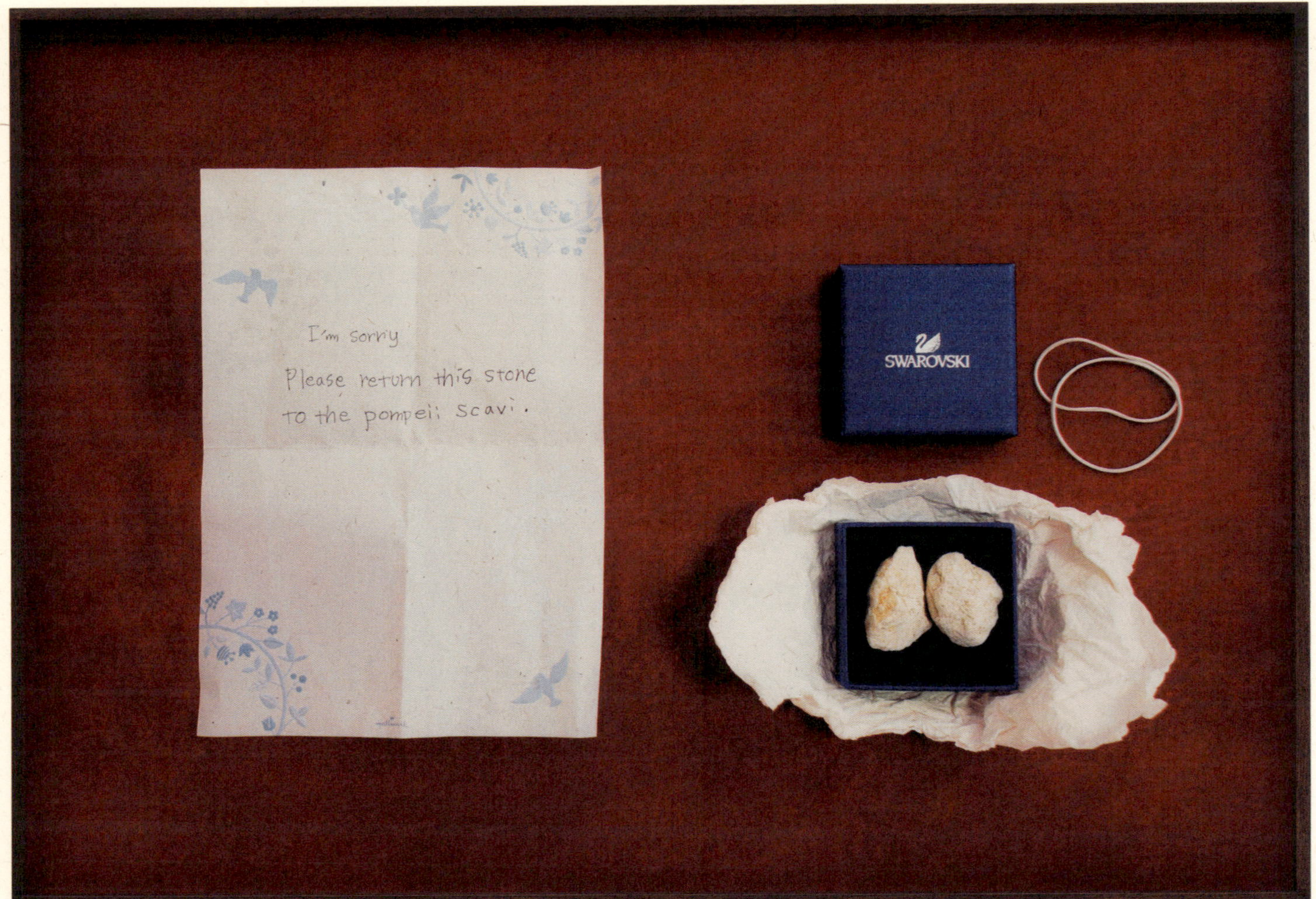
I'm sorry
Please return this stone
to the pompeii scavi.
SWAROVSKI

3.1

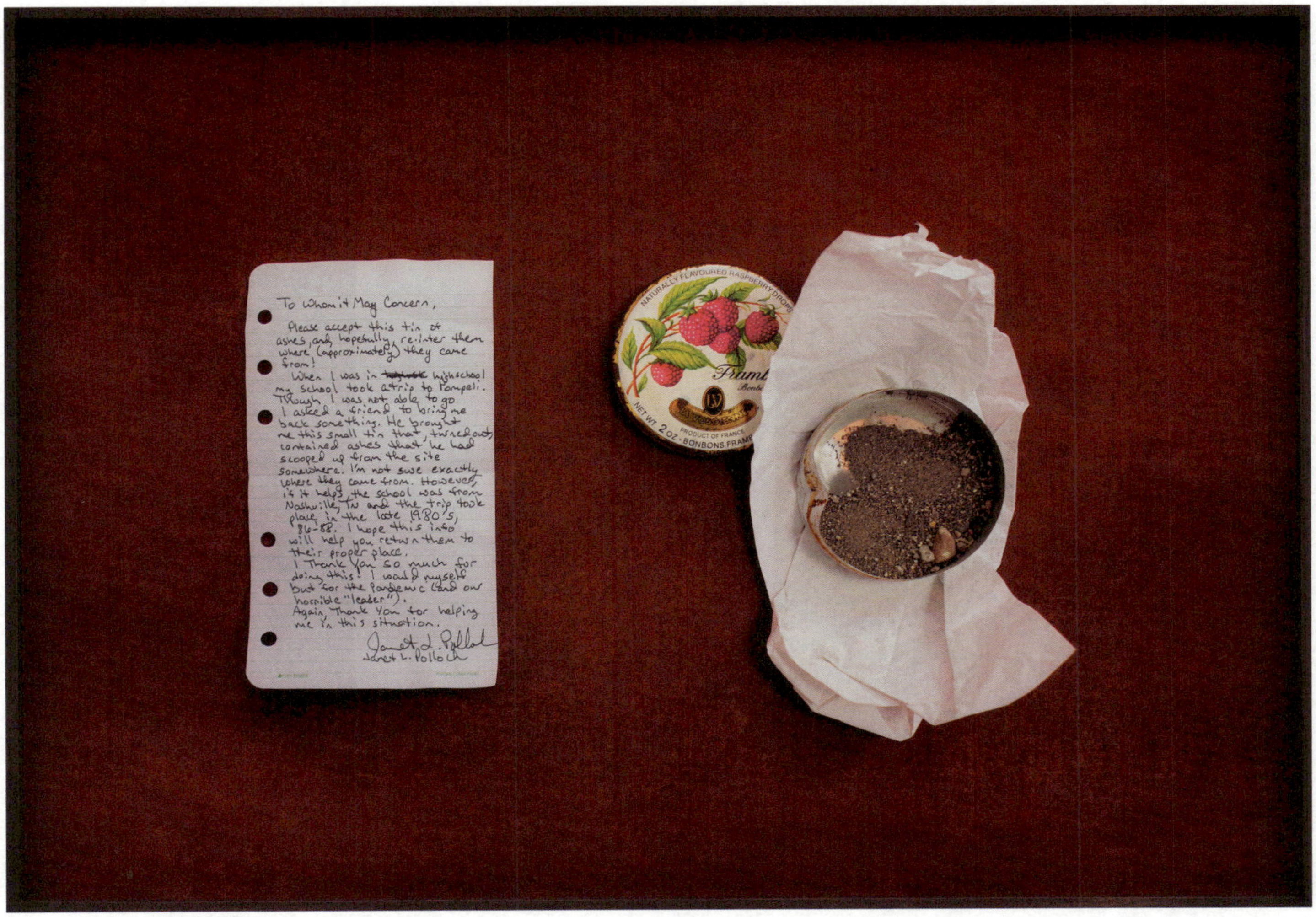

3.2

3.3

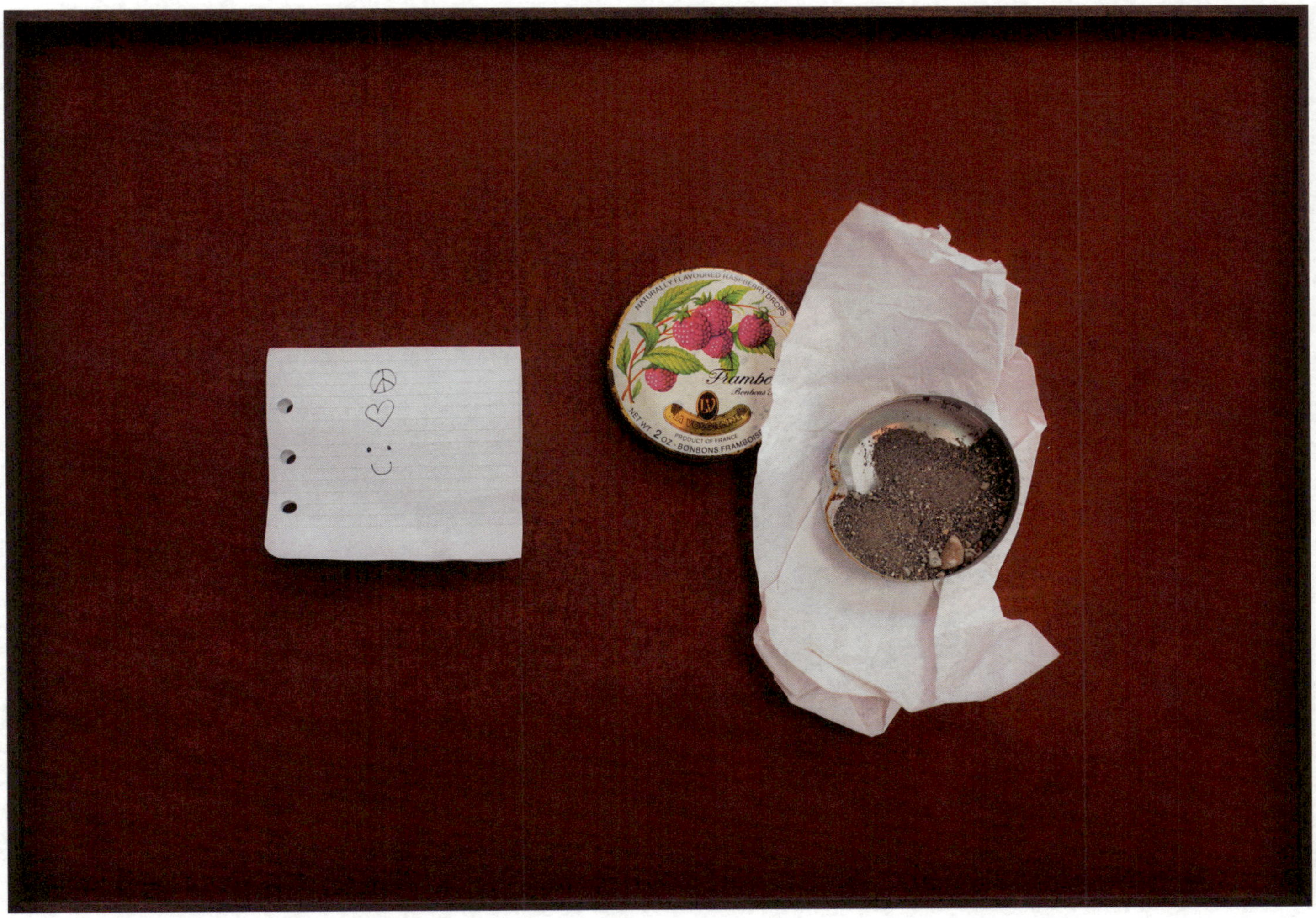

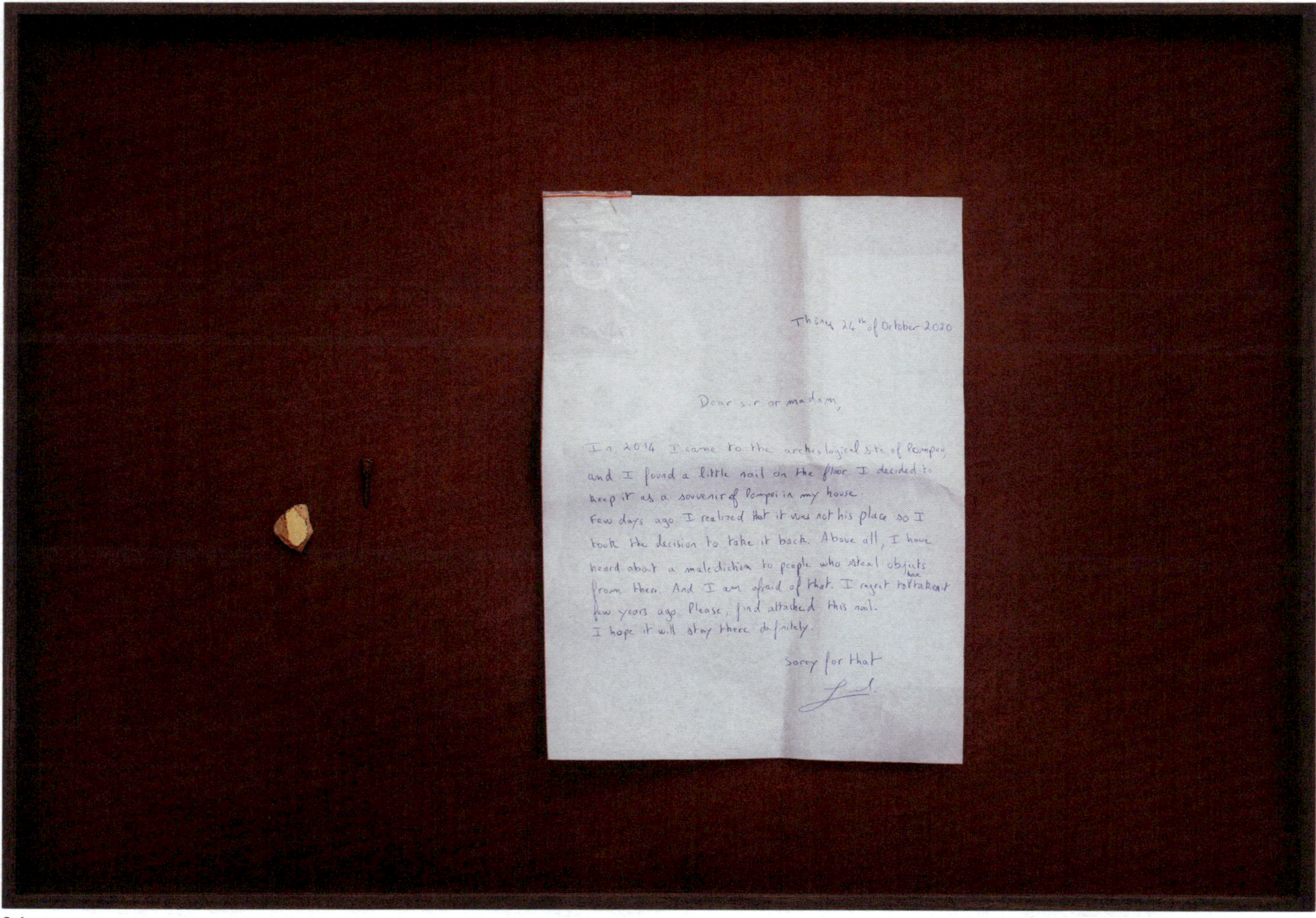


3.4

Dear Sir, Mrs,

I Herewith send you a peace of a marmera floor I took 10 years ago from the site in Pompeii. I am sorry it took so long returning it. As a child I was inspired by Pompei and felt I was familiar with the city and by visiting it three times I felt at home and I know that is not an excuus taking a peace of it with me. I am sorry for my fault.
Regards.

3.5

Rose Salane

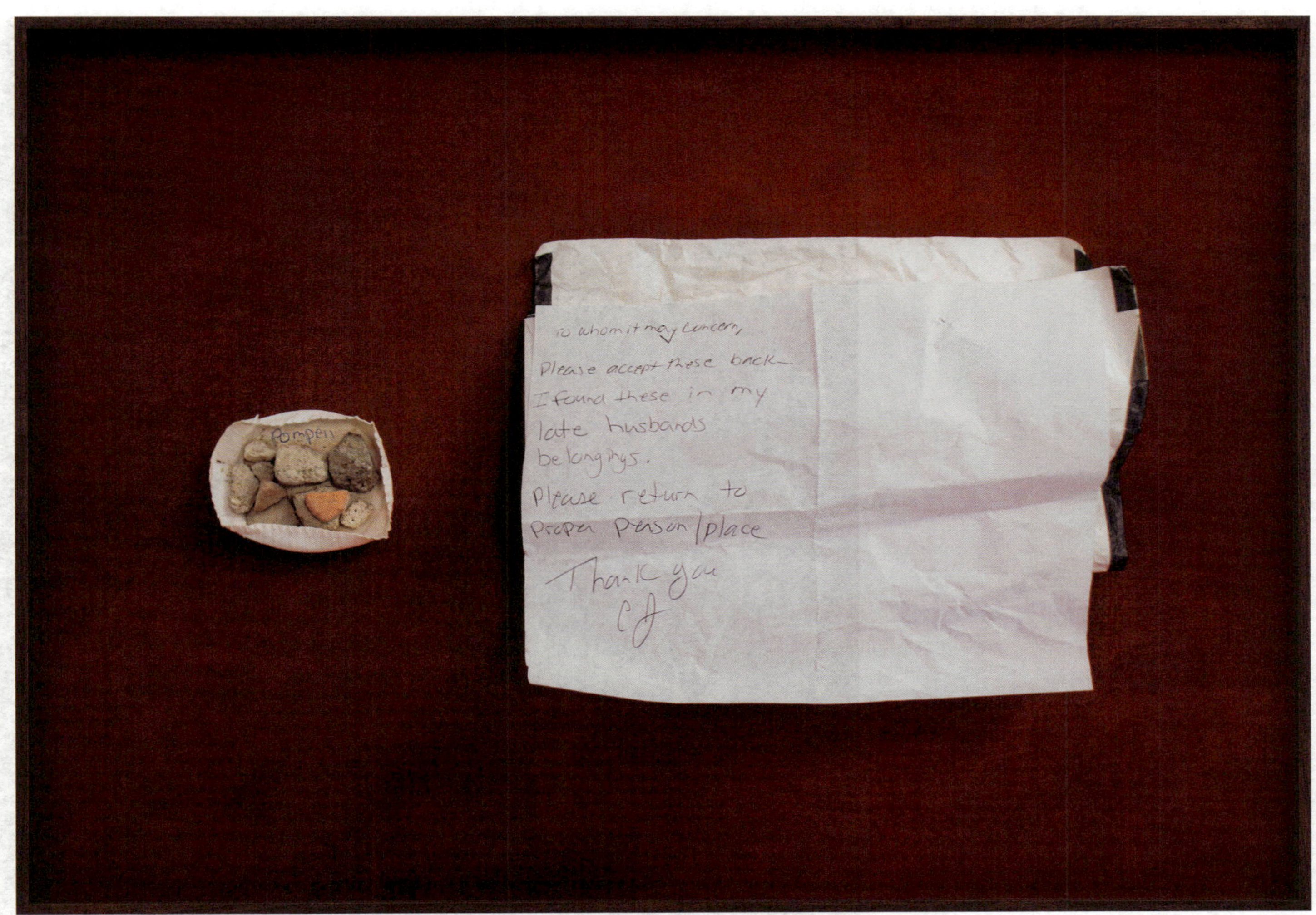


3.6

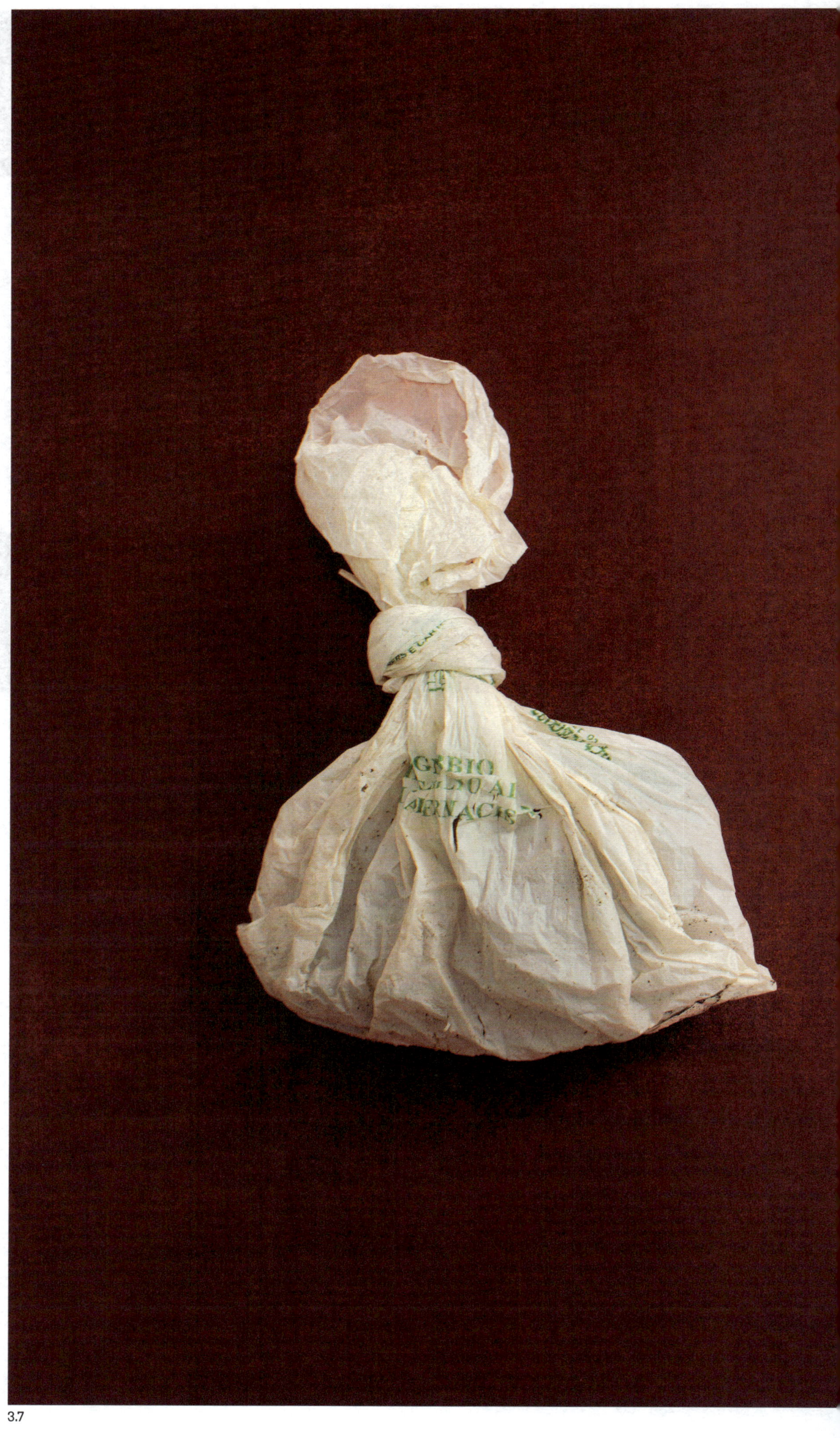

3.7

Rose Salane

People of Pompeii

I took these stones in July 2019. I was visiting c̄ my fiance. I was amazed and in awe of Pompeii. I took them because I was stupid and thought it was cool.

Since then, I have had numerous personal tragedies including the death of my daughter. This has caused me to look at the universe differently.

I understand that the people of Pompeii died in awful circumstances and they deserve to be left at rest.

I am truly sorry. Please forgive me

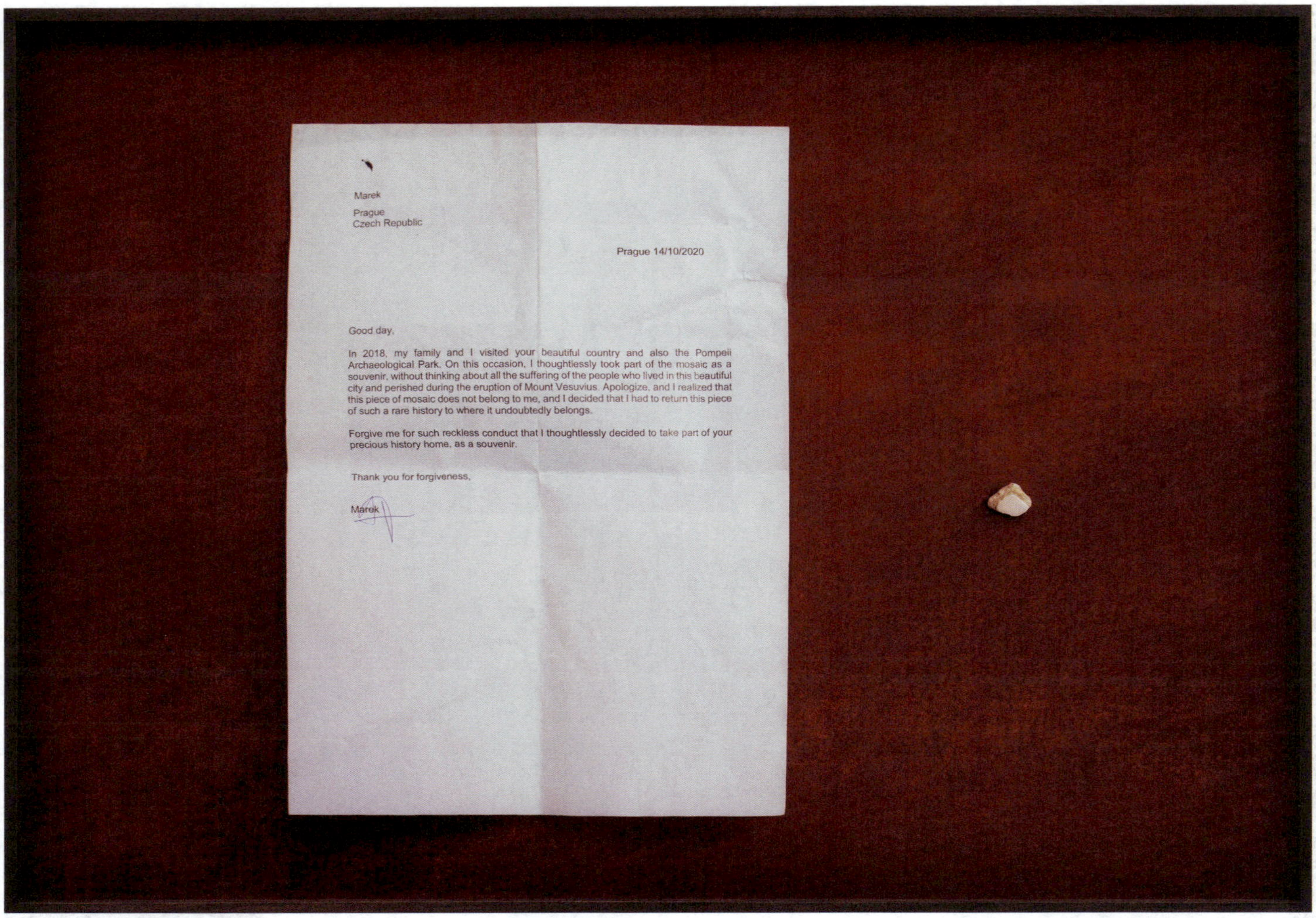

Marek

Prague
Czech Republic

Prague 14/10/2020

Good day,

In 2018, my family and I visited your beautiful country and also the Pompeii Archaeological Park. On this occasion, I thoughtlessly took part of the mosaic as a souvenir, without thinking about all the suffering of the people who lived in this beautiful city and perished during the eruption of Mount Vesuvius. Apologize, and I realized that this piece of mosaic does not belong to me, and I decided that I had to return this piece of such a rare history to where it undoubtedly belongs.

Forgive me for such reckless conduct that I thoughtlessly decided to take part of your precious history home, as a souvenir.

Thank you for forgiveness,

Marek

3.8

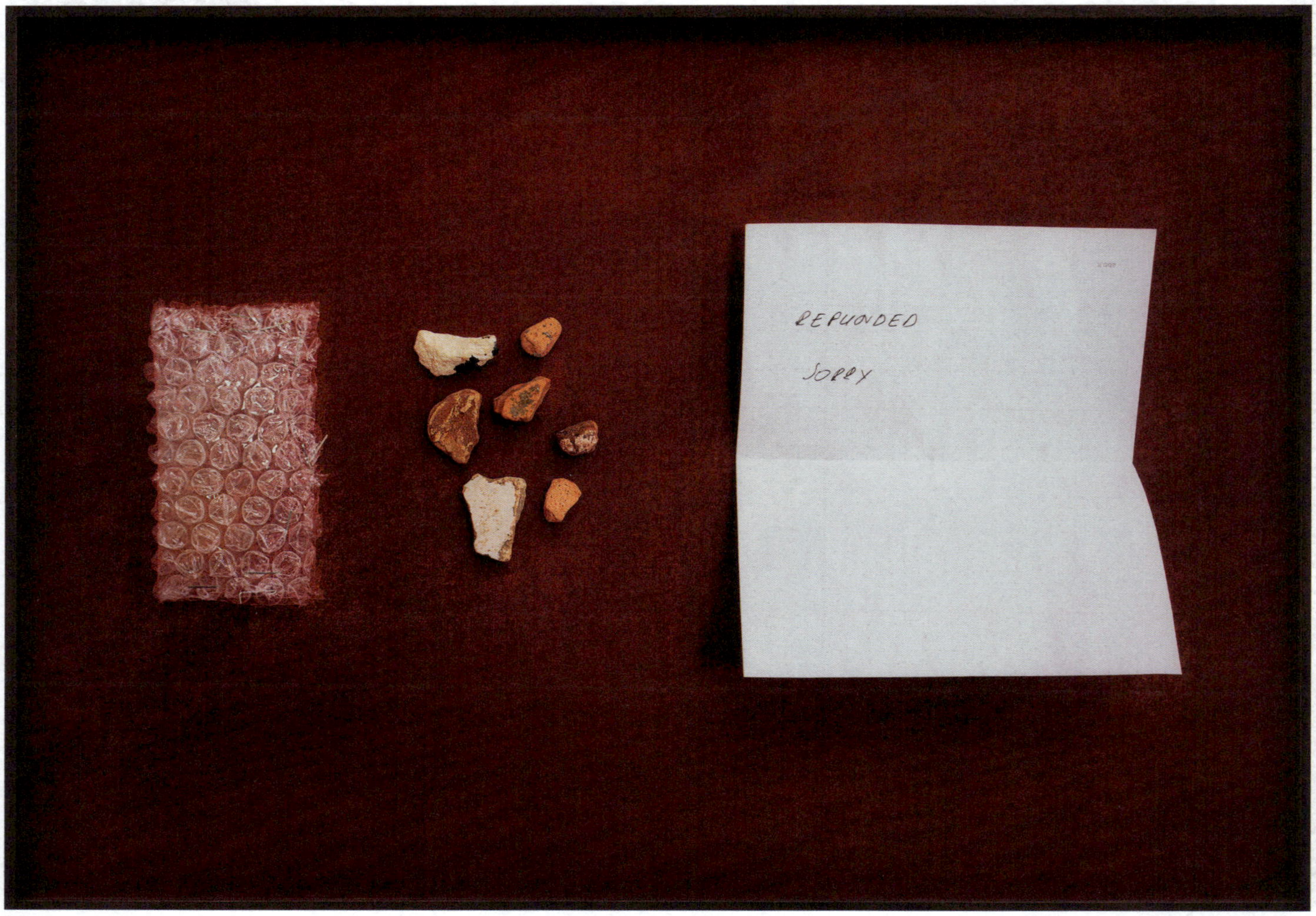

REFUNDED

SORRY

3.9

Rose Salane

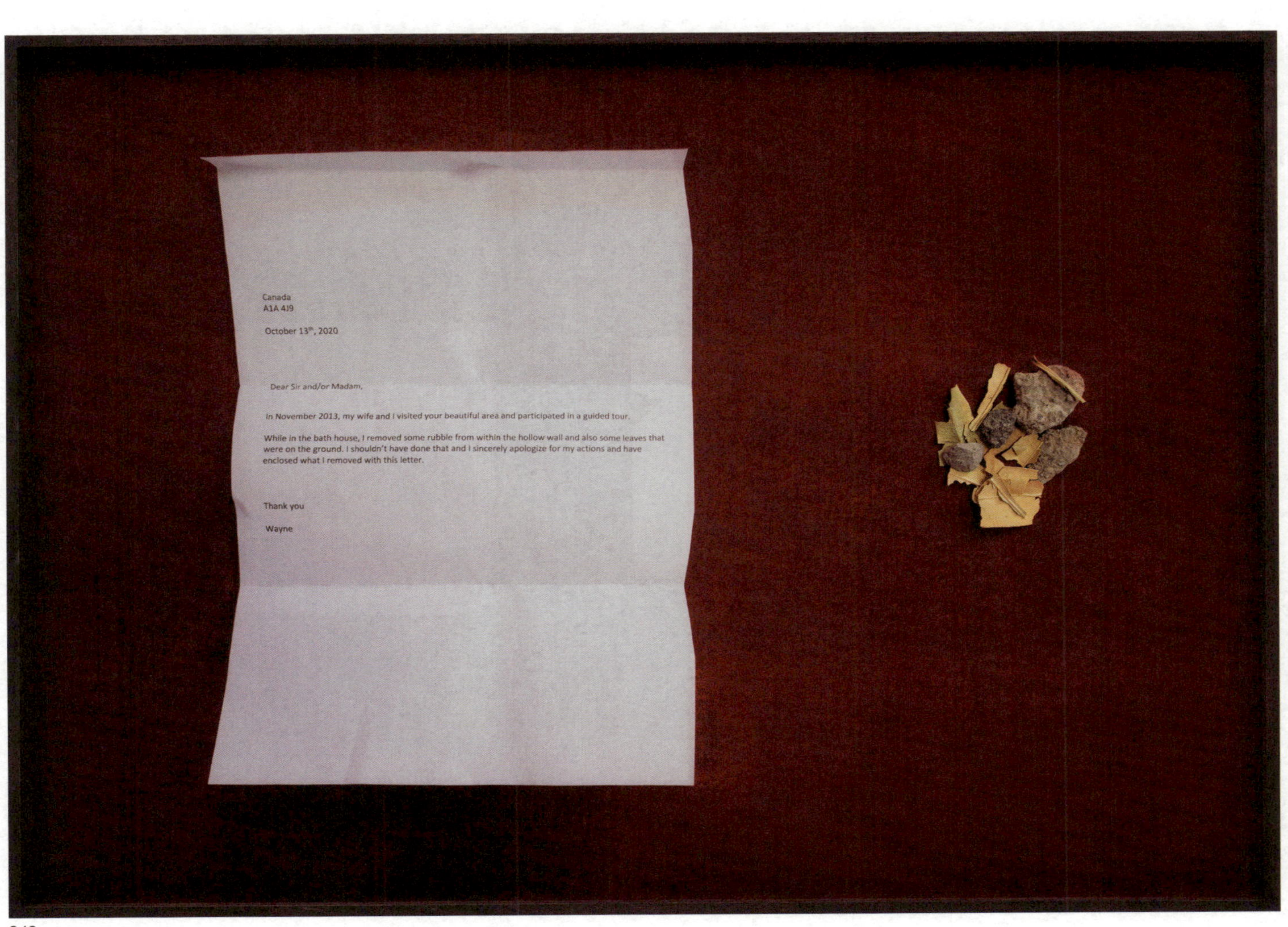

Canada
A1A 4J9

October 13th, 2020

Dear Sir and/or Madam,

In November 2013, my wife and I visited your beautiful area and participated in a guided tour.

While in the bath house, I removed some rubble from within the hollow wall and also some leaves that were on the ground. I shouldn't have done that and I sincerely apologize for my actions and have enclosed what I removed with this letter.

Thank you

Wayne

3.10

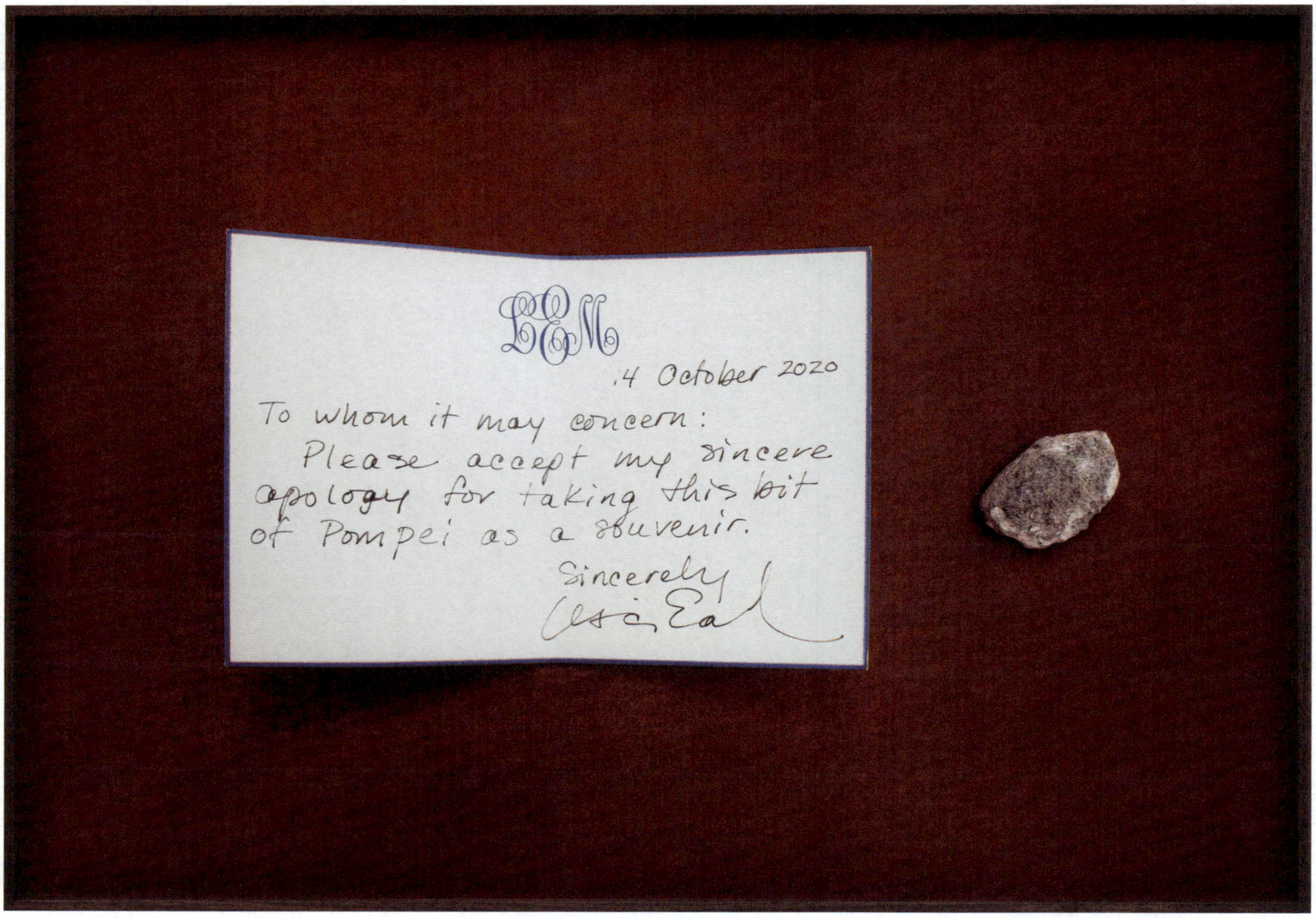

3.11

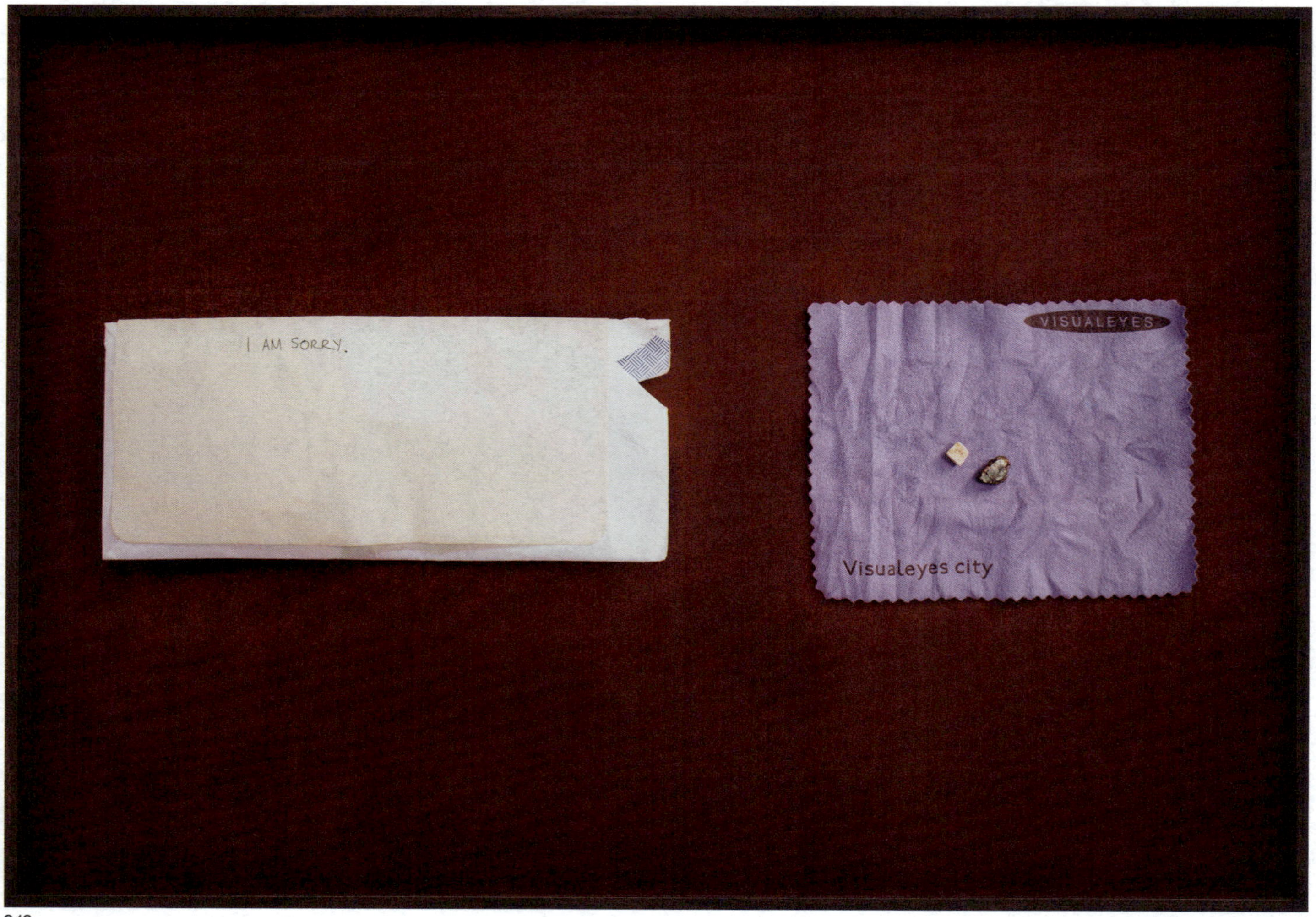

3.12

Rose Salane

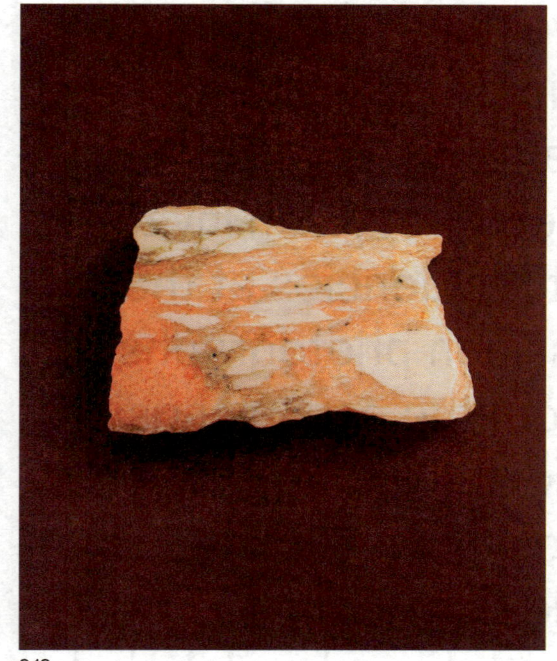
3.13

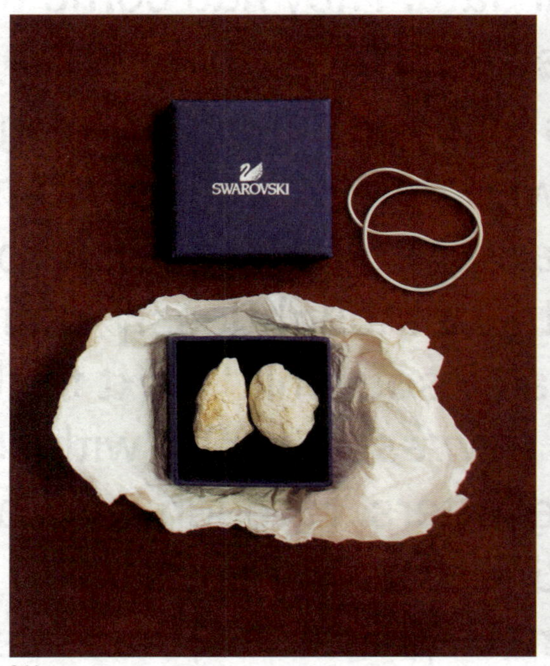

3.14

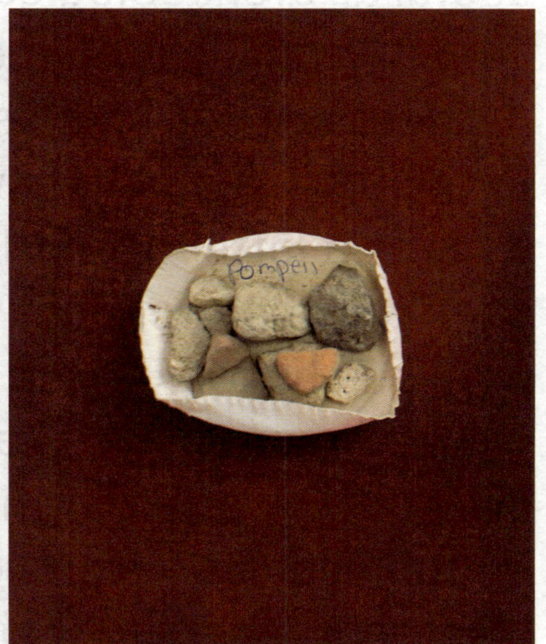

3.15

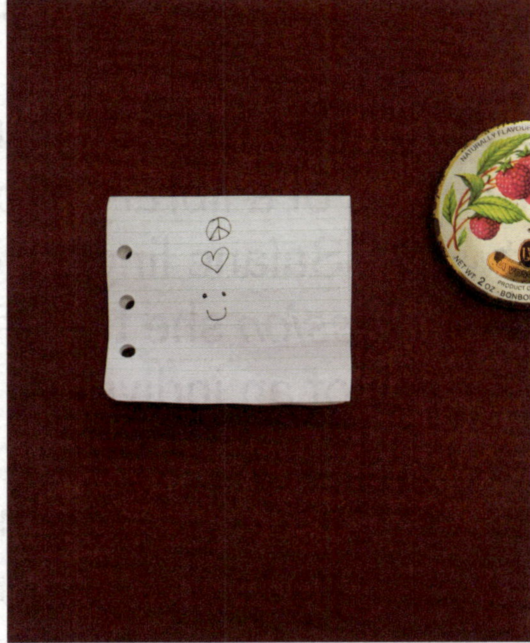
3.16

Rose Salane's work is deeply invested in the lives and afterlives of ordinary objects. Her research draws on object biographies to introduce the viewer to affective histories that often appear curiously minor in scale. Salane's *Confessions* (2023) were developed through an invitation in 2022 to participate in the first cohort of artist residencies at the Archaeological Park of Pompeii. Each of the fourteen photographs in the series presents an object or material taken from the park alongside a letter written by a regretful visitor seeking to make the ancient city whole. The objects pictured are not impressive treasures, however, but rather unidentifiable bits of soil, stone, mosaic, or marble that cannot be made useful as archaeological data. They had come to rest in a box labeled "reperti restituiti" (returned artifacts), where Salane found them during her residency. These objects (and the act of returning them) were meaningful to the fourteen people who removed them from the site. *Confession 6* depicts a letter from Marek (from Prague), who wrote, "Forgive me for such reckless conduct that I thoughtlessly decided to take part of your precious history home, as a souvenir." Next to the letter sits a single chipped mosaic tile. The *Confessions* play with scale, as the tesserae are invariably dwarfed by the letters. Through language and narrative these tiny objects are freighted with sentimental value and moral weight vastly disproportionate to their size, materials, and scientific significance.

Salane's earlier work reveals a preoccupation with different forms of loss; she has taken the role of researcher into microhistories of lost or forgotten objects or sites, among them rings found in the New York City subway system and the remains of a library once housed in the World Trade Center. In those artworks Salane lingers on the mystery of an object's past lives. In each *Confession* she transforms an archive of small stories into an abstract portrait of an individual in text and image. The writer in *Confession 12* notes that the impetus for their returns included "numerous personal tragedies" that caused them to "look at the universe differently," implying that their own losses spurred them to make this act of restitution. The photographs also capture the packaging of these materials, including a Swarovski jewelry box, a small square of bubble packaging, and a purple microfiber cleaning cloth for eyeglasses. These all suggest the care and reverence accorded to these objects. The letters expressing a desire for forgiveness and adherence to a higher ethical code are all photographed from above on a rich red background that fittingly evokes Catholic clerical garments or the curtains of a confessional booth. In recent years demands for the repatriation of cultural property have spread across the globe. The *Confessions* examine the limits and possibilities of restitution; reparation is paradoxically impossible for these small thefts. While these materials cannot be restored to their original context, the gesture of repair speaks to the universal quest for moral absolution and the ever-present promise of a change of heart. (BE)

CHANG YUCHEN Selections from *Coral Dictionary (Sentences)*, 2019–, pencil on paper, selection of up to 76 drawings: 17 × 14 in. (43.2 × 35.6 cm) each unframed, courtesy the artist, New York, and Beijing Commune

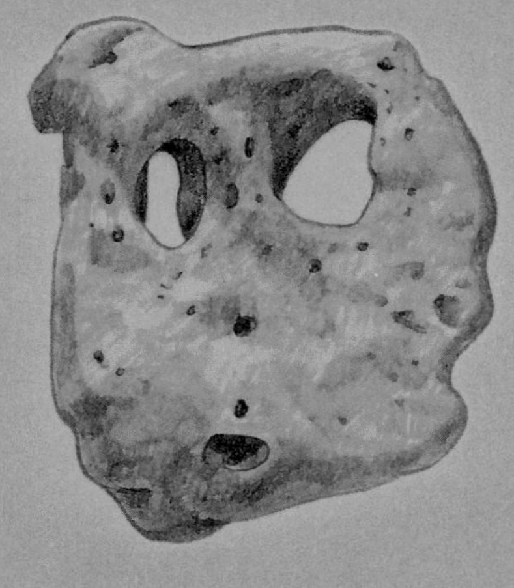

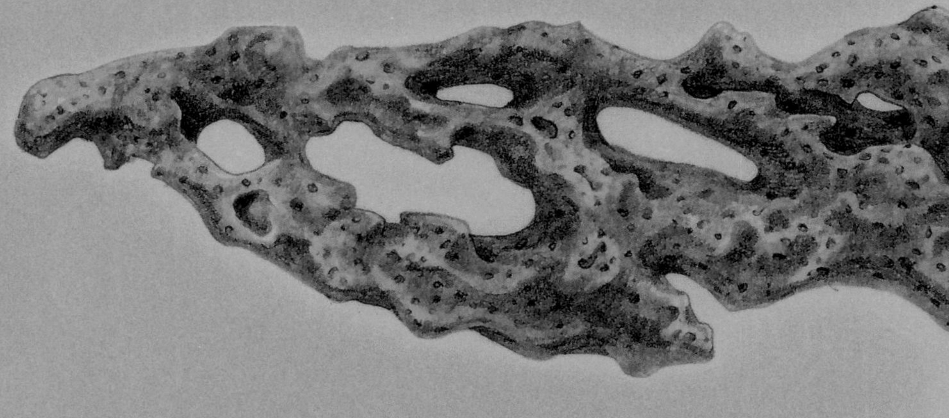

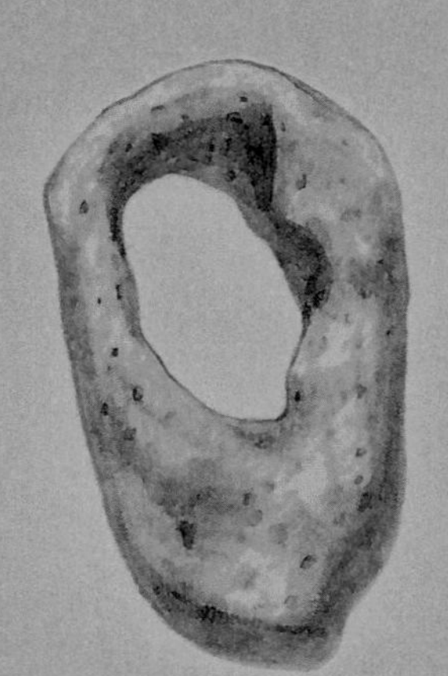

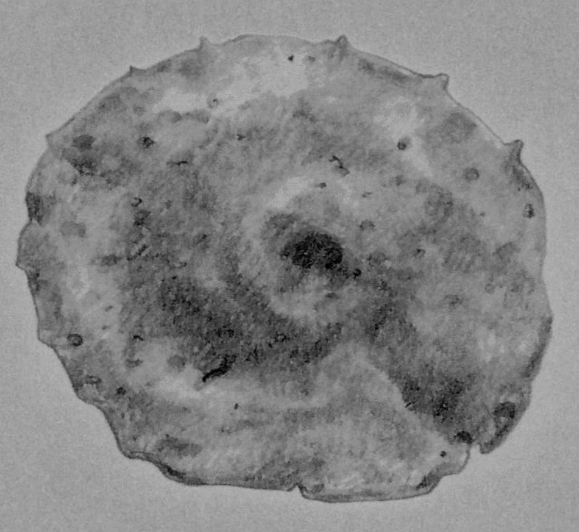

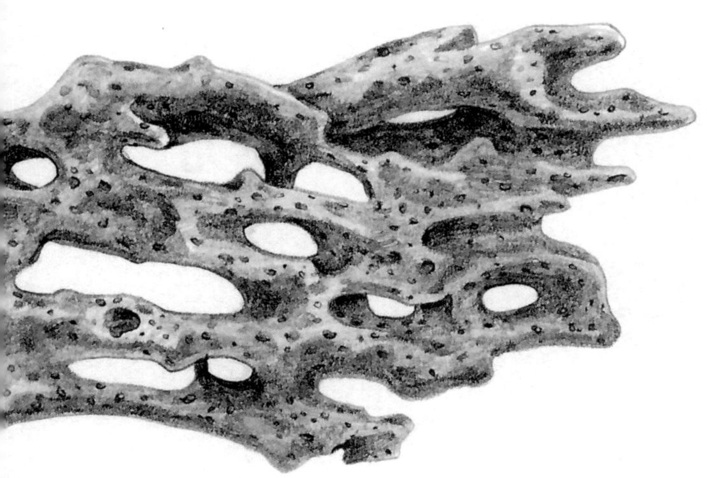

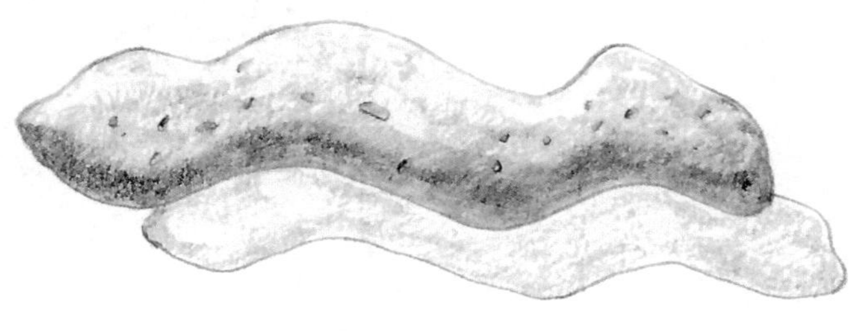

Luasnya cakerawala itu tidak terbatas.
The vastness of the sky is unbound.
天空是无限广阔的。
luasnya (luas)
vastness (wide, broad / area)
广阔 (广阔的 / 面积)
cakerawala
the sky
天空
itu
that / the
那个
tidak
no, not
不，没有
terbatas (batas)
limited / restricted (limit / boundary)
有限的 / 受限的 (界限，限度)
.
.
。

4.2

Reriang yang berdengung sungguh bising.
Cicadas' buzzing is really noisy.
蝉发出的鸣叫声真吵闹。
reriang
cicadas
蝉
yang
who / which / that
那个
berdengung (dengung)
to buzz (buzzing)
发出嗡嗡声 (嗡嗡声)
sungguh
true / really / indeed / earnestly
确实的 / 真的 / 实在 / 认真的
bising
noisy
吵闹
.
.
。

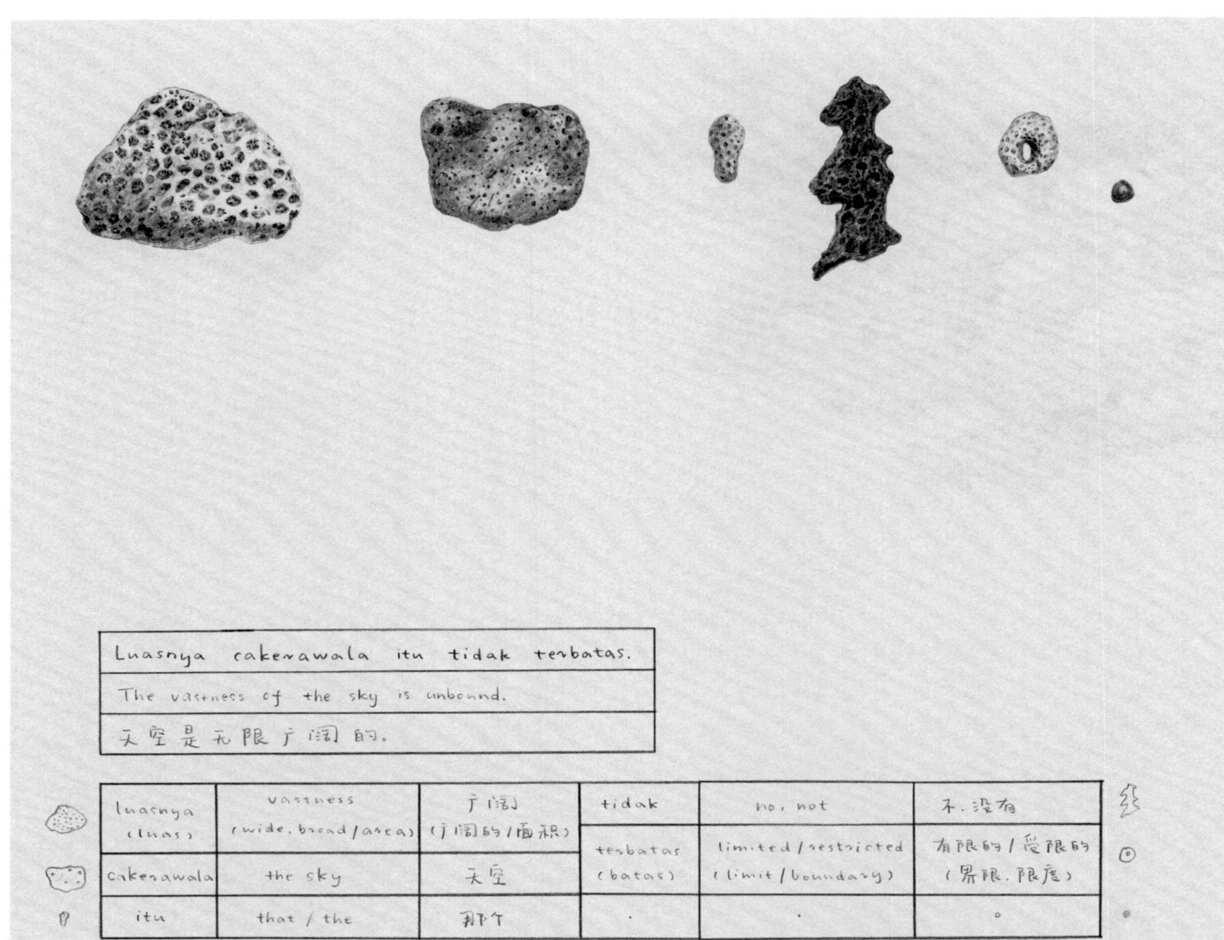

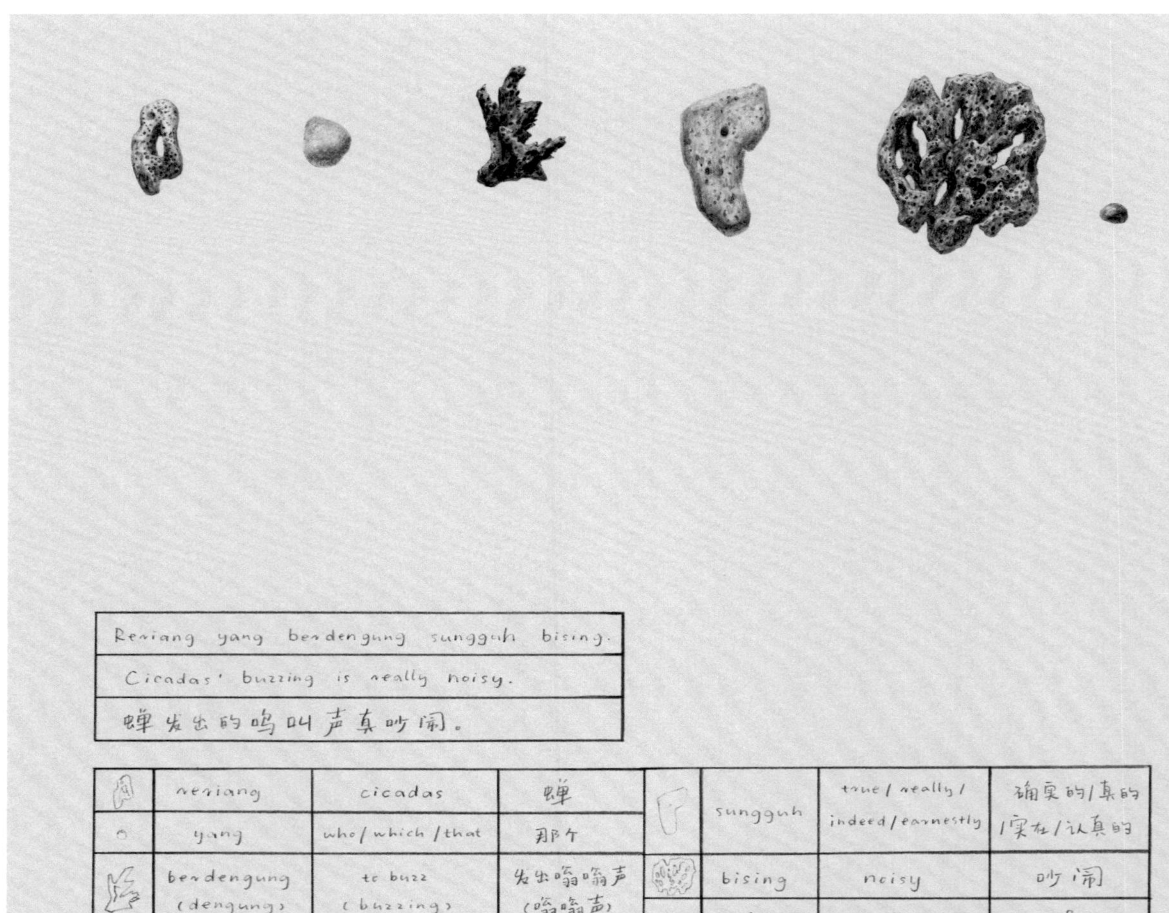

4.3

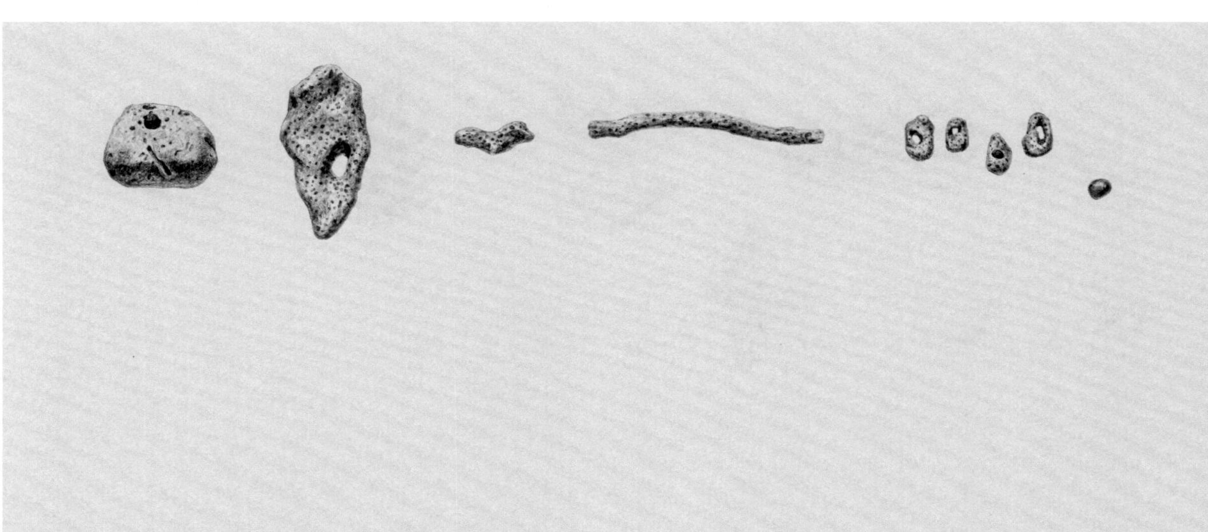

| Matahari terbenam di ufuk barat. |
| --- |
| The sun sets in the west horizon. |
| 太阳在西边落了。 |

| | matahari | sun | 太阳 | | di | in, at, on / by | 在，于 / 被 |
| --- | --- | --- | --- | --- | --- | --- | --- |
| | terbenam | to set (of the sun and moon) / immersed / be hidden | 沉落 / 陷落 / 被深藏 | | ufuk | horizon | 地平线 |
| | | | | | barat | west / western | 西方 / 西方的 |
| | | | | ○ | . | . | 。 |

4.4

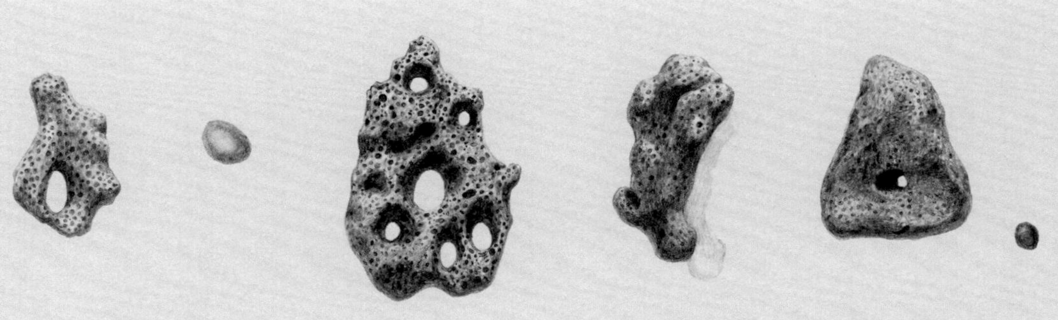

| Daun yang berembun segar-segar belaka. |
| --- |
| The dewy leaf is utterly fresh. |
| 沾了露水的叶鲜灵灵。 |

| | daun | leaf / lobe | 叶子 / 耳垂 | | segar | fresh / lively | 新鲜的 / 生动的 |
| --- | --- | --- | --- | --- | --- | --- | --- |
| ○ | yang | who / which / that | …的，那个 | | belaka | entirely / quite | 完全，全部 / 十分，非常 |
| | berembun (embun) | dewy (dew) | 有露水的 (露) | ○ | . | . | 。 |

4.5

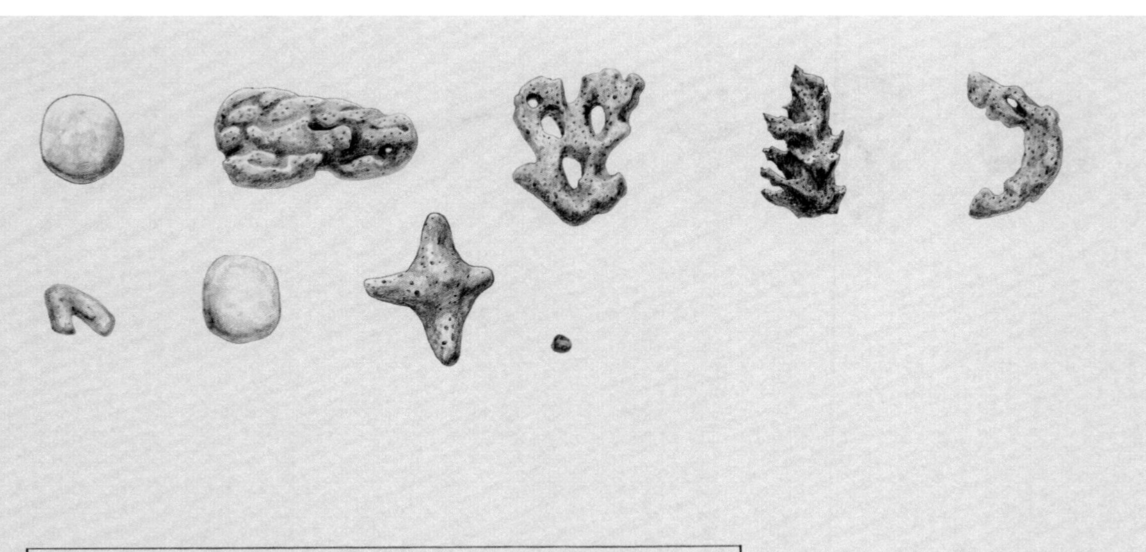


4.6

Chang Yuchen

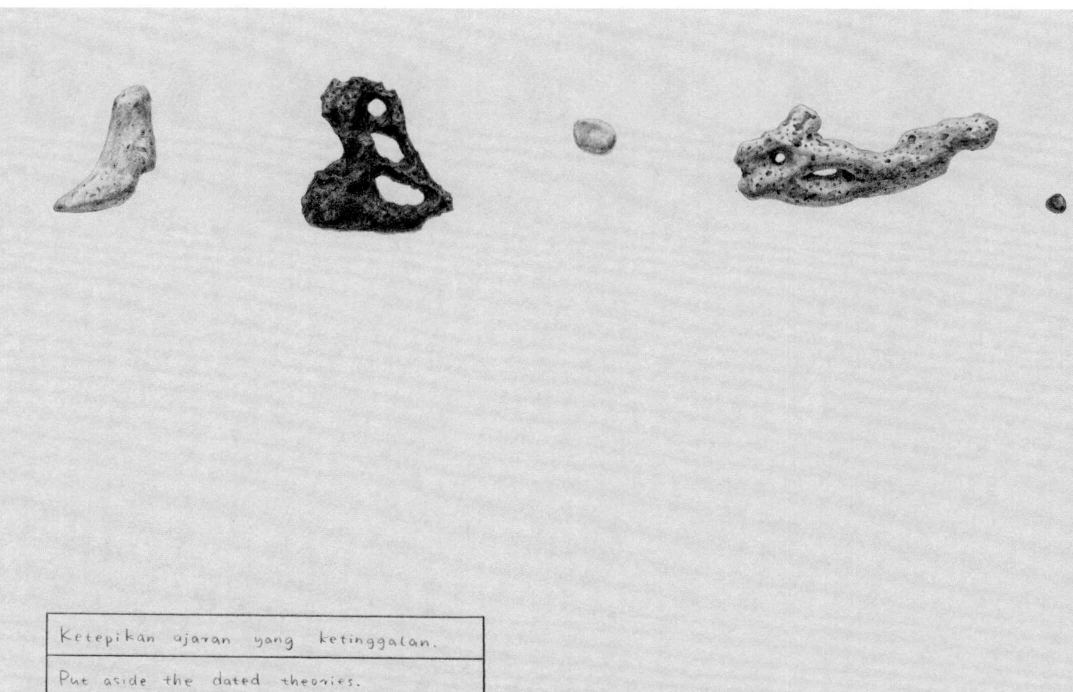

| Ketepikan ajaran yang ketinggalan. |
|---|
| Put aside the dated theories. |
| 把落后的学说搁在一边。 |

| | | | | | | | |
|---|---|---|---|---|---|---|---|
| | ketepikan (tepi) | to cast aside / ignore (side, edge) | 搁到一旁 / 忽略 (旁边, 侧) | | ketinggalan (tinggal) | remaider / to be left behind (to live at / to be left / to remain / past, gone | 剩下的 / 落后的 (住 / 剩下 / 依然 / 已过去的 |
| | ajaran (ajar) | warning / teaching, theory (to teach) | 教训 / 学说, 理论 (教, 教导) | | | | |
| o | yang | who / which / that | …的 | o | . | . | 。 |

4.7

| Ada orang bantah ada orang sokong cadangan itu. |
|---|
| There are people against that proposal, there are people for it. |
| 有人反对, 有人支持那项建议。 |

| | | | | | | | |
|---|---|---|---|---|---|---|---|
| | ada | to have / to exist | 有 / 存在 | | sokong | to support | 支持, 支撑 |
| | orang | human being, people / measure word for people | 人 / 位, 个, 名 | | cadangan (cadang) | proposal / project / reserve | 建议, 提案 / 计划 / 储备 |
| | bantah | oppose, protest | 反对, 抗议 | o | . | . | 。 |

4.8

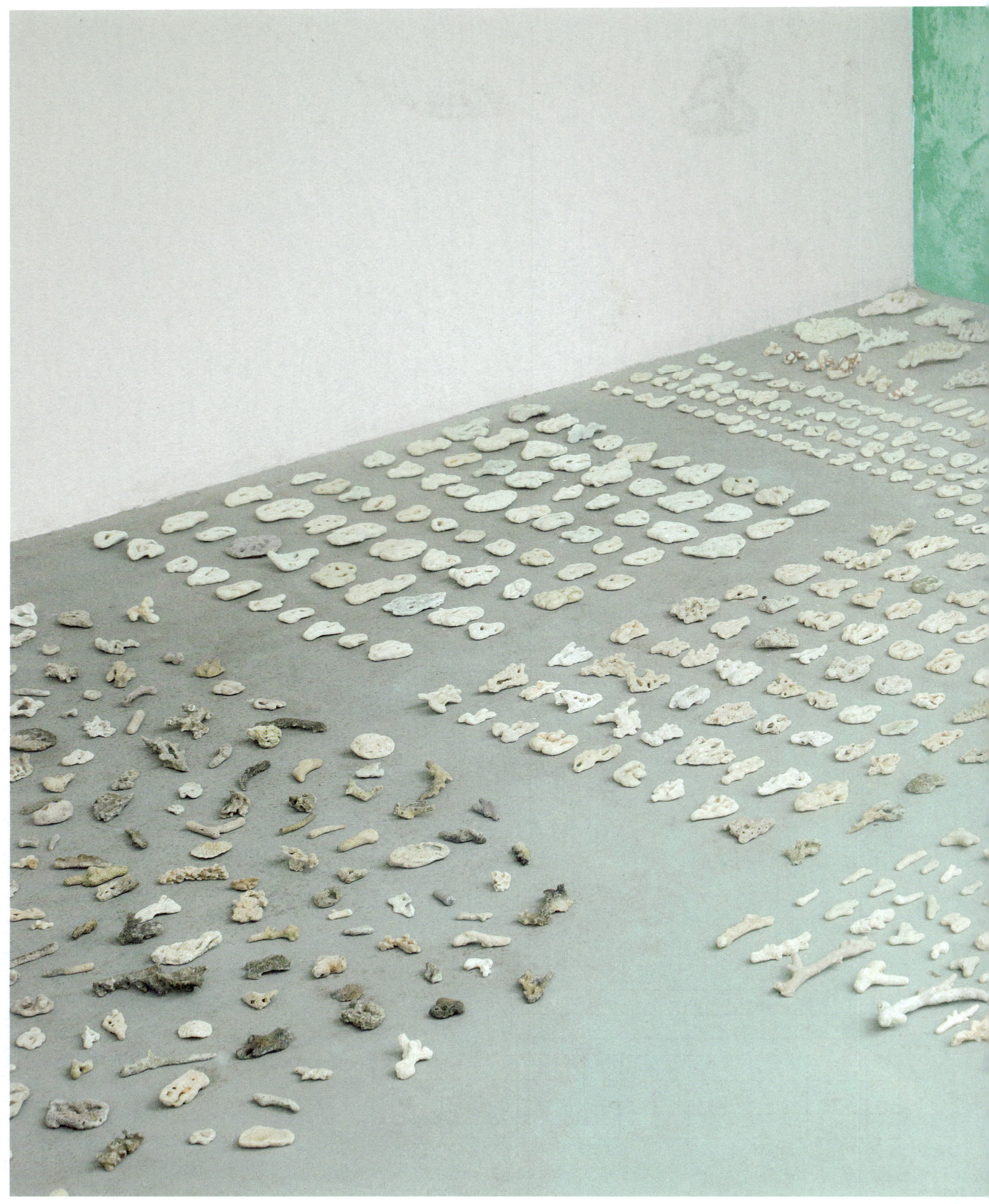

*Coral Dictionary (words)*, date unknown 4.9

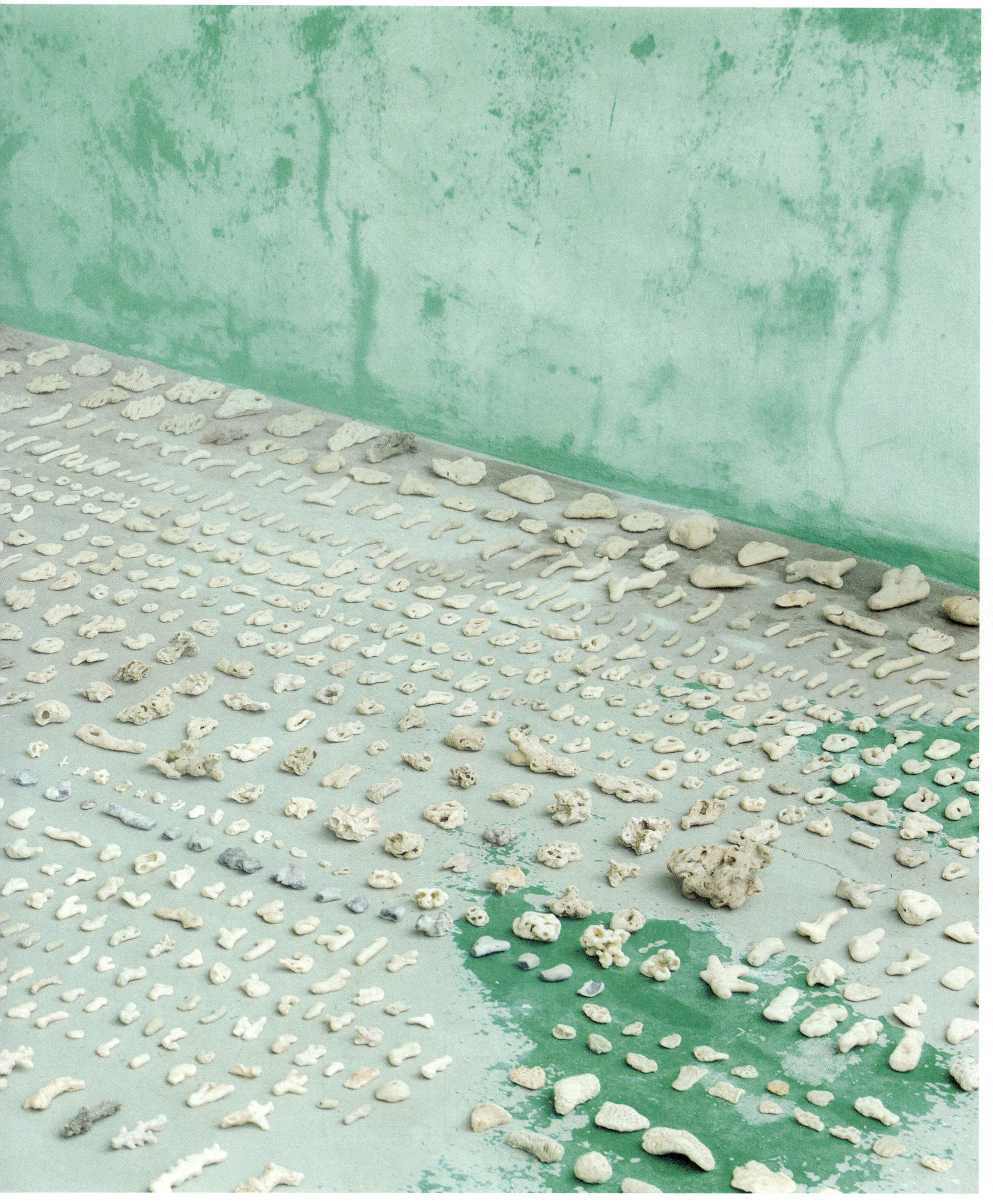

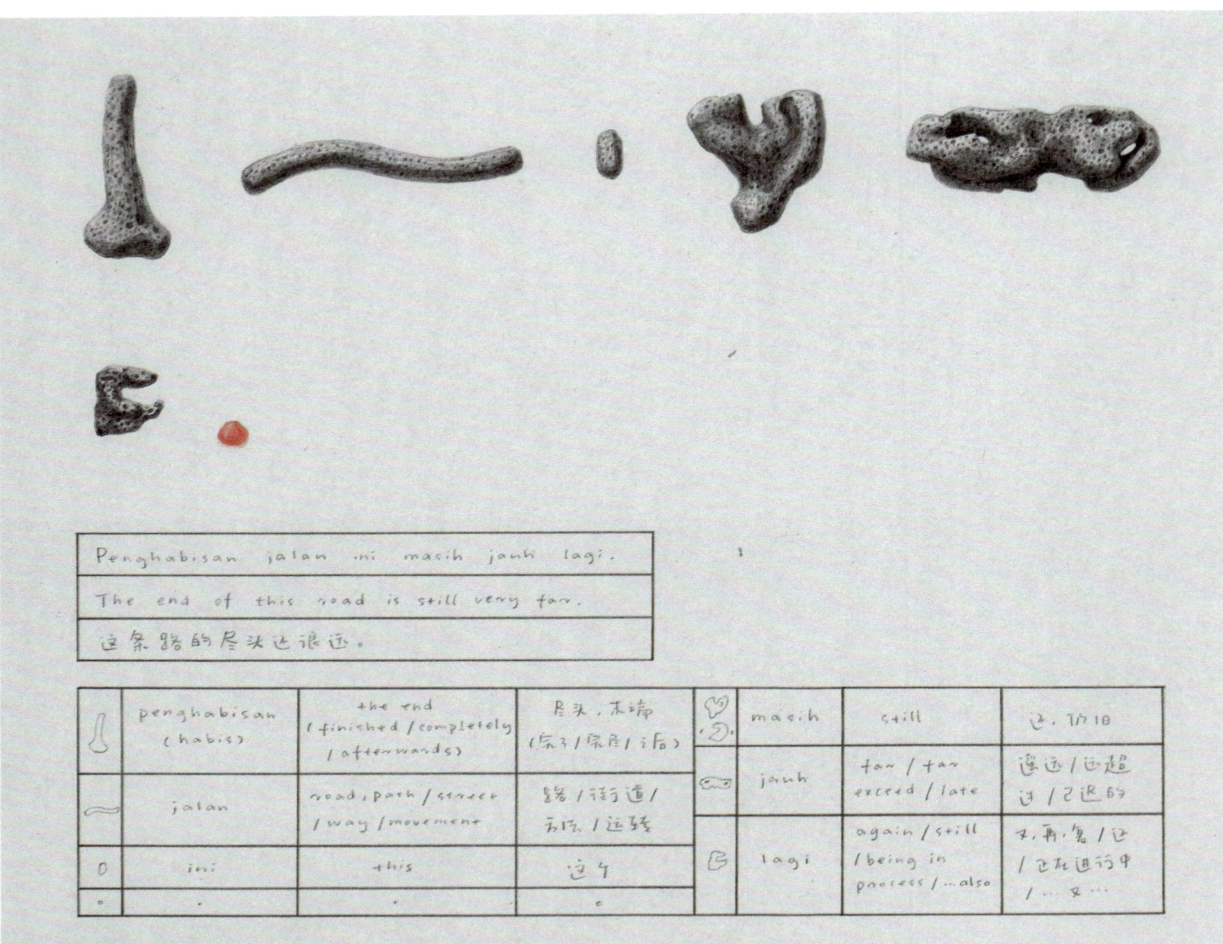


4.10

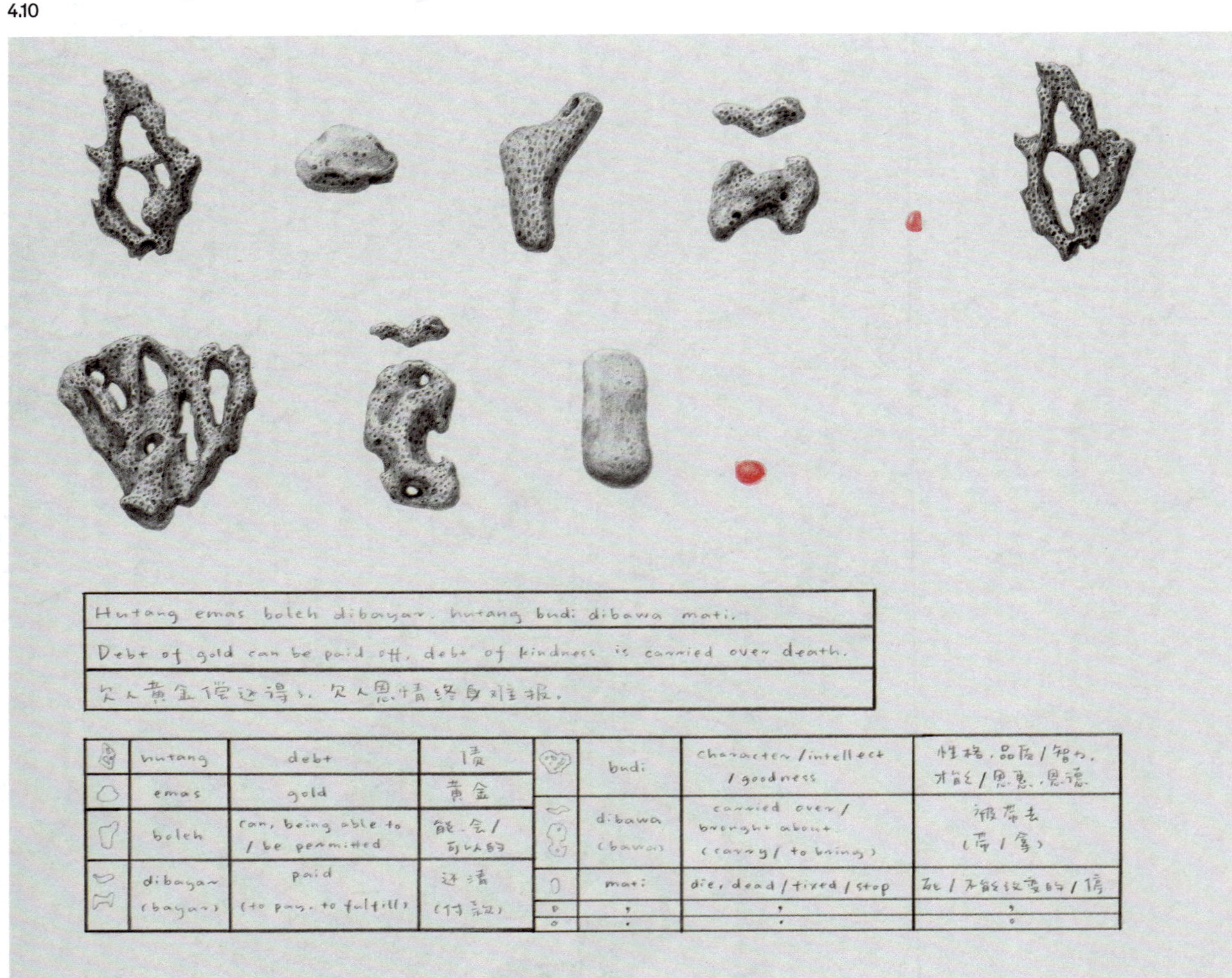


4.11

## Chang Yuchen

Kerana hawa itu bergerak terjadilah angin.
It's the movement of the air that causes wind.
空气流动即生风。
kerana
because of / reason
因为，由于 / 理由，原因
hawa
air / climate
空气 / 天气，气候
itu
that / the
那个
bergerak (gerak)
change position / to be in operation (movement)
移动，走动 / 活动（动作）
terjadilah (jadi)
to happen / made up of, consist of / finished / happen, occur / as a result / to be born
发生 / 组成（完成 / 发生，实现 / 结果，所以 / 诞生）
angin
wind / air
风

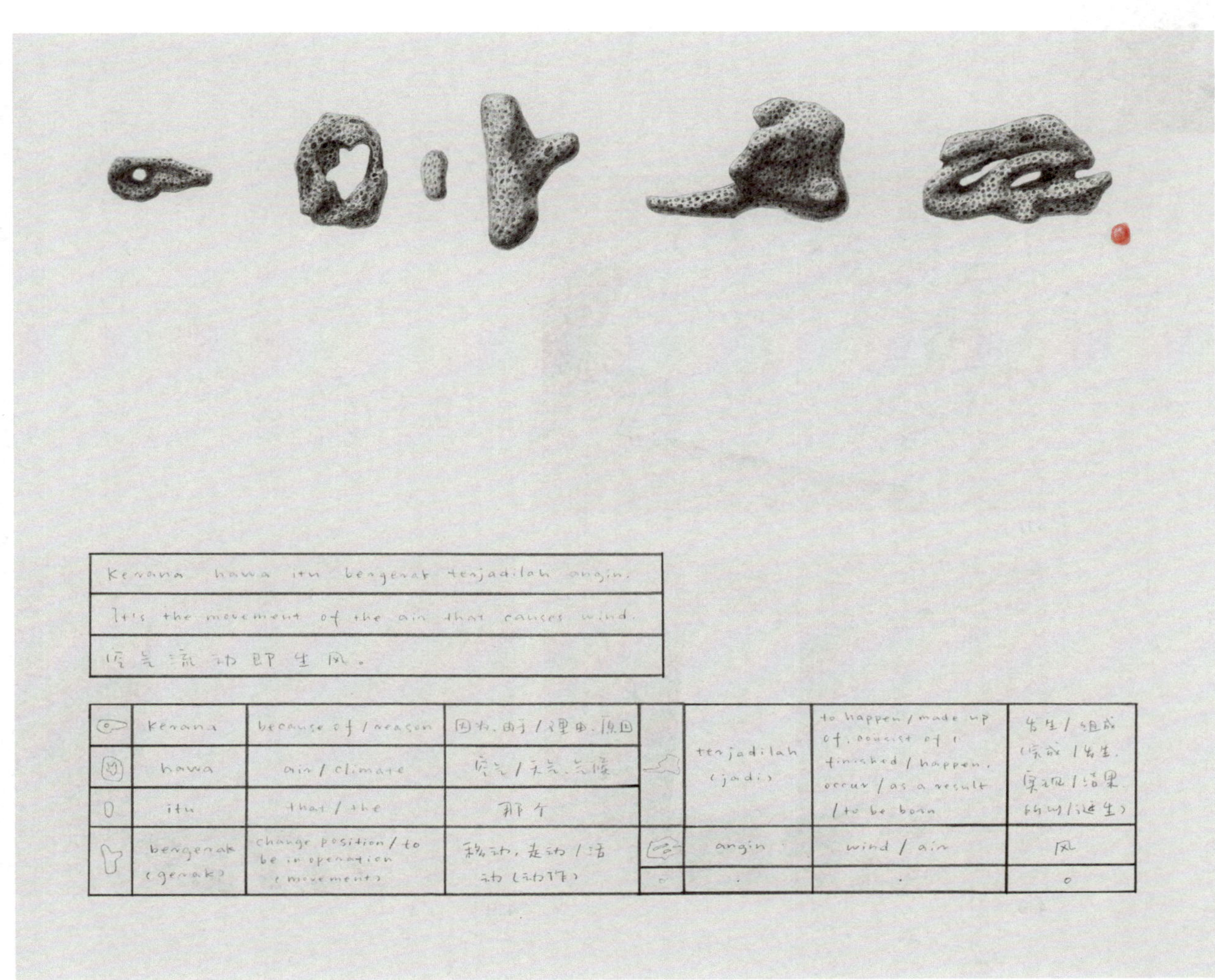

4.12

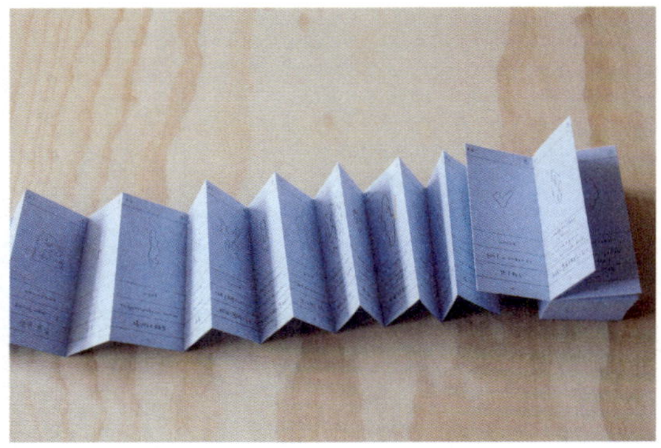

4.13

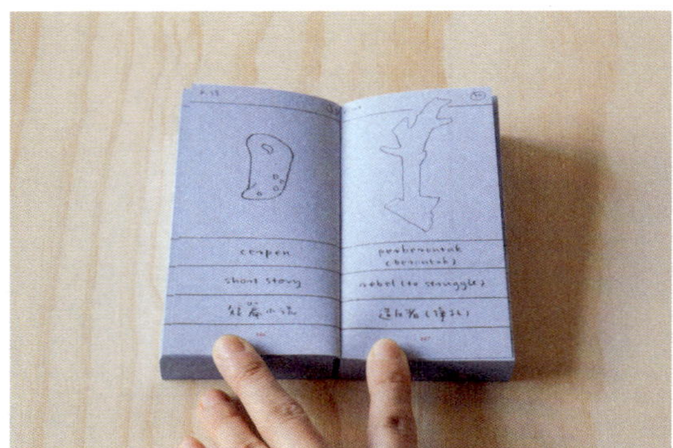

4.14

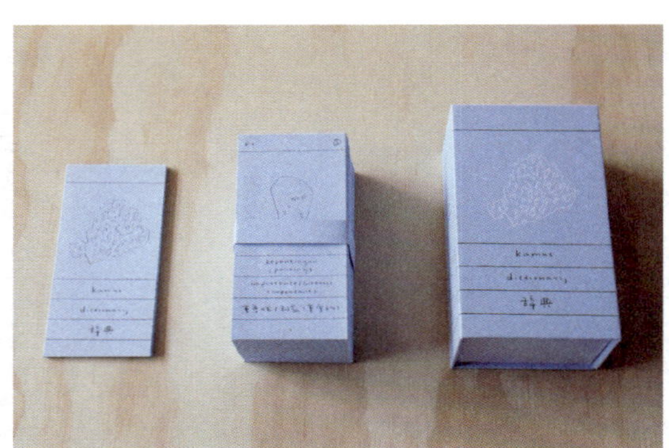

4.15

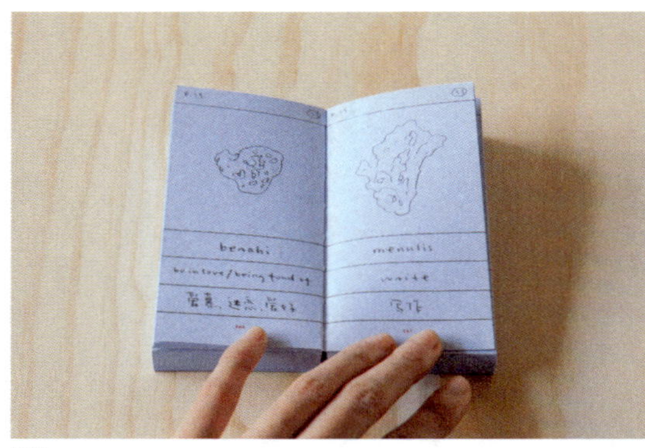

4.16

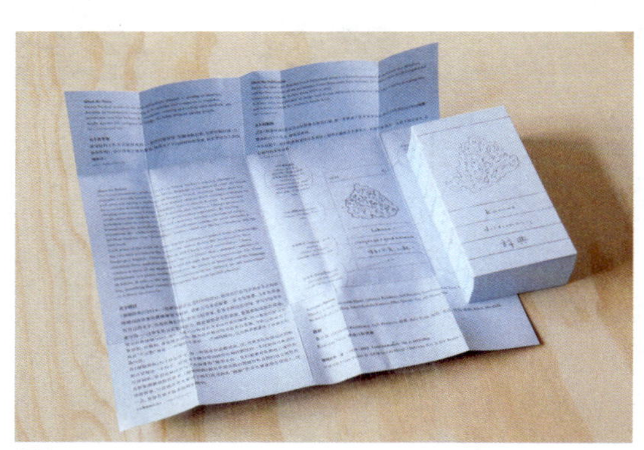

4.17

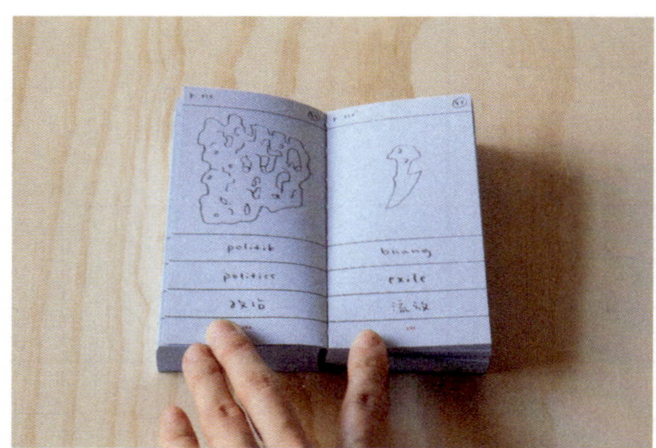

4.18

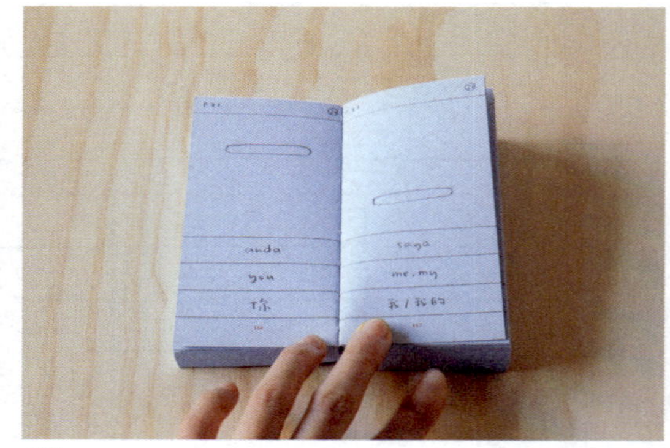

4.19

*Coral Dictionary Vol. 1: 2019–2022 (Accordion)*, printed 2022

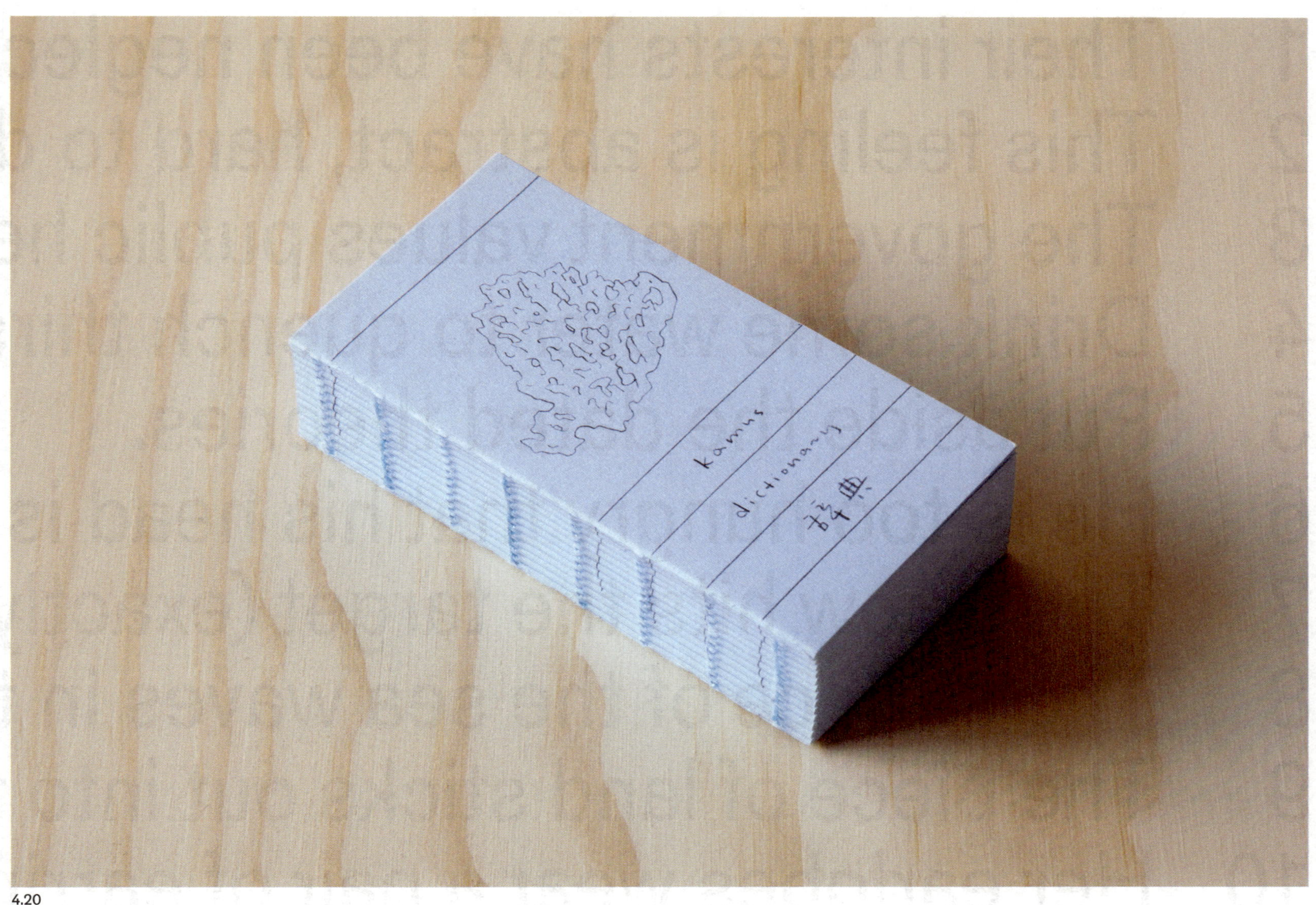


4.20

1 Their interests have been neglect

2 This feeling is abstract, hard to de

3 The government values public hea

4 Drink some water to quench thirs

5 Put aside the dated theories.

6 He is too hungry that his head is

7 The arrow hits the target (exactly

8 The surface of the sea waves in th

9 The piece of land sticks out into t

10 Her earlobes wear a pair of earrin

11 Why doesn't this child attend sch

12 Natural rubber is facing serious c

13 Salt can preserve food avoiding s

14 It seems like he didn't hear my ca

15 Thick mist has vanished, as the s

16 Take good care of your younger b

17 That injury left a scar.

ribe.

n.

zy.

morning.

sea.

?

petition from synthetic rubber.

lage.

becoming hotter.

ner (sister).

18 My letter received no response.
19 His salary matches his capability.
20 People from various ethnic groups
21 There are many tall buildings in do
22 There are people against that pro
23 He is sleeping with his arm as pill
24 Wherever you go, I will be able to
25 I can do any kind of work.
26 He doesn’t reveal inner sorrow of
27 Please take a look at your shadow
28 Behaviors reflect one’s thoughts.
29 It is said, he wants to liberate the
30 He often defends poor people.
31 The sun sets in the west horizon.
32 Have you obtained permission fro
33 His head felt dizzy when he left th
34 Take good care till total recovery,

e connected through national language.
ntown area.
sal, there are people for it.

d you.

heart.
that mirror.

pressed people.

the authorities yet?
inema.
order to prevent relapse.

35 My elder brother likes writing sho

36 The rebel has been arrested by th

37 Even though I keep working, actu

38 We study as usual in the rainy sea

39 He has whipping scars on his bac

40 The darkness of the night increas

41 Why do you cry secretly?

42 They are all colonizers' puppets.

43 All political prisoners were exiled

44 The government launches the car

45 The vastness of the sky is unbour

46 His home is painted with blue pai

47 The night is deep, his eyes are sti

48 Once we get there, we split up.

49 He waded shallow river to the opp

50 Princess misses the lost mouse c

51 She can smell flower's fragrance.

tories.
olice.
I'm very tired.
n.

the anxiety in his heart.

an island.
aign to wipe out illiteracy.

ide-open.

ite bank.
r very much.

52 My heart is beating in fear.
53 Stubbornness obstructs one’s pr
54 Cicadas buzzing is really noisy.
55 I’ve been wanting to go home to t
56 She uses a small stem of candle t
57 That ancient architecture has bee
58 She thinks about things with her
59 The dewy leaf is utterly fresh.
60 Apples are imported from foreign
61 The way a society changes is evo
62 Of course it is difficult if we want
63 We must think carefully before we
64 This film offered a false descriptio
65 Mother is worried when father is
66 The end of this road is still very fa
67 It’s the movement of the air that c
68 He is searching for magic to capt

ess.

village for long.
luminate her room.
estroyed by dynamite.
d up.

untries.
onary.
understand other people's ideas.
eak.
of the native people.
d to be missing.

ses wind.
e his fiancé's heart.

69 That ship disappeared from sight
70 Birds perch on top of the branch.
71 Fisherman on the sea often get ca
72 Debt of gold can be paid off, debt
73 Knowledge is like the torch of our
74 Foreign workers are tied by speci
75 He dreams even in day time.
76 Why do you keep asking over and

ht by the rain.
kindness is carried over death.
es.
conditions.

ain!

Made up of dozens of drawings, several artist's books, and a series of performances, Chang Yuchen's ongoing project *Coral Dictionary* began in 2019 during a residency on the Malaysian island of Dinawan. Located off the northwestern coast of the island of Borneo, Dinawan is largely undeveloped. During an evening visit to its western coast, the artist found a beach covered in fragments of small white corals. Chang noted that each "bleached and dehydrated" coral was an index of natural forces, including "sunshine, moonlight, ocean currents, [and] time."[1] She began collecting and sorting the corals, grouping them according to their formal characteristics. As she spent time with her growing collection, she created small drawings that functioned as a mode of study.

Soon afterward, on a resupply trip off the island, the artist purchased a copy of the *Kamus Sari*, a Malay to English and Mandarin dictionary first published in 1973. In response to the dictionary, Chang began to develop her *Coral Dictionary*, an artist's book that has taken several formats to date, including a small, palm-sized paperback and an accordion-fold book, both of which feature illustrations of individual corals with their "translations" in Malay, English, and Mandarin. The *Kamus Sari* contained not only the definitions of words in Malay but also a set of several hundred sentences translated between Malay and Mandarin. As a Mandarin speaker who does not speak Malay, Chang felt a connection to this text. Its history tethered her presence on Dinawan to the longer history of the Chinese diaspora in Malaysia and across Southeast Asia. Each sentence is a ready-made narrative fragment, a set of fictive conversations that might transpire between two speakers of different languages.

These sentences gave a new structure to the corals as Chang began to use them as a new script. In a still-growing series of drawings, each sentence is laid out in a graphite drawing of coral fragments above two charts. One shows the sentence in Malay, English, and Mandarin, and the other shows the meaning of each individual coral fragment, translated across the three languages. Some sentences describe or characterize elements of Malay geography. "The surface of the sea waves in the morning" is represented by a large, horizontally oriented fragment with dozens of holes, which readily evokes the shifting surface of a choppy sea. The coral for "morning" is a small, smooth oval shape with an opening that suggests the dynamic opening of the day.

Dinawan and many surrounding islands are fringed by reefs that gradually expand the island's usable area. By writing with corals, Chang employs the material of the land itself and evokes the relationship between landscape and language. Other sentences chart charged emotional interactions. "He doesn't reveal inner sorrow of his heart" includes a dark, pockmarked fragment that represents negation, and a solid rectangular coral with a small hole that represents "inside/in/deep/profound." Still other sentences allude to political struggle and analysis. "It is said, he wants to liberate the oppressed people" suggests that ideas like "liberation" and "oppression" were part of a shared vocabulary that might have built mutual understanding between a Mandarin speaker and a Malay speaker in the 1970s. In total the visual lexicon of the *Coral Dictionary* draws together affect, land, migration, and history in ways that emphasize the open possibilities of language. (BE)

1 "Coral Dictionary (a Lecture)," lecture at Tai Kwun Contemporary, Hong Kong, 2020, Vimeo video, 24:08, posted by Chang Yuchen, 2020, https://vimeo.com/389488407.

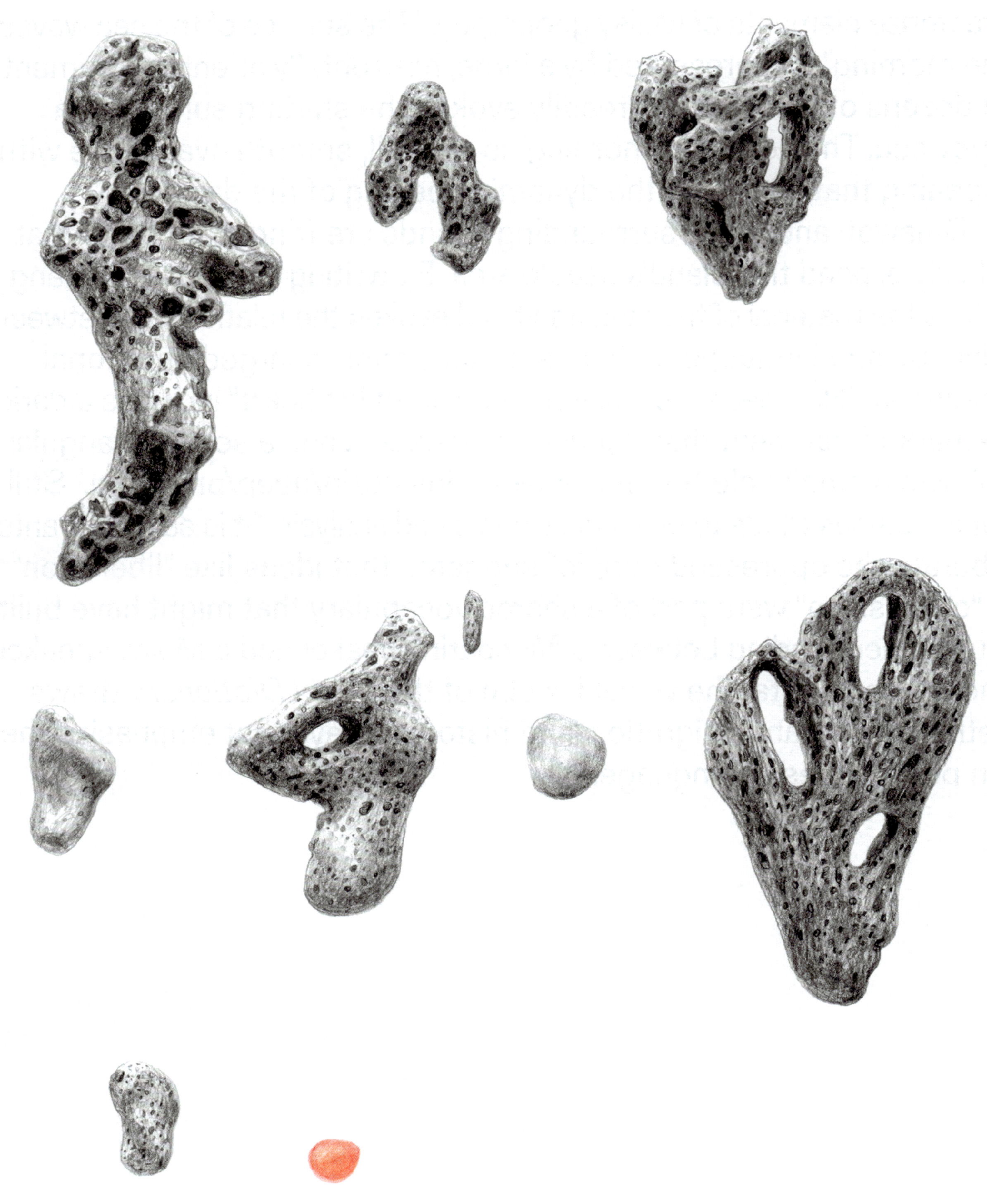

Chang Yuchen 4.21

# WAYS OF (UN)KNOWING

Rosario Güiraldes

A group exhibition of contemporary art, given its discursive and subjective nature, is a challenging curatorial exercise.[1] I would argue that group shows that don't whittle down the overwhelming amount of contemporary art produced today through the lens of a specific medium or some other regional, generational, stylistic, or thematic criterion can be even trickier. Faced with this difficulty, such exhibitions are often developed by choosing a theme or thesis beforehand and the artworks afterward, based on whether they confirm a hypothesis clearly outlined in advance. *Ways of Knowing* takes the opposite approach: beginning directly with the artworks and adopting more intuitive, more uncertain, and more capacious methods to guide the selection process; discovering shared artistic strategies; and using those as a basis to construct a thematic framework.

The Walker Art Center is renowned for providing a platform for curatorial work as a method of inquiry and a vehicle to examine ideas. In this sense, *Ways of Knowing* is the latest in a long history of exhibitions that have elucidated tendencies in contemporary art by exploring affinities between works of art. A preliminary description of *Ways of Knowing* could state that it brings together works produced by a multigenerational group of artists from around the world who are united by a new way of conceiving knowledge and who work within an expanded notion of research-based art. This description does not say much about what kind of knowledge these artists produce, however, nor about how they conceive it, what strategies they use, and how they present their knowledge visually. *Ways of Knowing* is about the useless, rebellious, playful, and irreverent ways in which artists engage with knowledge at a time when the viewer's attention is waning, a period that the art historian and critic Claire Bishop has described as characterized by "disordered attention."[2]

Research has become a fundamental element in certain artistic practices, in which it does not merely inform the making of the work but is presented to the viewer as an integral part of the work. Literature on research-based art is still scarce in the United States, however.[3] Moreover, there have been no exhibitions to date that consider research-based art as an artistic genre in its own right. Recent publications such as *Reclaiming Artistic Research* (2019) and Bishop's *Disordered Attention: How We Look at Art and Performance Today* (2024), along with essays such as Sara Callahan's "When the Dust Has Settled: What Was the Archival Turn, and Is It Still Turning?" (2024), have begun to elucidate how what the curator Cuauhtémoc Medina has referred to as "this particular daughter of conceptualism" became one of the most prevalent art modalities of the last thirty years.[4]

Research-based art is related to the phenomenon that the critic Hal Foster identified in an essay from 2004 titled "An Archival Impulse." Foster begins by describing works of the late 1990s and early 2000s that he identifies with this tendency:

> Consider a temporary display cobbled together out of workday materials like cardboard, aluminum foil, and packing tape, and filled, like a homemade study-shrine, with a chaotic array of images, texts, and testimonials devoted to a radical artist, writer, or philosopher. Or a funky installation that juxtaposes a model of a lost earthwork with slogans from the civil rights movement and/or recordings from the legendary rock concerts of the time. Or, in a more pristine register, a short filmic meditation on the huge acoustic receivers that were built on the Kentish coast between the World Wars, but soon abandoned as outmoded pieces of military technology. However disparate in subject, appearance, and affect, these works—by the Swiss Thomas Hirschhorn [fig. 5.2], the American Sam Durant, and the Englishwoman Tacita Dean—share a notion of artistic practice as an idiosyncratic probing into particular figures, objects, and events in modern art, philosophy, and history.[5]

The development of both the "archival" practices identified by Foster and research-based art more broadly has been significantly influenced by the professionalization of art during the 1990s. This period saw a rise in MFA and doctoral programs for artists across North America and Europe. Additionally, the biennial boom of the 1990s and particularly the influence of internationally known curators such as Ute Meta Bauer, Carolyn Christov-Bakargiev, Catherine David, and Okwui Enwezor, who popularized the concept of the thesis-driven

1 See Laura Hoptman, foreword to *Drawing in the Continuous Present* (New York: Drawing Center, 2022), 6.

2 Claire Bishop, *Disordered Attention: How We Look at Art and Performance Today* (London: Verso, 2024).

3 This is unlike the situation in Europe, where the sheer number of postgraduate programs for artists that integrate research into art practice has contributed to it being an assiduously discussed topic in academia.

4 Lucy Cotter, ed., *Reclaiming Artistic Research* (Berlin: Hatje Cantz, 2019); Bishop, *Disordered Attention*; Sara Callahan, "When the Dust Has Settled: What Was the Archival Turn, and Is It Still Turning?," *Art Journal* 83, no. 1 (2024): 74–88. Cuauhtémoc Medina's comment is from the roundtable discussion in this volume.

5 Hal Foster, "An Archival Impulse," *October*, no. 110 (Fall 2004): 3.

Fig. 5.1
Mary Kelly, *Post Partum Document: Introduction*, 1973, Perspex units, white card, wood vests, pencil, ink

Fig. 5.2
Thomas Hirschhorn, *Deleuze Monument (Library)*, 2000

Fig. 5.3
Hans Haacke, *Shapolsky et al. Manhattan Real Estate Holdings, a Real-Time Social System, as of May 1, 1971*, 1971 (detail), 9 photostats, 142 gelatin silver prints, 142 photocopies

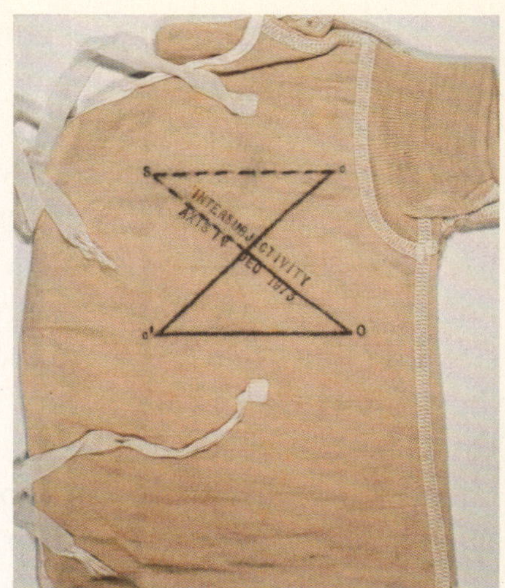


5.1

5.2

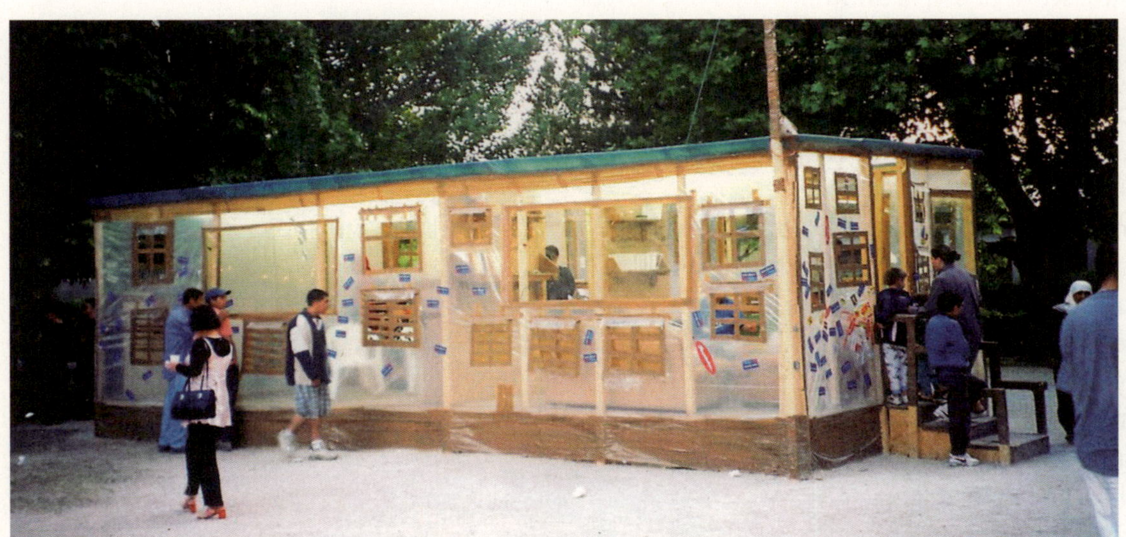

5.3

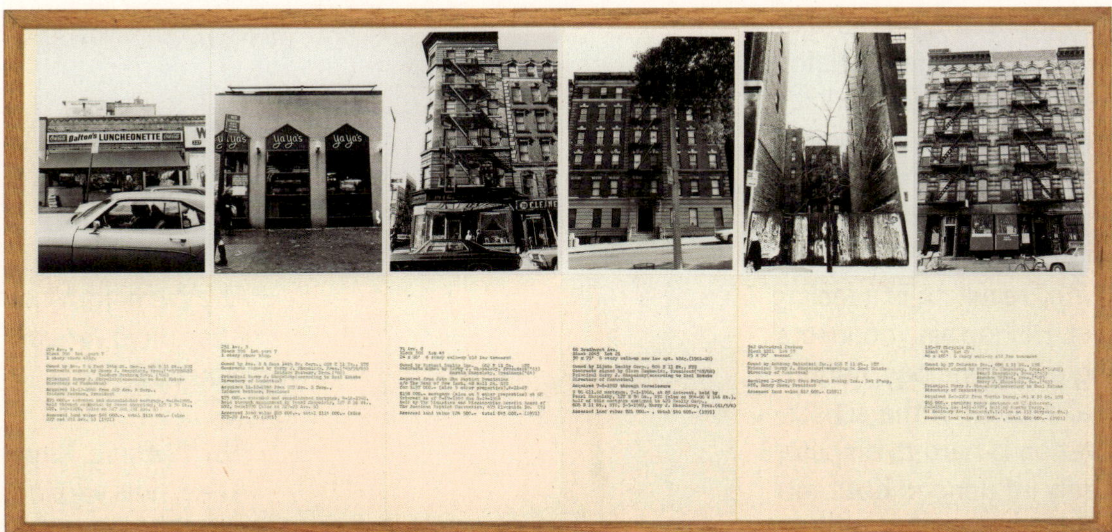

exhibition, fostered a closer convergence between artistic 5.4
practice and research. 5.5

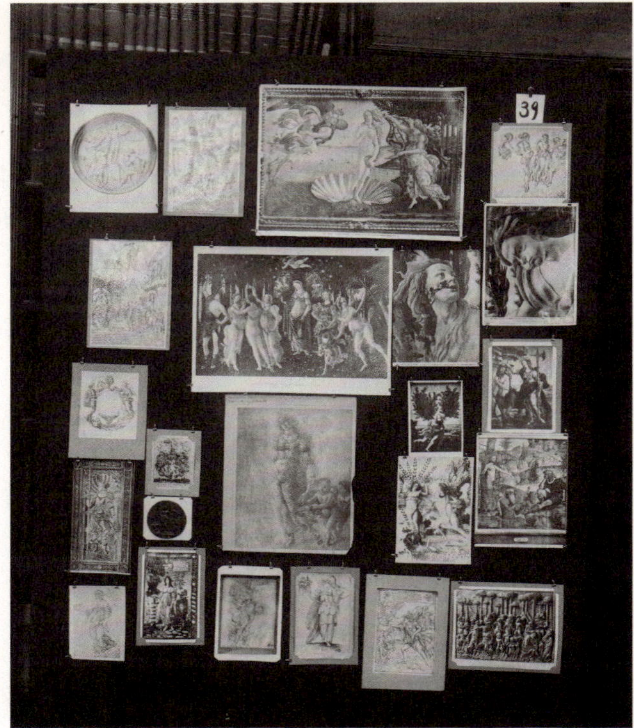

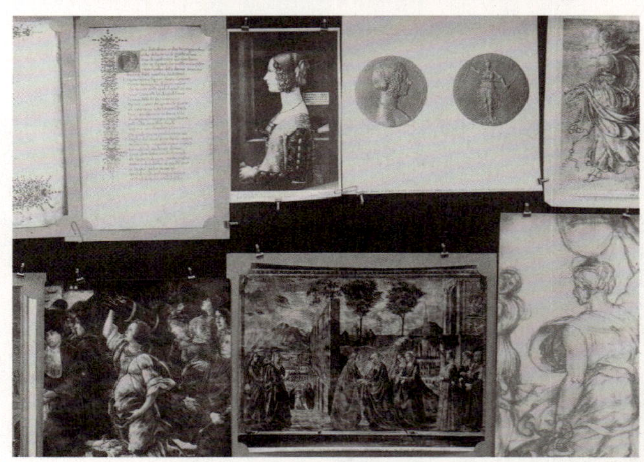

Many scholars and critics have traced the origins of research-based art to earlier twentieth-century movements. The artist Hito Steyerl has observed that such practices tend to emerge during "moments of crisis or reform," and she identifies the Soviet avant-garde of the 1920s as an early precursor. Steyerl points out that a group known as "factographers"—including Dziga Vertov, Sergei Tretyakov, and Alexander Rodchenko—argued that facts are not objective truths but are constructed, an idea that anticipates postmodern theorists' questioning of objective truth or reality. As Steyerl notes, the word *fact* is derived from the Latin *facere*, meaning "to make or to do."[6] These artists, writers, and filmmakers sought to chronicle modern life not by presenting it in a matter-of-fact way but by seeking to "actively transform reality through ideological acts of signification," as Kavior Moon notes in a recent essay.[7] Steyerl sees their work as an early form of research-based art and connects it to the genre of the film essay (or essay film), a term coined by the artist and filmmaker Hans Richter in 1940.[8] Notable later practitioners of this genre include Harun Farocki and Steyerl herself.

Conceptual art of the 1960s and 1970s, with its profound reexamination of the materiality of the work of art, is another significant predecessor. Early conceptual artists—including Robert Barry, Hanne Darboven, Douglas Huebler, Joseph Kosuth, and Art & Language—incorporated photographs, diagrams, grids, and especially text and language into their works. By the 1970s and 1980s, influenced by Marxist, poststructuralist, feminist, and postcolonial theory, artists began to expose power structures. Their critiques initially targeted art institutions, as seen in Hans Haacke's work (fig. 5.3), and later addressed issues related to race, gender, and multiculturalism, as seen in the works of Mary Kelly (fig. 5.1), Adrian Piper, and Renée Green. Some artists, such as Walid Raad, even created fictional archives to critique hegemonic narratives and highlight the biases inherent in traditional archives.

The abundance of artists incorporating research into their practices in recent decades has led to significant skepticism about these approaches. Noting the plethora of research-based works at Documenta 13 in 2012, the art historian Susanne von Falkenhausen labeled it "didactic overkill."[9] Claire Bishop, for her part, has argued that many such works amount to mere "information aggregation." She contends that research-based art often presents information without a discernible "authorial voice or position" or offers "positions that can't be contested, only agreed with," resulting in a feeling of "information overload" for the viewer. Bishop also connects research-based art to advances in digital technology, noting that "the Internet is the technological enabler of the artist's connectionist mindset."[10] This observation is hard to dispute, as our online behavior has undoubtedly influenced both the production and the reception of art. Bishop does not critique

Fig. 5.4
Aby Warburg, Mnemosyne Atlas, final version, 1929, panel 39

Fig. 5.5
Aby Warburg, Mnemosyne Atlas, final version, 1929, panel 46 (detail)

the term itself as a nonneutral or problematic concept, however, nor does she explore how artists might engage with research in ways that subvert, expand, or hybridize its conventional uses.

Many recent research-based artworks challenge the strict conventions of the genre, which often emphasize the display, accumulation, and spatialization of information while taking for granted research's assumed neutrality. These works advocate for a more personal and intentional approach to artistic research: a methodology that humanizes information, a strategy that reduces the distance between academic abstraction and the viewer. While the artworks included in *Ways of Knowing* span multiple mediums and varied subject matter, they share anomalous approaches to the use of information and a sly sense of curiosity. Many of these works also align with what Medina, in the roundtable discussion included in this volume, describes as "supplementary research": artworks that develop methodologies that both extend and deconstruct traditional modes of knowledge and representation, addressing the sense of "information overload" that Bishop describes.

The artists represented in *Ways of Knowing* reject the conventional assumption of the researcher's neutrality, challenging the notion that knowledge production should faithfully represent an external truth without intervention or interpretation. Echoing historical modes of representation of knowledge, some artworks in the exhibition maintain outward affinities with taxonomies and historical methods of visual categorization, but the artists employ these methods with a renewed sense of irony. Another group of artworks directly challenges and rejects these traditional frameworks and practices. They seek to dismantle the white, patriarchal, colonial gaze that historically shaped such systems. Instead these artworks propose more rebellious and confrontational methods of organizing knowledge, aiming to highlight marginalized perspectives and alternative narratives. Works in a third category employ fiction, imagination, and play as critical tools. These artworks not only redefine minor or personal archives but also create new informal archives and embodied knowledges through collaborative methods. *Ways of Knowing* prompts us to consider what happens when artists step into territories of knowledge production traditionally associated with disciplines like anthropology, science, or history, opening up new possibilities for how knowledge can be understood, represented, and disseminated through contemporary art.

*Ways of Knowing* includes artworks created by eleven artists from nine countries, each employing distinct artistic strategies. It is not a survey and does not try to encompass the extraordinary diversity of research-based art being practiced today. Rather, it focuses on how some of the most engaging contemporary artists are not merely creating knowledge about the world but doing so in ways that challenge conventional methods of collecting, documenting, and sharing information.

## POETIC TAXONOMIES

The human impulse to visually categorize knowledge reflects a profound desire to comprehend the world. The Greek philosopher Aristotle is credited with conceiving the first taxonomic systems, which he used to classify plants and animals, laying the groundwork for later developments in categorization practices. During the Renaissance, taxonomies expanded to encompass broader areas of human knowledge. Leonardo used his notebooks to record his observations in fields as diverse as anatomy, astronomy, botany, and cartography. This inclination persisted through the sixteenth century with the emergence of cabinets of curiosities, in which collectors organized and displayed different types of cultural and natural objects. These cabinets were the forerunners of modern museums, which began to take shape in the eighteenth century, further institutionalizing the practice of categorizing and displaying objects.

Aby Warburg, a German art historian and cultural theorist, offered one of the most radical interpretations of taxonomy in the early twentieth century. Drawing on techniques from the natural sciences, he pioneered the method of iconology in art history. His last and most significant project, the Mnemosyne Atlas (1924–1929; figs. 5.4, 5.5), involved the collection and juxtaposition of different types of visual material from various historical periods. He pinned these images to wooden panels covered with black cloth to show the recurrence of ideas and visual motifs throughout history. Naming the work after the Greek goddess of memory, Warburg created a "'comparative view' of objects and visual perspectives to highlight the 'afterlight of antiquity.'" Fittingly, he described his project as "the foundation for a new theory on the function of human

6 Hito Steyerl, "Aesthetics of Resistance? Artistic Research as Discipline and Conflict," in "Art/Knowledge: Overlaps and Neighboring Zones," special issue, *Transversal*, March 2011, https://transversal.at/transversal/0311/steyerl/en.

7 Kavior Moon, "Research Art Is Everywhere. But Some Artists Do It Better than Others," *Art in America*, March 8, 2023, https://www.artnews.com/art-in-america/features/what-is-artistic-research-1234660125/.

8 Hans Richter, "The Film Essay: A New Type of Documentary Film" (1940), in *Essays on the Essay Film*, ed. Nora M. Alter and Timothy Corrigan (New York: Columbia University Press, 2017), 89–92.

9 Susanne von Falkenhausen, "The Rules of Research," *Frieze*, no. 6 (August 1, 2012), https://www.frieze.com/article/forschung-mit-folgen.

10 Claire Bishop, "Information Overload," *Artforum* 61, no. 8 (April 2023), https://www.artforum.com/features/claire-bishop-on-the-superabundance-of-research-based-art-252571/.

visual memory."[11] The Mnemosyne Atlas was not merely a visual record but also a means of examining the role of visual culture in the formation of collective consciousness.

Several of the artists represented in *Ways of Knowing*—such as Iosu Aramburu, Gala Porras-Kim, Rose Salane, and Chang Yuchen—often draw on classification methodologies from traditional disciplines of knowledge, lending their works a certain familiarity. They approach the task with a sense of irony and an awareness of the limitations of such efforts, however, and their application of these practices tends to result in a kind of useless erudition. Bringing together thousands of images drawn from diverse publications on modern art in the extensive Andean region, dating from the nineteenth century to 2018, Aramburu's *Atlas of Andean Modernism* (2022–; pp. 13–25) constructs a visual chronology. He presents images of artworks in a grid-like structure, printed on loose sheets with a digital stamp containing information about the publication from which the image originates, including its title, author, year, and country. Aramburu's fingerprints on the scanned images and their arrangement on the wall using small pieces of adhesive tape suggest the construction of the region's cultural history as an incomplete, tentative, and provisional process—one that can be easily reorganized (figs. 5.8, 5.9).

Aramburu proposes a utopia: the disorganized rewriting of independent art histories in the Andean region as a complete entity. Unlike Warburg, who grouped images according to predetermined categories, Aramburu takes images from a broad set of panoramic publications on modern art, breaks them down, and reconstructs them. In doing so, he dismantles existing narratives and proposes a new disorder as order. This approach not only highlights the gaps between various historical narratives but also emphasizes the works not included in official narratives and the voices lost along the way. *Atlas of Andean Modernism* is a work about absences: the artworks that are not part of official historical accounts, the historical events that haven't been accounted for, the artworks that were displaced and ignored. Aramburu underlines the idea that historical narratives are malleable, susceptible to change and transformation, the product of a personal vision of what history might be. "It has always been important to me to approach the idea of modernity with open questions," he has said, "seeking dialogue rather than imposing a critical agenda."[12] His *Atlas* is not a singular, hegemonic art historical narrative but a tapestry of overlooked images and unknown artworks, including the gaps between them.

Gala Porras-Kim also explores interstitial spaces, particularly those between cultural artifacts and the institutions that preserve them. She is known for her drawings of clusters of objects that reveal how museological cataloging and conservation practices recontextualize their original functions. Her largest series to date, *530 National Treasures* (2023; pp. 27–39), consists of a drawing depicting eleven long shelves that display 530 objects and sites from North and South Korea that have been designated National Treasures. Originally conceived in 2015 as a handwritten document (p. 28) in which Porras-Kim enumerated these cultural artifacts and sites, the series was inspired by her interest in the origin of the cultural preservation system that was introduced in Korea during the Japanese occupation in the late nineteenth and early twentieth centuries.

Arranged across a nearly forty-foot-long (twelve-meter-long) four-panel composition, the treasures have been meticulously drawn in a hyperrealistic style that employs the language of scientific illustration (figs. 5.6, 5.7). This approach produces an entirely different interpretation, however, a sort of by-product of research into the extensive cultural history shared between the two Koreas. Porras-Kim's method involved exhaustive research using public records dating back to the Japanese occupation and the subsequent division of Korea. Through the painstaking process of drawing each National Treasure and arranging them across the four panels, she traces the shifting motivations of generations of collectors but also the visual and cultural continuities between them. For example, the top shelves predominantly feature images of architectural sites copied from photographs—such as temples, tombs, pagodas, and pavilions—which gradually give way to vases, jewelry, documents, and figurines on the lower shelves (p. 29).

The lower half of the drawing is sparser due to the lack of availability of North Korean records after the nation's division; even some of its treasures consist of nondescript landscape images in which it is virtually impossible to identify the National Treasure originally photographed by North Korean authorities, pointing to the opacity of their cultural preservation systems (p. 37). Porras-Kim has emphasized that "categorization is important because it reflects more contemporary priorities of what we want history to do, rather than what might have happened in the past."[13] Indeed, *530 National Treasures* emphasizes the notion of cultural heritage as a product of Japanese colonial influence despite the context of a nation in flux.

11 Martha Schwendener, "This Atlas of Art and Memory Is a Wonder of the Modern World," *New York Times*, May 14, 2020, https://www.nytimes.com/2020/05/14/arts/design/aby-warburg-memory-atlas.html.

12 Elise Chagas, "On the B-Side of Modernity: An Interview with Iosu Aramburu," *MoMA Magazine*, December 28, 2022, https://www.moma.org/magazine/articles/822.

13 Gala Porras-Kim, in "Mediating between the Past and Present: A Conversation with Gala Porras-Kim," *Eazel Magazine*, January 26, 2024, https://www.eazel.net/magazine/206.

5.6

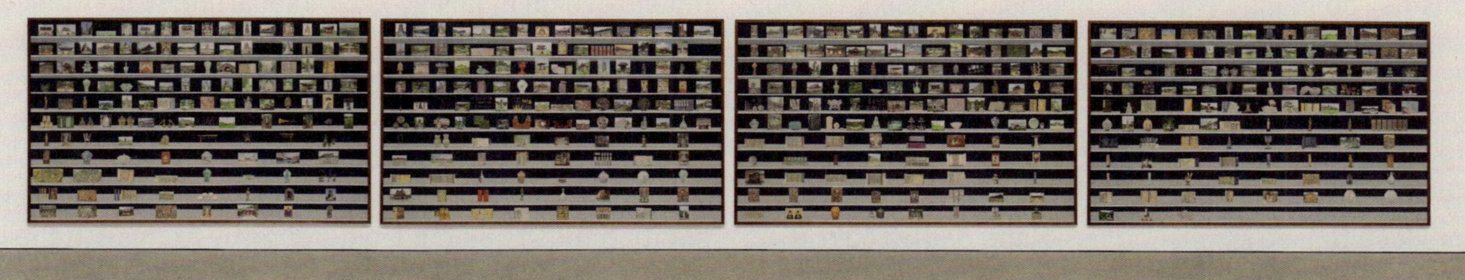

5.7

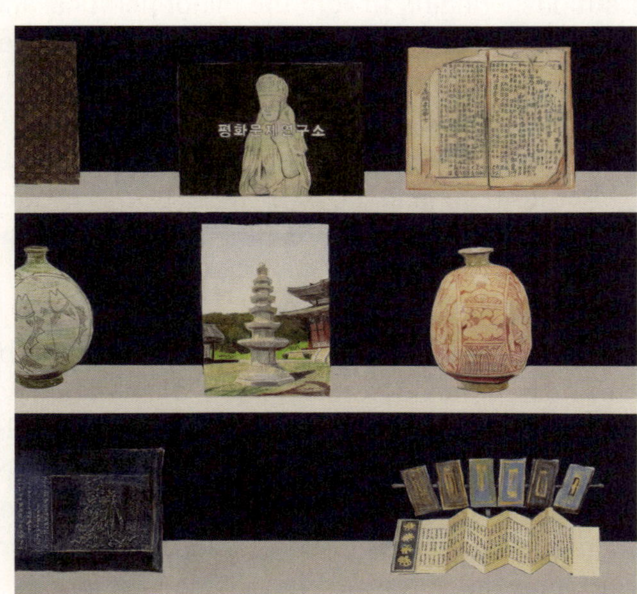

5.8

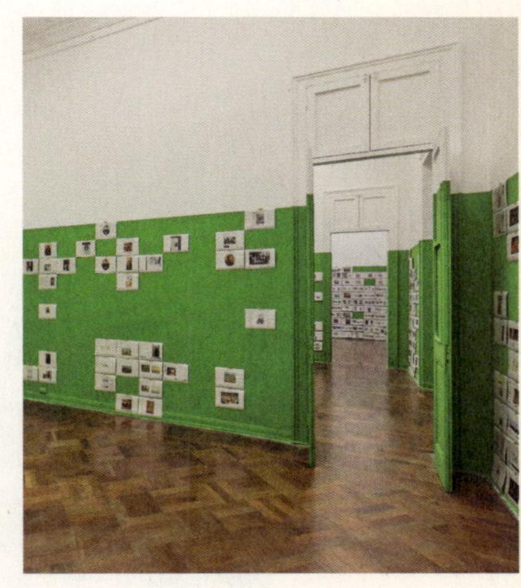

5.9

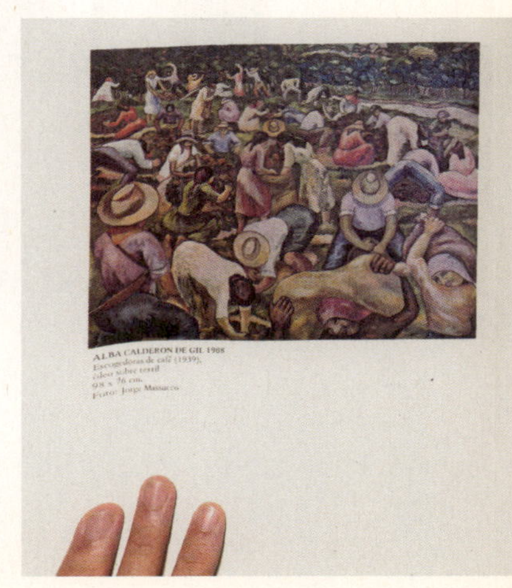

Fig. 5.6
Gala Porras-Kim, *530 National Treasures*, 2023, colored pencil and Flashe on paper

Fig. 5.7
Gala Porras-Kim, *530 National Treasures*, 2023 (detail), colored pencil and Flashe on paper

Fig. 5.8
Iosu Aramburu, *Atlas of Andean Modernism*, 2022–, printed paper, taped to the wall; number of pages variable

Fig. 5.9
Iosu Aramburu, *Atlas of Andean Modernism*, 2022– (detail), printed paper, taped to the wall; number of pages variable

Fig. 5.10
This box contains artifacts that were taken from Pompeii by visitors and later returned in the mail. These objects became source material for Rose Salane's *Confessions*.

Fig. 5.11
Rose Salane, *60 Detected Rings (1991–2021) (Person 41–45)*, 2021 (detail), silkscreen on mat board, found rings of varying metals

Fig. 5.12
Chang Yuchen, *This feeling is abstract, hard to describe.*, 2021, pencil on paper

Fig. 5.13
Chang Yuchen's copy of the *Kamus Sari*, a Malay to English and Mandarin dictionary.

In many ways Porras-Kim's explorations of how institutions assign meaning to cultural artifacts contrast with Rose Salane's interest in the past lives of ordinary objects. Salane is intrigued by what she calls "dynamic assemblages of objects," large collections of lost or forgotten objects that she often discovers by chance or obtains at public auctions in her native New York City.[14] Her process involves granting these objects a biography by examining their histories through a variety of methods, from the scientific to the superstitious, bringing to light the minor personal and emotional histories embedded in seemingly mundane items. Many of her earlier works look at various forms of loss. *Panorama 94* (2019) and *60 Detected Rings 1991–2021* (fig. 5.11), for example, both feature collections of rings. Those in *Panorama 94* were found in the New York subway system and never reclaimed by their owners; the artist subsequently acquired them at a public auction by the Metropolitan Transit Authority. The rings in *60 Detected Rings* were discovered on the shores of Atlantic City, New Jersey, by a woman using a metal detector and sold at an estate sale in Queens. In both instances Salane developed methods to analyze the rings with the assistance of pawnshop owners, genetic scientists, and fortune tellers. Her findings were presented in multipanel series, with each panel displaying five rings arranged in a grid-like composition. Beneath each ring, she detailed its material properties and melt value, results of DNA analysis, and an intuitive interpretation of the ring's previous life. Through this approach she transformed each found ring and its related data into a portrait of its previous owner.

During her residency at the Archaeological Park of Pompeii in 2022, Salane produced a series titled *Confessions* (2023; pp. 41–53). The series comprises fourteen photographs, each pairing a handwritten letter from a tourist with a small object or fragment that was stolen from the park. The returned fragments (fig. 5.10) include small pieces of volcanic rock, stones, tiny mosaic bits, a rusted nail—objects of seemingly insignificant archaeological value and with no identifiable place of restitution (p. 51). Salane's photographs also play with scale, contrasting the small, unassuming fragments with the emotionally charged letters. As the series' title suggests, each letter expresses the visitor's remorse and pleads for forgiveness. In *Confession 2* (p. 43), for example, the sender writes: "Please accept these back—I found these in my late husband's belongings. Please return to proper place." By photographing the objects and accompanying correspondence from above, set against a quasi-institutional red velvet backdrop, Salane plays with notions of neutrality in scientific archaeology to convey how these seemingly mundane objects become charged with personal histories and emotional weight as they are reintroduced into the institutional archive. *Confessions* underscores the cycles of disruption and redefinition that

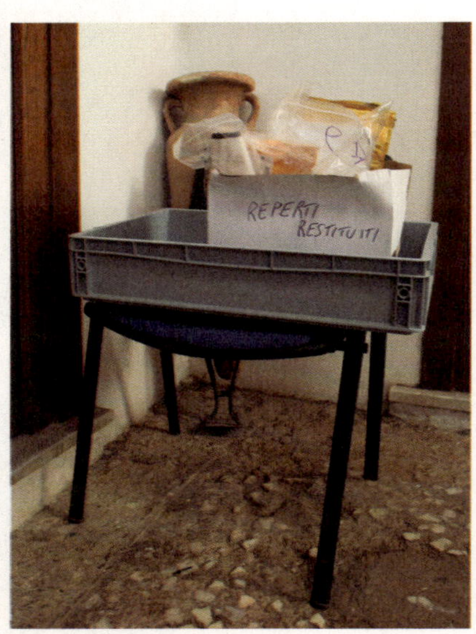

5.10

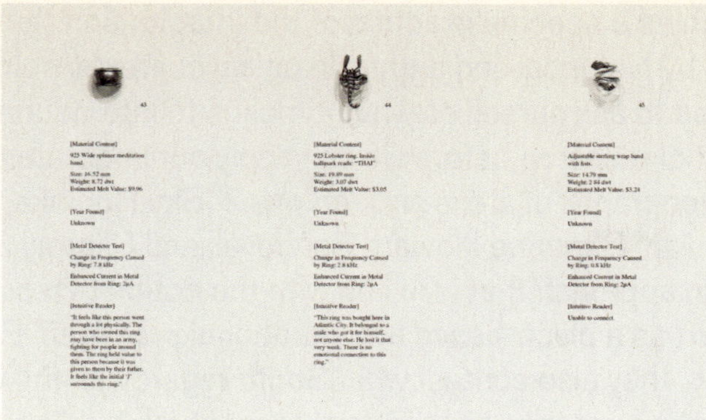

5.11

5.12

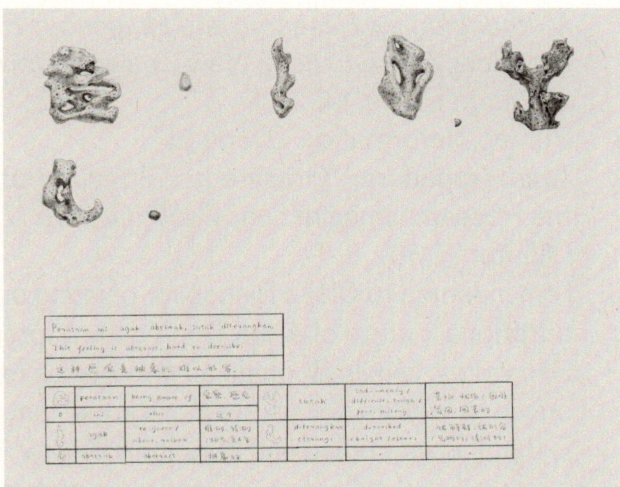

5.13

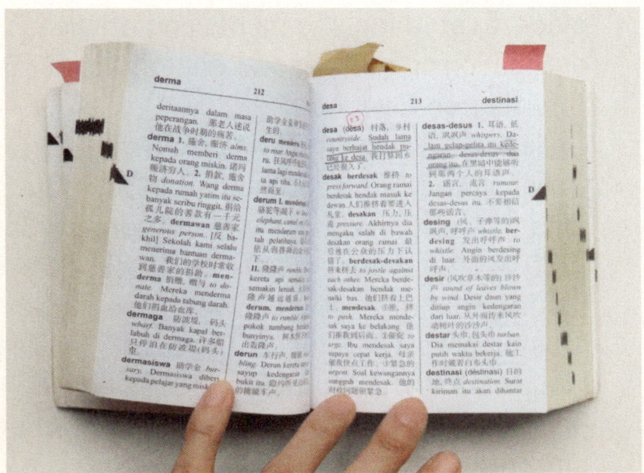


continually shape personal ways of understanding and valuing objects and places.

For nearly five years, Chang Yuchen has been developing a writing system for the spoken Malay language, using as words fragments of coral she gathered during her residency on Dinawan, a small reef island off the coast of Borneo, in Malaysia (pp. 62–63). Malay, belonging to the Austronesian language family, has a rich oral tradition yet historically lacks a standardized writing system of its own. Over time it has adopted and adapted several writing systems—such as the Sanskrit, Arabic, and Roman alphabets—reflecting the language's resilience in spite of its being marked by a sense of impermanence and uprootedness.

Chang's approach is as intricate as it is poetic. As Maya Hayda has pointed out, her method is pictographic, associating coral fragments with words in an emotive, metaphoric, and performative process.[15] She acts as an interpreter who navigates the subtle interplay between the essence of each coral fragment—reflected in its shape, size, and texture—and the linguistic expression it represents (figs. 5.15, 5.16). Her ongoing project *Coral Dictionary* (2019–; pp. 55–80), inspired by her personal experiences across languages and cultures (she was born in China but lives in the United States), involves translating 182 phrases selected from the *Kamus Sari*, a dictionary for the Chinese diaspora in Malaysia originally published in 1973. Chang came across a copy of the fourth edition, issued in 2018, during a trip to the mainland to shop for supplies (fig. 5.13).

The phrases are recorded in a series of graphite drawings on paper (fig. 5.12). In each drawing, the coral fragments become words that make up a sentence rendered at the center of the sheet. Below each coral-drawn phrase is a precisely rendered chart, which presents each coral word in a simplified style, followed by its translation into Malay in Roman script, then English, and finally Mandarin. These drawings exhibit a structure reminiscent of traditional alphabets and the intricate details typical of botanical illustrations, but they can't be reduced to either of these forms. Chang felt an immediate connection to many of the phrases, which embody "sediments of a lived experience."[16] They capture her

14 Rose Salane, in Livia Russell, "Work in Progress: Rose Salane—'A Love Poem to the City of New York'" (interview), Frieze New York, April 11, 2024, https://www.frieze.com/article/work-progress-rose-salane-interview-frieze-new-york.

15 Maya Hayda, "Coral Tongues: On Chang Yuchen's 'Coral Dictionary Vol. 1,'" *Los Angeles Review of Books*, November 4, 2023, https://lareviewofbooks.org/article/coral-tongues-on-chang-yuchens-coral-dictionary-vol-1/.

16 Chang Yuchen, correspondence with the author, October 8, 2024.

own experiences on the island, with some phrases reflecting nature ("The vastness of the sky is unbound"), while others address economic conditions or political upheaval: ("Natural rubber is facing serious competition from synthetic rubber," "The rebel has been arrested by the police"). Still others are more poetic encapsulations of everyday life: "This feeling is abstract, hard to describe."

DURATIONAL AND PLACE-BASED KNOWLEDGES The classification and representation of new knowledge during the period spanning the sixteenth to the nineteenth centuries were often driven by a profound desire to comprehensively understand the world. These pursuits were inextricably linked with colonial and imperial expansion, however, serving as positivistic tools to represent the Other through an essentialist lens: that of the white Western man. While the Renaissance saw the beginning of visually ordered knowledge, the artists whose work appears in this section of the exhibition try to deconstruct colonial narratives and linear temporalities using alternative frameworks of knowledge. In this sense, *Ways of Knowing* seeks to create a space for diverse approaches to organizing knowledge, which can at times be playful and useless or rebellious and anomalous.

In addressing the Indigenous experience and the relationship between colonized and colonizers, the Maori cultural writer Linda Tuhiwai Smith has critiqued the outcomes and effects of Western research on Indigenous communities, proposing instead the concept of "indigenous research" as a practice aligned with the perspectives and priorities of these communities.[17] While Smith discusses the evolution of research in the Western context as a social science, her argument is relevant to contemporary art discourse, especially with regard to the conceptual and formal strategies present in some of the works in this exhibition. Bishop's analysis of research-based art further enriches this discussion by distinguishing between two contrasting approaches. One is centered on the accumulation of data and information, often overwhelming the viewer with literal content. Another approach embraces a more imaginative and engaging conception of research as embodied and extended in time. Bishop distinguishes between the mere collection of data and a more immersive, emotional, intimate, and profound connection with history and its significant spaces.[18] This distinction is certainly illuminating.

Arjun Appadurai, like Smith, adopts a more critical view of research, particularly in the context of colonialism. Smith critiques research as a practice historically intertwined with colonial agendas, often disregarding or distorting Indigenous knowledge and perspectives. She argues that research has been complicit in perpetuating colonial dominance and marginalizing Indigenous voices, thus viewing it as a problematic concept. Appadurai, in contrast, characterizes research as a specific practice of the imagination that is shaped by historical and anthropological contexts, pointing to the "need to ask ourselves what it means to internationalize any sort of research before we can apply our understandings to the geography of areas and regions."[19] Sky Hopinka, Anna Boghiguian, Christine Howard Sandoval, and Sammy Baloji adopt an approach that is in line with the notion of research-based art as a place-based and durational practice.[20] But in doing so, they also contest what Smith regards as the violent connotations of the very concept of research by disrupting conventional methodologies. In contrast to Aramburu, Porras-Kim, Salane, and Chang, who play with and employ traditional research methodologies with a certain irreverence, Hopinka, Boghiguian, Howard Sandoval, and Baloji take an autonomous, perhaps even rebellious approach to the generation of knowledge. They challenge the hegemonic structures of knowledge production, suggesting that conventional tools and methodologies may not be suitable for disrupting master narratives.[21]

A questioning of the use of information and knowledge methodologies runs through Sky Hopinka's artistic practice. His experience growing up in northern Washington, far from his parents' Indigenous lands, informs his approach to diverse places and histories in his role as "visitor." He defines the "liminal space" of belonging to the Native diaspora

17 See Linda Tuhiwai Smith, *Decolonizing Methodologies: Research and Indigenous Peoples* (London: Zed; Dunedin, New Zealand: University of Otago Press, 1999), 1.

18 Bishop, "Information Overload."

19 Arjun Appadurai, "Grassroots Globalization and the Research Imagination," *Public Culture* 12, no. 1 (Winter 2000): 8.

20 I am indebted to Claire Bishop for pointing out the durational nature of Anna Boghiguian's practice. She writes: "While Boghiguian undertakes research online as well as offline, the more important point is that it is embodied and durational: All her literary, historical, and philosophical reading is grounded in time spent on the sites where these events took place. Everything she paints and draws is made on location or from her own photographs." Bishop, "Information Overload."

21 Callahan, "When the Dust Has Settled," 84. Callahan writes in a footnote (84n30): "The phrase ['master narrative'], coined by Audre Lorde in 1979 was an urgent plea to embrace diversity in the feminist movement." See Audre Lorde, "The Master's Tools Will Never Dismantle the Master's House (1979)," in *The Essential Feminist Reader*, ed. Estelle B. Freedman (New York: Modern Library, 2007), 331–335.

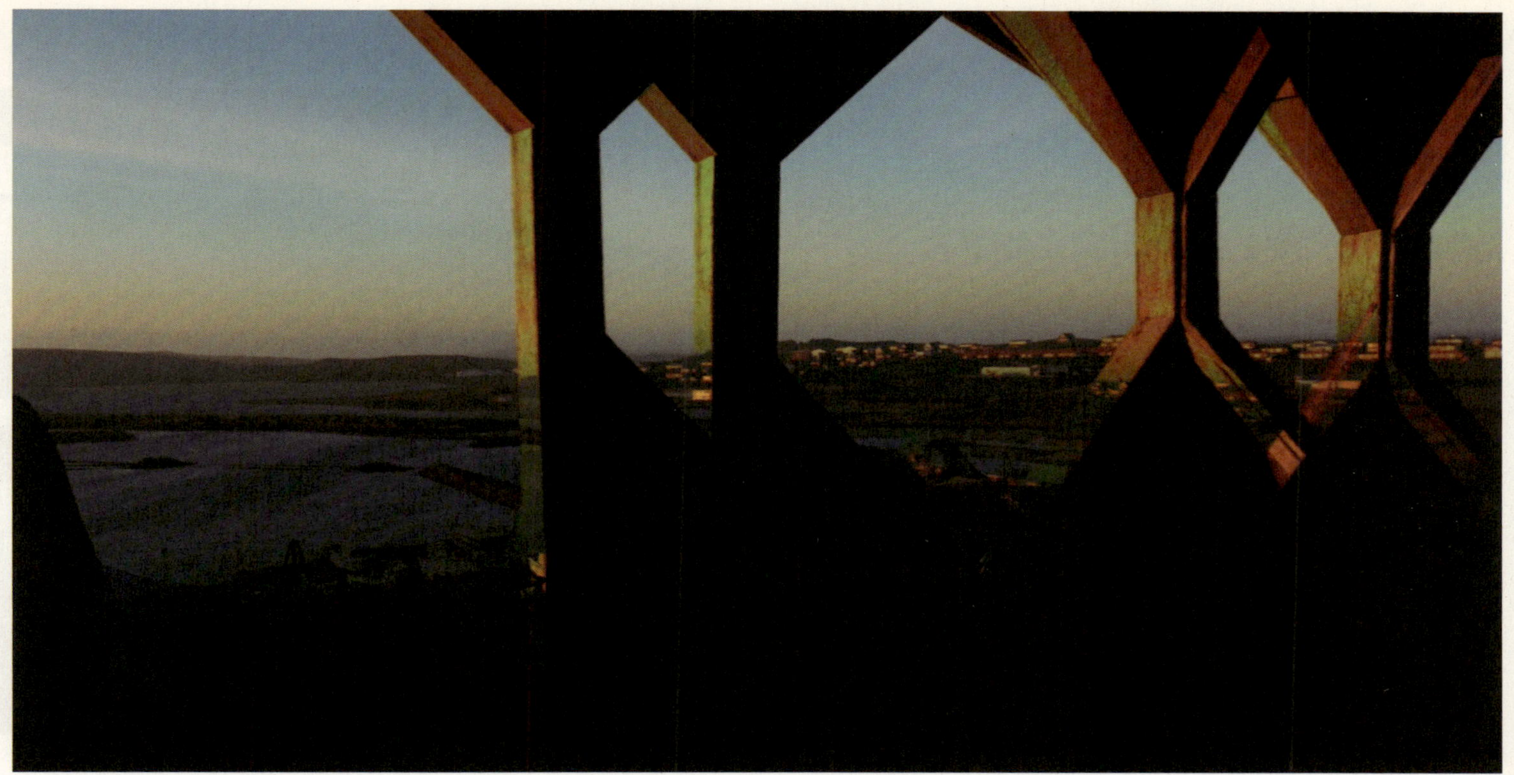

5.14

5.15
5.16

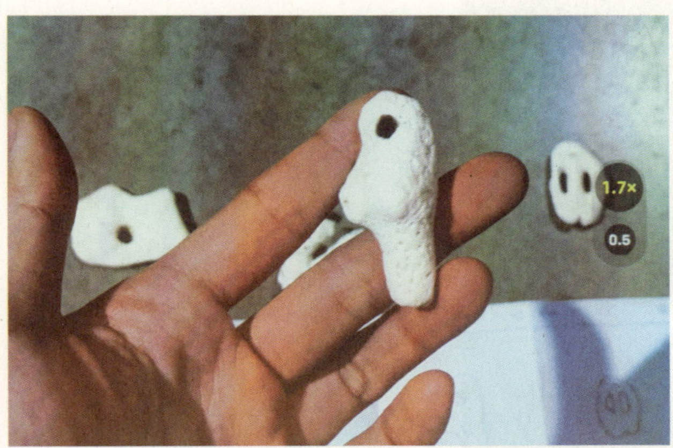


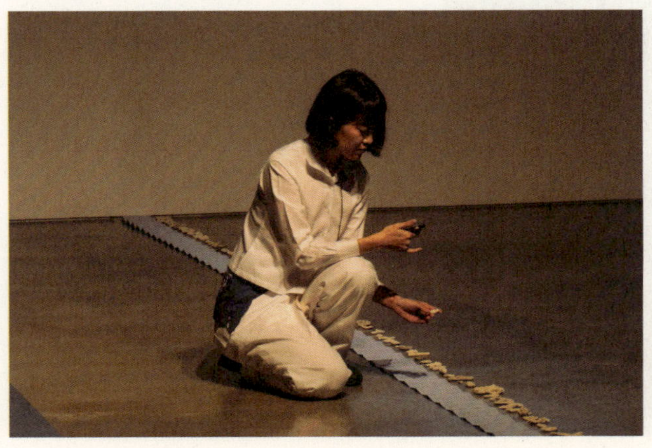

Fig. 5.14
Sky Hopinka, *Visions of an Island*, 2016, HD video (color, sound); 15:03 min.

Figs. 5.15, 5.16
Chang Yuchen, *Coral Dictionary—an Interpretation Performance*, 2022–, performance at Amant, New York. Chang has developed her Coral Dictionary project into a performance-lecture in which the artist handles her collection of Malaysian corals and describes her process of interpretation and translation.

Figs. 5.17–5.20
Sky Hopinka, *Visions of an Island*, 2016, HD video (color, sound); 15:03 min.

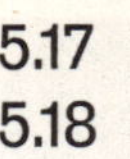

5.17
5.18

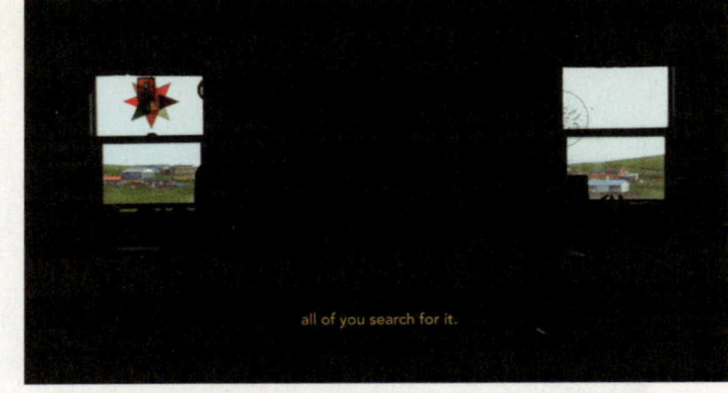


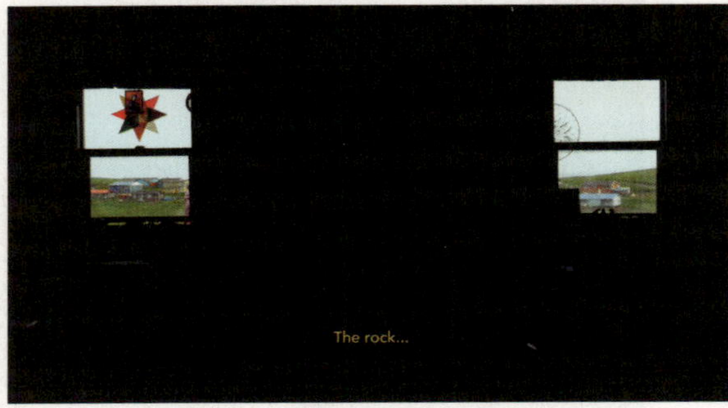


5.19
5.20

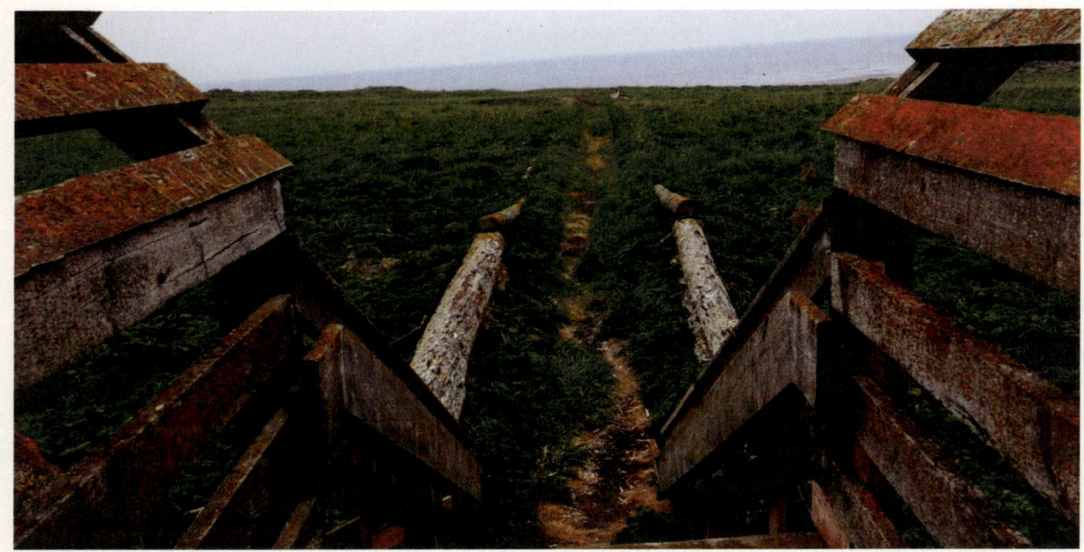

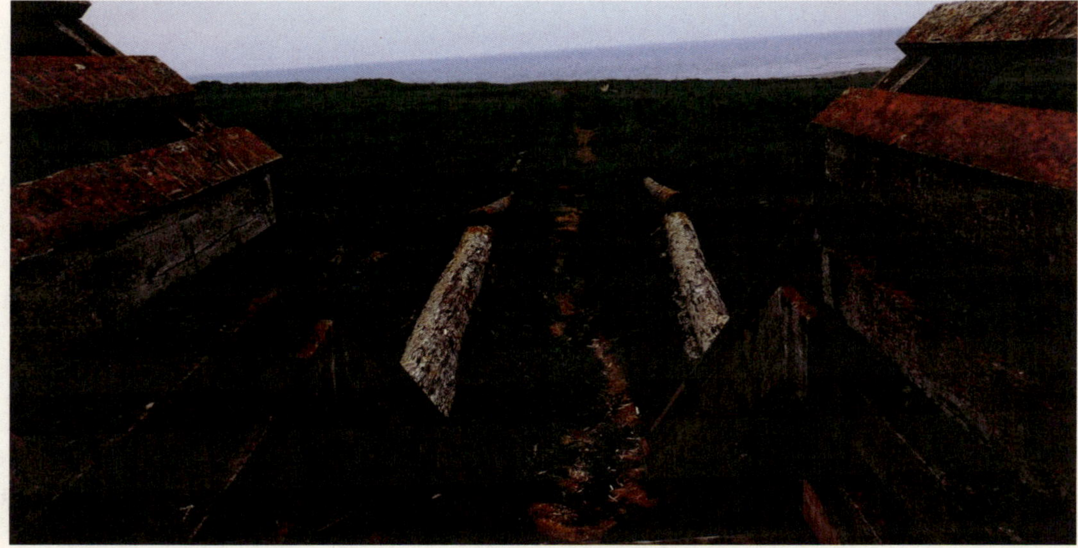

as simultaneously "inside and outside."[22] Hopinka employs various art forms, but his primary media are film and video, through which he addresses the relationship between "knowing and not knowing," between transparency and opacity, constructing poetic visual narratives that resist clarification.[23] At the same time, through image manipulation and color saturation (figs. 5.14, 5.19, 5.20), he challenges historical cinematic representations of Indigenous communities, which have often been shaped by colonial perspectives and ethnographic traditions. Rather than aiming to convey specific knowledge, he focuses on capturing seemingly mundane details: scenes of everyday life, fragments of spoken language, and partial views of landscapes. This results in a distinctive approach to exploring significant themes, such as the interrelationship of land, language, and culture in Indigenous communities.

*Visions of an Island* (2016; pp. 105–121) is an audiovisual collage that weaves images, sounds, and narrative fragments to express the multiple and complex layers of history inscribed in the land, specifically Saint Paul Island in Alaska, which is the ancestral home of the Unangax̂ (Aleut) people. The film serves as a meditation on language and its connection to place. Throughout the film Hopinka combines various linguistic and cultural markers: he accompanies images of coastlines, cliffs, landscapes, rock formations, and elevations of the land with a narrative in the voice of Gregory Fratis Sr., who, in Unangam Tunuu (Aleut), describes the land and wildlife. Other scenes involve linguistic activities, such as a language game centered on the word *rock* and children playing with rocks (figs. 5.17, 5.18).

The concept of failure as a form of disciplinary resistance, as articulated by Jack Halberstam, expands the notion of knowledge to an undisciplined, open, and relatively free form. Halberstam has written that the notion of failure "dismantles the logics of success and failure with which we currently live. Under certain circumstances failing, losing, forgetting, unmaking, undoing, unbecoming, not knowing may in fact offer more creative, more cooperative, more surprising ways of being in the world."[24] By not constructing linear narratives and not always translating the voices that appear in his documentaries, Hopinka underscores this idea of failure and, in doing so, invites viewers to experience more intuitive, more uncertain, messier—fundamentally incomplete—ways of knowing. He attacks the values that underpin the conventional documentary format—in which the material is explicit, follows a classic narrative, and above all is (or pretends to be) instructive—by deliberately obstructing any kind of straightforward reading. He eschews clarity and, instead of offering pristine images, inverts, confuses, alters, and distorts (pp. 110–111). Through this counter-documentary technique, the artist reflects on the complex legacies of colonial narratives and Indigenous stories sedimented in the earth.

Anna Boghiguian makes drawings, paintings, collages, books, and large-scale installations that range over diverse geographies and chronologies to examine historical events. Boghiguian's engagement with history is not simply academic, however; it is visceral and experiential. She is an avid reader, and her understanding of history is enriched by her direct relationship with the places where narratives take place, adding a lived dimension to her investigations into the past. Made in situ, from her own photographs, or from images found on the internet, her drawings tend to incorporate passages that alternate between figuration and abstraction, handwritten text, and organic materials such as cotton thread, beeswax, salt, and earth (p. 128).

*Time of Change* (2022; fig. 5.24) is a series of ninety-six drawings arranged linearly on easels in an expansive configuration. The individual drawings feature expressively rendered multitudes of figures, finely etched ghostly markings, scattered names of relevant places, and gestural floods of color, which merge as part of a synchronic experience. The series focuses on moments of social upheaval, from the tumultuous events leading up to the French and Russian Revolutions to the enigmatic figure of the Nazi physician Aribert Heim, who was known as Dr. Death among Jewish prisoners at the Mauthausen concentration camp (pp. 123–135).

One series of these drawings was created during Boghiguian's visit to the Palace of Versailles, where she depicted the signing of the peace treaty that ended World War II in the Hall of Mirrors (fig. 5.21). The narrative of another set was inspired by a trip to a Berlin apartment complex formerly owned by Heim; the rental proceeds from this property would fund his extended years as a Nazi fugitive (fig. 5.23). Heim's escape to Cairo after the war is depicted in Boghiguian's drawings, including scenes from the hotel room where he lived in hiding until his death (fig. 5.22). Through these varied contexts—in which characters, places, and events merge—Boghiguian suggests that history is an ongoing, interconnected process, never truly concluded nor existing apart from the self.

Christine Howard Sandoval conceives of research as an embodied practice, literally, through the act of walking. By repeatedly moving through the same areas while wearing a GoPro-type body camera, she incorporates herself into the substance of her ancestral homeland in Alta California.

22 Sky Hopinka, in Anaïs Duplan, "What Does It Mean to Be a Visitor," Art21, interview conducted September 2021, https://art21.org/read/big-question-what-does-it-mean-to-be-a-visitor/.

23 Adam Khalil and Zack Khalil, "Sky Hopinka" (interview), *Third Rail*, no. 10 (Spring 2017), http://thirdrailquarterly.org/sky-hopinka/.

24 Jack Halberstam, *The Queer Art of Failure* (Durham, NC: Duke University Press, 2011), 2.

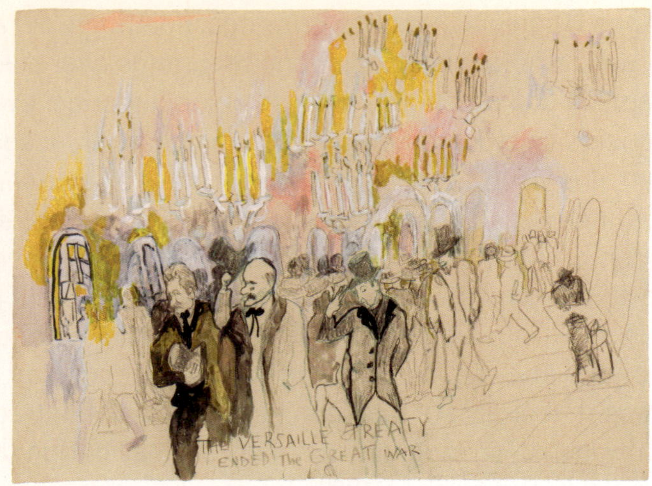


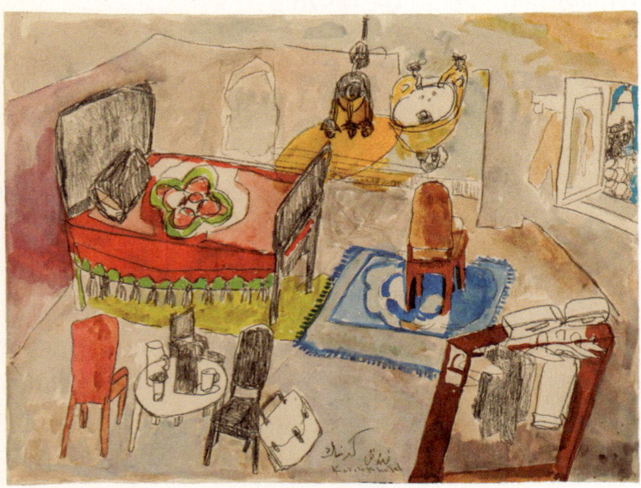

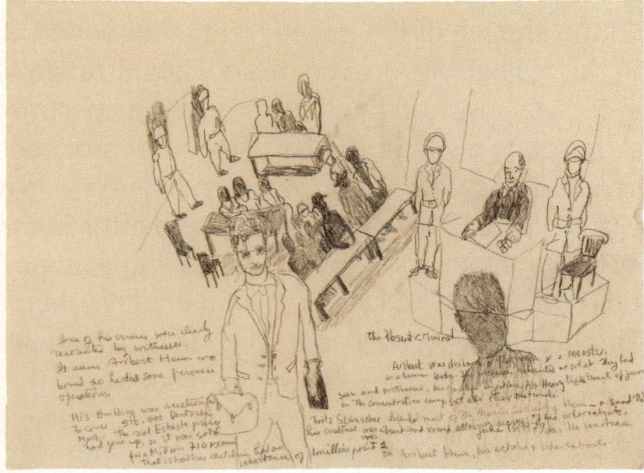

5.21
5.22
5.23

Her primary interest in these video works lies not so much in the disorienting visual content captured by the camera, however, as in how the images engage the viewer's body when projected, inviting a reevaluation of one's relationship to the land and its history (figs. 5.25, 5.26). Other works by Howard Sandoval directly integrate research. In sculptures such as *The Eaters* (2020; fig. 5.27), she mixes adobe with other materials, including, in some cases, archival documents. This atypical combination literally embodies what happens to history: in this case the very material of the sculpture, the adobe, contains physical vestiges of history (the documents). Thus the artist shows that adobe "contains" history and that art cannot dispense with it in order to be constituted.

Like Boghiguian, Howard Sandoval is known for her use of organic materials, including adobe mud, graphite, water, and fire. Adobe has particular significance for Howard Sandoval, as it symbolizes "how people inhabit desert land," but it also has personal significance, as her grandmother made adobe bricks (p. 147).[25] Adobe carries historical weight as the material used by Spanish missionaries, often through the labor of enslaved Indigenous people, to erect the kinds of structures Howard Sandoval references and abstracts in her drawings (pp. 137–149). She creates these drawings by tracing long lines with masking tape on handmade paper and then covering the surface with wet mud. When the tape is removed, thick, striated patterns are revealed that evoke both memories of the structures and the potential for their future (pp. 144–145). This act of resignification transforms the missions from relics of a traumatic past into symbols of reciprocity and renewal.

Sammy Baloji is also known for his ability to manipulate notions of time and space in his artistic practice, with a particular focus on his homeland, the Katanga province in the Democratic Republic of the Congo. His work examines the exploitation of labor and natural resources, critically reflecting on historical and contemporary power dynamics. Baloji differs from Hopinka in that his recognition of the complex legacies of photography and ethnography in relation to the perception of the Other does not deter him from using these tools in a more straightforward fashion; in fact, his practice is firmly rooted in archival research.

In *Tales of the Copper Cross Garden: Episode 1* (2017; pp. 151–168), Baloji subtly unravels the intertwined issues of labor exploitation, colonialism, and religious influence in Congo. Throughout the film he narrates the laborious process of transforming copper into an industrial product for the global market as a means to reference the historical exploitation of Congolese workers by colonial

25 Christine Howard Sandoval, in Louis Bury, "Embodied Practice: Christine Howard Sandoval" (interview), *Bomb*, April 21, 2021, https://bombmagazine.org/articles/2021/04/21/embodied-practice-christine-howard-sandoval-interviewed/.

Figs. 5.21–5.23
Anna Boghiguian, *Time of Change*, 2022 (details), mixed media on paper

Fig. 5.24
*Anna Boghiguian: Period of Change*, installation view, Kunsthaus Bregenz, Austria, 2022

Figs. 5.25, 5.26
Christine Howard Sandoval, *CHANNEL*, 2017 (video stills), three-channel HD video (color, sound); 07:43 min.

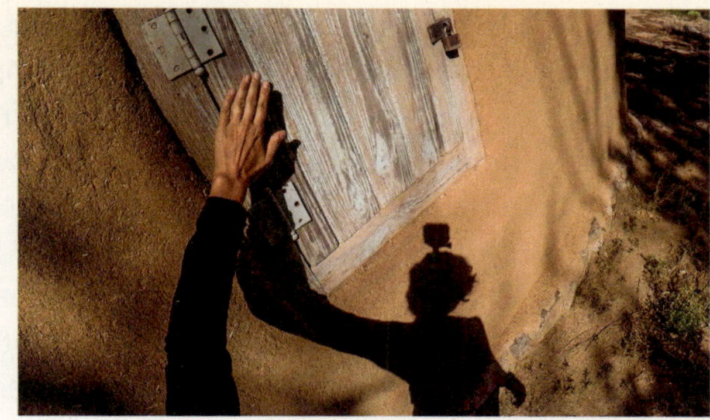

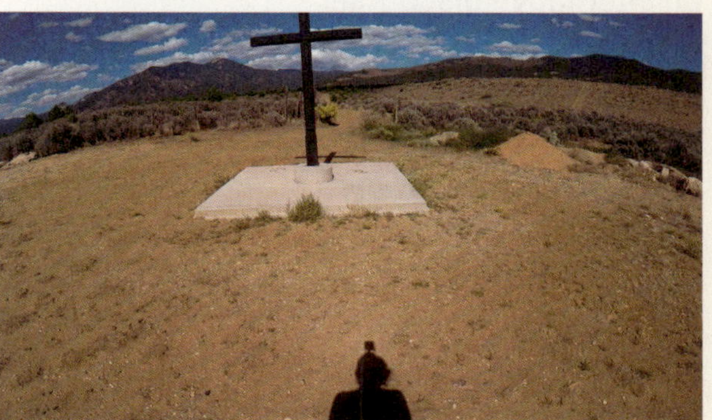

5.25
5.26

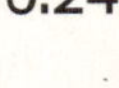

5.24

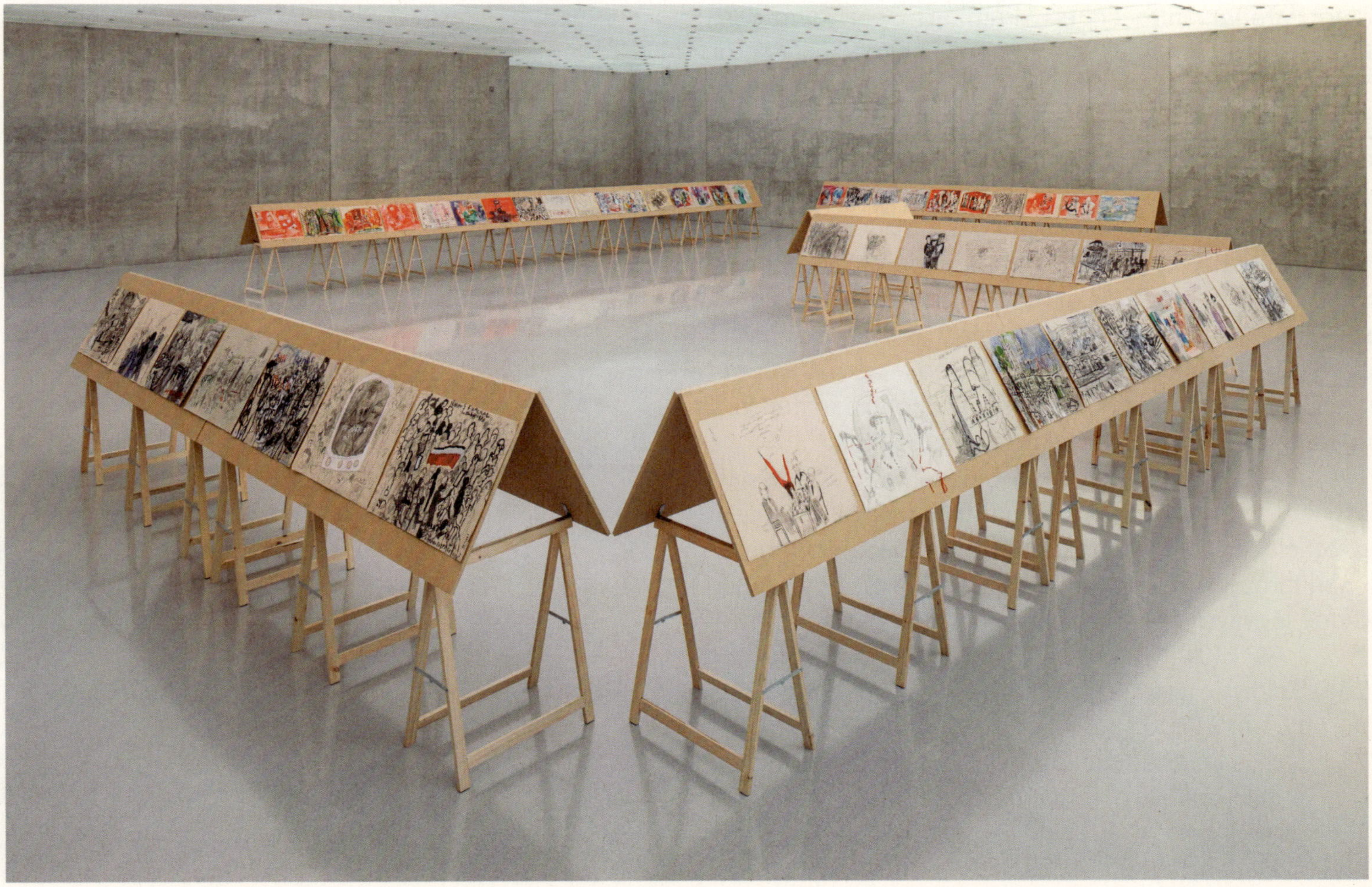

powers. Accompanied by a soundtrack composed of syncretic church music from the 1930s, the film also emphasizes the important role of the Catholic Church in shaping Congolese society. The fusion of Christian church music with bodily movements creates a unified and synchronous experience, underlining the interconnection of religion and labor exploitation (figs. 5.28–5.30). By bringing together visual and material remains, Baloji challenges the dominant narrative of the colonial era while opening up a space for the emergence of an alternative discourse.

Fig. 5.27
Christine Howard Sandoval, *The Eaters*, 2020, adobe mud, masking tape, postcard, steel

Figs. 5.28–5.30
Sammy Baloji, *Tales of the Copper Cross Garden: Episode 1*, 2017 (video stills), HD video (color, sound); 42 min.

PARAFICTIONS The creation of alternative archives and knowledges through the use of imagination and fiction as a critical tool is a common strategy in a third group of works. This work has parallels with the concept of "critical fabulation," proposed by the cultural historian Saidiya Hartman to describe the use of invention as a way of confronting the limitations and exclusions of archives, particularly in relation to the lives and deaths of two enslaved girls during the Middle Passage, as she elaborates in her essay "Venus in Two Acts." Hartman writes: "It is a history of an unrecoverable past; it is a narrative of what might have been or could have been; it is a history written with and against the archive."[26]

Beyond its historical specificity, this use of storytelling and narrative speculation is also connected to the notion of "parafiction," proposed by Carrie Lambert-Beatty to describe a genre of artworks that combines both real and fictional elements. "Fiction or fictiveness has emerged as an important category in recent art," Lambert-Beatty wrote in 2009. "But, like a paramedic as opposed to a medical doctor, a parafiction is related to but not quite a member of the category of fiction as established in literary and dramatic art. It remains a bit outside. It does not perform its procedures in the hygienic clinics of literature, but has one foot in the field of the real."[27] Sara Callahan cites the work of Pamela Corey, who applied the concept of parafiction to the work of "artists who use methods of microhistory and layered and associative narratives as strategies to represent locally based memory practices that are anchored in non-Western temporalities and associated notions of historical materials" through play, affect, and transhistorical practices.[28]

*Ways of Knowing* holds similar ideas: to push against the partiality of archives to show that there are alternatives to their official histories, that knowledge is capable of being expressed through art, and that art is capable of constructing knowledge in ways other than the canonical. Although

5.28 5.29 5.30

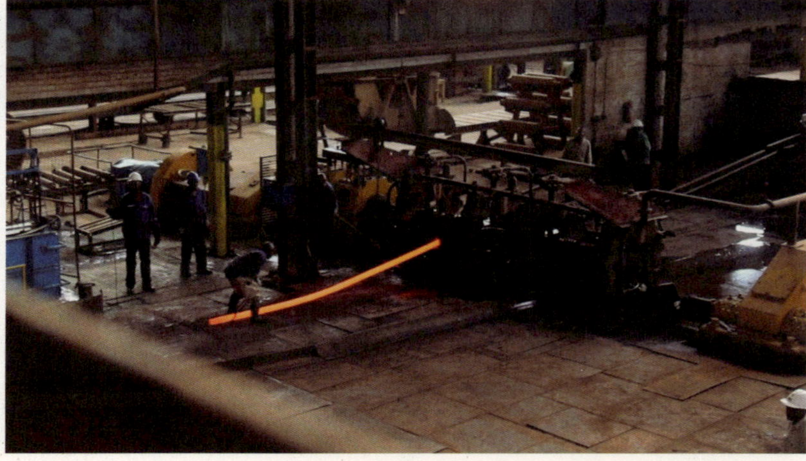

26 Saidiya Hartman, "Venus in Two Acts," *Small Axe* 12, no. 2 (2008): 12.
27 Carrie Lambert-Beatty, "Make-Believe: Parafiction and Plausibility," *October*, no. 129 (Summer 2009): 54.
28 Callahan, "When the Dust Has Settled," 84.

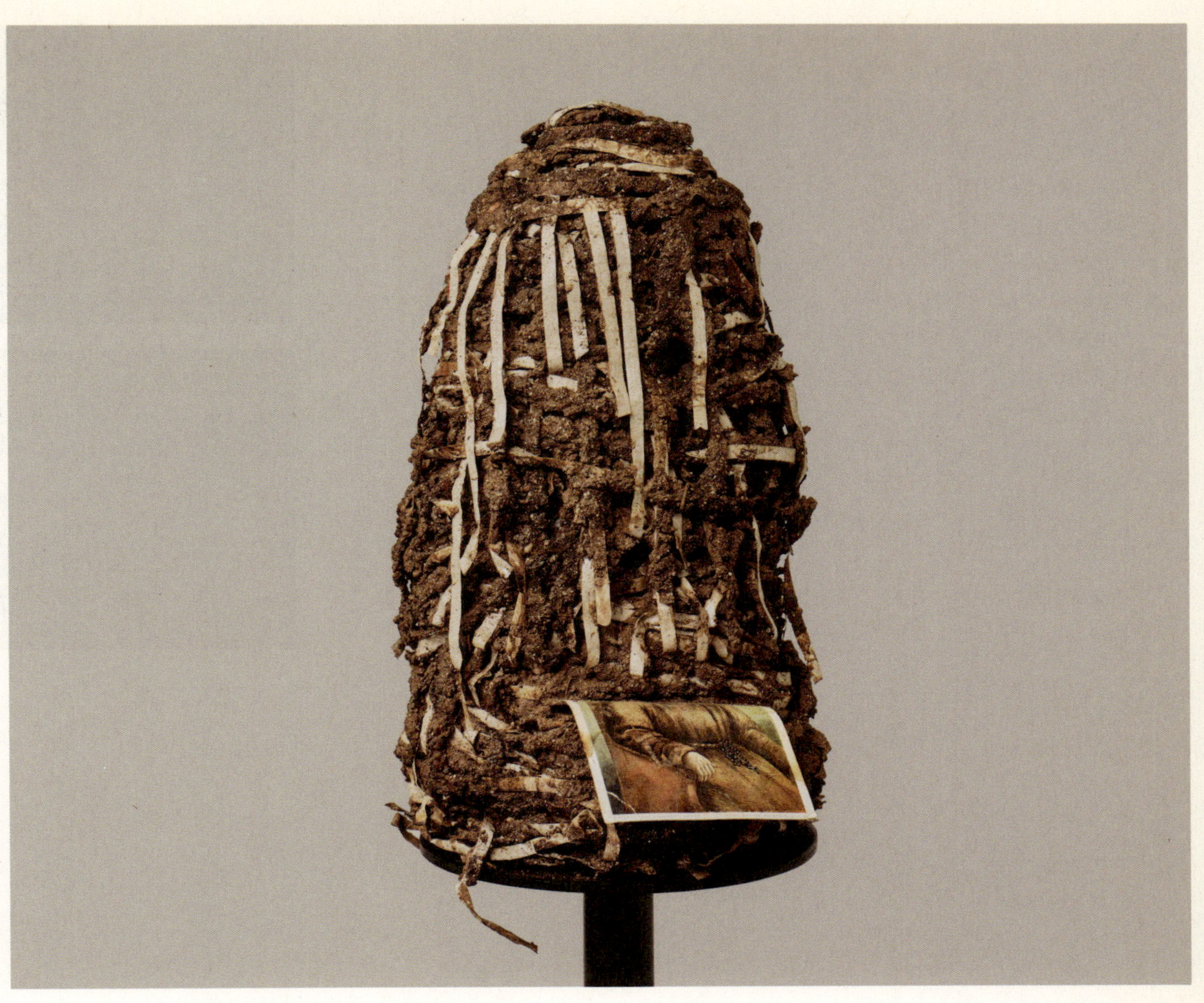

5.27

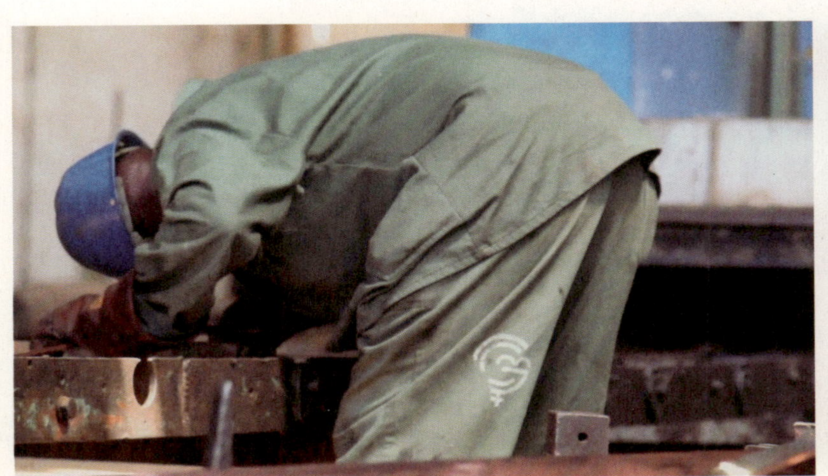

It is useful to note that given the tensions described by the colonial literature between the 'night' of the village in its carnal thickness and the 'day' of the mission in all its saving light, the 'evolved' African between 1930 and 1945 —symbolized, at least, by my father— almost always chooses the call of the mission.

He often interiorized these material and directly visible signs of the new power: the new codes of living (on the ethical and social plane), the hierarchy of languages (some even went so far as to learn Latin, to the point that they spoke it better than French), and the capitalist choreography of profitability and competition.

Figs. 5.31, 5.32
Cabello/Carceller, *Una voz para Erauso. Epílogo para un tiempo trans* (A voice for Erauso. Epilogue for a trans time), 2021–2022 (video stills), two-channel 4K video transferred to HD video (color, sound); 28:15 min.

Fig. 5.33
Petrit Halilaj, *Very volcanic over this green feather*, 2021, UV-printed felt, spray-painted ink, thread, metal pipe

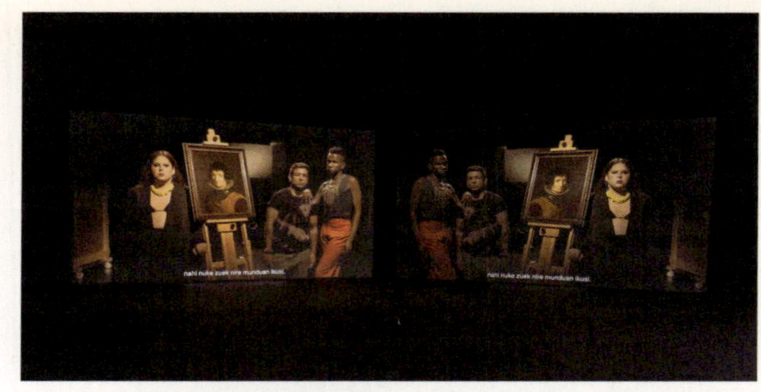

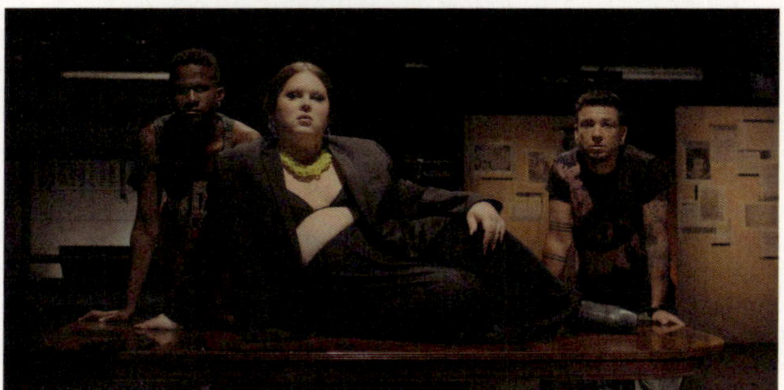

5.31
5.32

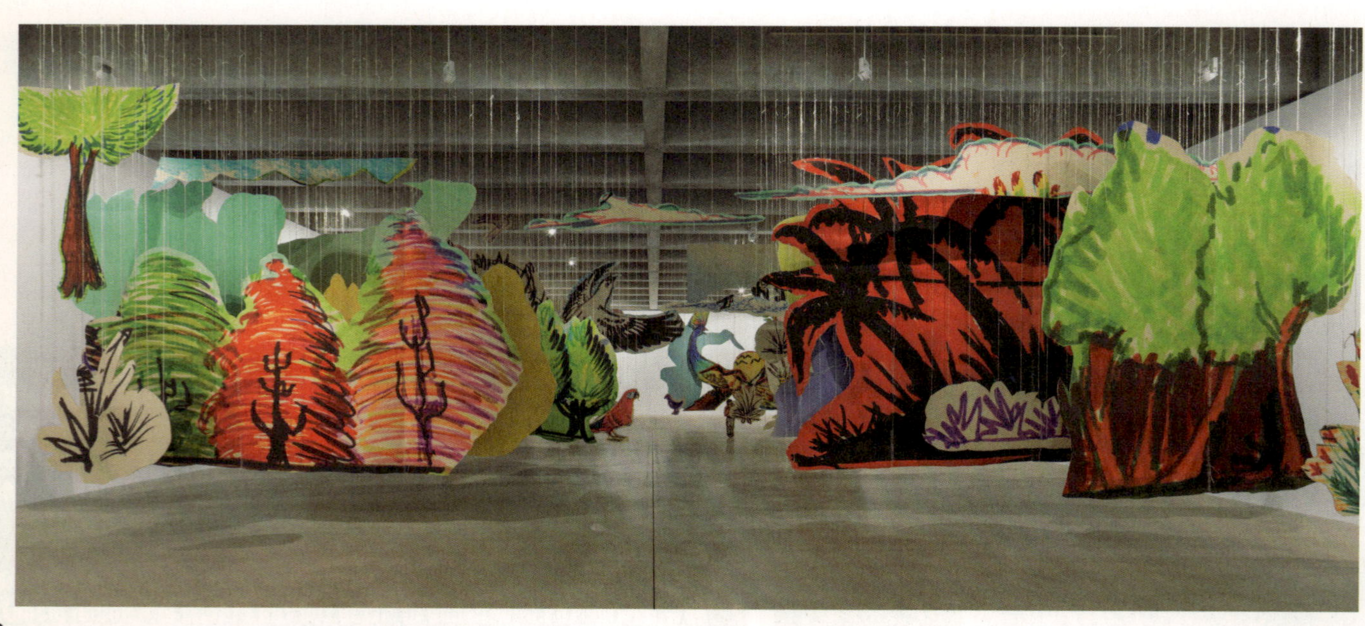

5.33

Cabello/Carceller, Petrit Halilaj, and Eduardo Navarro each approach the topics of their interest in their own unique ways, the thread that unites their works is the use of imagination and fiction and the rejection of traditional methods of seeking knowledge in favor of introducing new vocabularies and embodied modes of understanding.

Cabello/Carceller construct highly innovative narratives in which both history and the present are seen "as conditions that are not 'given,' as public narratives that must be fought for."[29] Using fiction and other formal resources as tools, as well as collaborative structures, Cabello/Carceller explore historical thought, especially the dominant binaries in relation to gender identity and sexuality. *Una voz para Erauso. Epílogo para un tiempo trans* (A voice for Erauso. Epilogue for a trans time, 2021–2022; pp. 185–197) addresses the complex biography of Antonio de Erauso, a prominent figure in colonial Spain in the seventeenth century due to his transition from female to male and his bloody participation in the wars in the Americas. The work focuses on the portrait painted around 1630 by Juan van der Hamen y León of Erauso dressed as an officer in the Spanish navy (p. 189) and weaves a complex temporal narrative in which the figure of Erauso is intertwined with that of three contemporary nonbinary characters, who claim their right to be recognized (p. 188). Visually the installation consists of two screens arranged at an angle and joined in the center, allowing the images to come closer or to coincide as the narrative moves through time, creating a sort of visual and temporal kaleidoscope (figs. 5.31, 5.32). Rejecting notions of critical distance, Cabello/Carceller use Erauso—an uncomfortable character, a "site in which a multiplicity of conflicting identities are constructed and deconstructed"—to investigate the historical condition of gender identity at a time when it is in conflict.[30]

The use of imagination as a critical tool also permeates the production of Petrit Halilaj, whose work delves into personal and collective histories as a means to create new scenarios that claim space for freedom, desire, and intimacy. Born in 1986 in Kostërrc, a village outside the town of Runik, in Kosovo, Halilaj grew up during the Kosovo War (1998–1999), and the consequences of the political and cultural tensions of that time often serve as the starting point for large, immersive installations that weave together personal relationships, memories, dreams, and stories.

In *Very volcanic over this green feather* (2021; pp. 199–215), drawings of scenes, people, and plant and animal life are transformed into a large installation set up as a theatrical stage, inviting the viewer to become the protagonist of an imagined and lived world. These drawings, clearly made by a child, were scanned, cut out, enlarged, and printed on felt panels, which were also cut out following the silhouettes of the images. The resulting elements hang from the ceiling at varying heights, creating a sort of suspended forest (fig. 5.33). The installation is linked to a set of drawings (figs. 5.34, 5.35) that Halilaj made as a child under the instruction of Giacomo Poli, an Italian psychologist who visited the refugee camp to which Halilaj's family was relocated after their house was bombed by Serbian soldiers. Provided with drawing materials by Poli, who was researching the effects of war on children, Halilaj drew colorful landscapes, flowers, and various birds—including parrots, peacocks, and doves—but also soldiers, military paraphernalia, and scenes of torture and executions. With the exception of a single figure, that of a child, printed on both sides and placed flush with the floor in the installation, Halilaj arranged the imagined scenes on the front side and the remembered scenes on the back side, so that the viewer has to pass through the imagined scenes before turning to be confronted with the war scenes on the back. If, like memories of the past, visions of the future also occur in fragments, his work proposes that our vision of the world to come is a collective dream, built from the fragments of what was and what might have been.

Throughout an artistic practice spanning more than fifteen years, Eduardo Navarro has created works of art that invite a broadening of human perception. Although his projects often differ greatly from one another, they all begin from a position antithetical to the academic rigor of the sciences and the methodologies of more traditional branches of knowledge. Navarro calls this approach, which is deeply empathetic and leavened by a healthy dose of absurdity and humor, "transmuting." It usually involves collective experiences that propose new ways of relating to the world—mostly nonhuman life-forms—through unconventional uses of the senses. Some of his transmutations have involved treating water homeopathically, as if it were a living entity; creating edible drawings to decentralize the primacy of sight over other senses; imitating the movements of a turtle, a horse, an octopus, and, most recently, a seal, using protheses based on the anatomies of these animals; and creating artworks in collaboration with the wind, the sun, the sky, and plants. These projects are typically presented as preparatory and finished drawings and physical objects that take on a sculptural character when shown in exhibition spaces, as well as prostheses or costumes when used by people.

Commissioned specifically for *Ways of Knowing*, Navarro's *Cloud Museum* (2025; pp. 217–230) takes up recurring elements of his practice, such as using natural forces as the impetus for his works and translating intuitions and perceptions into poetic diagrams. In previous works such as

29 Paul B. Preciado, "A Voice for Erauso—Epilogue for a Trans Time," exhibition brochure, Azkuna Zentroa Alhóndiga Bilbao, March 2022, https://issuu.com/azkunazentroa/docs/brouchure-a-voice-for-erauso.

30 Paul B. Preciado, *Una voz para Erauso: Epílogo para un tiempo trans* (Bilbao: Azkuna Zentroa Alhóndiga, 2022), 14.

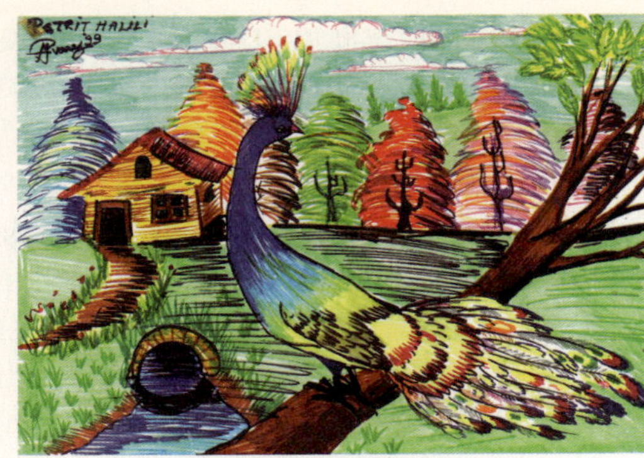

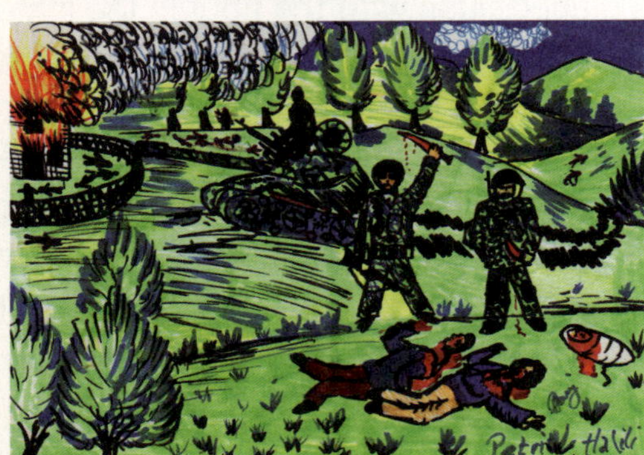

5.34
5.35

*Instructions from the Sky* (2016; fig. 5.40), *In Collaboration with the Sun* (2017/2019; figs. 5.36–5.38), and *Instant Weather Prediction* (2019; fig. 5.39), Navarro created sets of costumes to be worn by groups of dancers who could improvise choreographies in relation to the direction of the wind and the reflections of the sun or the sky on their costumes. In a more recent work, *Sonic muscle* (2023), he arranged a group of people equipped with stethoscopes in a circle to transcribe the heartbeats of their companions on the elastic suits they wore, creating a kind of poetic electrocardiogram. *Cloud Museum* integrates several of these elements, particularly a movement exercise or a choreography and a drawing exercise, as a means to foster a contemplative state of perception as a form of collective knowledge. But this work specifically explores this experience across a broader spectrum of abilities. In the margin of a notebook, Navarro wrote, "How would you describe the sky to a blind person?" (p. 223). One drawing shows two figures with spools of blue thread on their heads, each connected to a cloud. They use their fingertips to trace cloud shapes on the back of a person (p. 219). Another drawing depicts two feathers descending from clouds, suspended from blue threads, as they trace a face on the back of a figure who is making a drawing on a pool of water (p. 219). A third drawing shows two figures drawing clouds on the palms of a person lying on their back, with the sky reflected on their body (p. 227).

Regarding his process, Navarro shared during a visit that "grasping an idea is like catching a lion, poetically closing it until it is built."[31] This method, he explains, allows him to remain detached from conventional notions of artistic research. Appropriately, the preliminary stages of *Cloud Museum* consisted of sketches of a modular structure with mirrored surfaces enabling participants to transcribe the reflections of the sky. Later drawings depict a system of interconnected suits akin to a parachute that allow participants to share the experience of "becoming a walking collective cloud" and then to transcribe the experience through drawing or journaling. In yet a more recent instance, Navarro wrote a letter to *Cloud Museum* (p. 218), expressing his belief that works of art have their own consciousness and that he would assist in its manifestation, so that we can temporarily become "a cloud of gathered stories, feelings, emotions, anecdotes, memories, and shared mythologies." He notes that each of his works addresses a "nonexistent problem" and has stated that he sees himself more as a "diviner" than an artist, as one who creates a shared experience by bringing together disparate elements, much like clouds converging in the sky. While Navarro's artworks may propose solutions to nonexistent problems, *Cloud Museum* (p. 230) synthesizes his

Fig. 5.34
Petrit Halilaj, *Fantastic Landscape*, 1999, felt-tip pen on paper

Fig. 5.35
Petrit Halilaj, *These are two Serbian soldiers who massacred a couple and their baby. That's a tank with other soldiers who killed people in their garden and others further down. They also burned down the house*, 1999, felt-tip pen on paper

Figs. 5.36–5.38
Eduardo Navarro, *In Collaboration with the Sun*, 2017/2019, seven mirrored suits, solar synchronization

31 All quotations from Eduardo Navarro in this paragraph are from the artist's conversation with the author, January 12, 2024.

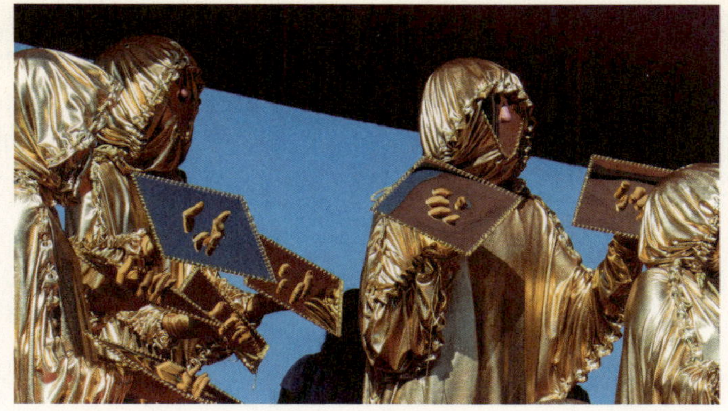
5.36

5.37
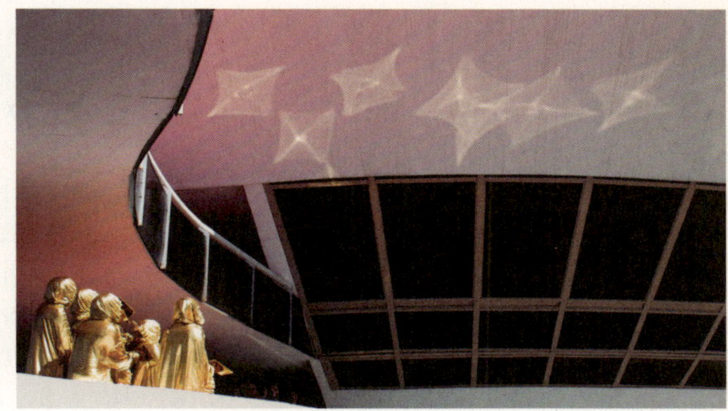

5.38
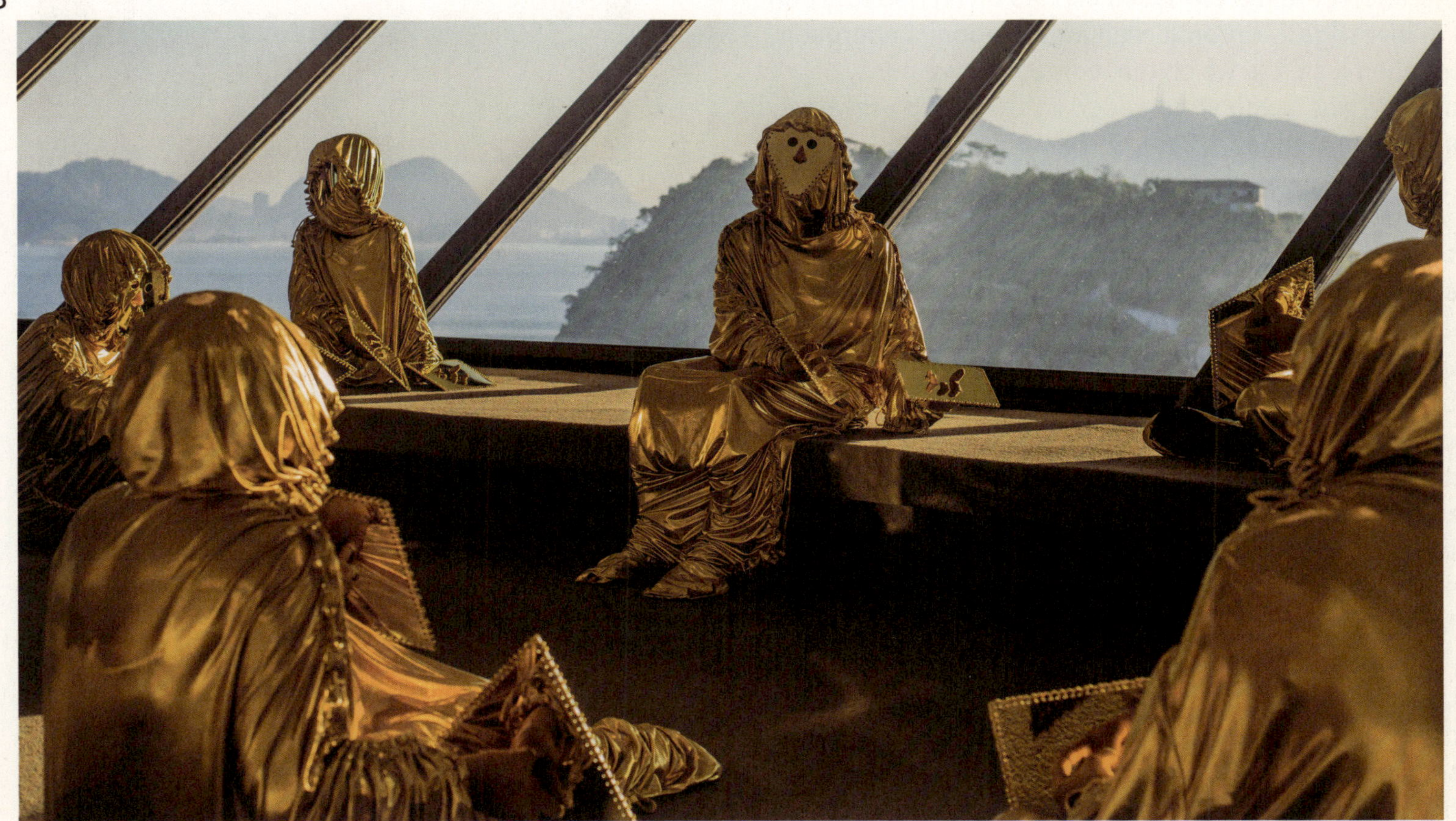

research into a collective experience that is emotional, intuitive, and extrasensorial while offering an embodied way of understanding that transcends traditional modes of perception.

In 2017 I curated the first museum survey dedicated to Forensic Architecture, an interdisciplinary collective, born out of the "open source revolution," that develops methods to uncover and expose hidden truths. Pushing architecture beyond its traditional boundaries into the realms of human rights advocacy, art, and law, Forensic Architecture's practice involves geolocating videos and images within interactive 3D models and using a variety of existing and newly invented techniques—such as satellite imagery analysis, "remote sensing," and "situated testimony"—to create evidence files in cases of state and corporate malfeasance (fig. 5.41).[32]

Although the collective's findings have frequently been presented in legal and political platforms, its work is most prominently shown in contemporary art institutions. Forensic Architecture's work operates on a very different register from relational art or social practices, however, as its investigations have directly demonstrated the culpability of states and corporations in various abuses of power. Indeed its work has been replicated not only within contemporary art contexts but also by mainstream media. The exhibition *Forensic Architecture: Towards an Investigative Aesthetics* (p. 181) emerged at a moment when the notion of truth was increasingly questioned and facts were seen as subject to varying degrees of manipulation, signaling the erosion of the very concept of transparency. The exhibition aimed to examine, through the lens of the collective's groundbreaking work, how this iteration of research-based art had given rise to a new kind of investigative practice, an interventionist approach that marked a shift in which the "contemplative purity of past aesthetics" was being superseded by the sharp precision of "sensitive knowledge."[33]

The nature of Forensic Architecture's work led at least one visitor to the exhibition to ask, "Is this art?"[34] A skeptical visitor to *Ways of Knowing* would be more likely to wonder, "Where is the research?" In response I would argue that research can be as simple as walking in a specific territory, as Howard Sandoval suggests, or as imaginative as studying the sky by drawing it as a means of gaining collective knowledge, as seen in Navarro's work, in which the practice takes on its most expansive and open-ended form. Today research-based art encompasses a wide variety of approaches, from the factual to the fictional, from the playful to the anomalous. Artists have opened up and hybridized research-based methods by incorporating subtler and more intuitive ways of integrating information, creating a more nuanced and poetic expression of the genre. Most criticism of the genre suggests that it merely aggregates information, enacting a kind of redundancy. As Bishop notes, however, "the richest possibilities for research-based installation emerge

Fig. 5.39
Eduardo Navarro, *Instant Weather Prediction*, 2019

Fig. 5.40
Eduardo Navarro, *Instructions from the Sky*, 2016

Fig. 5.41
Image Complex—1: Multiple images and reconstructed bomb clouds are arranged within a 3D model of Rafah, Gaza. From the Forensic Architecture investigation "The Bombing of Rafah," commissioned by Amnesty International and published in 2015

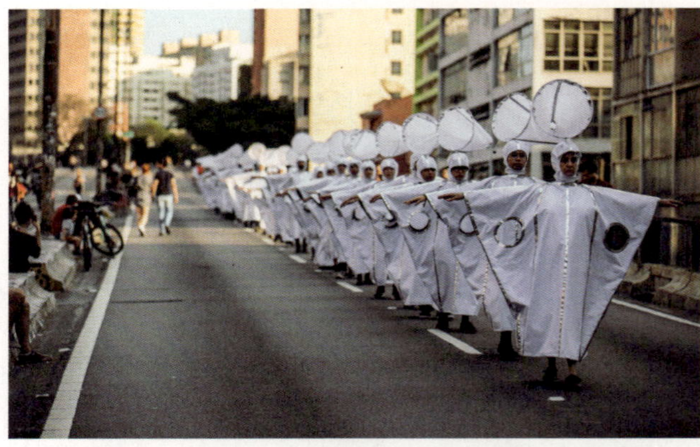

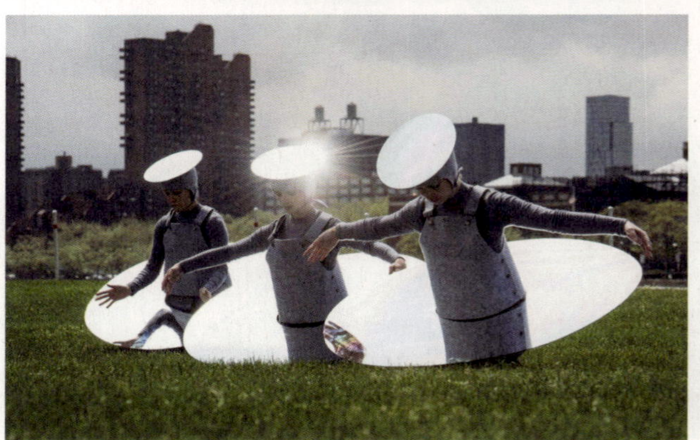

5.39
5.40

when preexisting information is not simply cut and pasted, aggregated, and dropped in a vitrine but metabolized by an idiosyncratic thinker who feels their way through the world."[35] *Ways of Knowing* highlights the work of artists who use research to synthesize their content, "metabolizing" information in ways that are highly individual and also playful, curious, rebellious, and lyrical.

In this essay and in the exhibition it accompanies, I look at how artists engage with information using approaches that reflect current shifts in culture, and I have tried to identify a few of the strategies they are adopting as they explore research as a relevant method to generate relatable ways of knowing. The artists featured in the first section, "Poetic Taxonomies," play on familiar tropes of organizing and representing knowledge, such as grids and taxonomies, thereby critically examining the lack of neutrality present in Western empirical knowledge systems. Their approach echoes the logic systems mined by artists associated with institutional critique but with a key difference: these artists infuse their systems with their own subjectivity. This often results in a sense of "useless" or "silly" erudition, a form of nonknowledge that is neither purely factual nor merely replicative.

The second section, "Durational and Place-Based Knowledges," presents works by artists who invoke alternative frameworks of knowledge to create a deeply poetic engagement with their source material. This is not to say that those frameworks are inherently poetic but rather that their disrupting of conventional methodologies of research enriches their narratives. By asserting their unique visual perspectives, these artists blur and complicate notions of otherness, place, and duration. This approach challenges and disrupts established methods of understanding, opening up the possibilities of what research can be.

The artists in the third and final section, "Parafictions," use even more unconventional forms of perception to investigate human experiences. Navarro, for example, specifically challenges the idea of human subjectivity as a mechanism for understanding or at least acknowledges the role of the subconscious in conscious thought processes. This is evident in the phenomenological nature of his works, which each re-create an

5.41

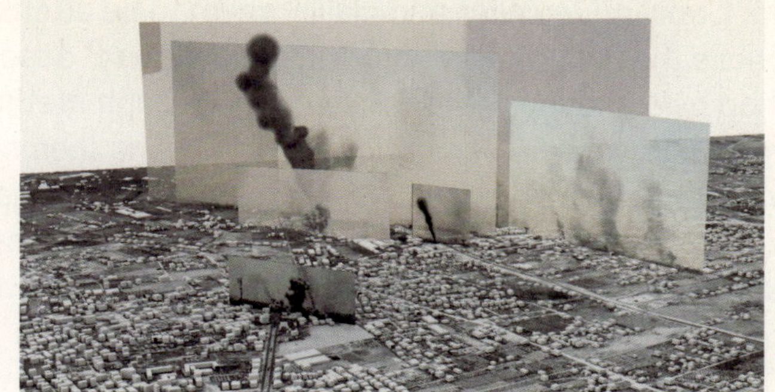

32 Forensic Architecture, "What Do We Do?," https://forensic-architecture.org/about/agency.

33 Ferran Barenblit and Cuauhtémoc Medina, "Una estética libre de estética," in *Forensic Architecture: Hacia una estética investigativa* (Barcelona: MACBA, Museu d'Art Contemporani de Barcelona; Mexico City: MUAC, Museo Universitario Arte Contemporáneo, UNAM, 2017), 18.

34 Rosario Güiraldes, "Arte en la era de la posverdad: *Hacia una estética investigativa*, de Forensic Architecture," in *Forensic Architecture*, 151.

35 Bishop, "Information Overload."

environment to capture the "dissonance" he seeks to express. Navarro, Cabello/Carceller, and Halilaj seem to be attempting to reconcile the condition of "information overload" described by Bishop by engaging with their material through methods that evoke extrasensory perception. By immersing themselves in their content and using tools such as fiction, imagination, or play, they come to a more nuanced and embodied way of understanding. This dynamic approach positions their work as a critical tool in an era saturated with information.

The three strategies that provide the organizing principle for *Ways of Knowing* are only some of the research-based methodologies that artists can potentially adopt. Many artists, including those represented in this exhibition, combine elements of these strategies as well as employing others that are already at work or are in the process of being developed. This suggests that it may be time to acknowledge the persistence of research-based art as evidence of a significant shift in artistic practice, one whose evolving possibilities artists will continue to explore.

SKY HOPINKA *Visions of an Island*, 2016, HD video (color, sound); 15:03 min., Walker Art Center, Minneapolis, Ruben/Bentson Moving Image Collection

SKY HOPINKA *Visions of an Island*, 2016, HD video (color, sound); 15:03 min., Walker Art Center, Minneapolis, Ruben/Bentson Moving Image Collection

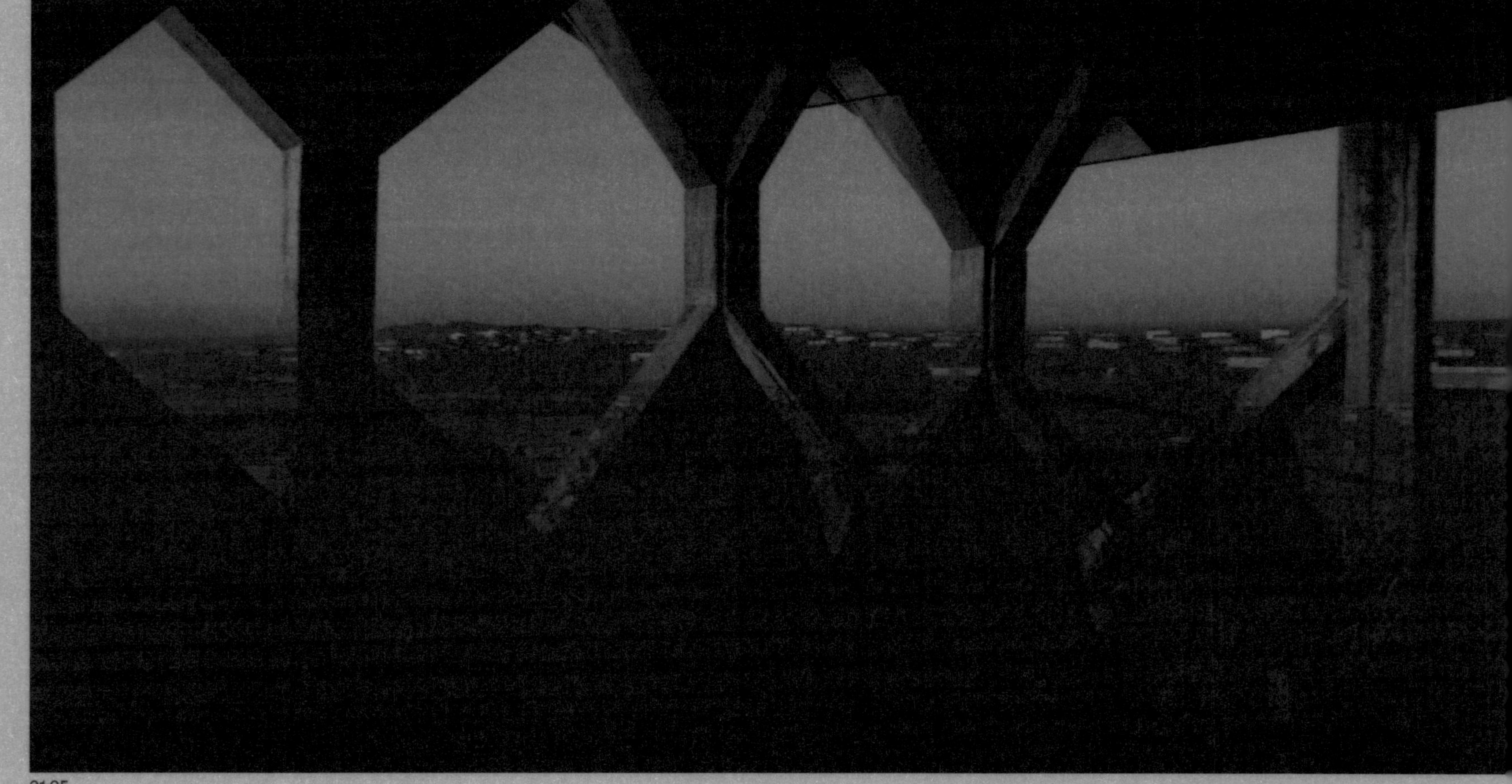

01:05

Stills from *Visions of an Island*, 2016 61

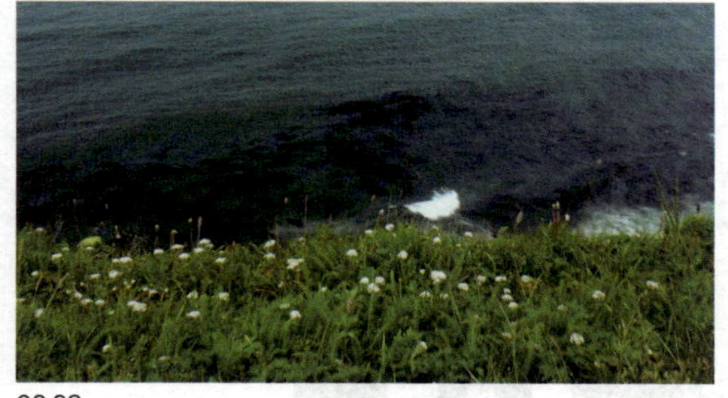

03:38

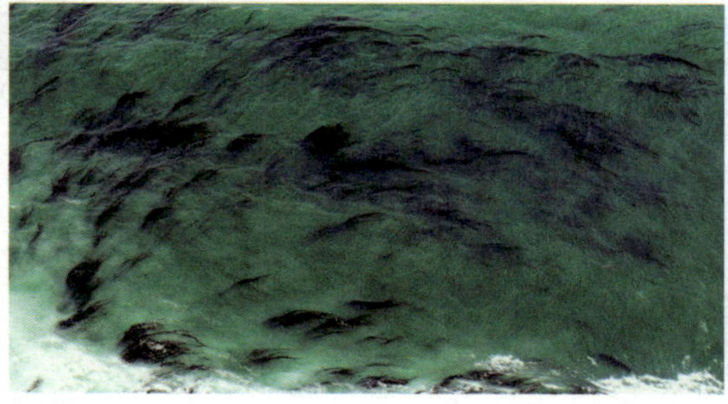

04:42

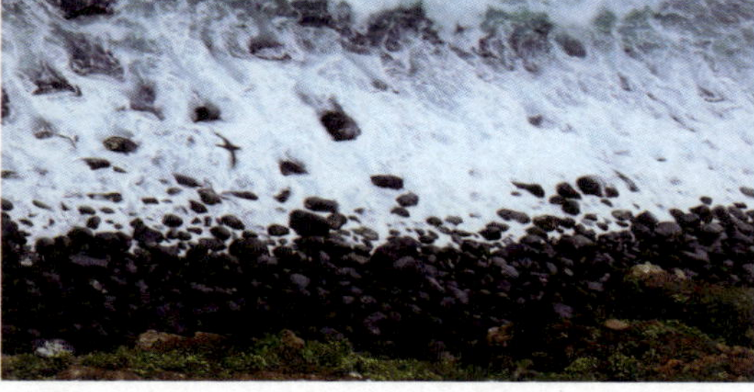

04:04

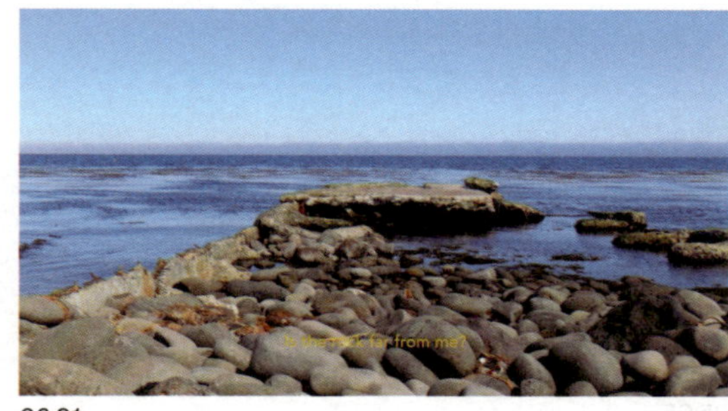


06:31

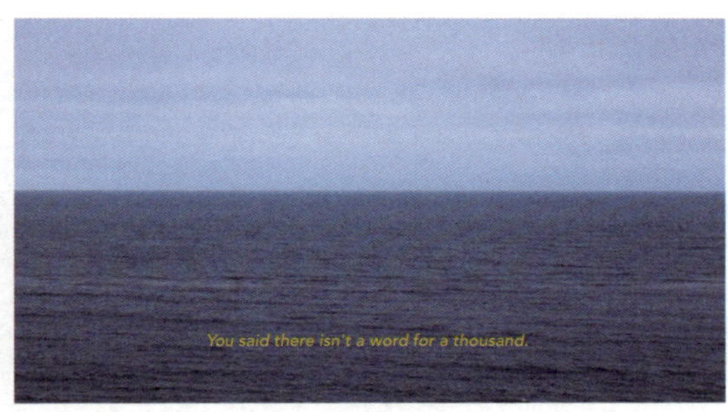


07:16

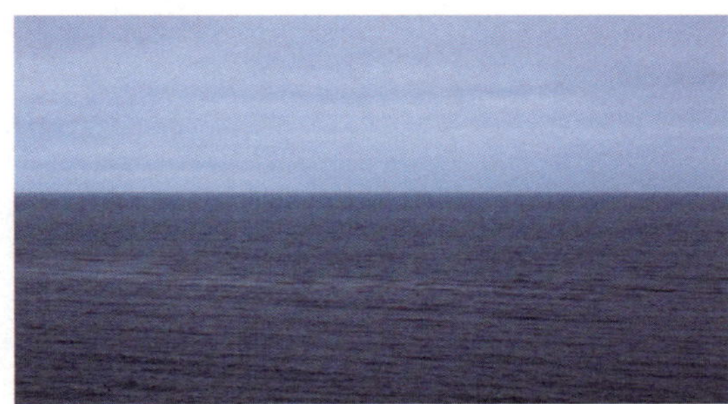

07:30

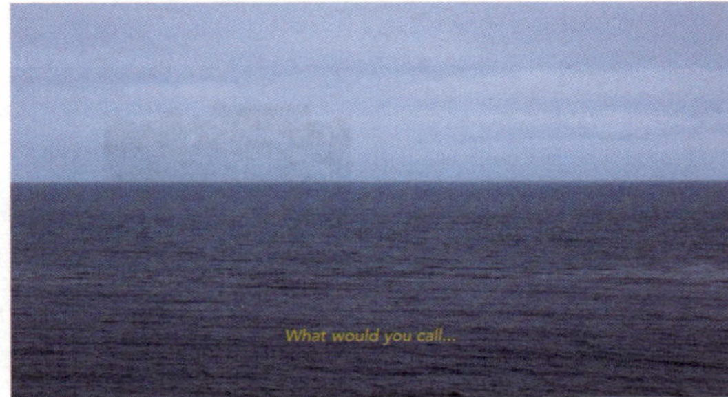


07:23

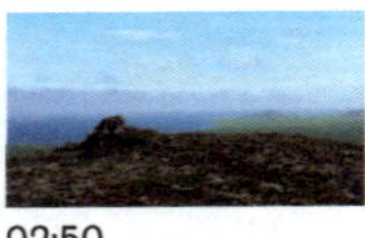
02:50

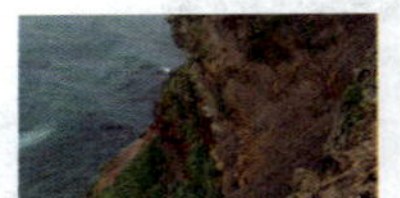
04:30

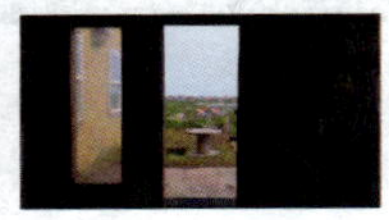
10:43

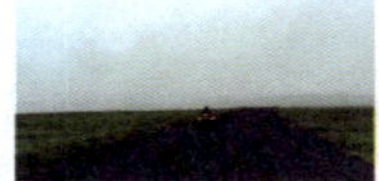
09:27

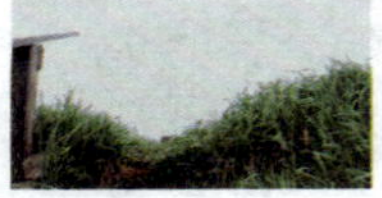
05:05

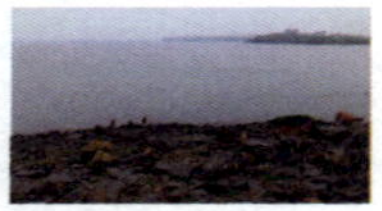
12:56

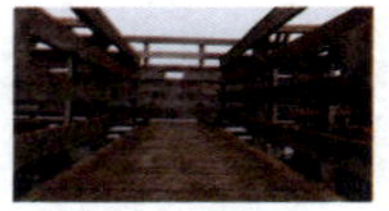
13:14

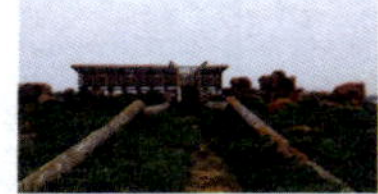
13:35

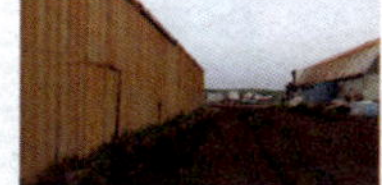
11:01

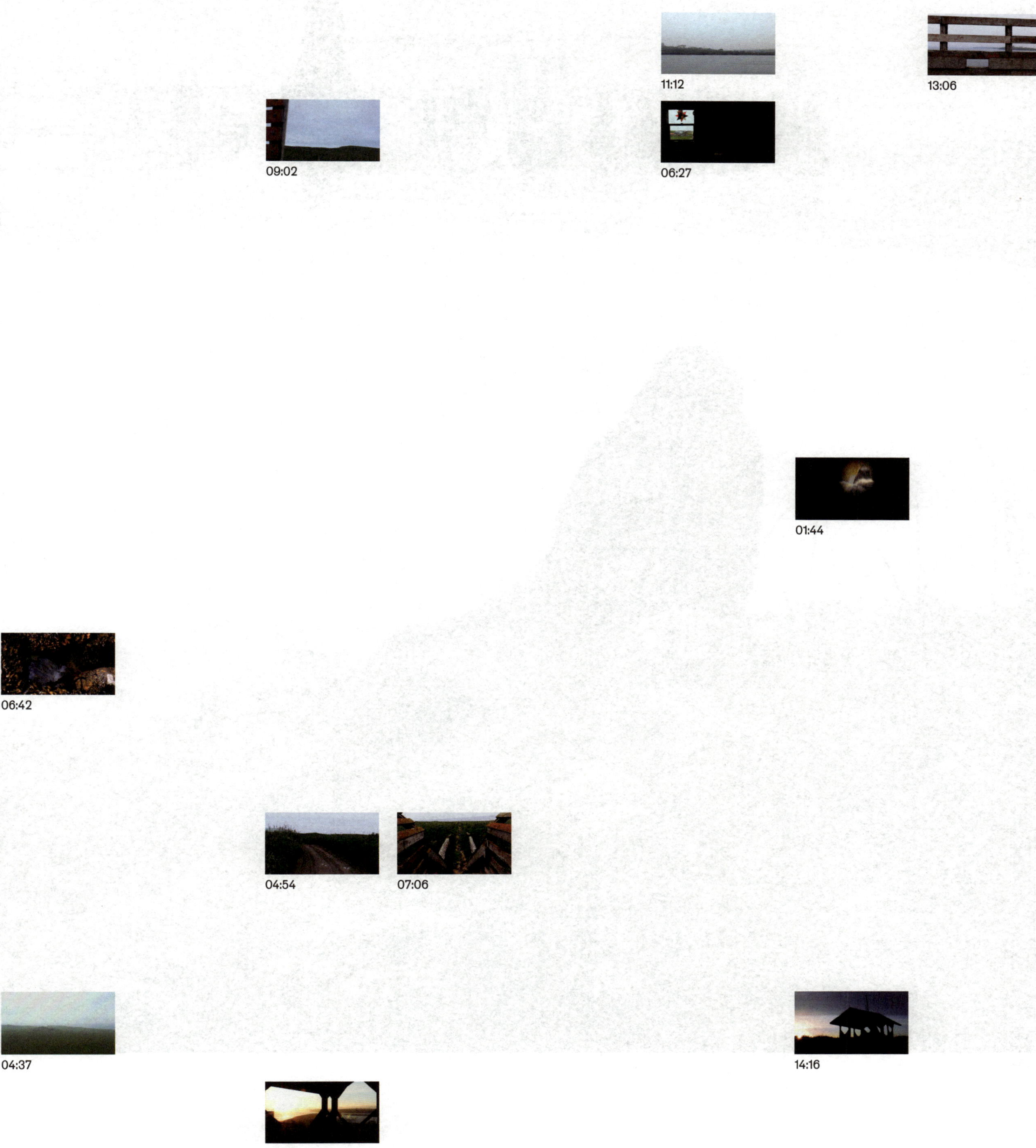
11:12
13:06
09:02
06:27
01:44
06:42
04:54
07:06
04:37
14:16
01:25

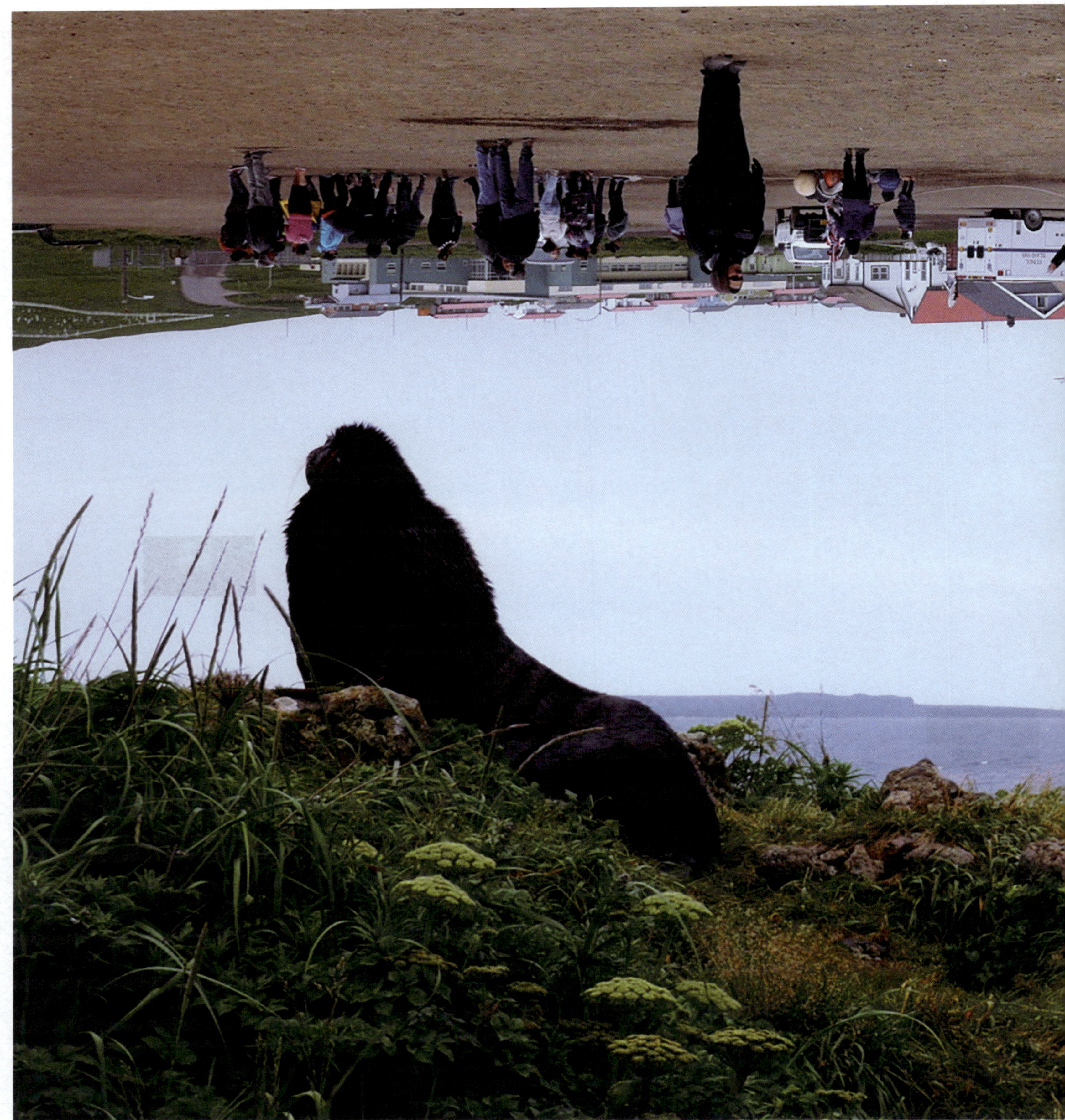

09:54

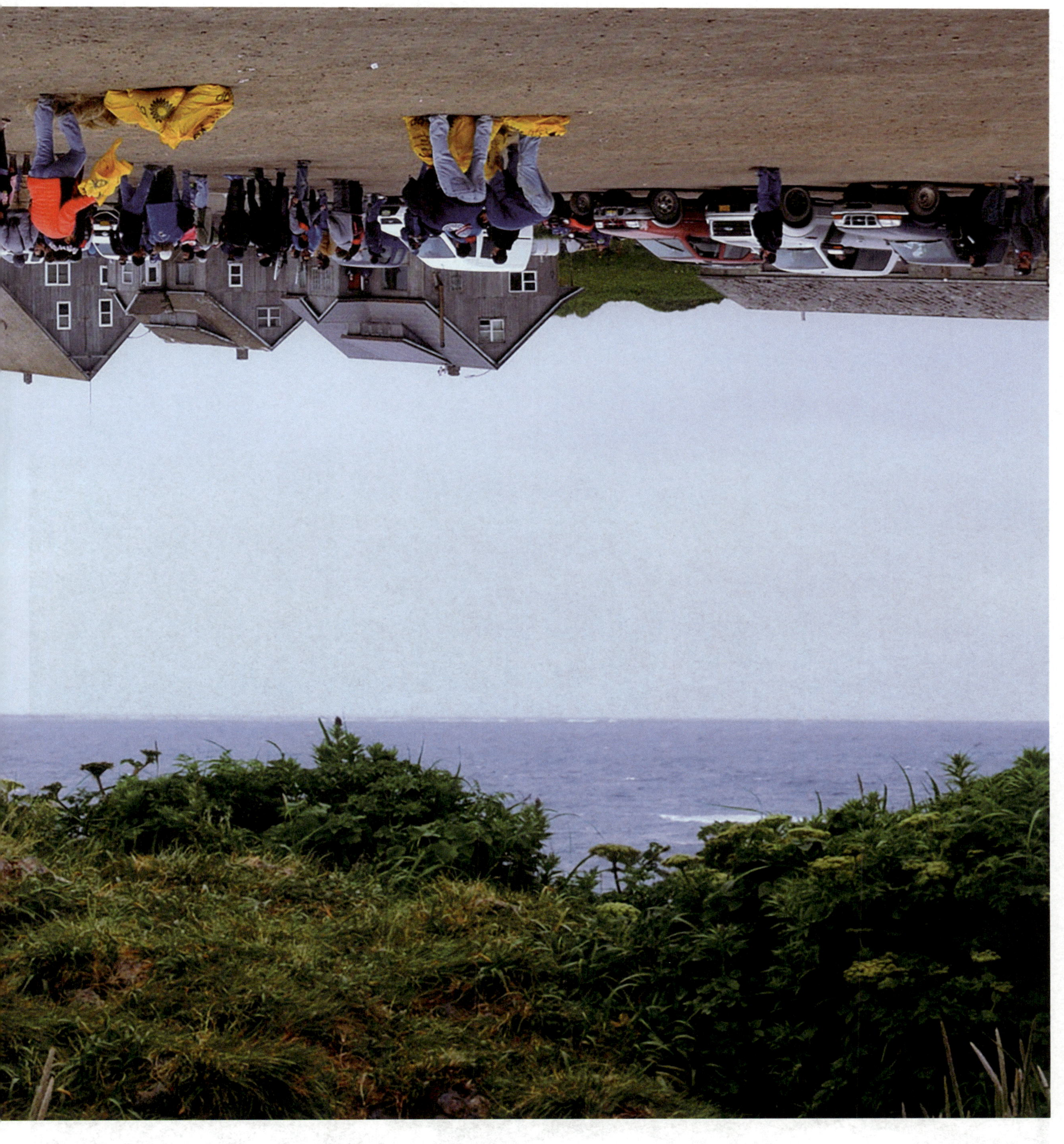

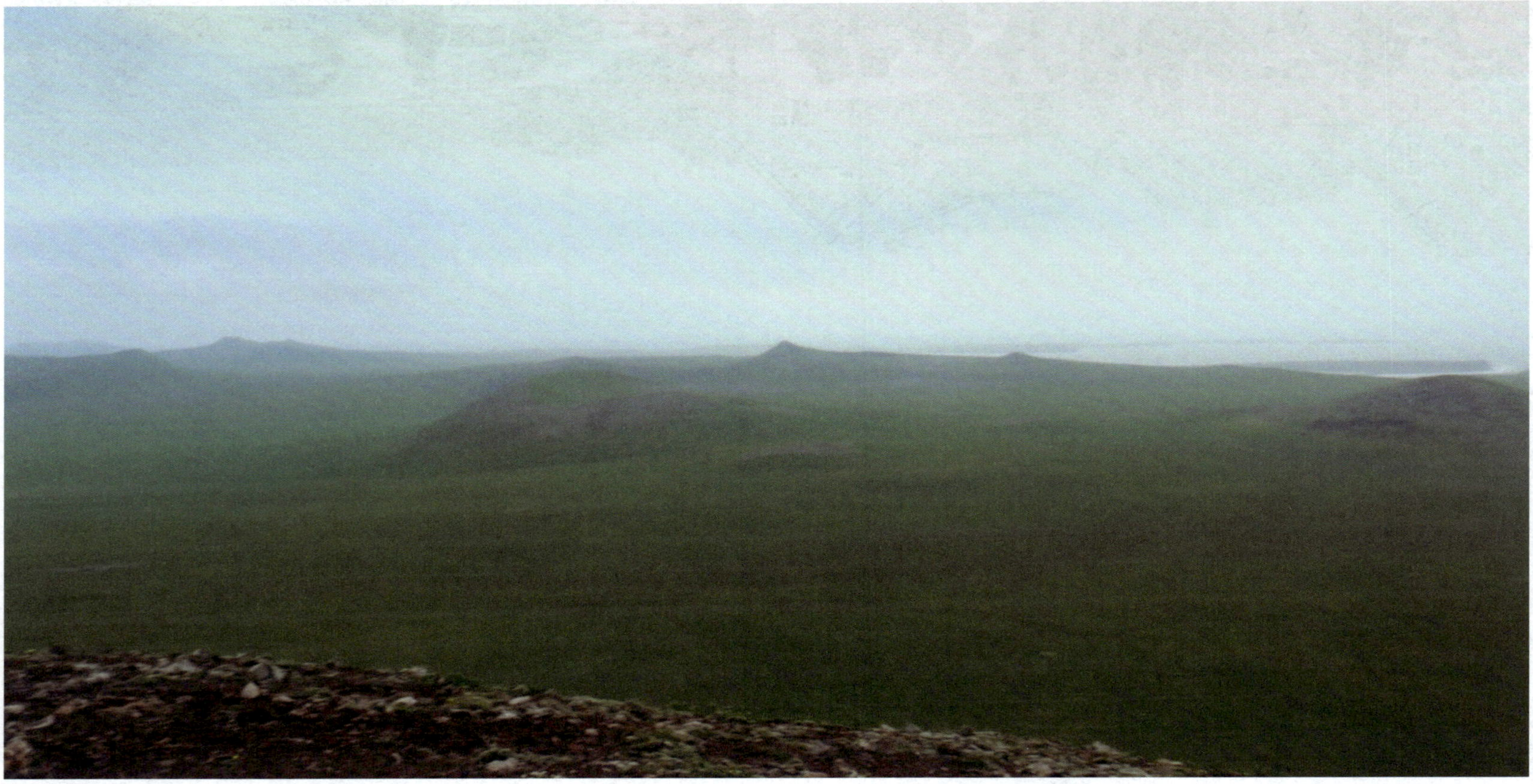

03:13

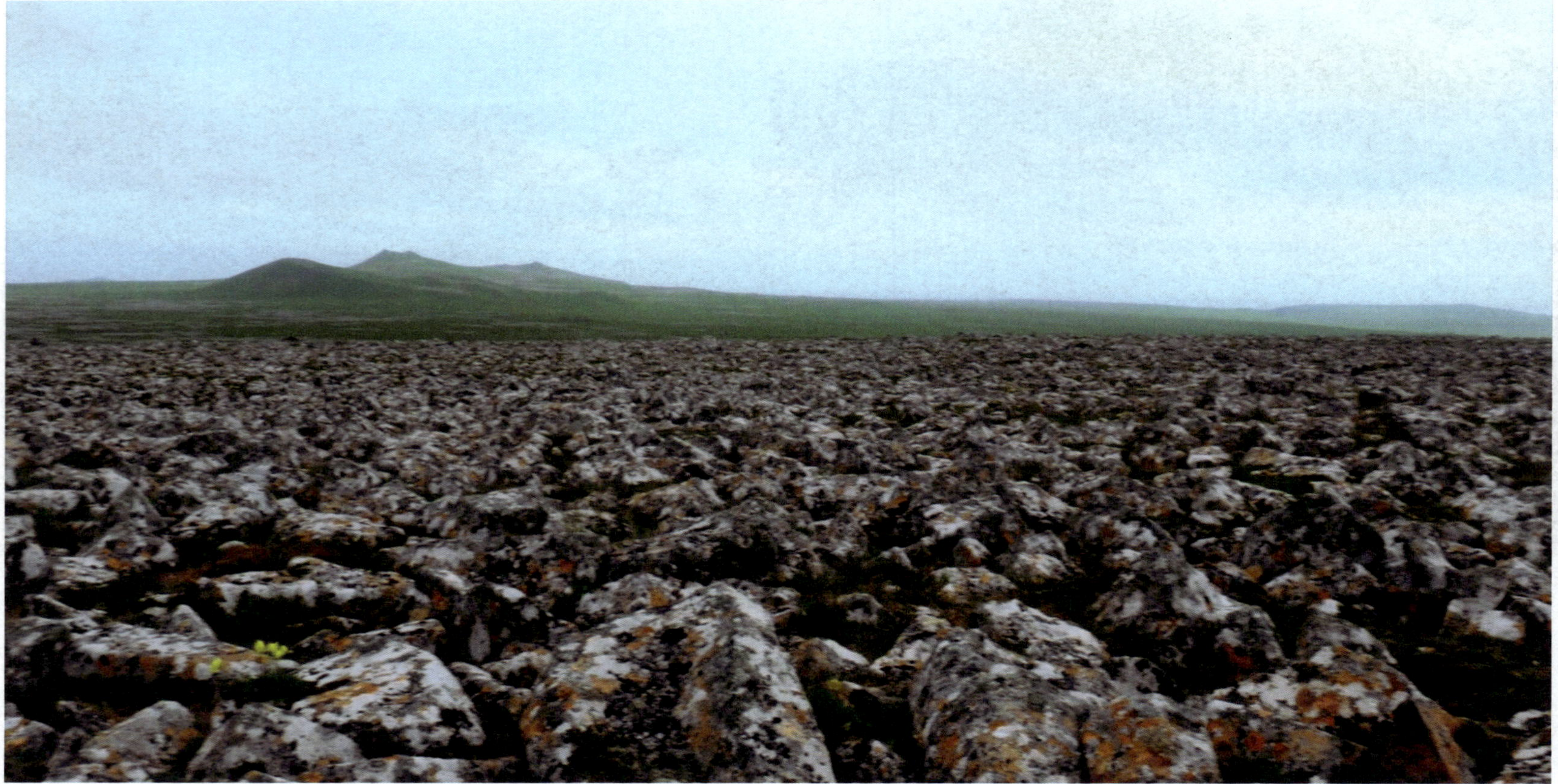

10:41

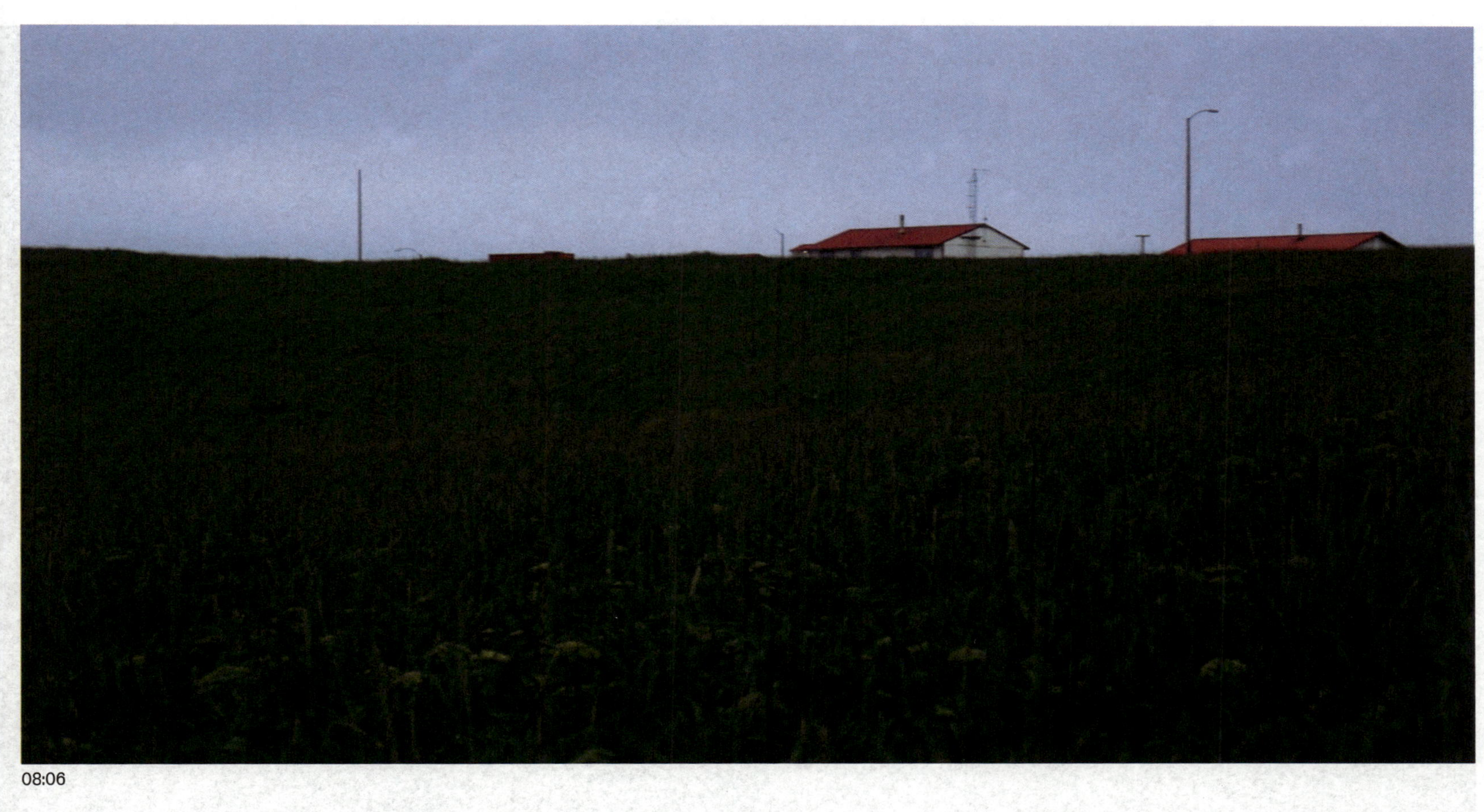
08:06

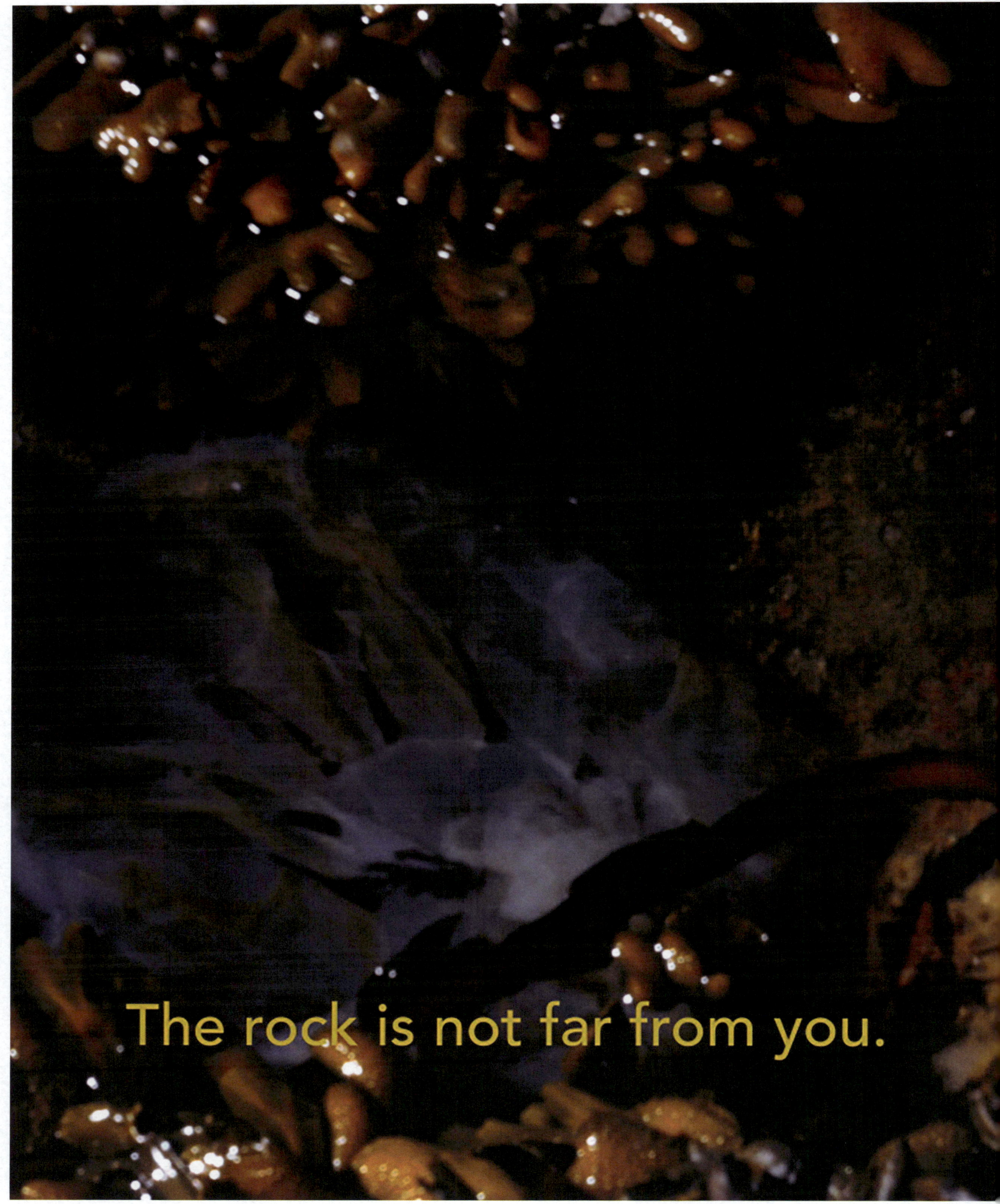
The rock is not far from you.

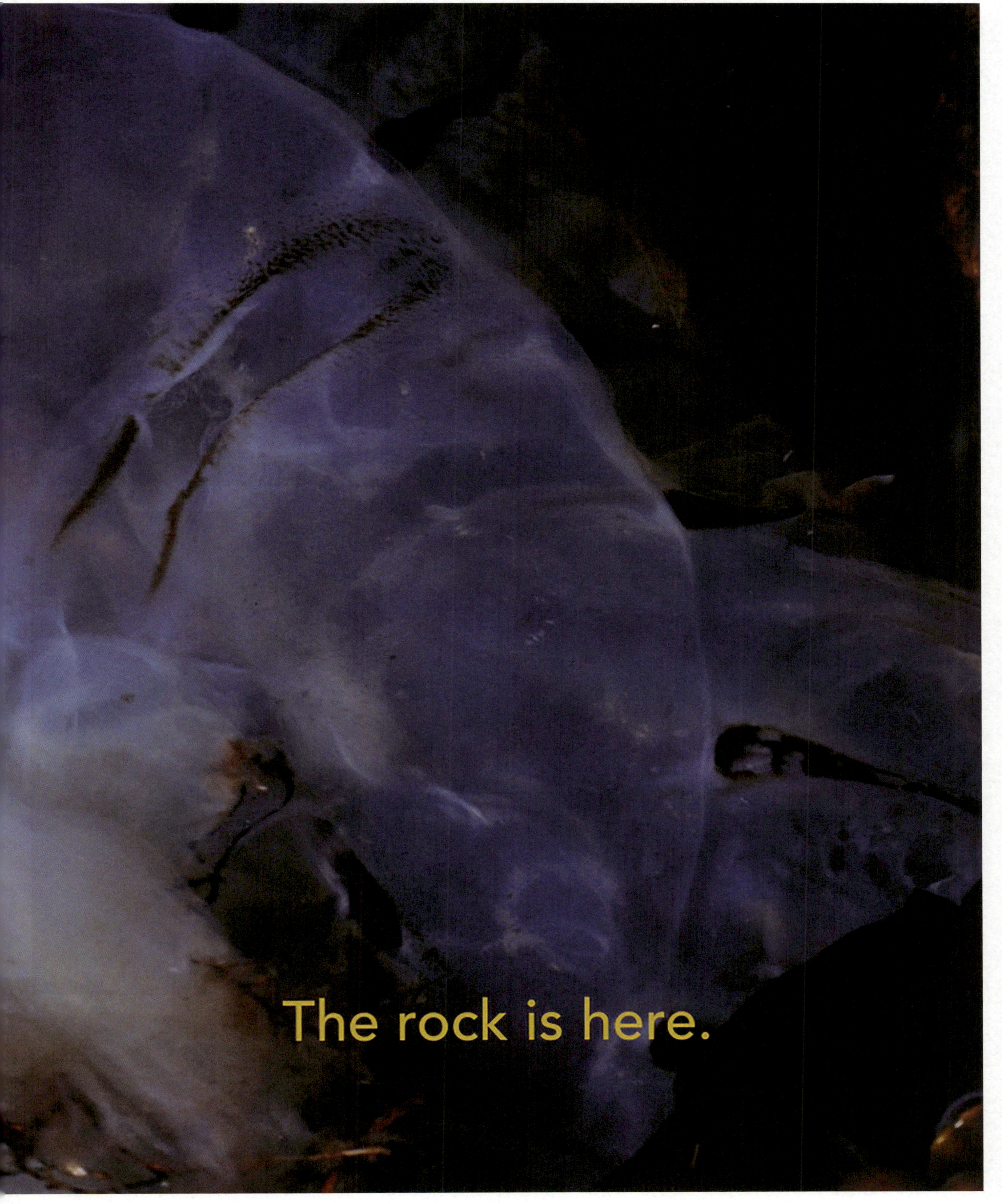
The rock is here.

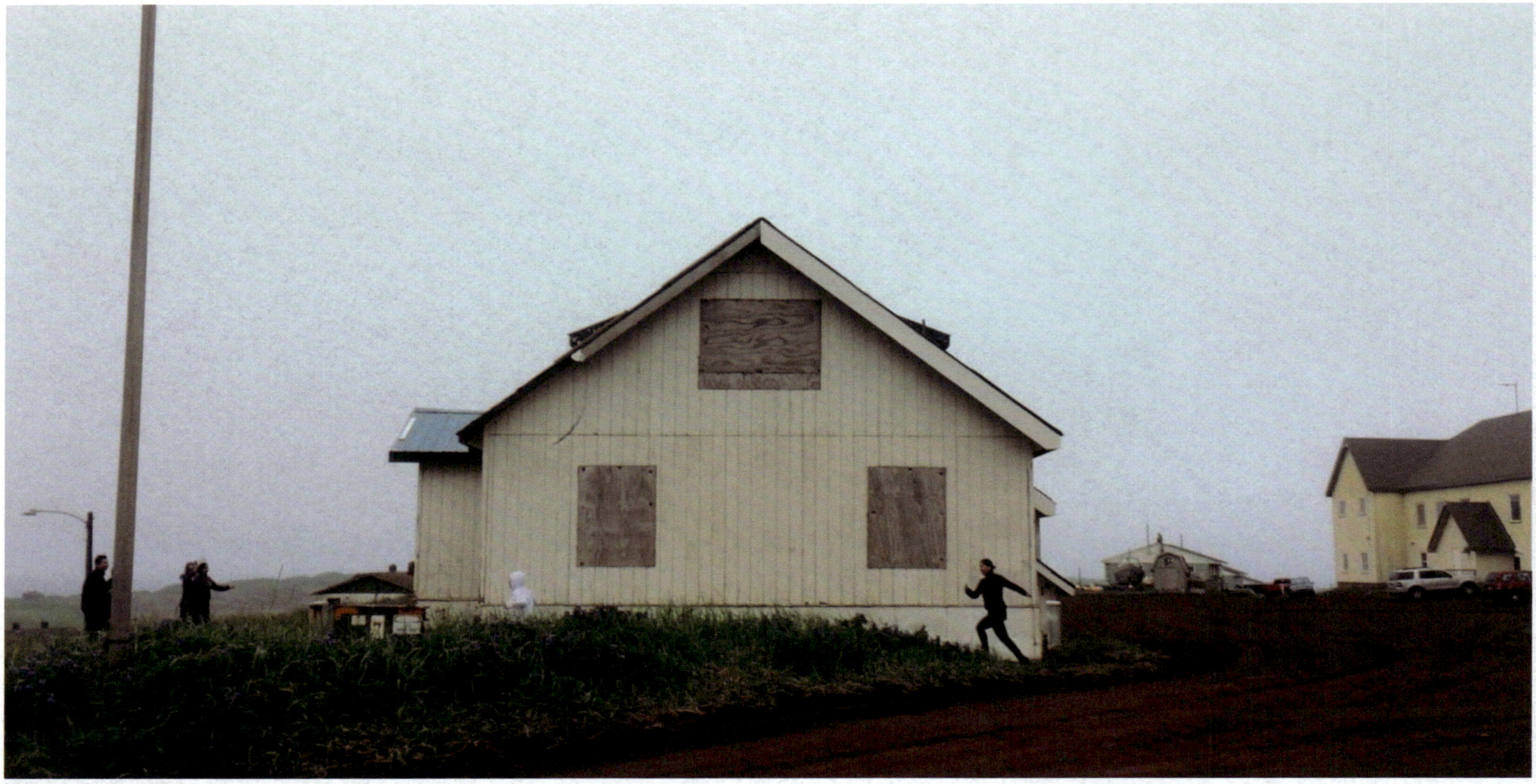

11:37

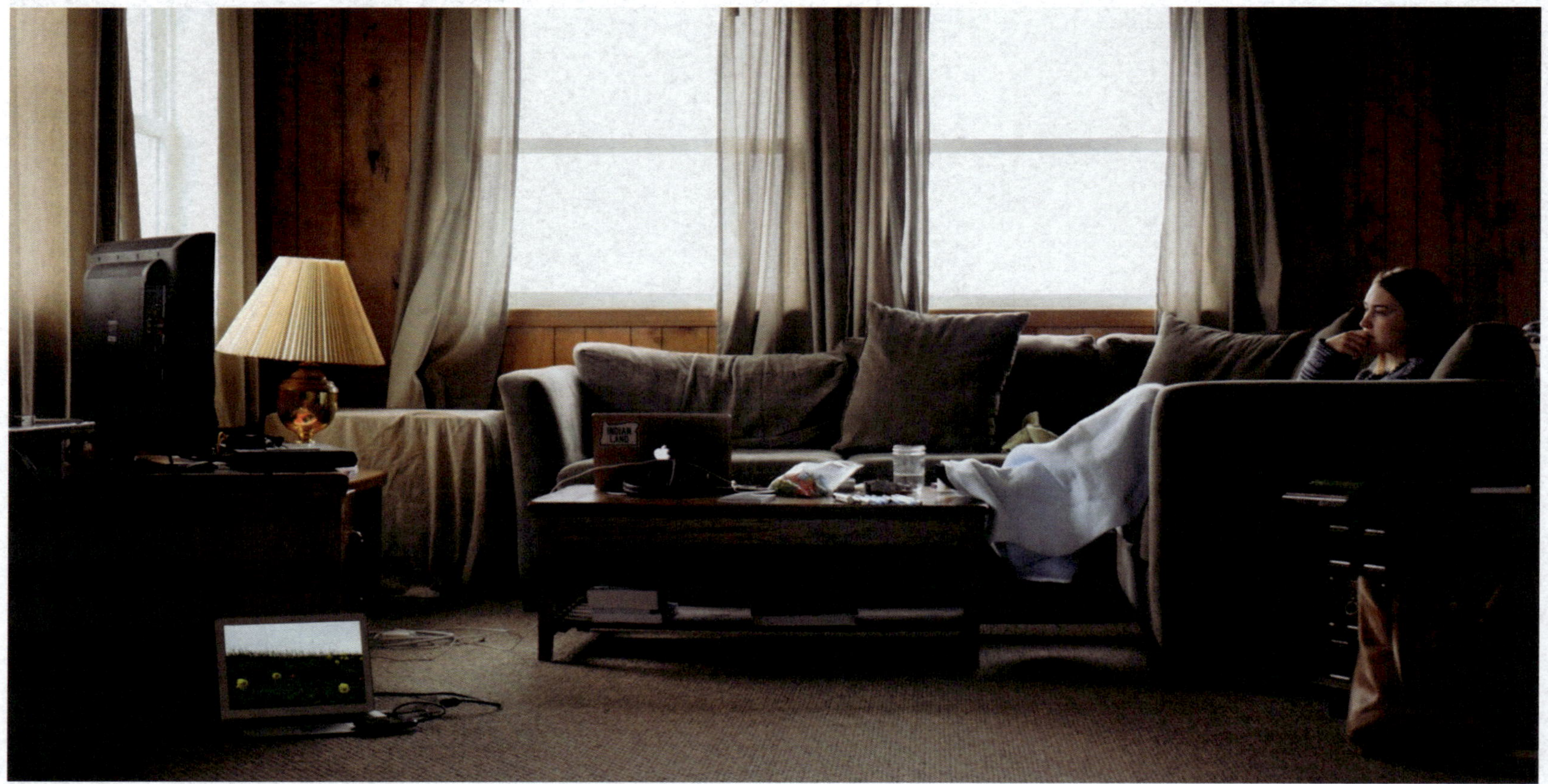

05:16

12:14

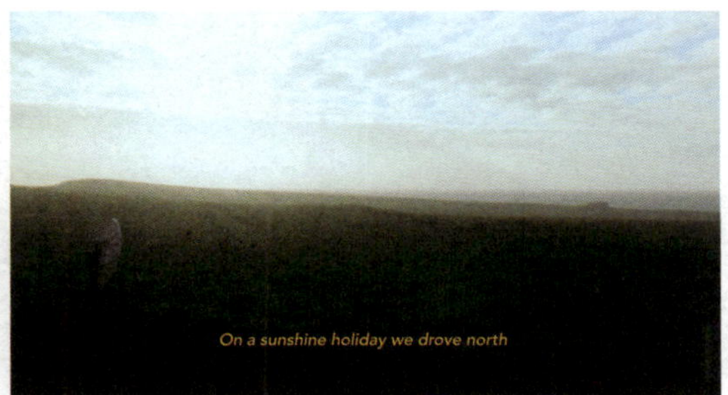


12:17

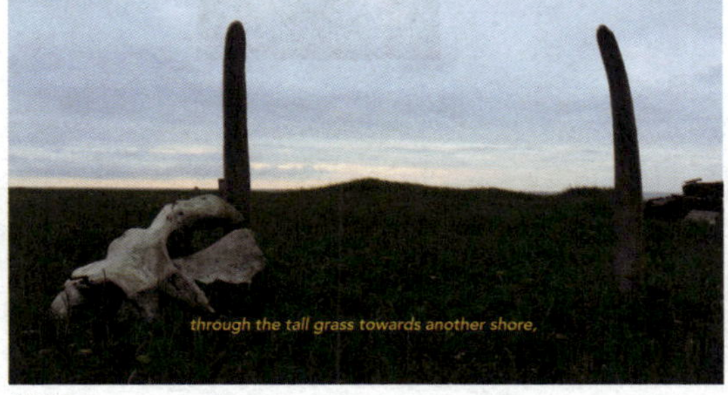


12:26

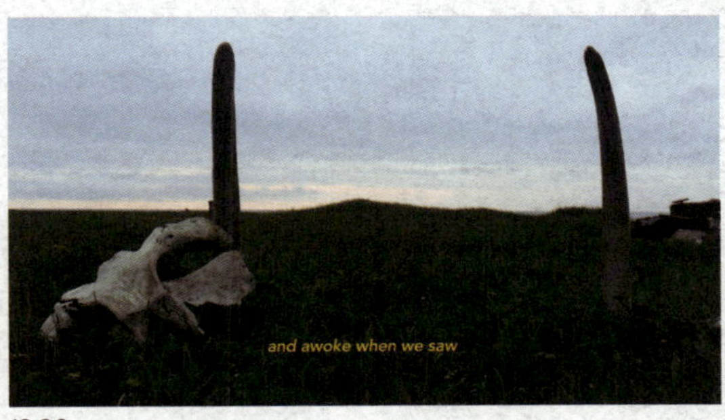


12:30

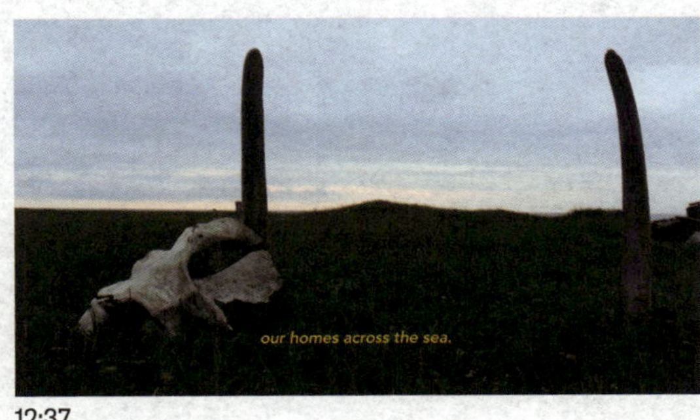


12:37

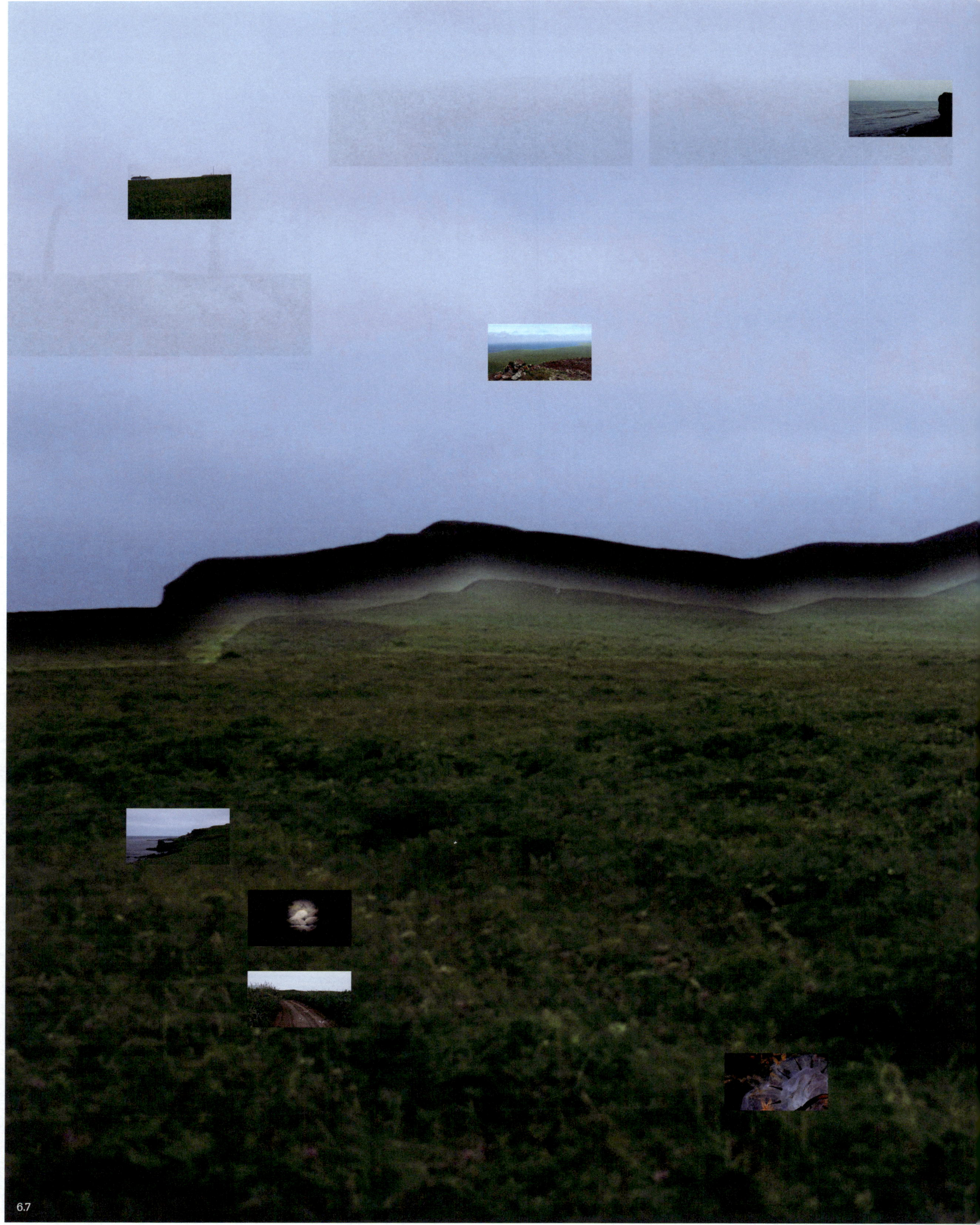

6.7

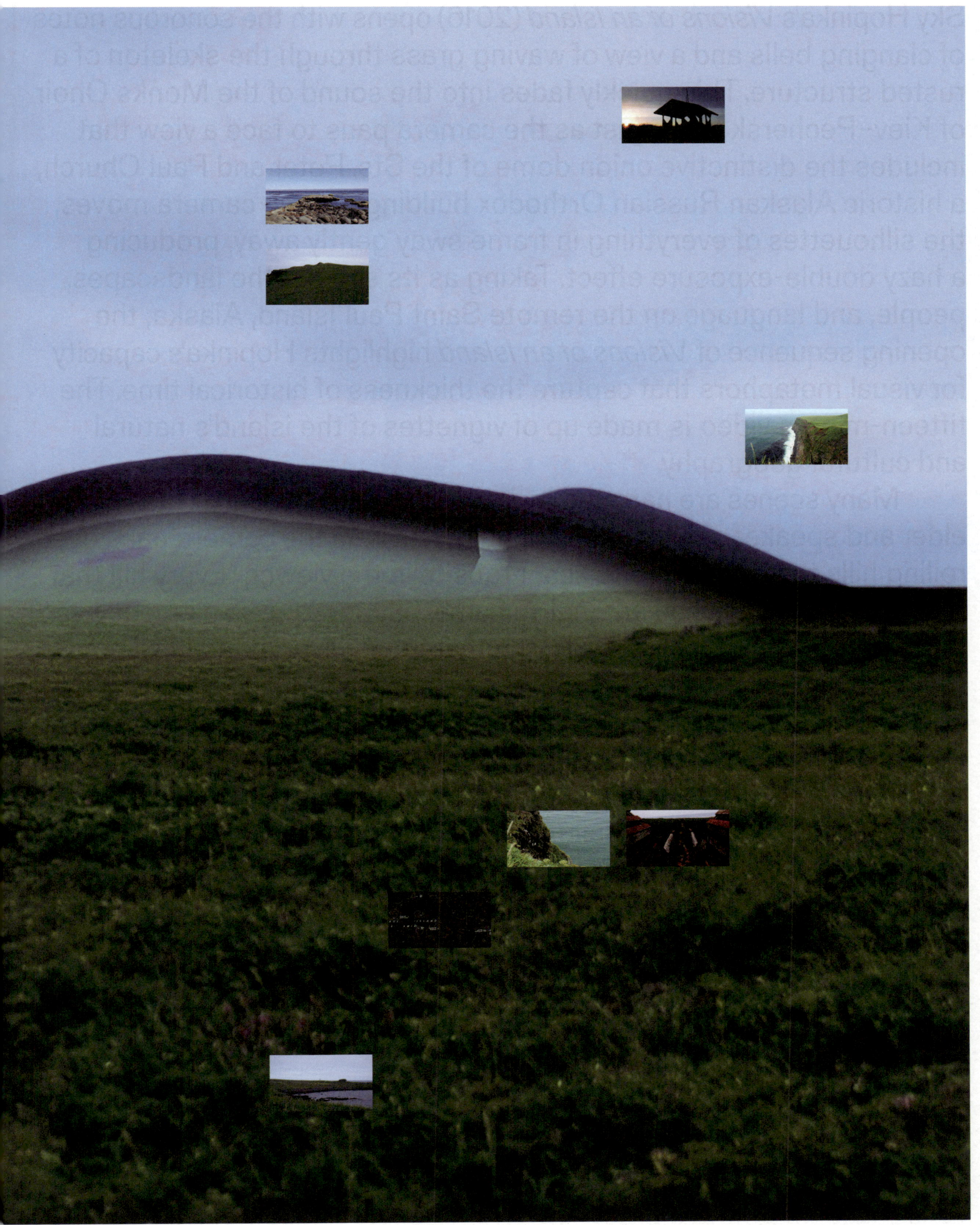

Sky Hopinka's *Visions of an Island* (2016) opens with the sonorous notes of clanging bells and a view of waving grass through the skeleton of a rusted structure. This quickly fades into the sound of the Monks Choir of Kiev–Pechersk Lavra just as the camera pans to face a view that includes the distinctive onion dome of the Sts. Peter and Paul Church, a historic Alaskan Russian Orthodox building. As the camera moves, the silhouettes of everything in frame sway gently away, producing a hazy double-exposure effect. Taking as its subject the landscapes, people, and language on the remote Saint Paul Island, Alaska, the opening sequence of *Visions of an Island* highlights Hopinka's capacity for visual metaphors that capture the thickness of historical time. The fifteen-minute video is made up of vignettes of the island's natural and cultural geography.

Many scenes are narrated by interviews with Gregory Fratis Sr., an elder and speaker of Unangam Tunuu (Aleut). As the camera pans over rolling hills that rise over the sea, Fratis tells the viewer, "Every hill that you see has a name, had an English name, but now they're all Aleut, even the sea you see there, the birds, the mammals, everything is all now in Unangam Tunuu." As Fratis describes the history of place-names on the island and their transition from Russian to English to Aleut, Hopinka's double exposure allows one hill to rise slowly over itself, in a hallucinatory repetition of the initial motif. Layering and inversion express the ways in which landscapes are a palimpsest of colonial histories that are not visible to the naked eye but remain reflected in the memories held by language. Like many of Hopinka's works, *Visions of an Island* explores the relationship between filmmaking and knowledge, between vision and obscurity. In one scene we hear a group of people practice Unangam Tunuu, but the language learners are hidden from view, hinting at the value of listening without seeing.

The artist's long-standing interest in the relationships between language, culture, and place comes in part from his own lived experience. Hopinka grew up in Washington State, away from his parents' respective

Indigenous homelands. This has driven him to ask, "What does it mean to be a visitor?" from the perspective of a Native person in the "liminal space" of diaspora.[1] One answer to this question involves learning Indigenous languages. Hopinka spent years studying Chinuk Wawa while living in Portland, Oregon, and in 2020 completed *małni—towards the ocean, towards the shore*, a feature-length film largely in that language. The frequent use of abstraction and visual distortion reflects his attitude toward the complex legacies of documentary and ethnographic filmmaking in Indigenous communities. The artist has noted that he "resist[s] the idea that just because something exists, just because something has the opportunity to be studied or documented, then it should be." He states that he is "a big fan of the mystery of culture, and how certain people have access to information that others don't."[2] Near the close of *Visions of an Island*, Hopinka suggests that learning to love a place is an integral part of being a visitor. Fratis's voice is heard once more over a shot of seals on a foggy bay: "I love this island, this beautiful island, my island. And I'm pretty sure if you saw it you would have the same feeling." **(BE)**

1 Sky Hopinka, as told to Anaïs Duplan, "What Does It Mean to Be a Visitor?," Art21, September 2021, https://art21.org/read/big-question-what-does-it-mean-to-be-a-visitor.

2 Sky Hopinka, in Adam Khalil and Zack Khalil, "Sky Hopinka" (interview), *Third Rail*, no. 10 (Spring 2017), http://thirdrailquarterly.org/sky-hopinka.

ANNA BOGHIGUIAN *Time of Change*, 2022, mixed media on paper, 96 drawings: 8⅞ × 24 7/16 in. (48 × 62 cm) each, courtesy the artist and Milani Gallery, Brisbane, Australia

WELCOME TO CAIRO
PASSPORT

ARIBERT HEIM ARRIVED IN April
1963 THE NEWLY INNAGURATED
CAIRO
AirPort From Morocco ONE MONTH VIS

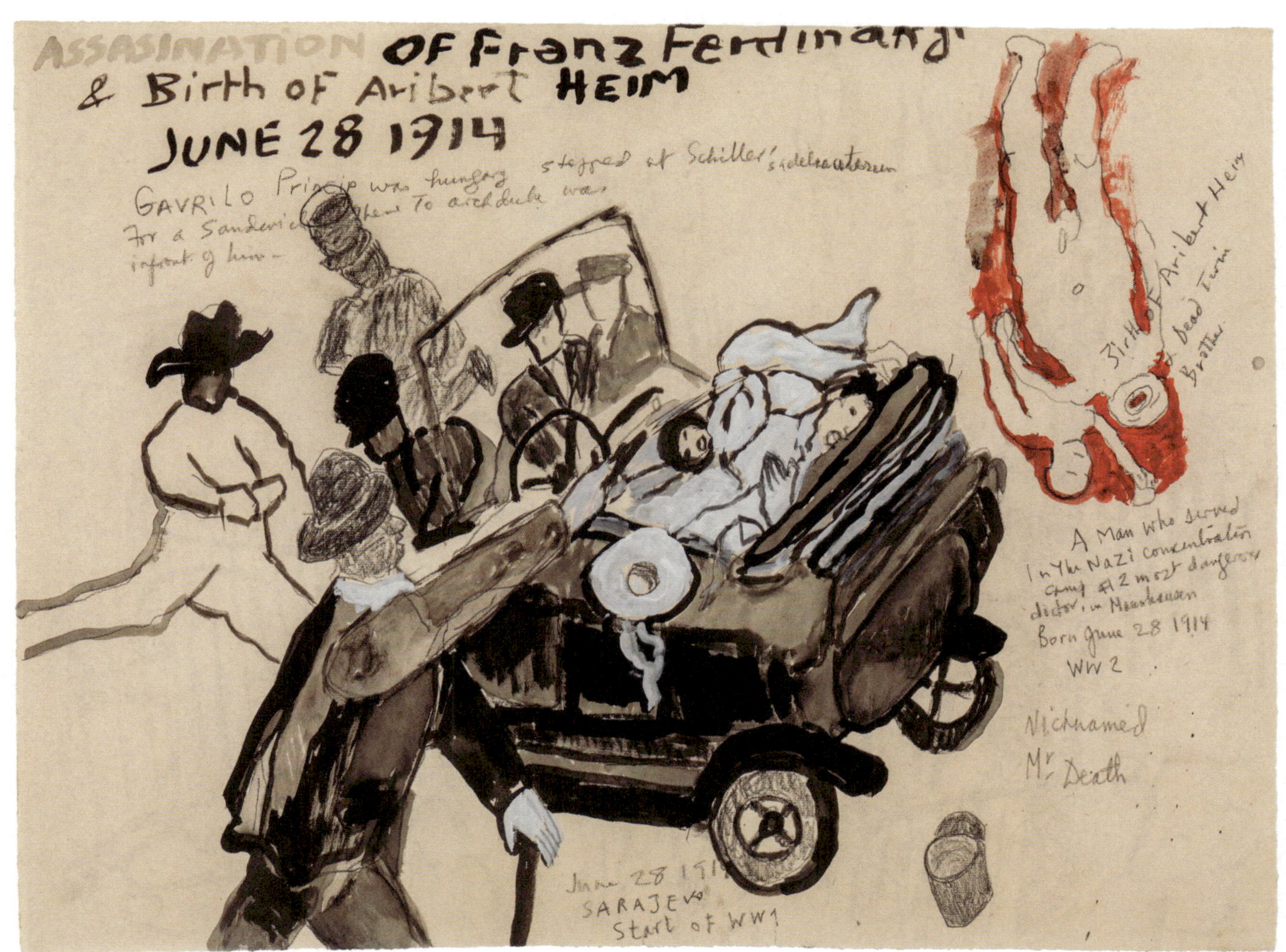


7.2

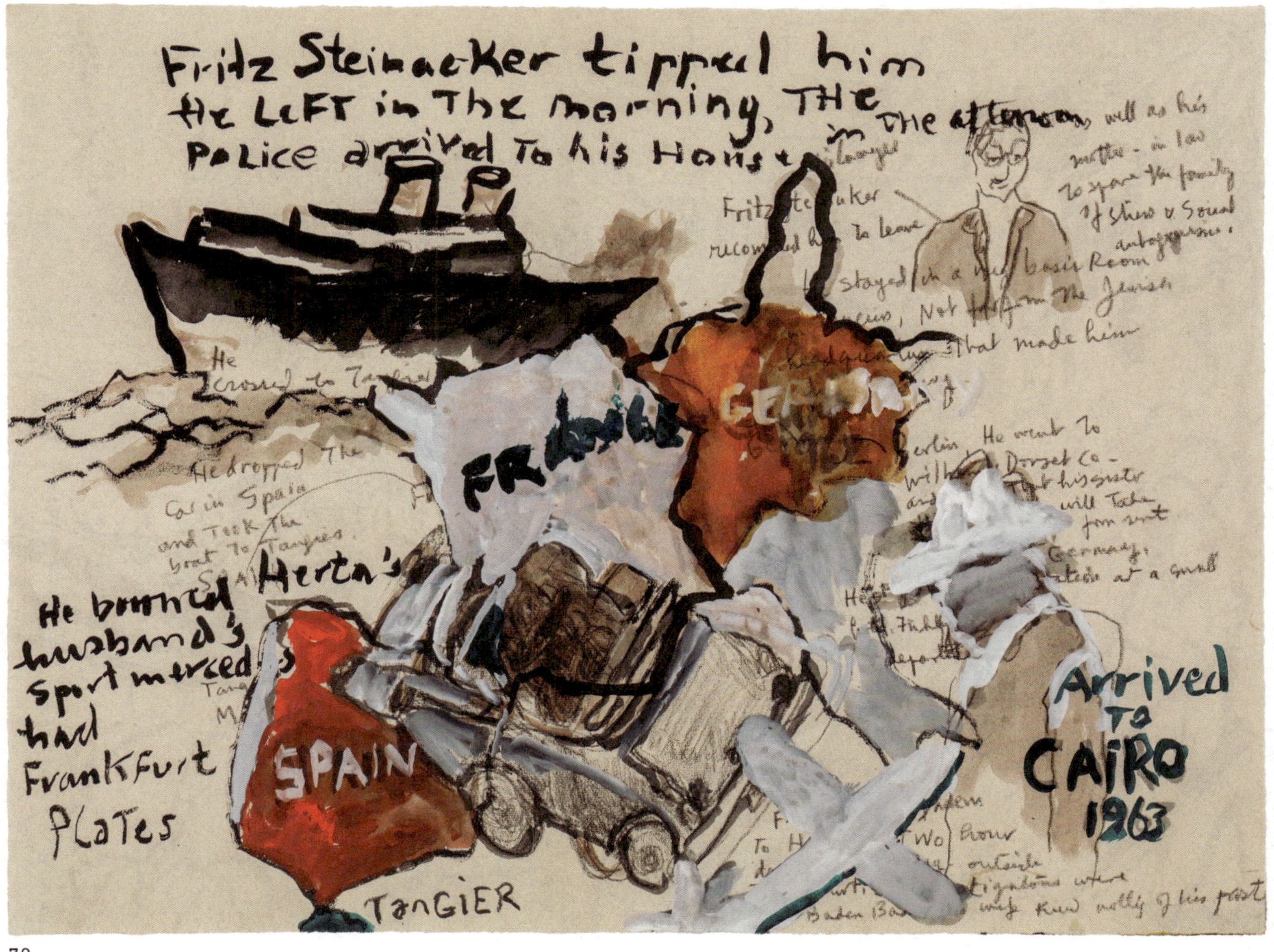


7.3

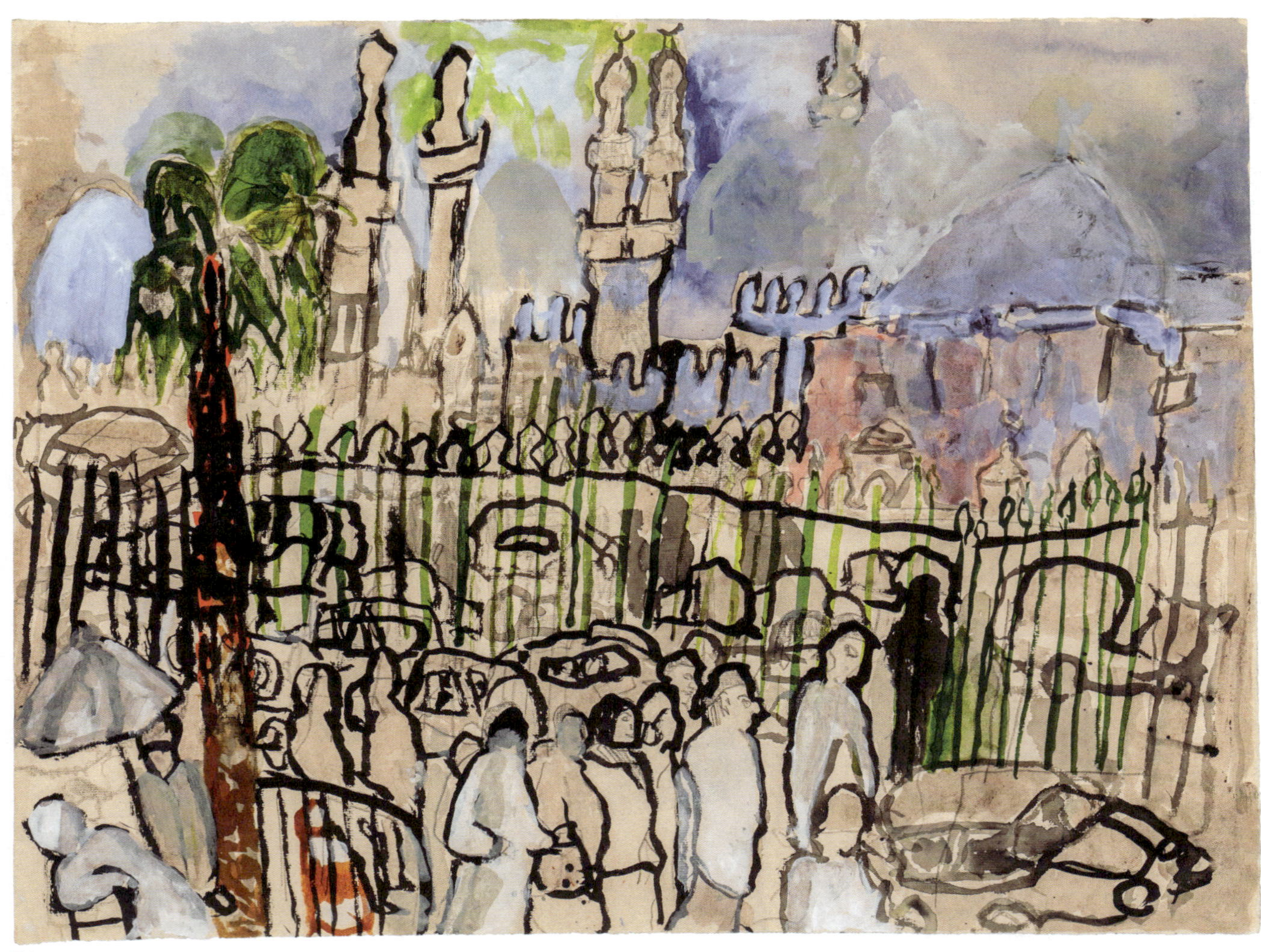

7.4

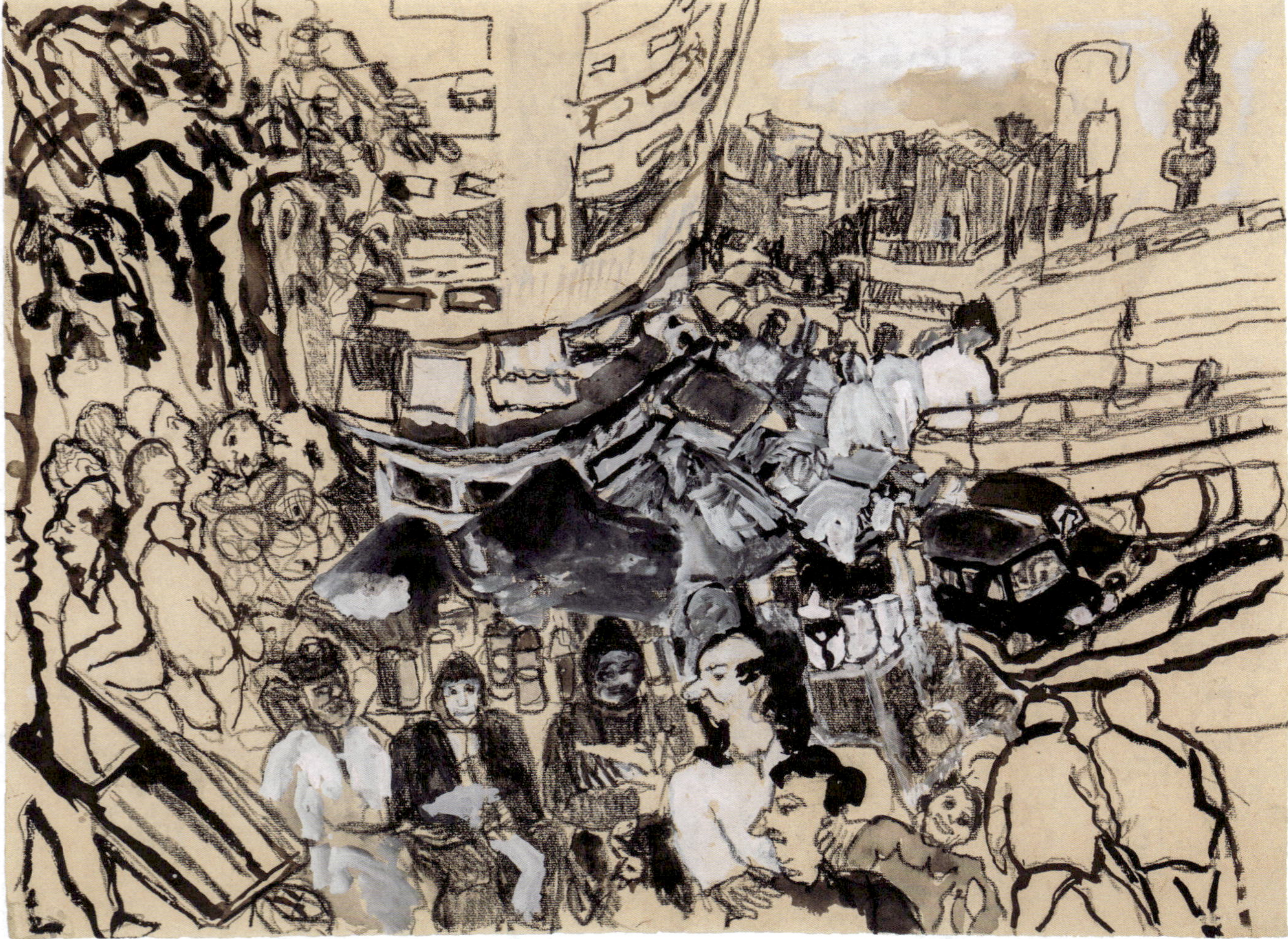

7.5

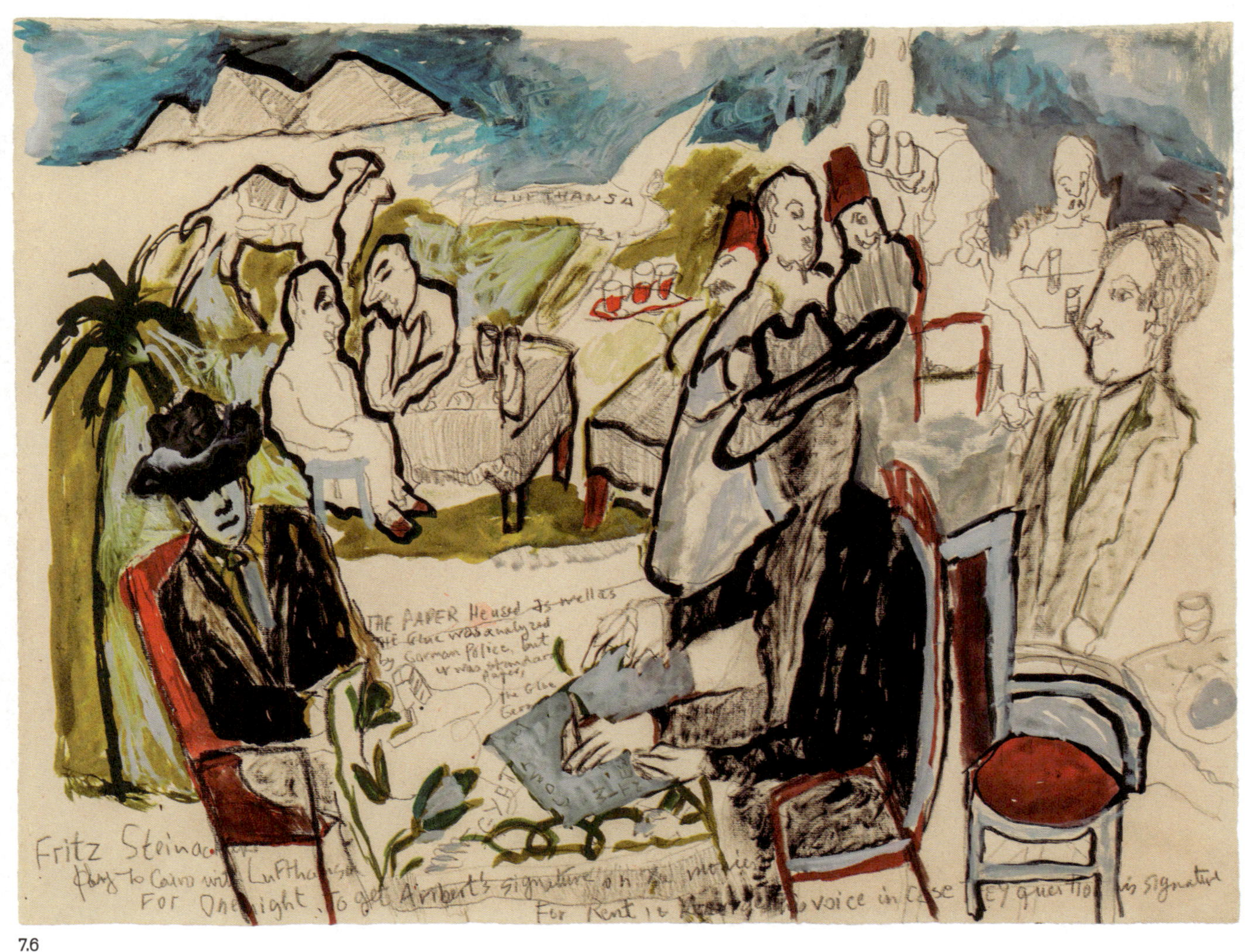

7.6

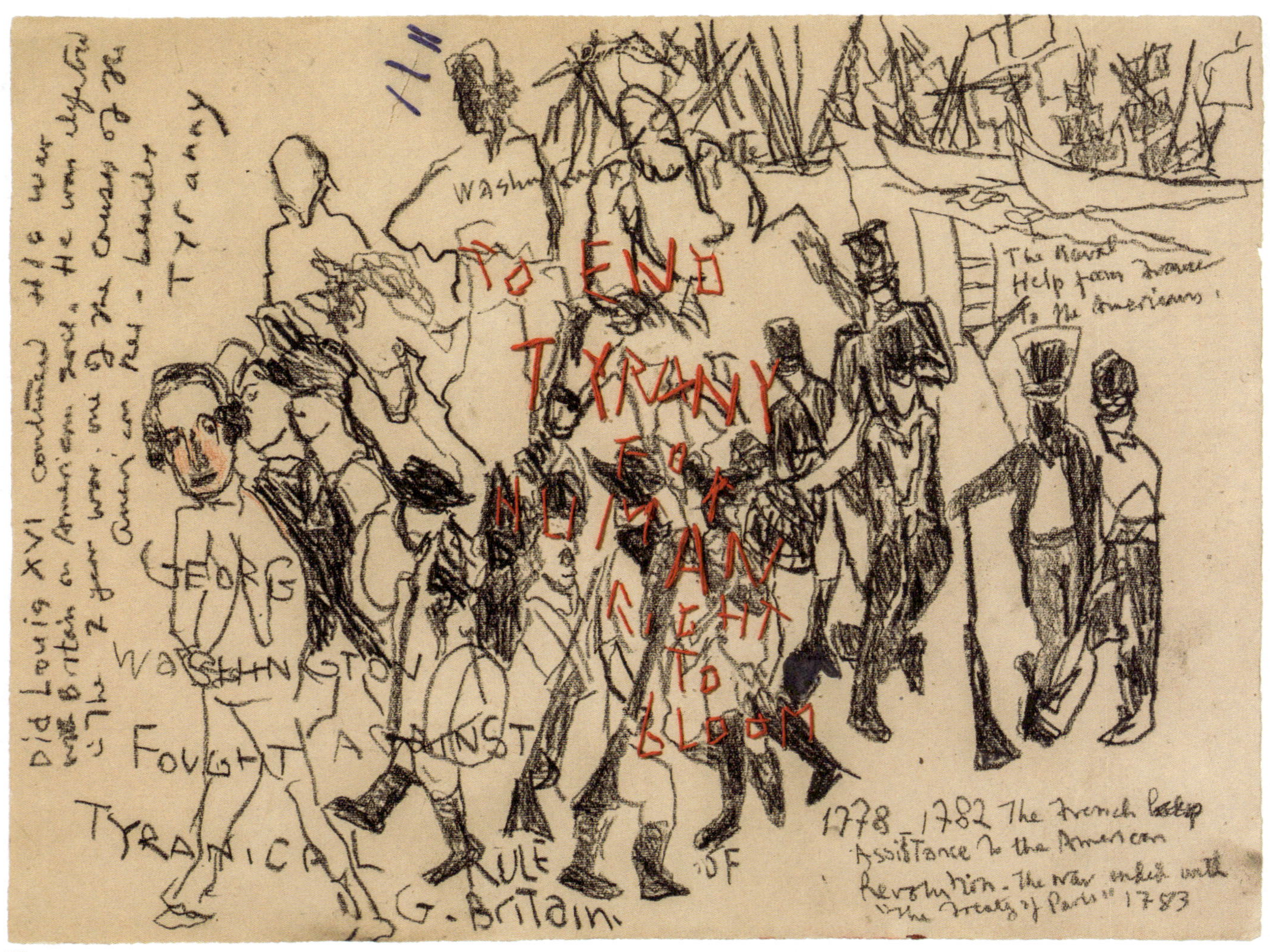


7.7

7.8

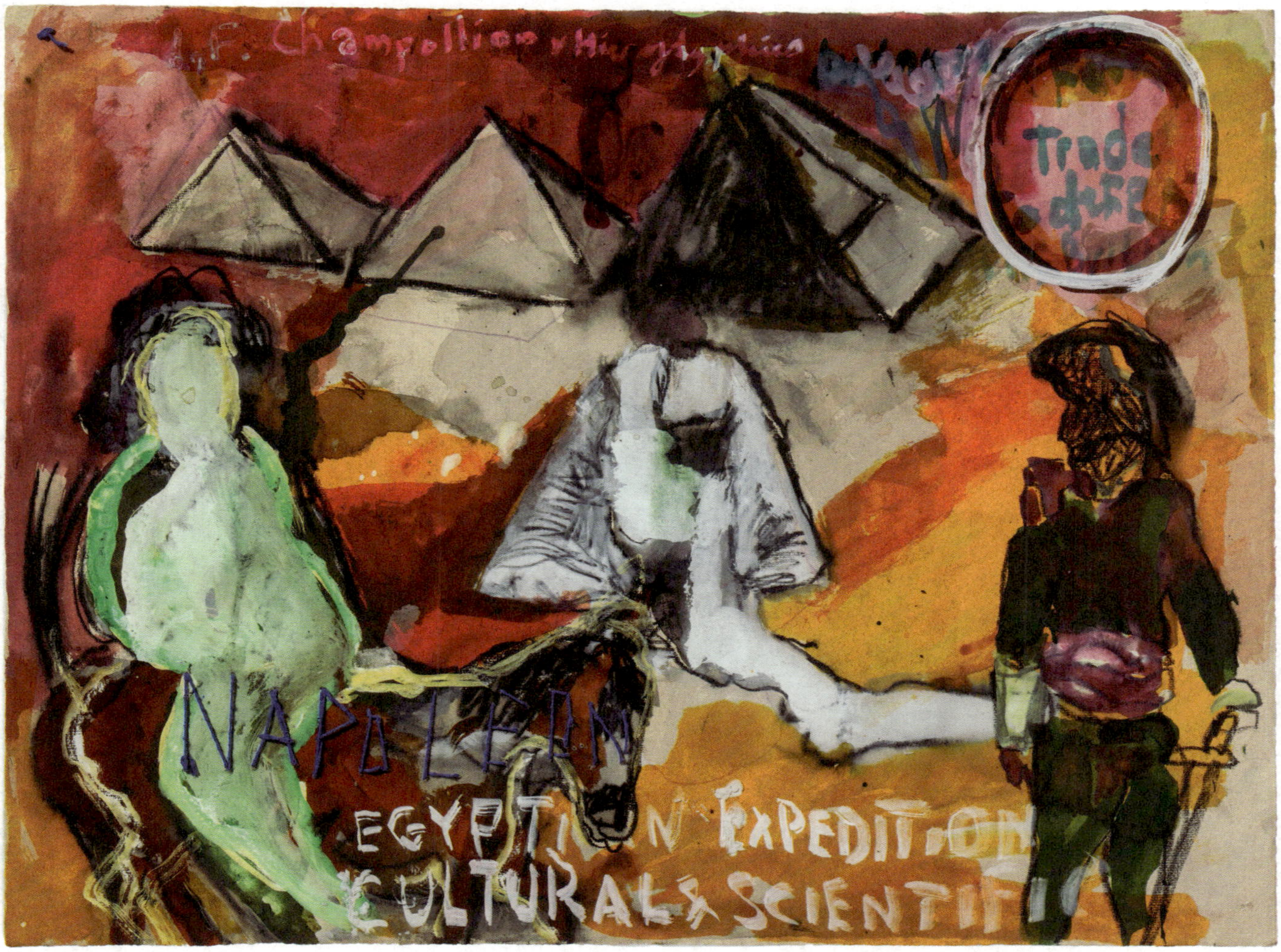

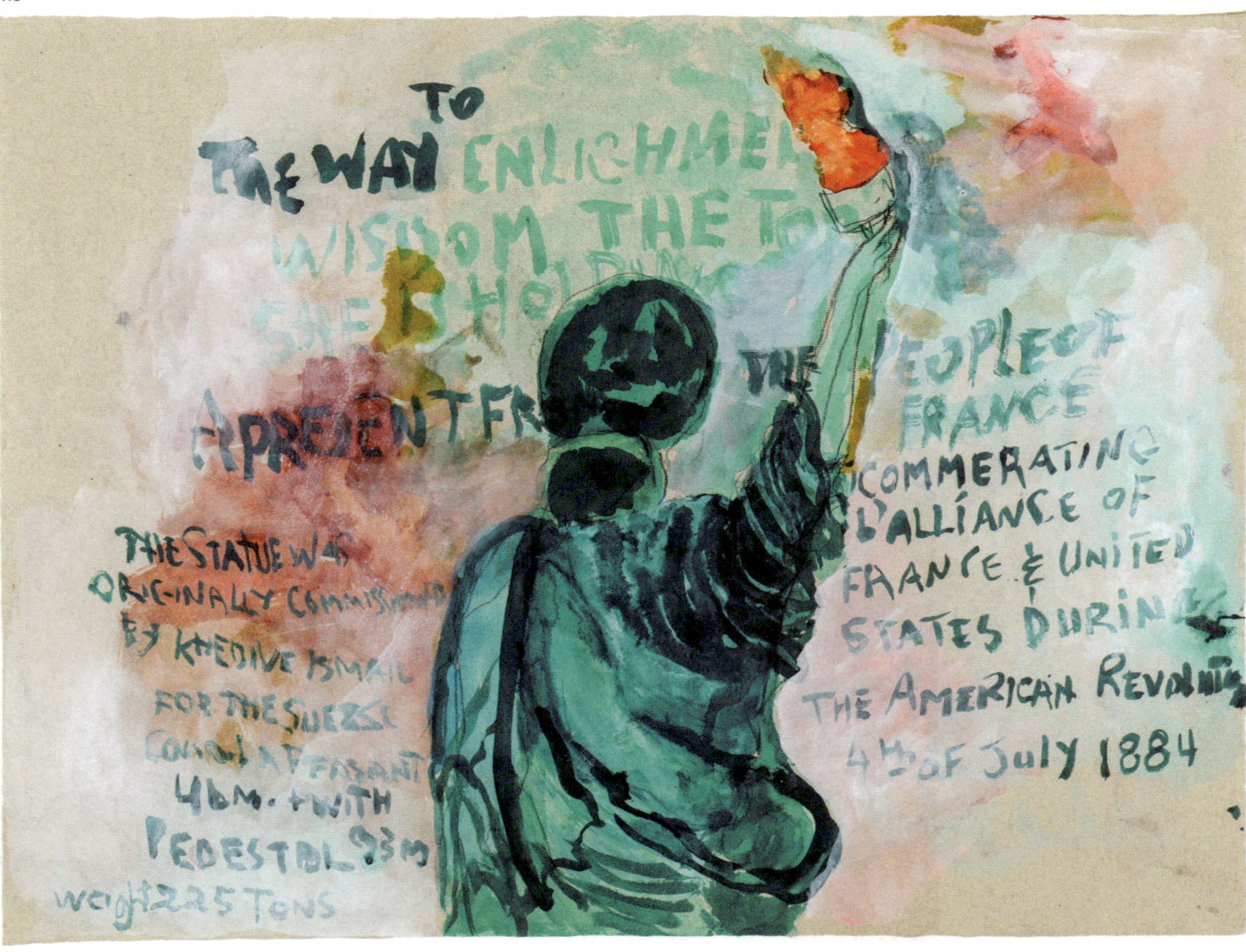
TO
THE WAY
WISDOM THE
PEOPLE OF
FRANCE
COMMERATING
L'ALLIANCE OF
FRANCE & UNITED
STATES
THE AMERICAN
4th OF July 1884
THE STATUE WAS
ORIGINALLY
BY KHEDIVE ISMAIL
46M. + WITH
weight 225 TONS

7.9

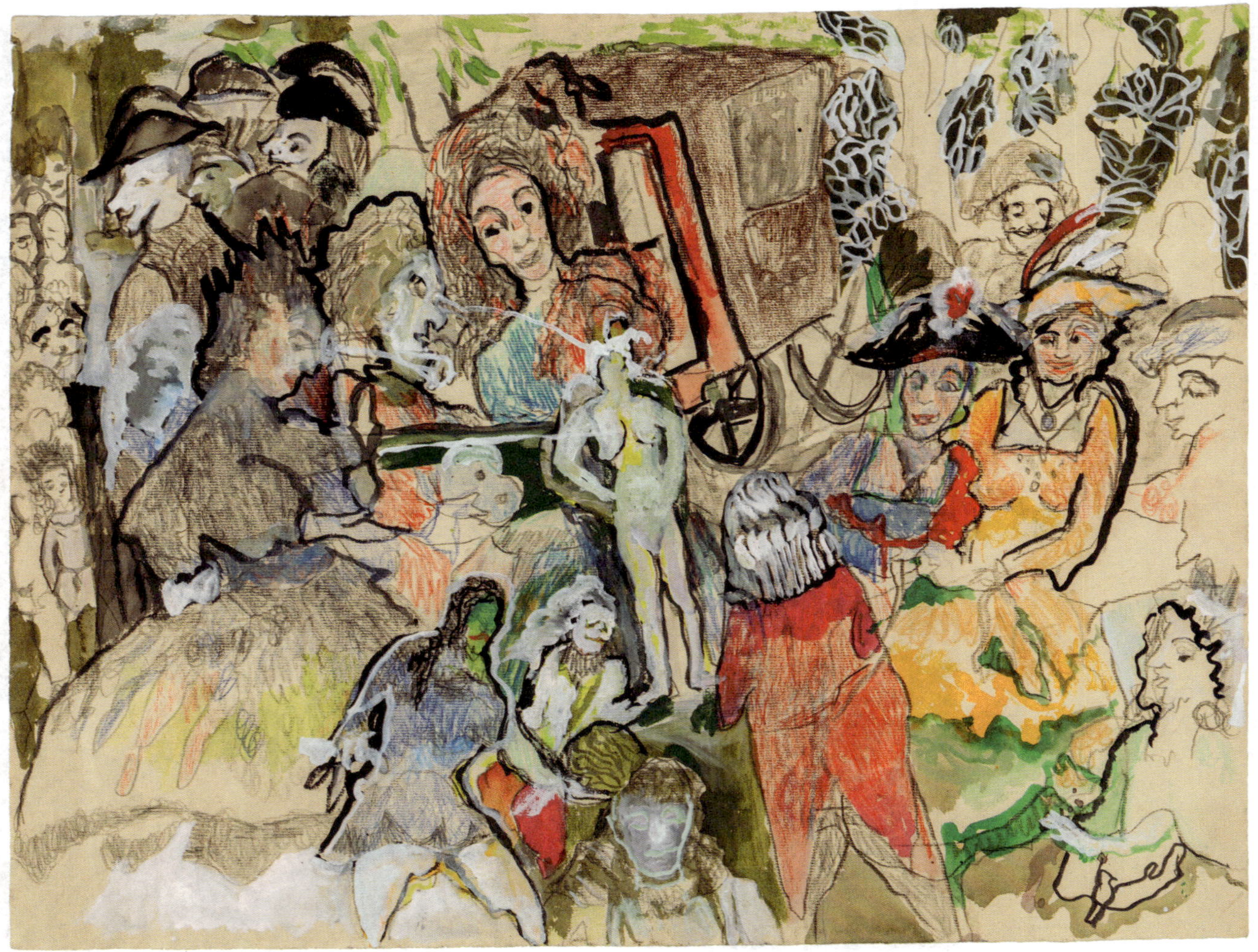

7.10

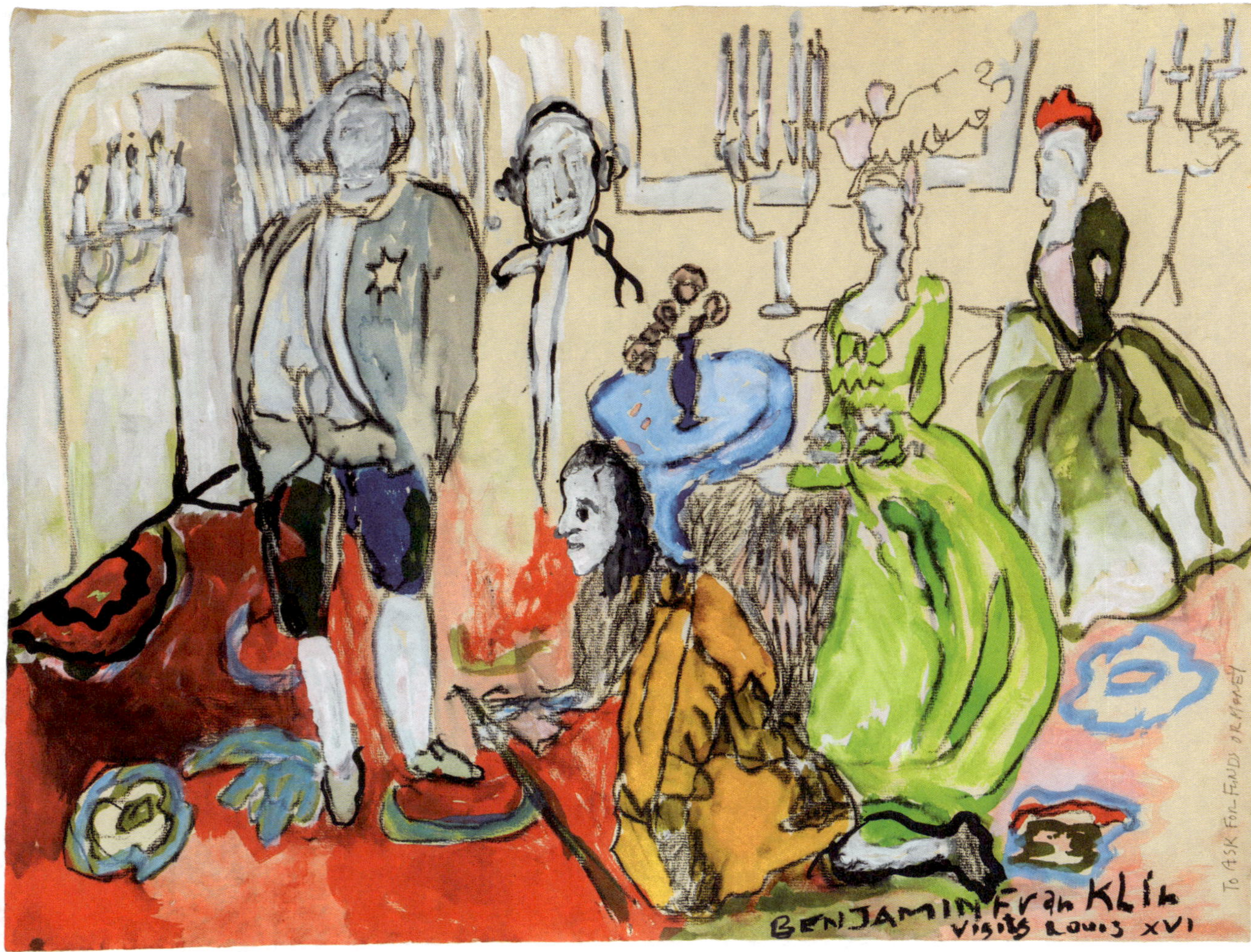
To ASK FOR FUNDS OR MONEY
BENJAMIN Franklin
visits Louis XVI

7.11

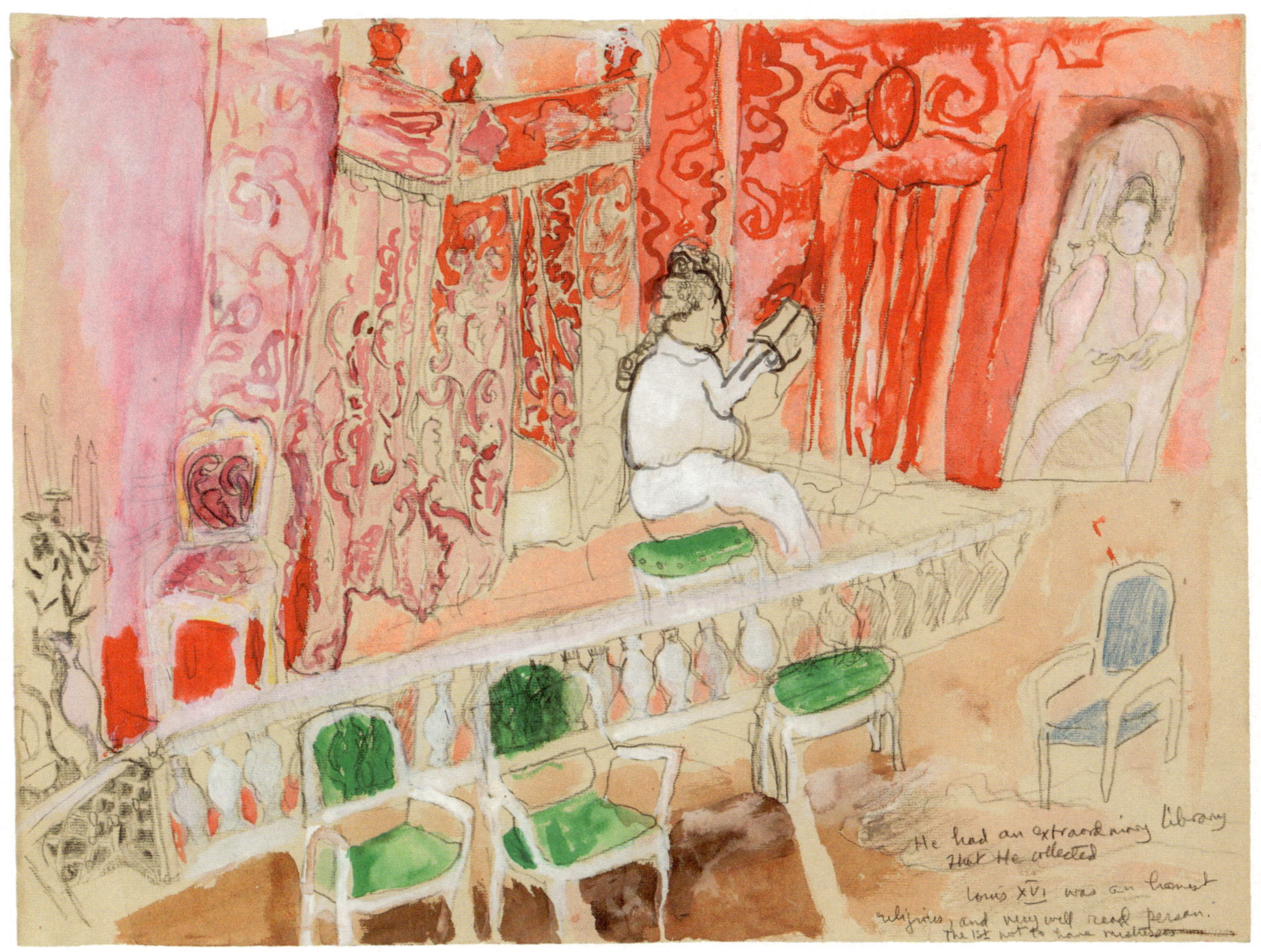


7.12

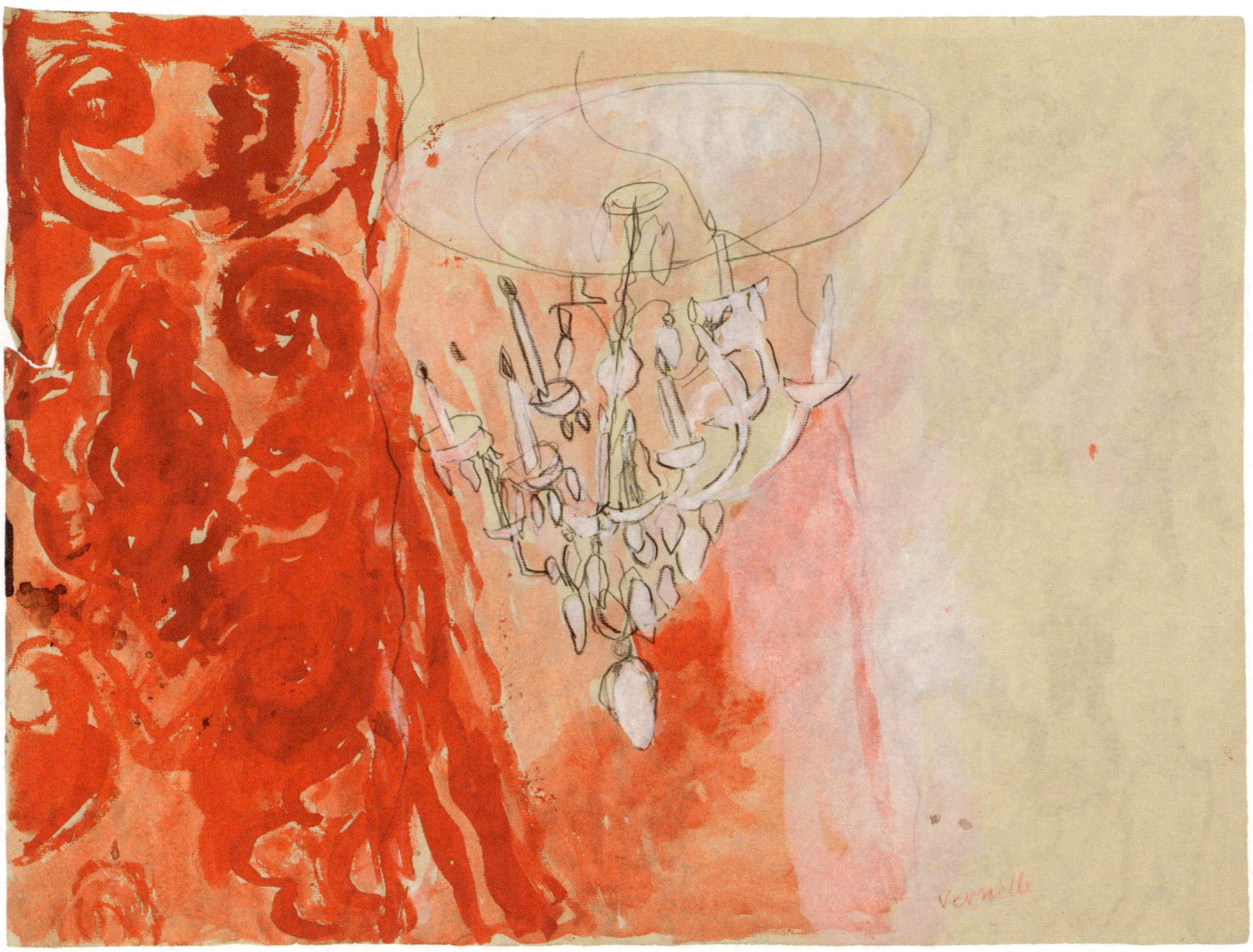


7.13

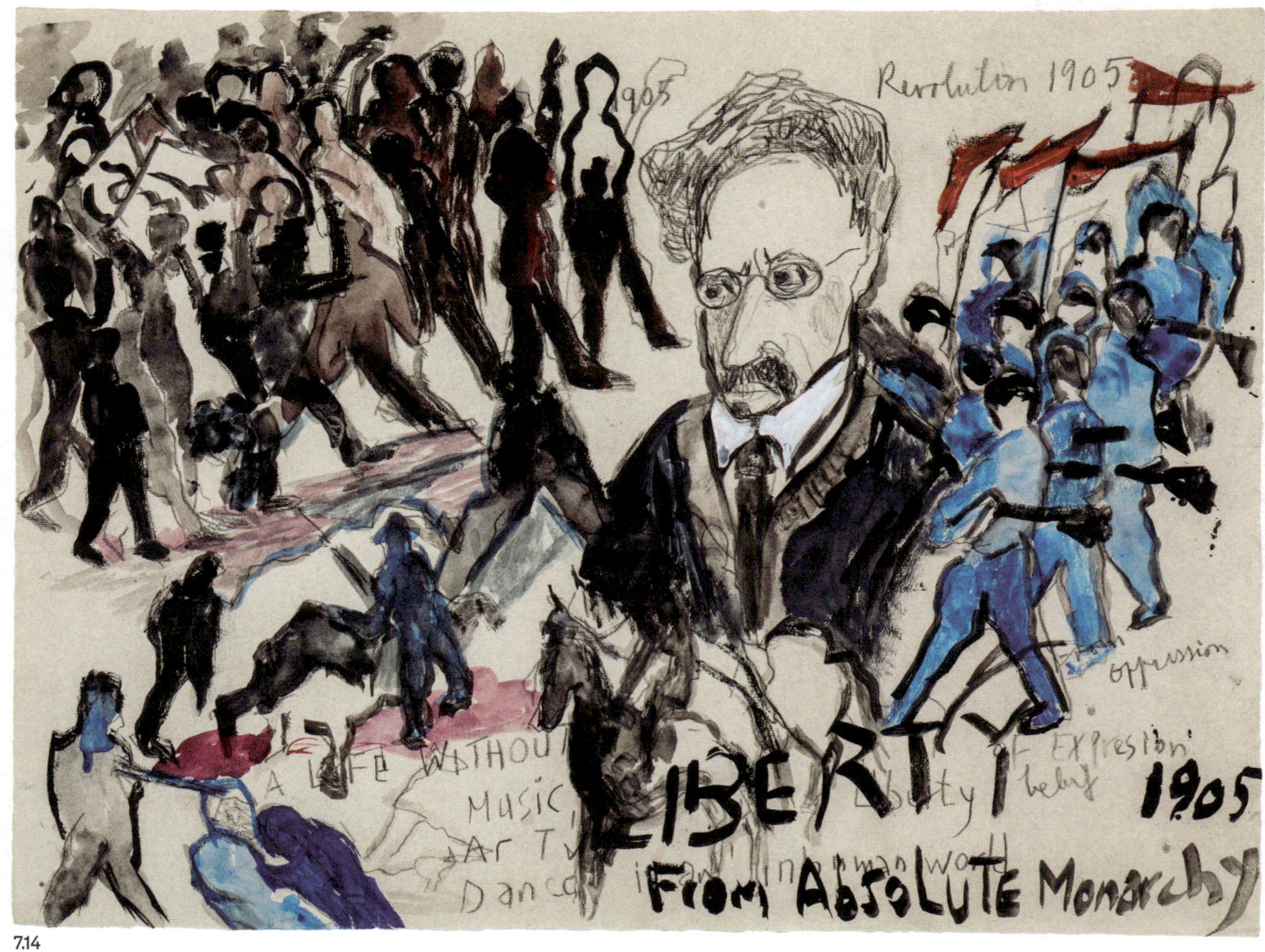


7.14

Anna Boghiguian

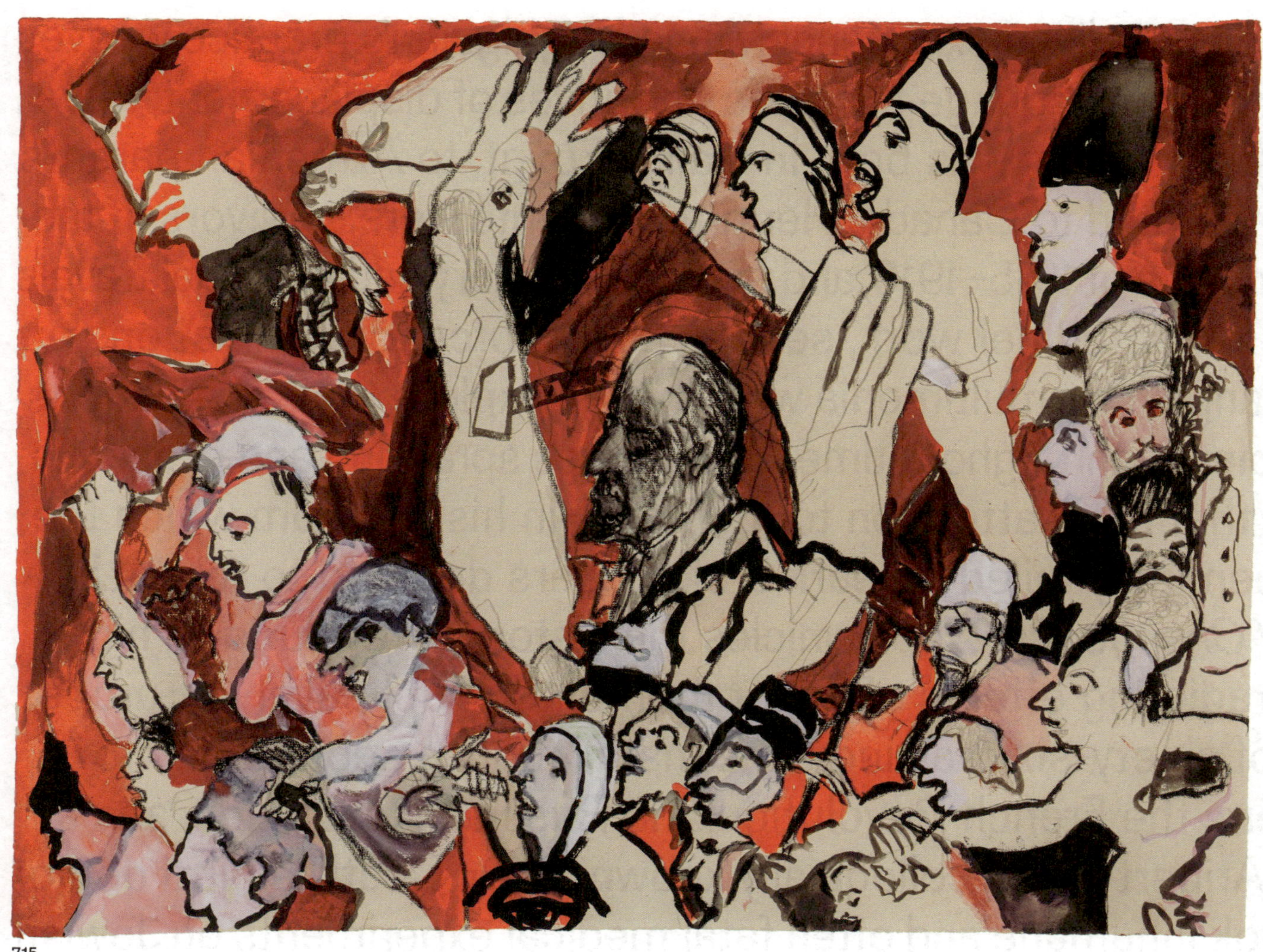

7.15

Deeply rooted in her lived experience, Anna Boghiguian's practice weaves together image and language to create narratives of displacement, travel, and history. Boghiguian was born in Cairo, Egypt, to Armenian parents who later immigrated to Canada. Her grandparents were survivors of the Armenian genocide of 1915–1916, and her family history and personal travels have greatly impacted her work, serving as a source for ruminations on place and change. Her multimedia works often explore the ramifications of war and violence throughout time. She creates sprawling and evocative installations that draw attention to moments in history from which the world has seemingly failed to learn and appears doomed to repeat.[1]

*Time of Change* (2022) chronicles the history of revolutions, highlighting the radiating effects of major moments of upheaval in Europe. Composed of ninety-six drawings, the installation is separated into three chapters: the French Revolution, the Russian Revolution, and a segment on Aribert Heim, colloquially known as Dr. Death, a Nazi doctor who undertook inhumane and often fatal medical experiments on Jewish prisoners during the Holocaust. Through these chapters, Boghiguian chronicles not only the initial moments of violence but also the resulting waves, such as the Haitian Revolution, the Cold War, and Heim's flight to Cairo to escape prosecution as a war criminal. The ramifications of the seismic shifts in political and social ideologies prompted by these events are still felt today.

Boghiguian utilizes a bright color palette for the drawings, with luminous pools of red appearing throughout the series, evoking recollections of blood. The works are often densely layered, figures and landscape compressed into a flat plane. The loose, caricature-like figures are overlaid with glitter and embroidery thread, commentary and historical information scrawled across the images. Powerful leaders bump up against the masses under their control, emphasizing the impacts of individual minds on global conflicts.

We are not far removed from the events that Boghiguian depicts. History folds into itself, a cyclical movement. "The world is always looking to restore itself," she has said, "while art stops and heals this."[2] Despite the violence shown, *Time of Change* acts as a space for reflection and growth. Although the works depict periods of change, so too are they a means of change, reminding the world of how we have arrived at our current state and urging a way out that avoids the same traps and pitfalls. (LRL)

1 "Anna Boghiguian: Time of Change | The Power Plant," YouTube video, 9:04, posted by The Power Plant, January 8, 2024, https://www.youtube.com/watch?v=J9WKVqmqYOM.

2 "Anna Boghiguian in Conversation with Thomas D. Trummer," in *Anna Boghiguian: Period of Change*, ed. Thomas D. Trummer (Bregenz: Kunsthaus Bregenz; Cologne: Verlag der Buchhandlung Walther & Franz König, 2022), n.p.

CHRISTINE HOWARD SANDOVAL

Selections from *A Wall Is A Shadow On The Land*, 2020–, adobe mud and graphite on paper, 4 drawings: 60 × 96 in. (152.4 × 243.8 cm) each, courtesy the artist, Vancouver, and Forge Project Collection, traditional lands of the Moh-He-Con-Nuck

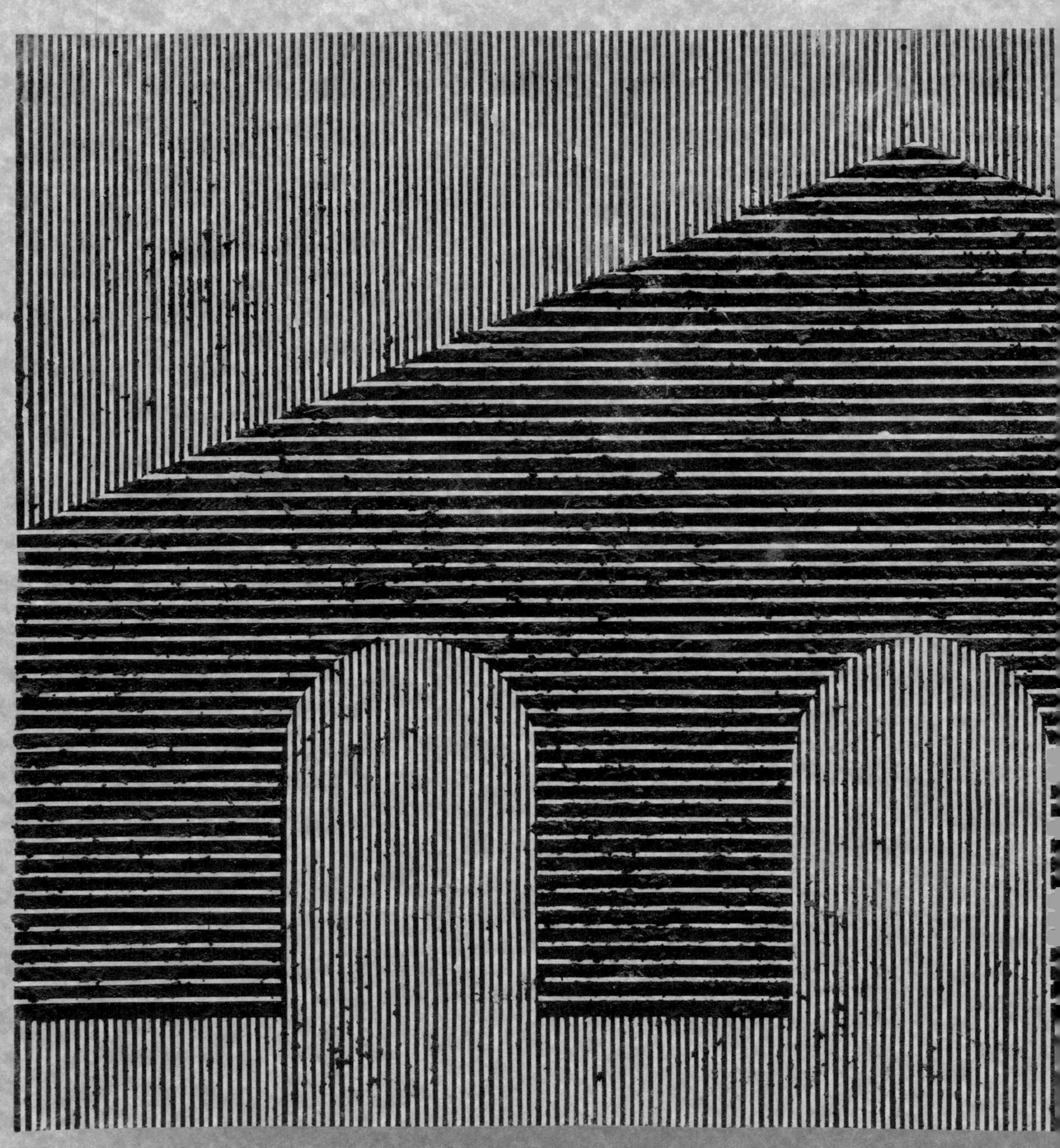

8.1

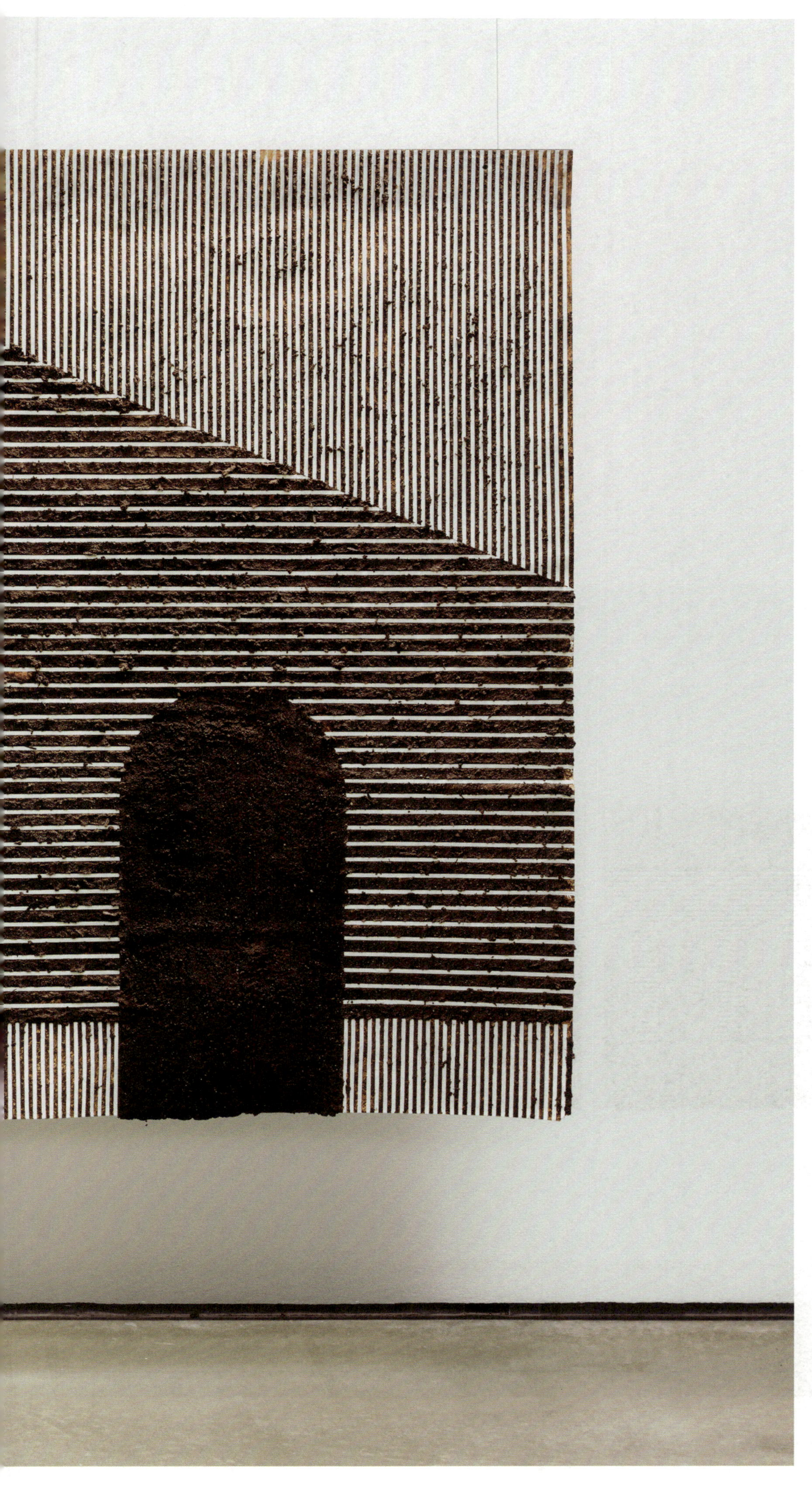

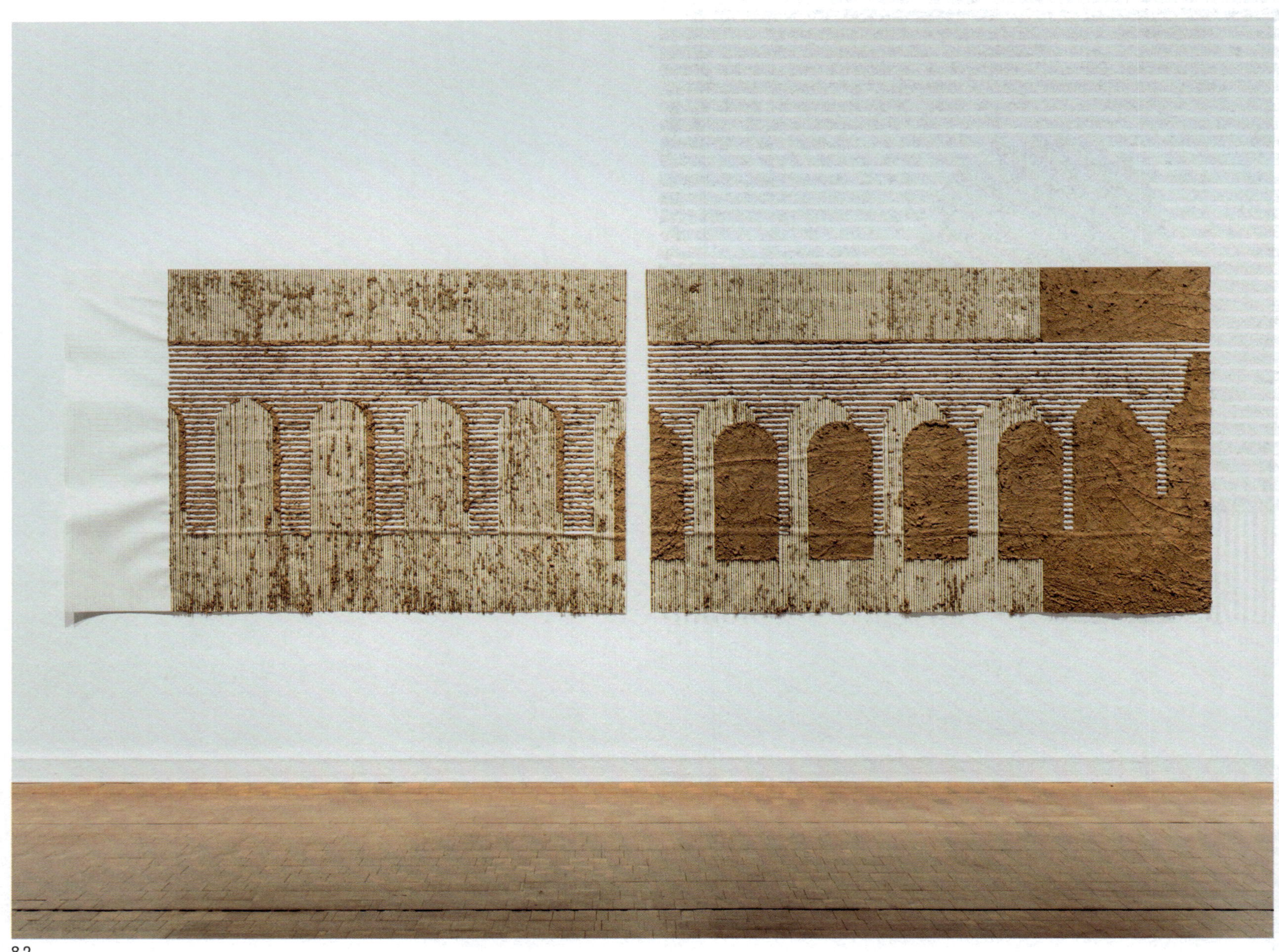

8.2

Christine Howard Sandoval

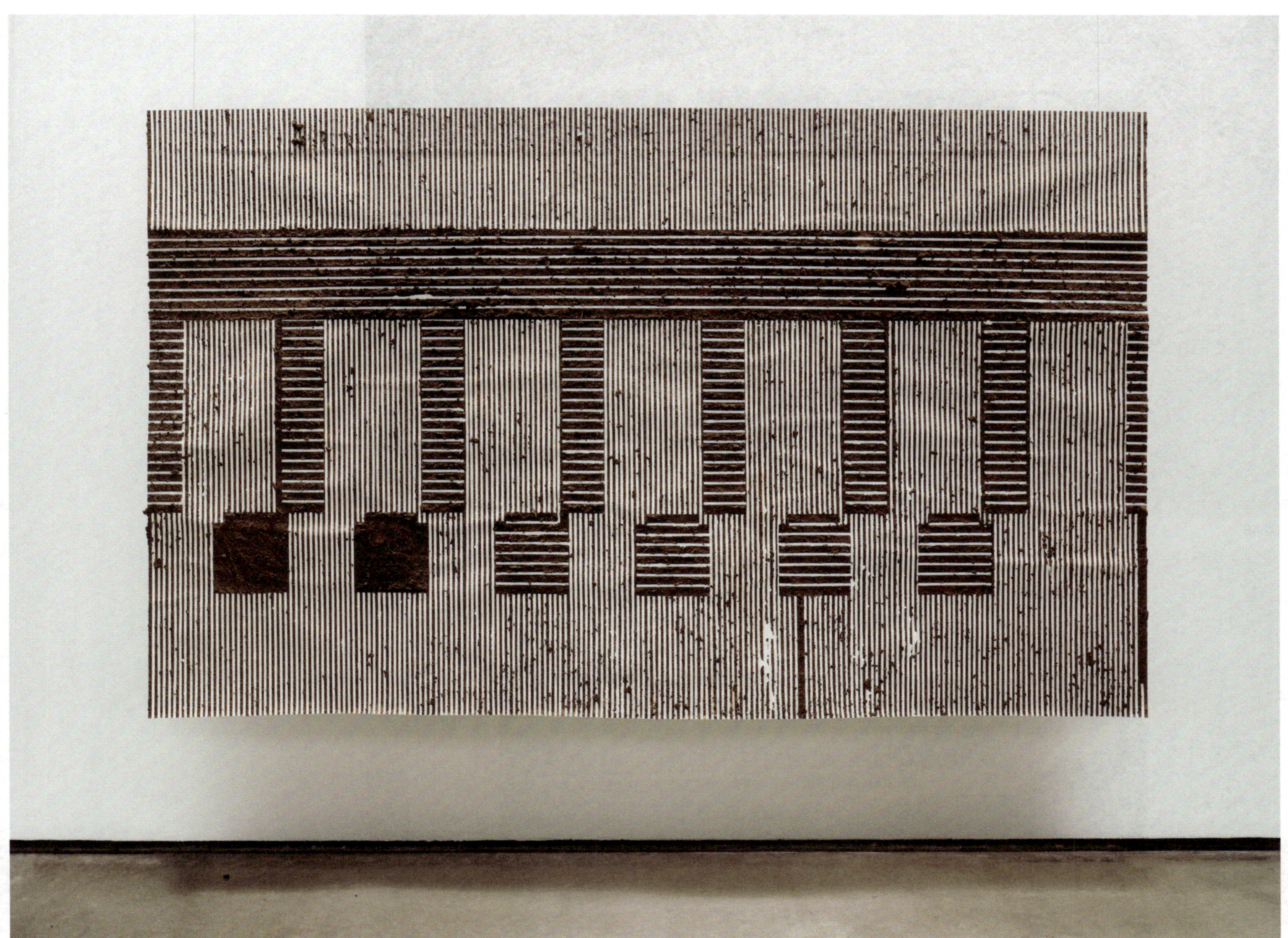
8.3

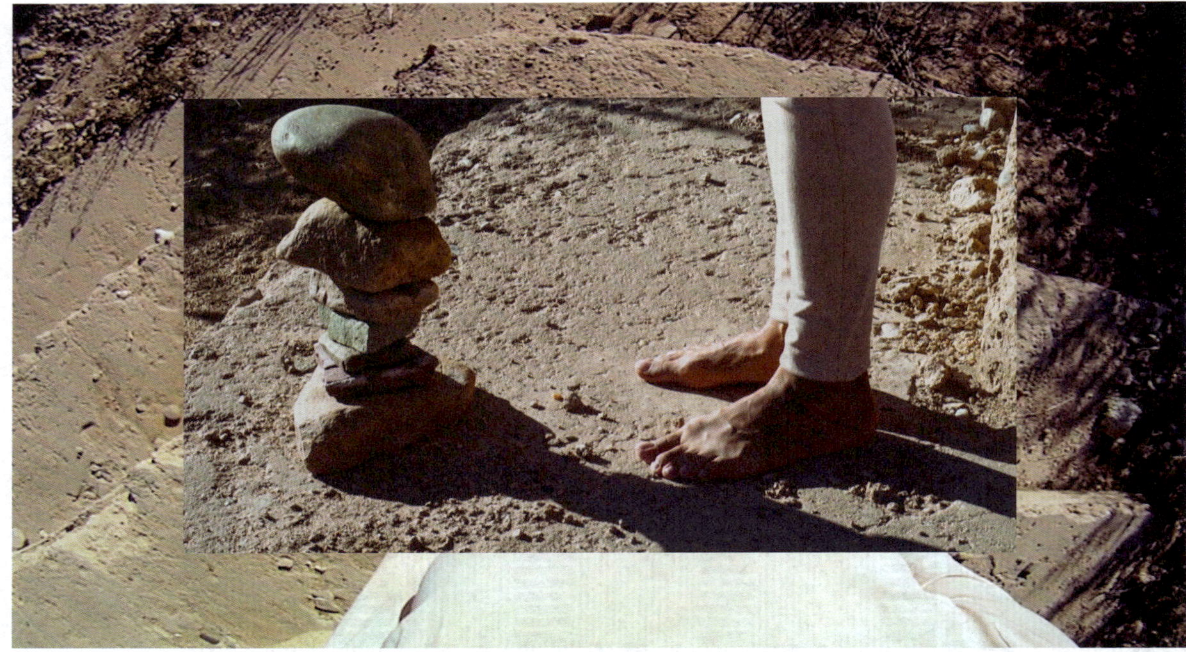

02:48

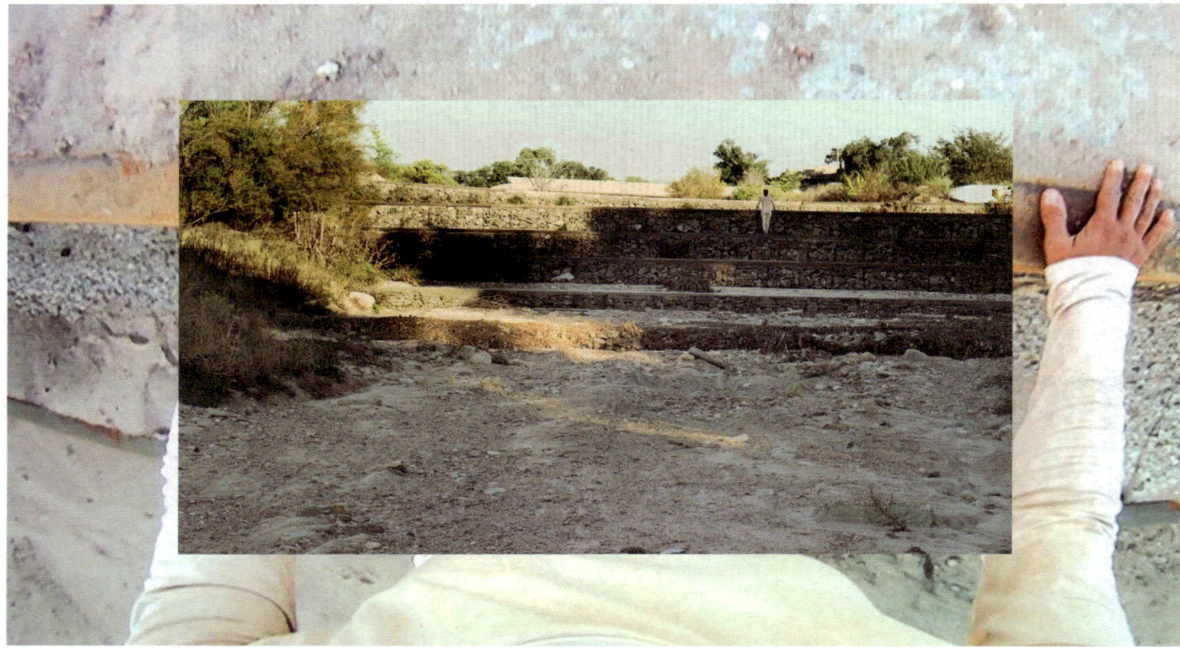

03:46

Stills from *CHANNEL*, 2017 

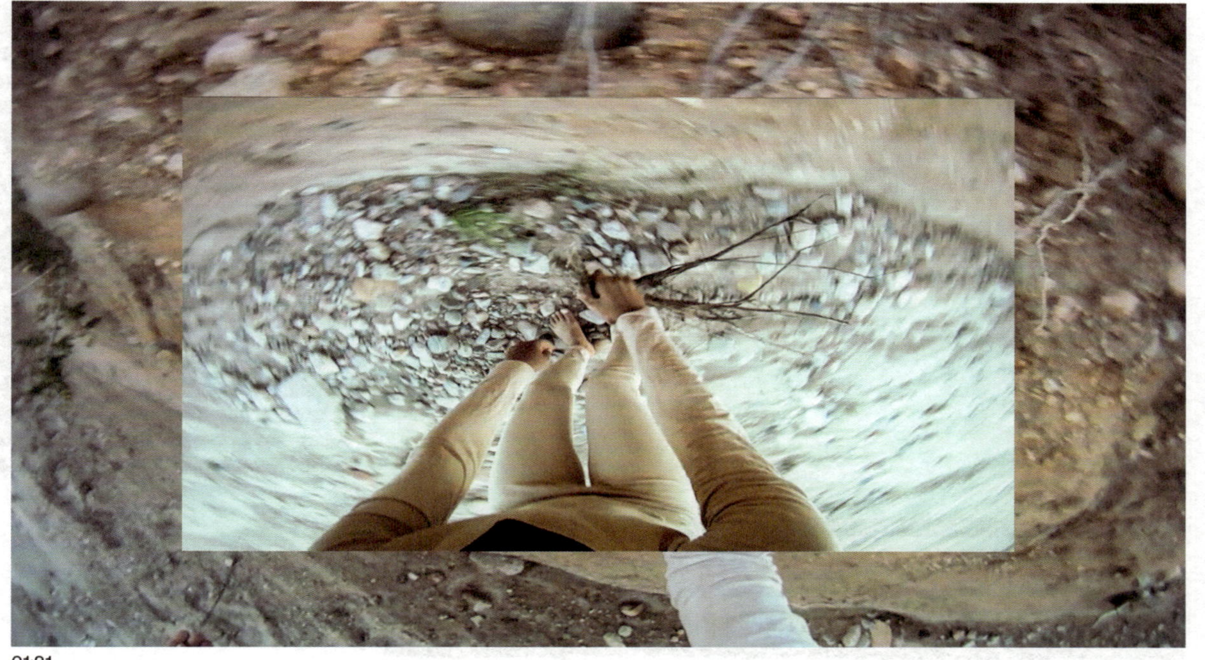

01:31

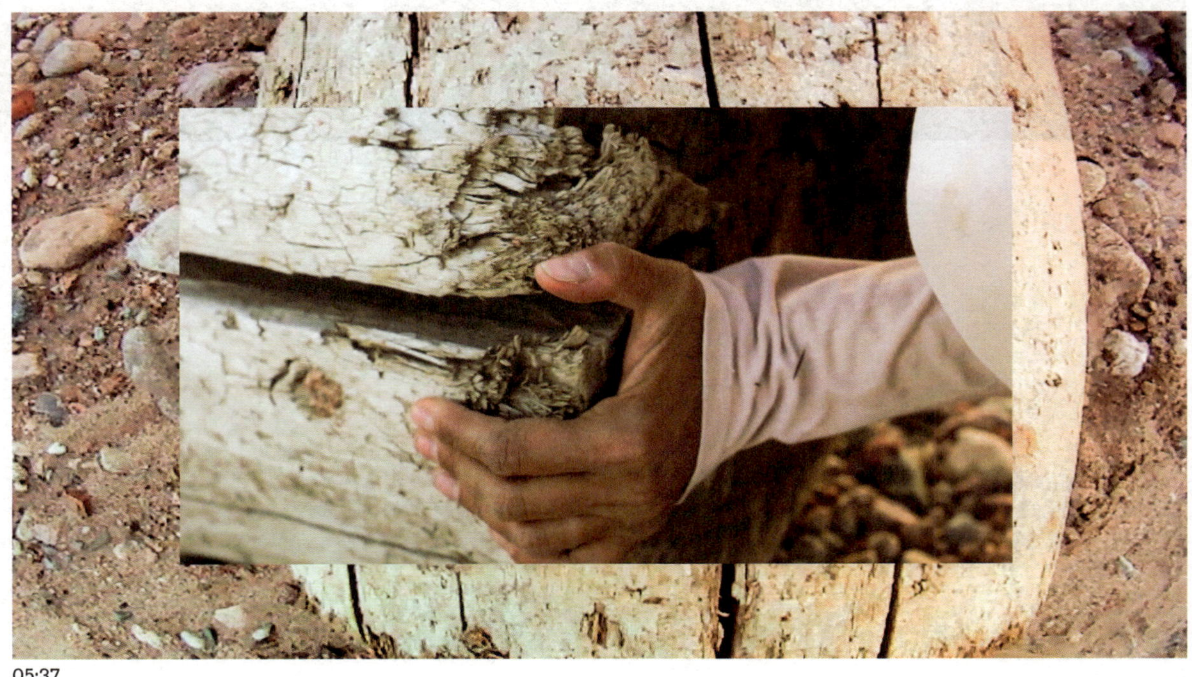

05:37

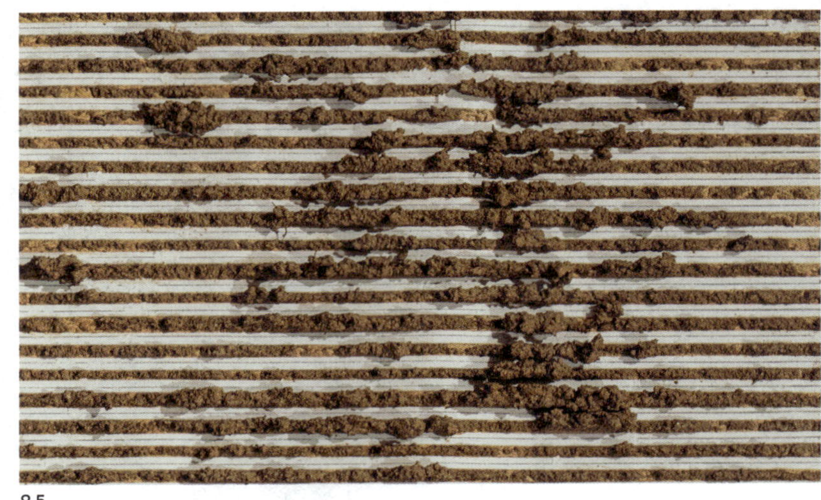
8.5

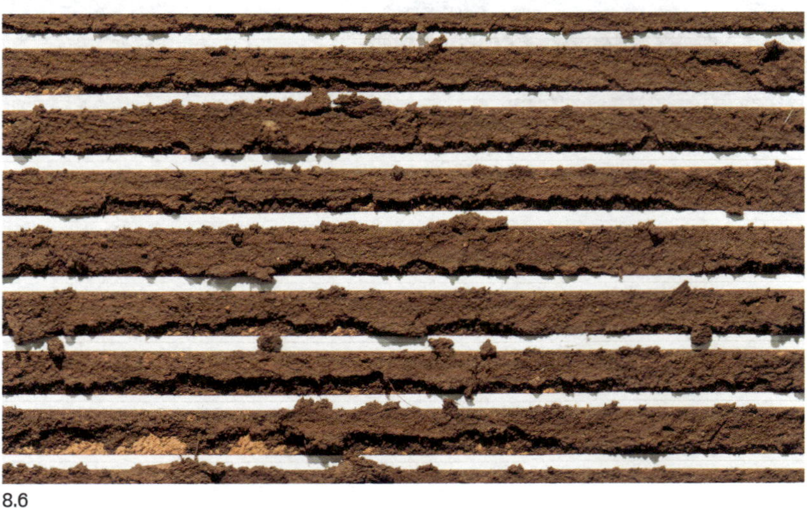
8.6

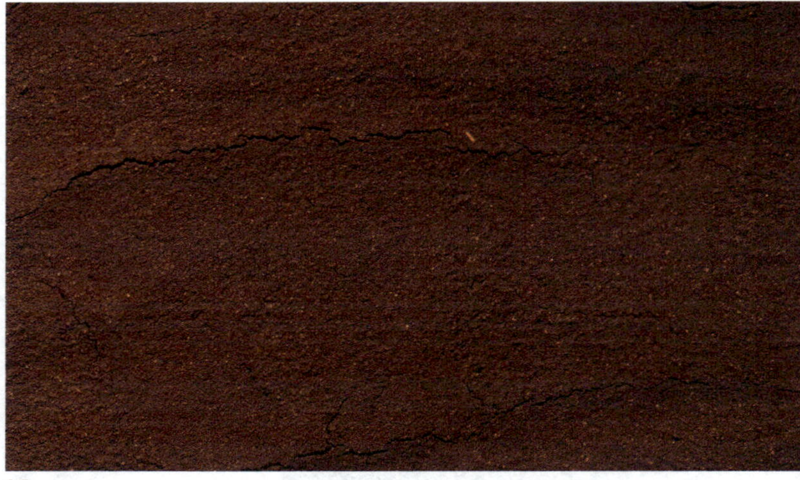
8.7

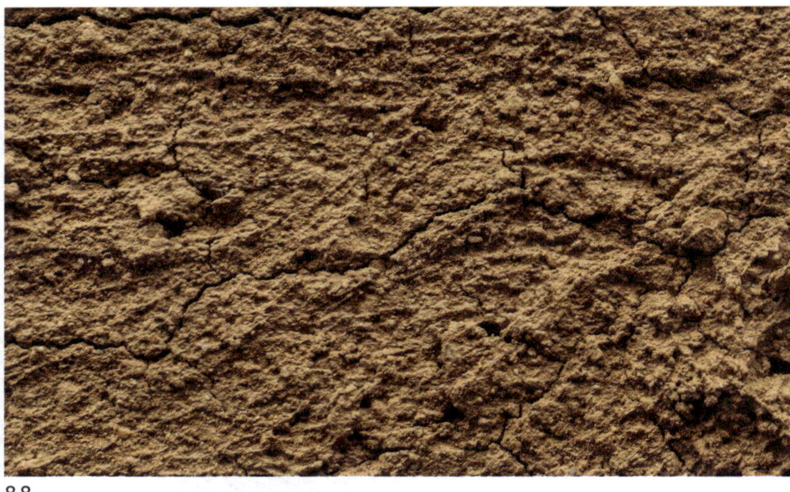
8.8

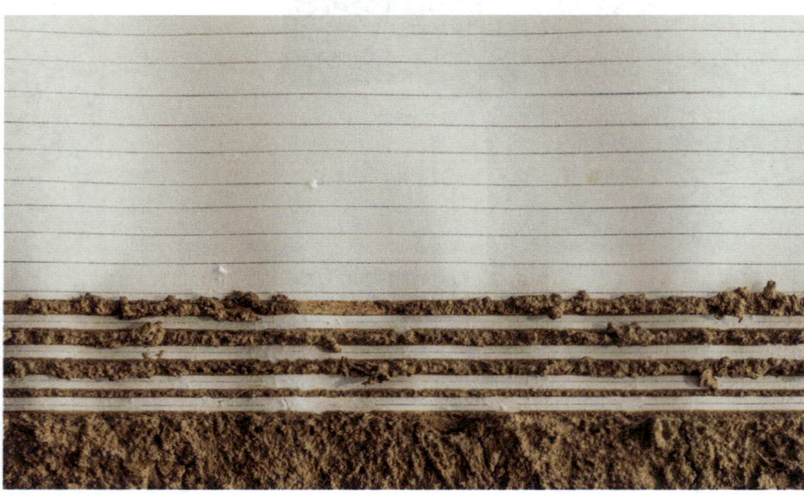
8.9

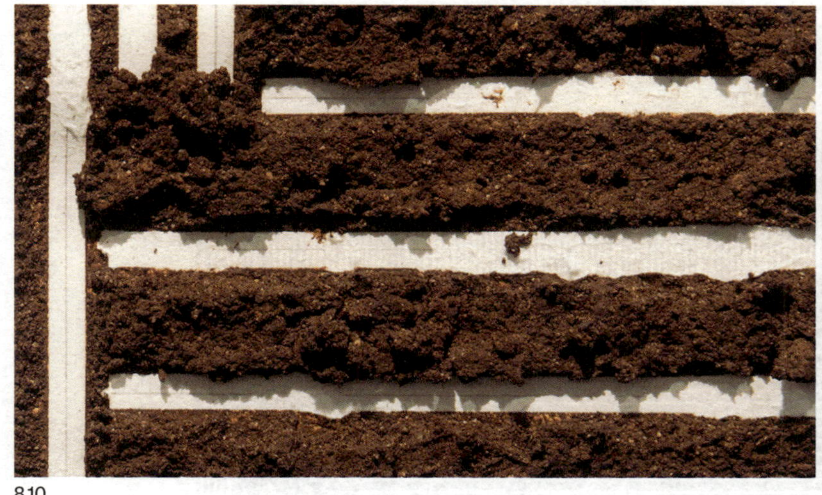
8.10

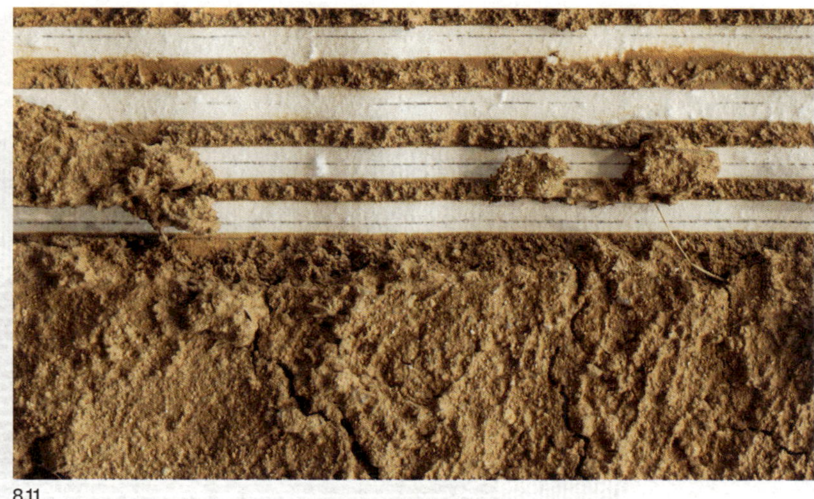
8.11

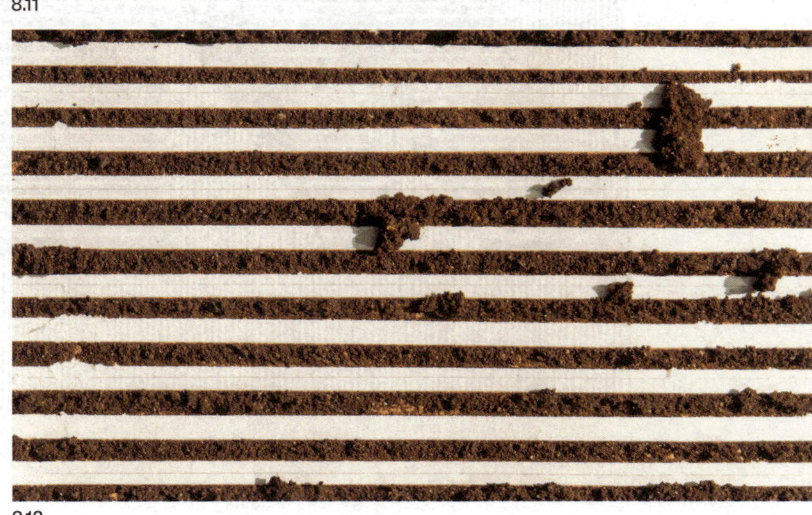
8.12

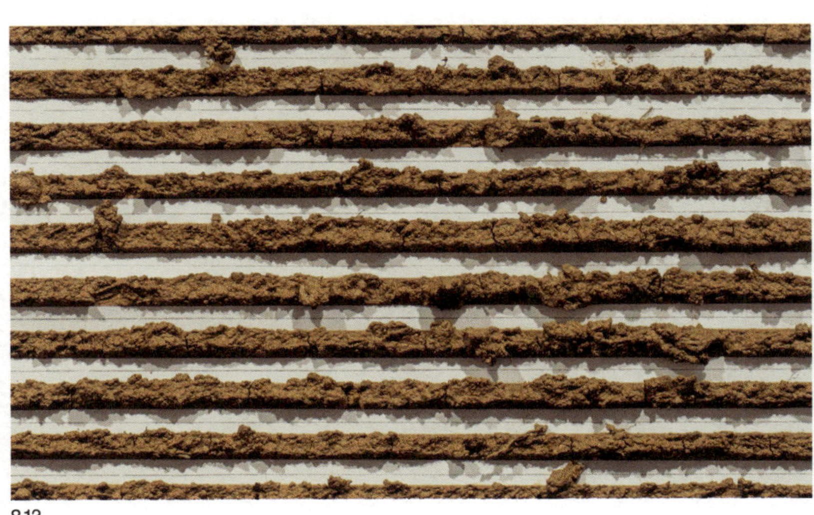
8.13

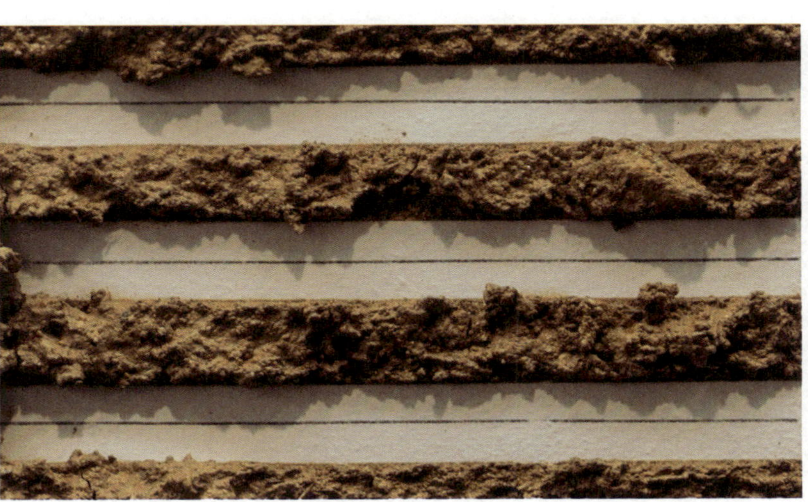
8.14

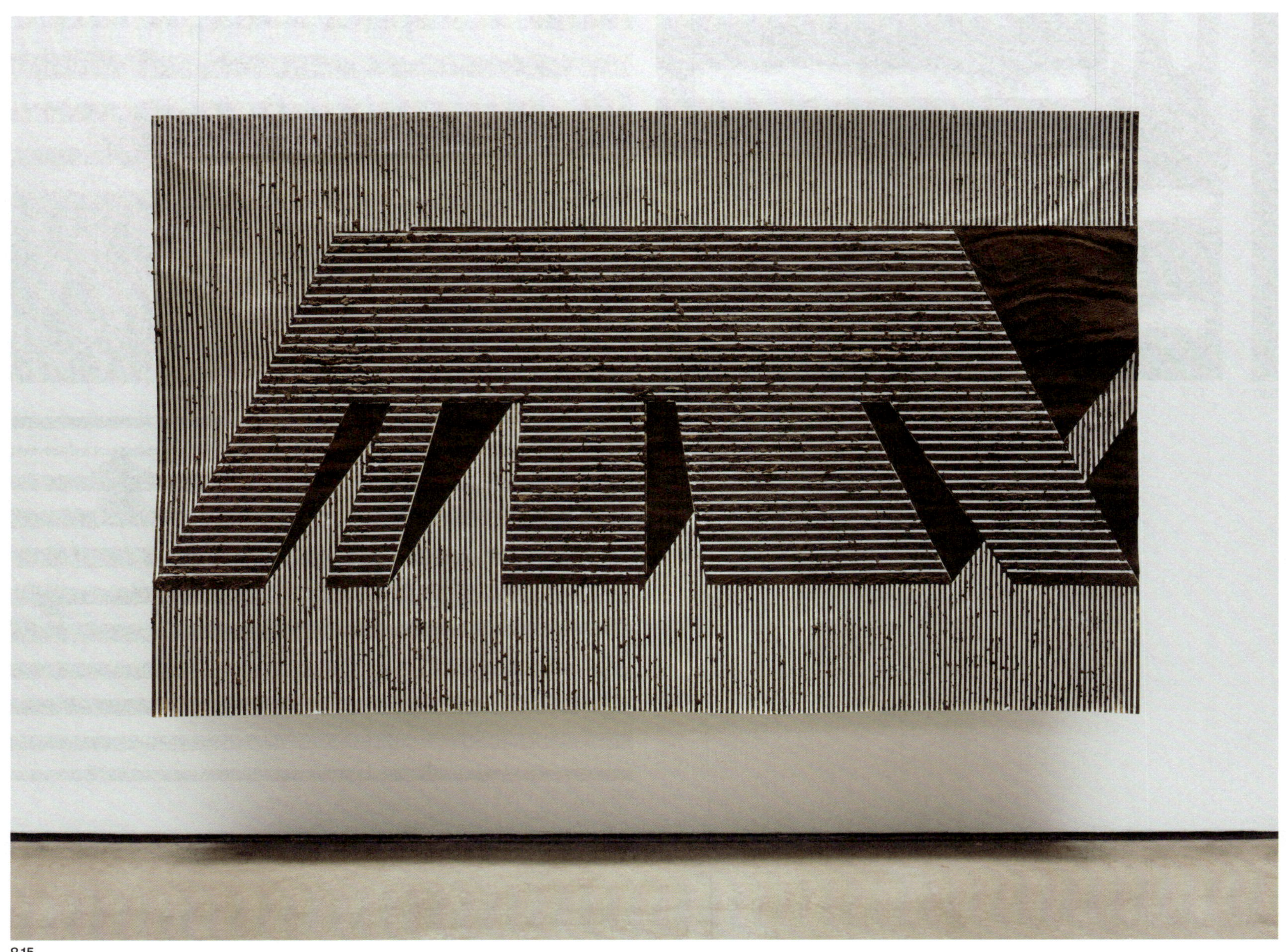

8.15

Christine Howard Sandoval

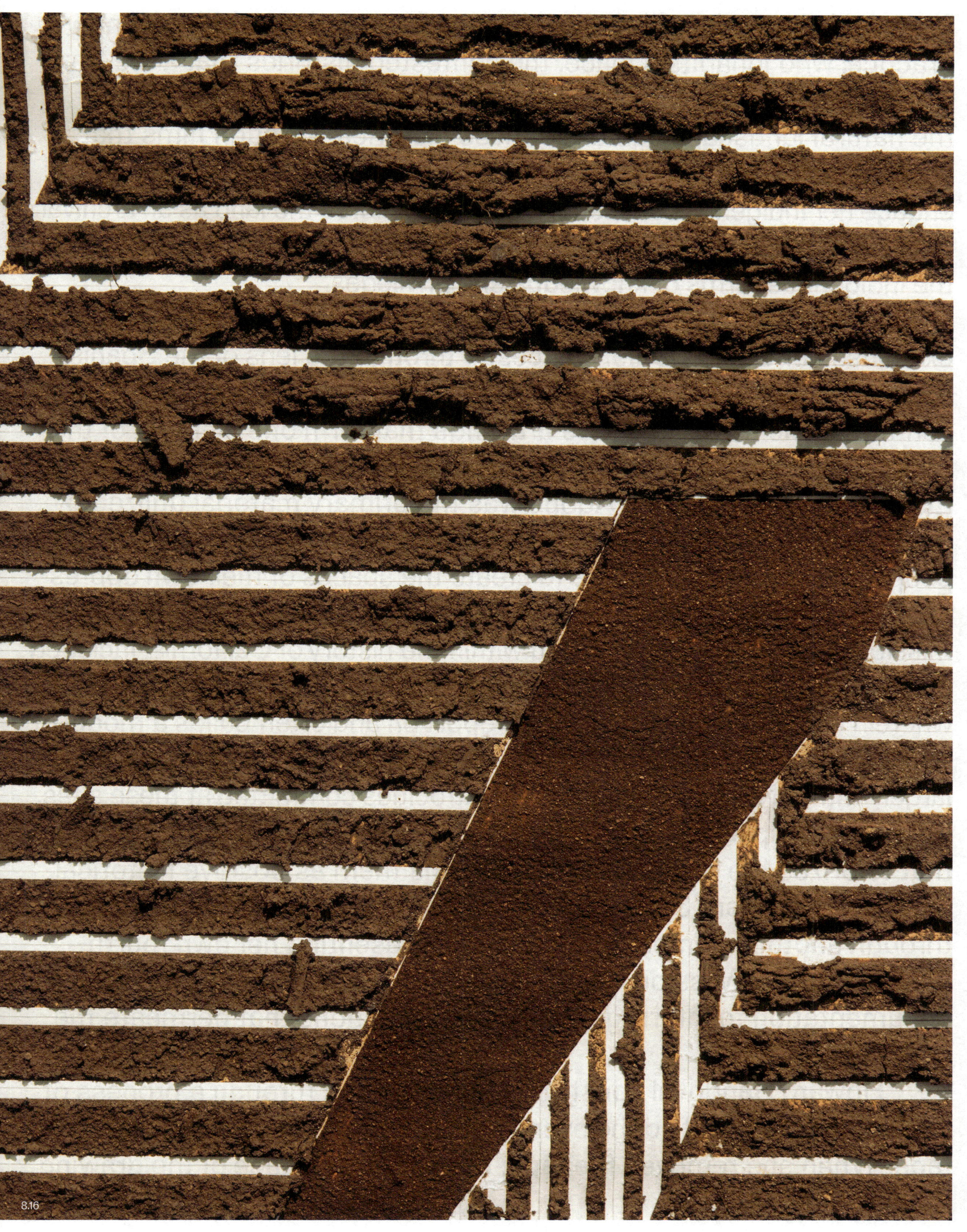

The land is central to Christine Howard Sandoval's multidisciplinary practice: who inhabits a place, the contested histories that arise from colonial incursions on Native lands, and how the use (or misuse) of the natural landscape can trace these histories. Through films that capture her movement across landscapes and through materials that engage her Indigenous ancestry, the artist explores the land as an archival presence, an equal to the state-sponsored archives that so often discredit the Indigenous forms of knowledge she privileges.

In *A Wall Is A Shadow On The Land* (2020–), Howard Sandoval examines her Chalon Ohlone ancestry through the lens of the Spanish missions established in California in the eighteenth and early nineteenth centuries. The massive adobe drawings that form one element of the project draw on a lineage of Indigenous labor that was co-opted by a European colonial power. Adobe was the primary material utilized by the Spanish to construct mission buildings, a practice that used Native people's labor and knowledge to create the spaces of their own oppression. Intended to colonize and convert the Native populace, Spanish missions have become canonized within the history of California. Included in the curricula of many California primary schools is a mission project, wherein each student completes a report on and often builds a model of one of California's twenty-one missions. Presented for many decades largely without critical insight into the atrocities committed at these sites, the project implicates each student in the continuing colonial practice that valorizes the missions and maintains them as positive historical landmarks. Howard Sandoval reflects on her complicity in this practice through another element of the project, presenting her own fourth-grade report on Mission San Francisco de Asís alongside historical documentation to interrogate the colonial fictions that permeate the education system.[1]

Howard Sandoval constructs her drawings through a process of removal, layering wet adobe over carefully delineated paper and masking tape. When she removes the tape, the striated surface of the drawing takes shape. The architecture depicted draws on the facades of the Mission San Luis Obispo, its arches and columns an echo of classical architecture, itself an imperial form.[2] Howard Sandoval quotes this colonial architecture only to deconstruct it, leaving gaps wherein the hidden histories of these spaces can be perceived. "What can be gained from the interstices," the artist writes, "or the blank spaces in between the lines?"[3]

*A Wall Is A Shadow On The Land* rejects the colonial modes of history in favor of an exploration of Indigenous modes of remembrance. Howard Sandoval's deep connection to her materials and references creates a rich foundation for exploration through which both the artist and the viewer can begin to confront and unlearn their engagement with colonial legacies. (LRL)

1 Julia Lamare and Kimberly Phillips, "Christine Howard Sandoval: *A wall is a shadow on the land*," Contemporary Art Gallery, Vancouver, January 2021, https://cag-cms-cdn.sfo3.cdn.digitaloceanspaces.com/strapi-uploads/1dbc2070ed2405dc00f842e14b27f5ed.pdf.

2 Louis Bury, "Embodied Practice: Christine Howard Sandoval" (interview) *Bomb Magazine*, April 21, 2021, https://bombmagazine.org/articles/2021/04/21/embodied-practice-christine-howard-sandoval-interviewed.

3 Christine Howard Sandoval, "A wall is a shadow on the land," STTLMNT, https://www.sttlmnt.org/projects/a-wall-is-a-shadow-on-the-land.

SAMMY BALOJI *Tales of the Copper Cross Garden: Episode 1*, 2017, HD video (color, sound), 42 min., wall vinyl (size variable), courtesy the artist and Galerie Imane Farès, Paris

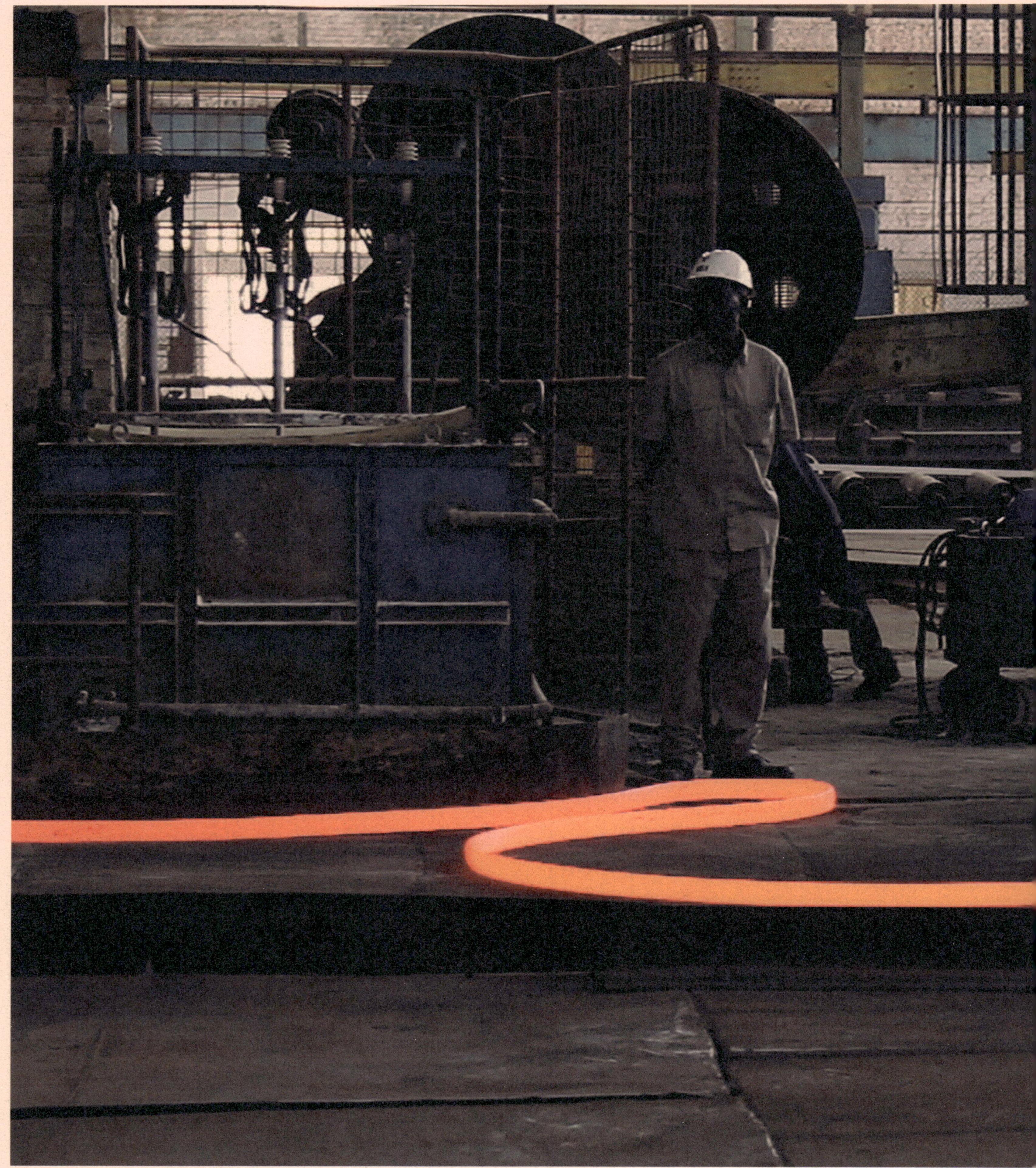

04:05

Stills from *Tales of the Copper Cross Garden: Episode 1*, 2017

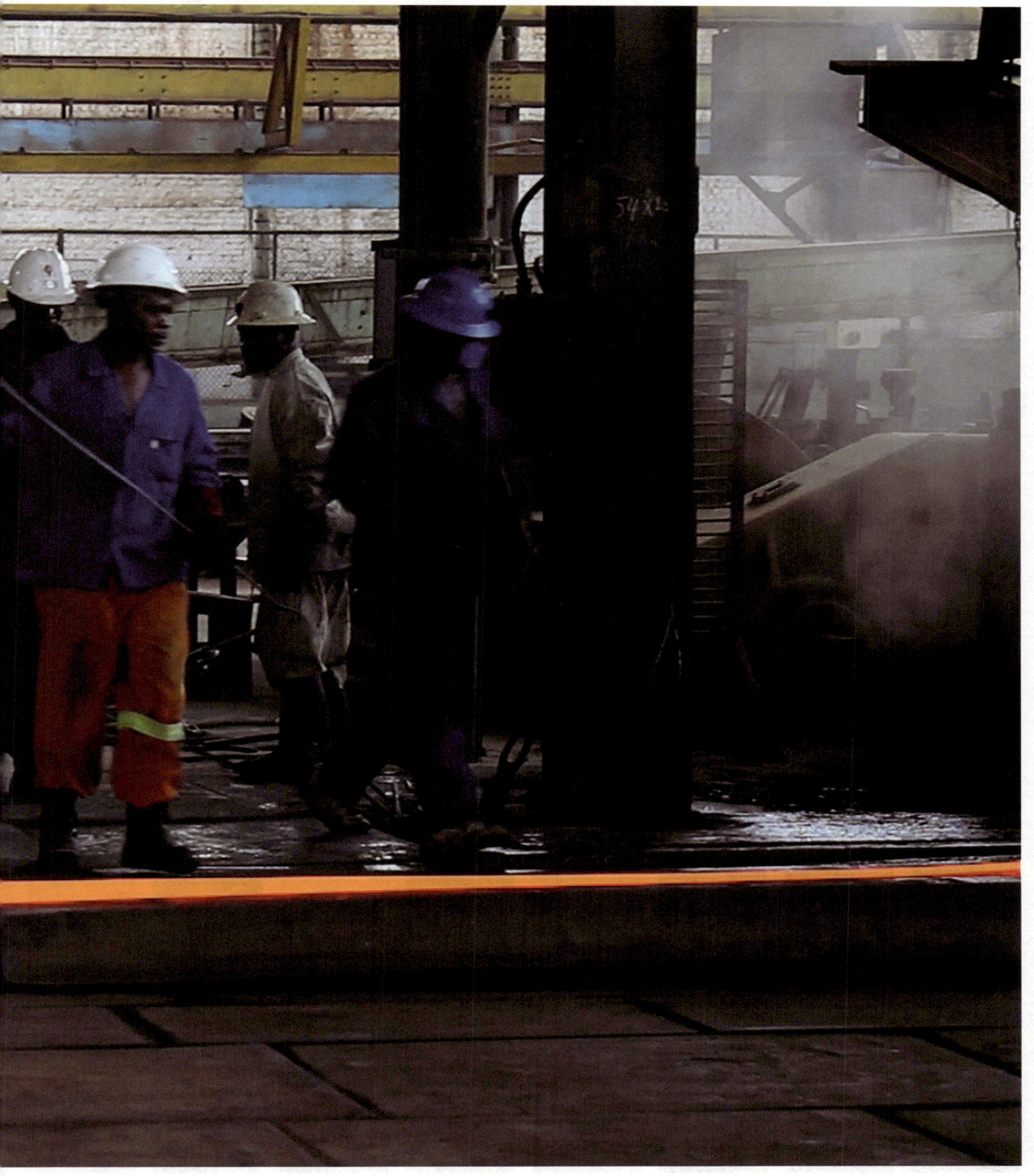

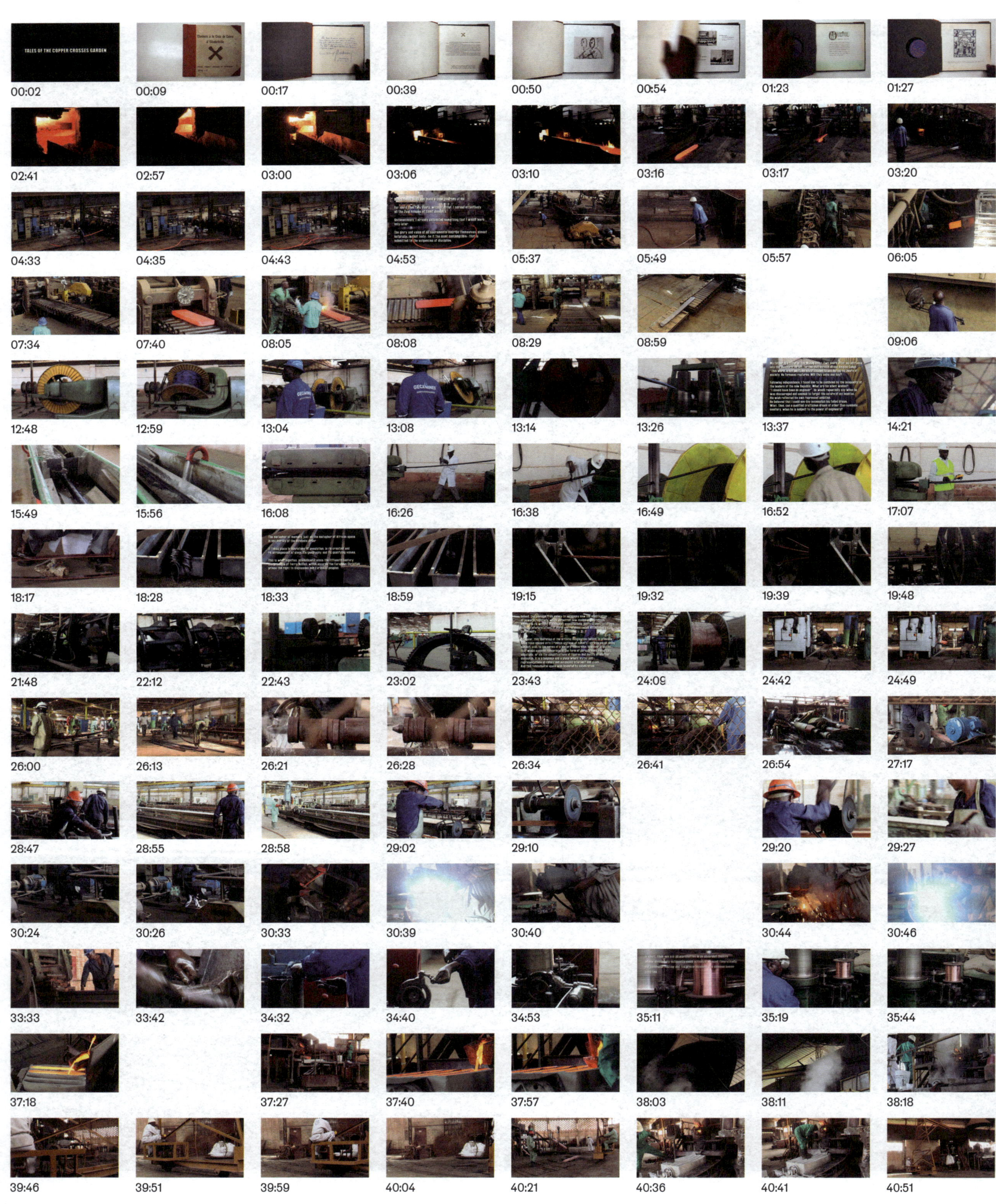
TALES OF THE COPPER CROSSES GARDEN
00:02
00:09
00:17
00:39
00:50
00:54
01:23
01:27
02:41
02:57
03:00
03:06
03:10
03:16
03:17
03:20
04:33
04:35
04:43
04:53
05:37
05:49
05:57
06:05
07:34
07:40
08:05
08:08
08:29
08:59
09:06
12:48
12:59
13:04
13:08
13:14
13:26
13:37
14:21
15:49
15:56
16:08
16:26
16:38
16:49
16:52
17:07
18:17
18:28
18:33
18:59
19:15
19:32
19:39
19:48
21:48
22:12
22:43
23:02
23:43
24:09
24:42
24:49
26:00
26:13
26:21
26:28
26:34
26:41
26:54
27:17
28:47
28:55
28:58
29:02
29:10
29:20
29:27
30:24
30:26
30:33
30:39
30:40
30:44
30:46
33:33
33:42
34:32
34:40
34:53
35:11
35:19
35:44
37:18
37:27
37:40
37:57
38:03
38:11
38:18
39:46
39:51
39:59
40:04
40:21
40:36
40:41
40:51

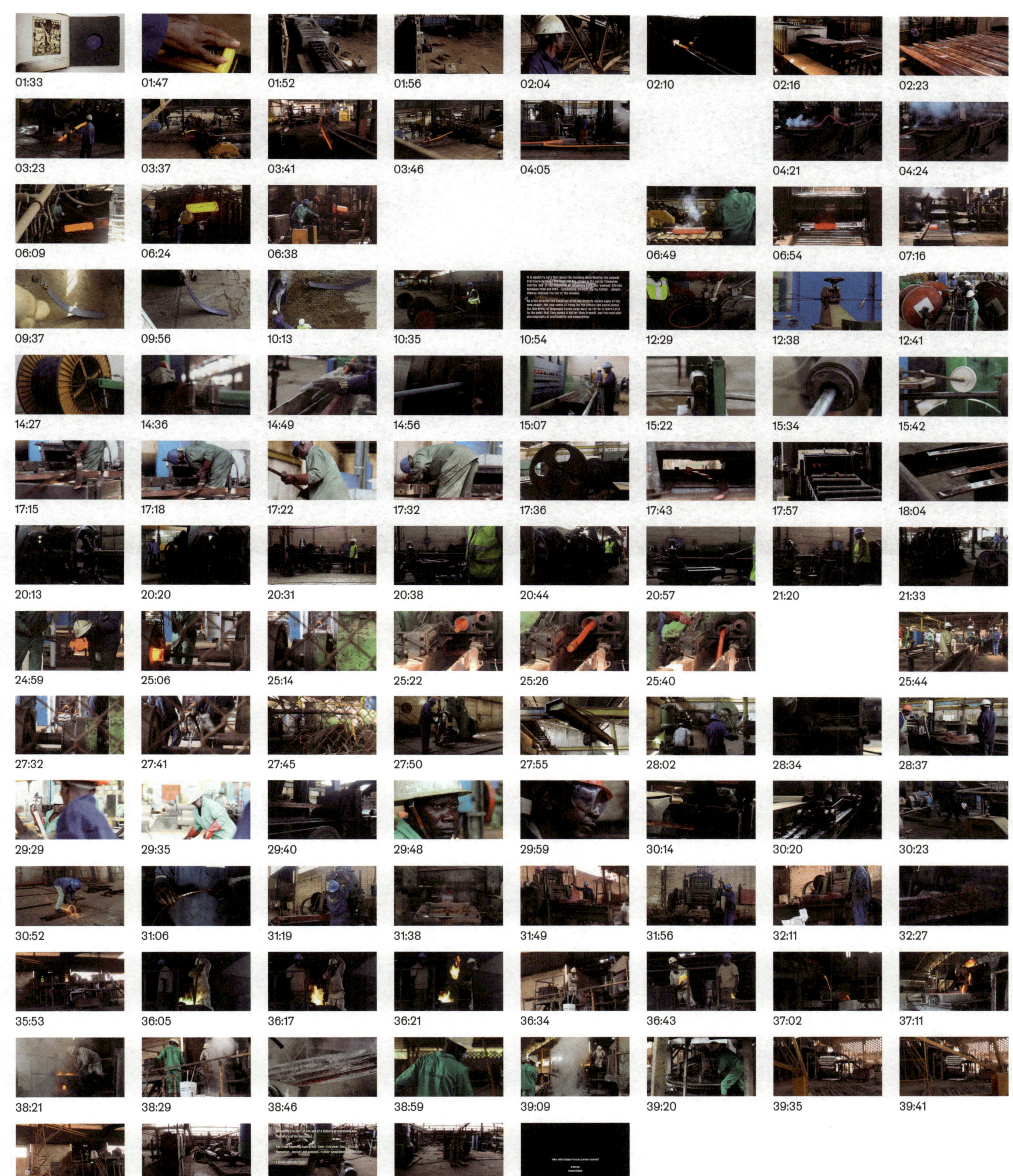
01:33 01:47 01:52 01:56 02:04 02:10 02:16 02:23
03:23 03:37 03:41 03:46 04:05 04:21 04:24
06:09 06:24 06:38 06:49 06:54 07:16
09:37 09:56 10:13 10:35 10:54 12:29 12:38 12:41
14:27 14:36 14:49 14:56 15:07 15:22 15:34 15:42
17:15 17:18 17:22 17:32 17:36 17:43 17:57 18:04
20:13 20:20 20:31 20:38 20:44 20:57 21:20 21:33
24:59 25:06 25:14 25:22 25:26 25:40 25:44
27:32 27:41 27:45 27:50 27:55 28:02 28:34 28:37
29:29 29:35 29:40 29:48 29:59 30:14 30:20 30:23
30:52 31:06 31:19 31:38 31:49 31:56 32:11 32:27
35:53 36:05 36:17 36:21 36:34 36:43 37:02 37:11
38:21 38:29 38:46 38:59 39:09 39:20 39:35 39:41
41:12 41:17 41:29 41:44 41:51

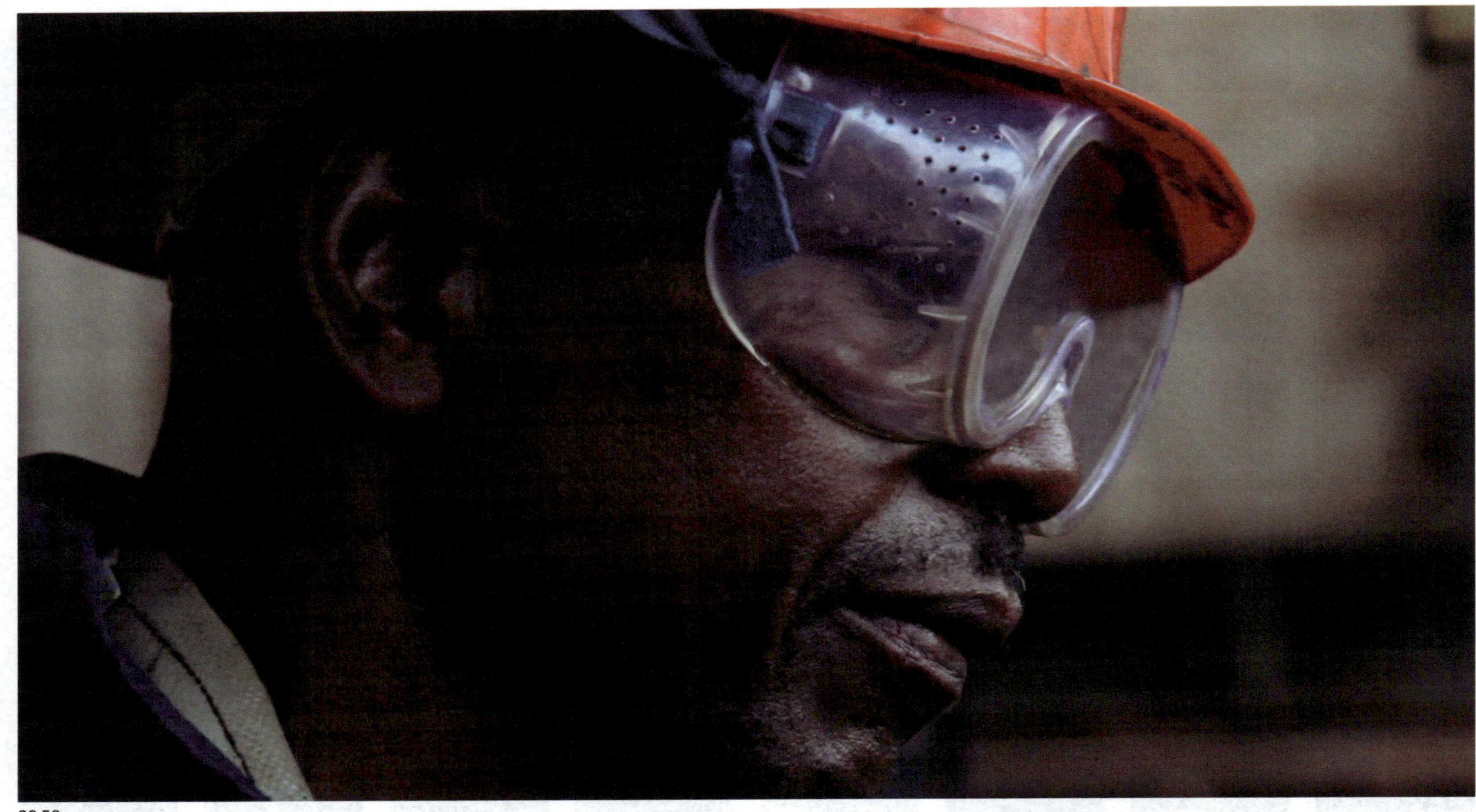

29:59

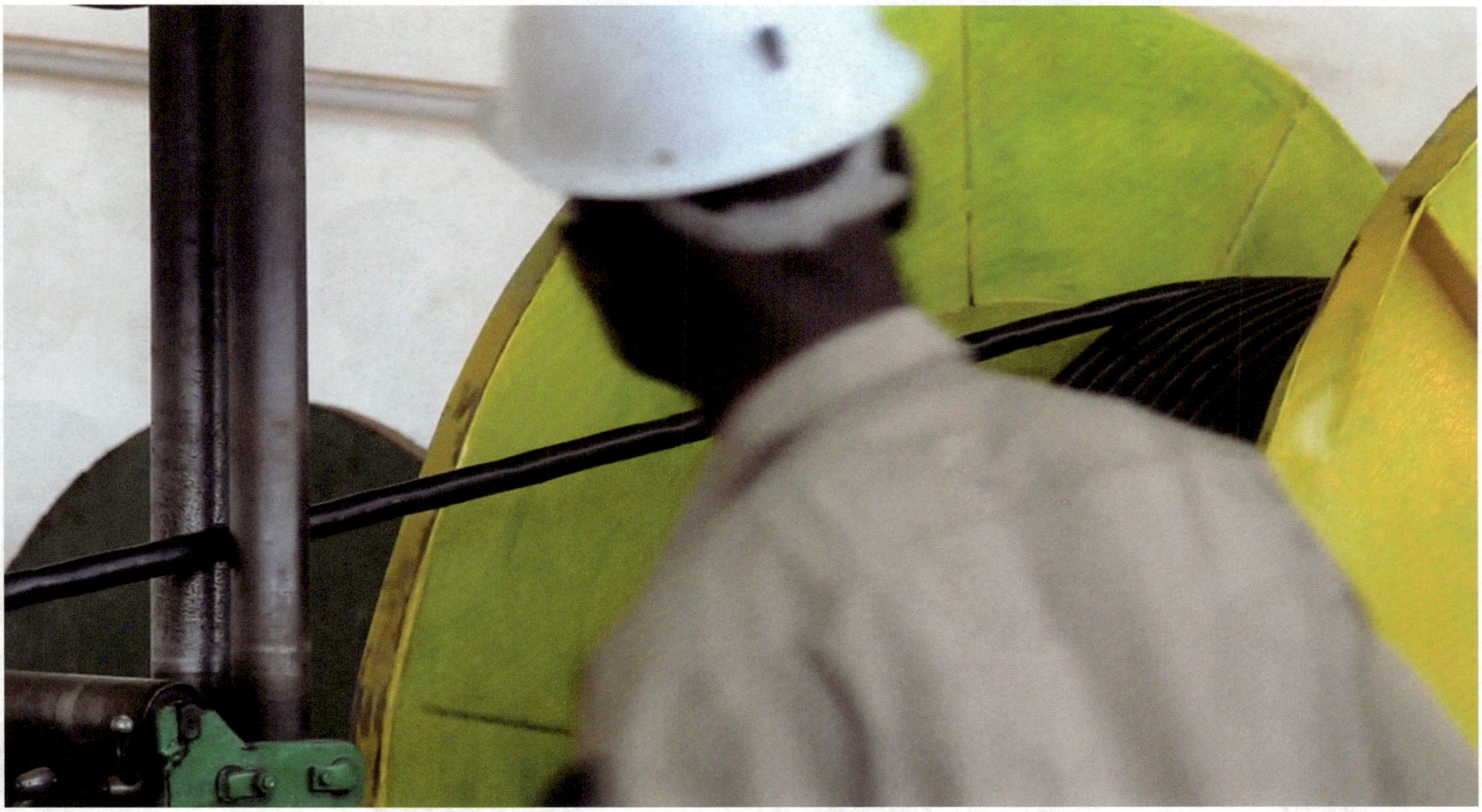

16:52

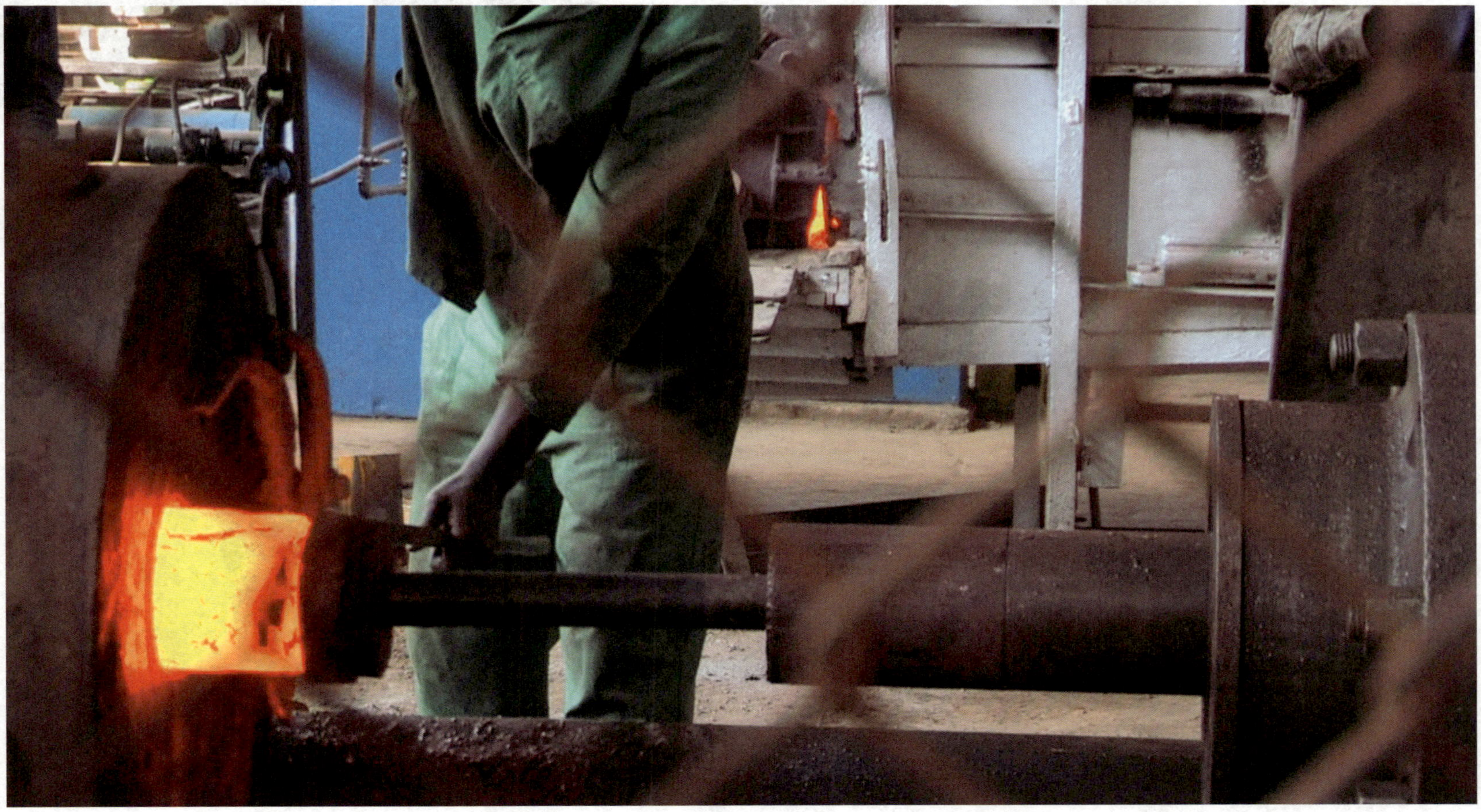

25:06

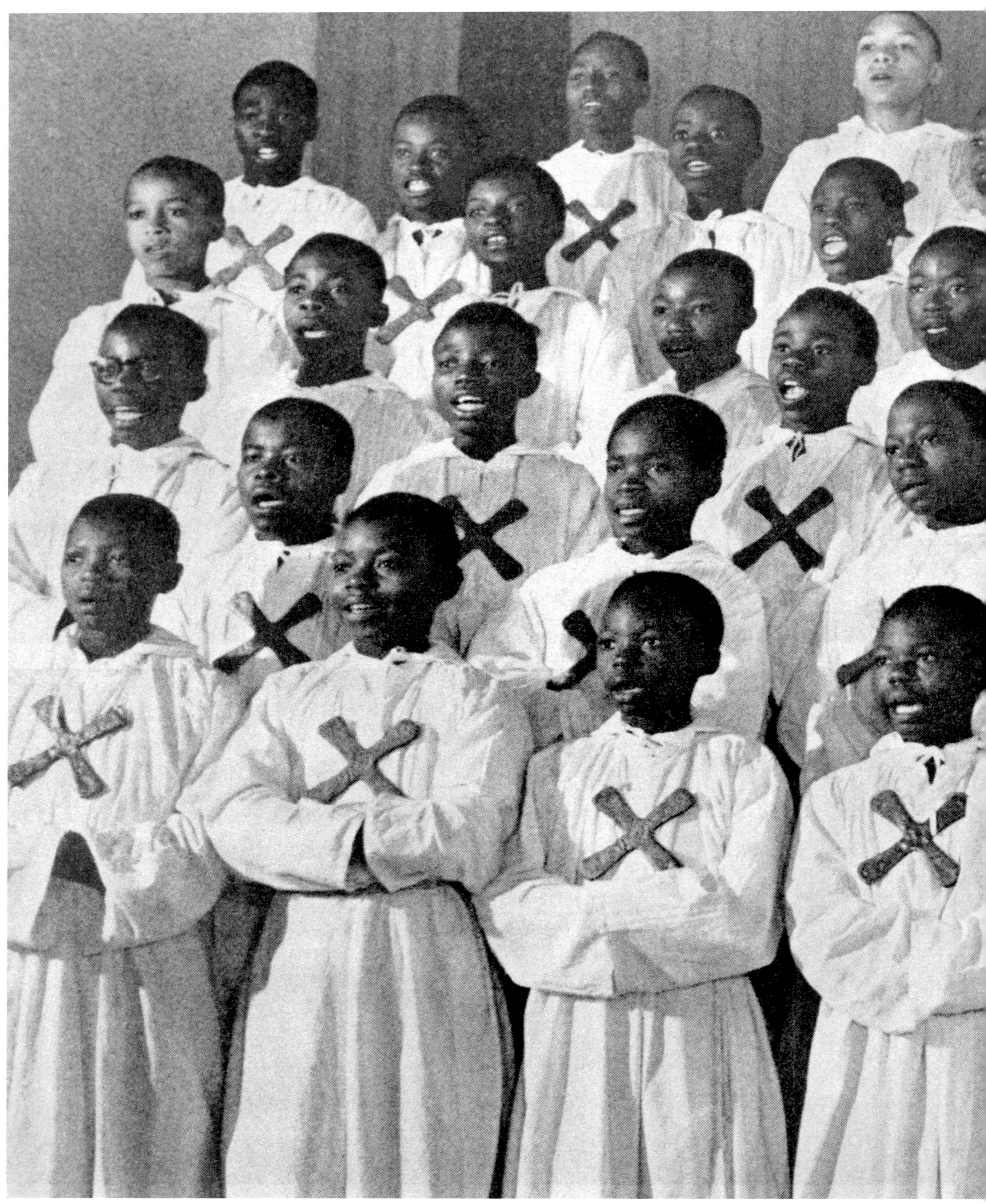

*Les petits Chanteurs à la Croix de Cuivre*, 1960 9.4

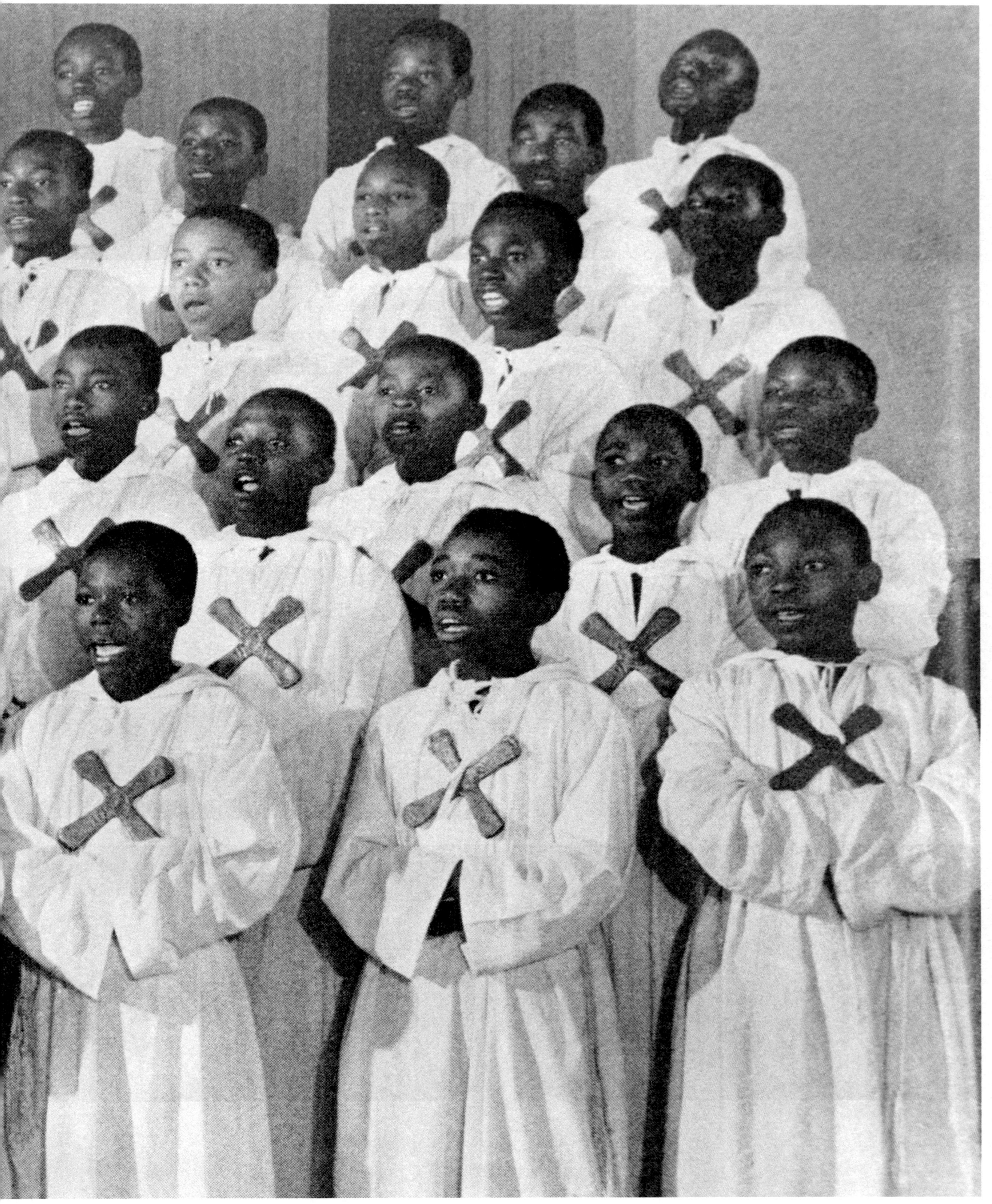

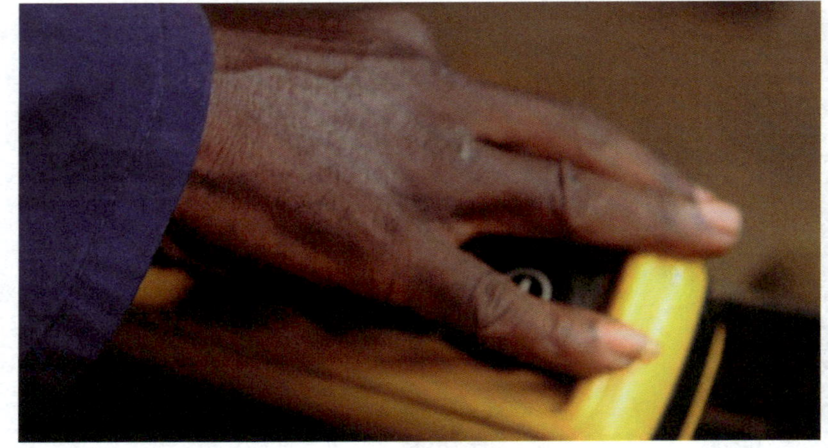
01:47

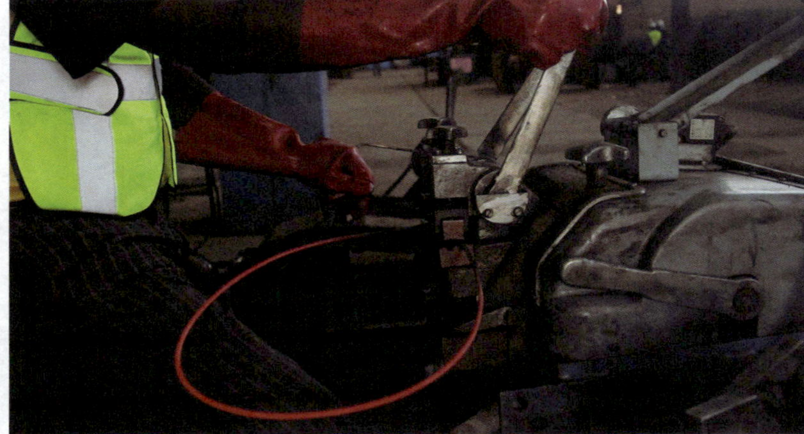
12:29

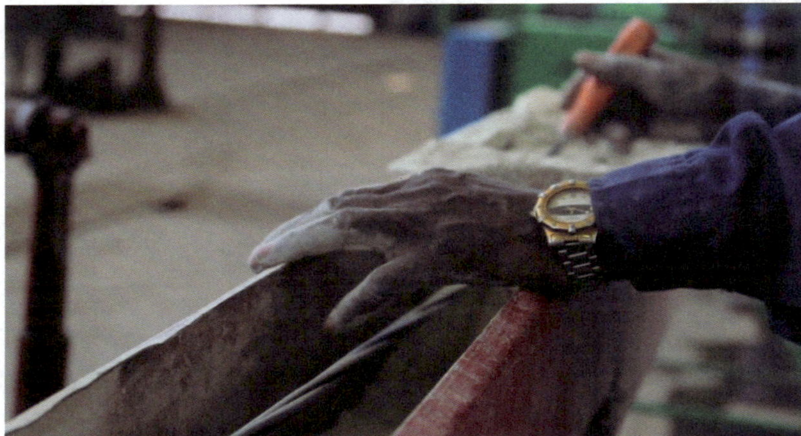
14:49

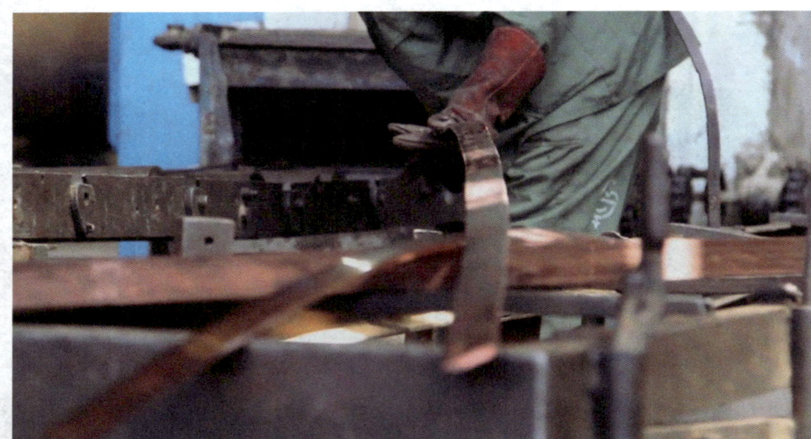
17:15

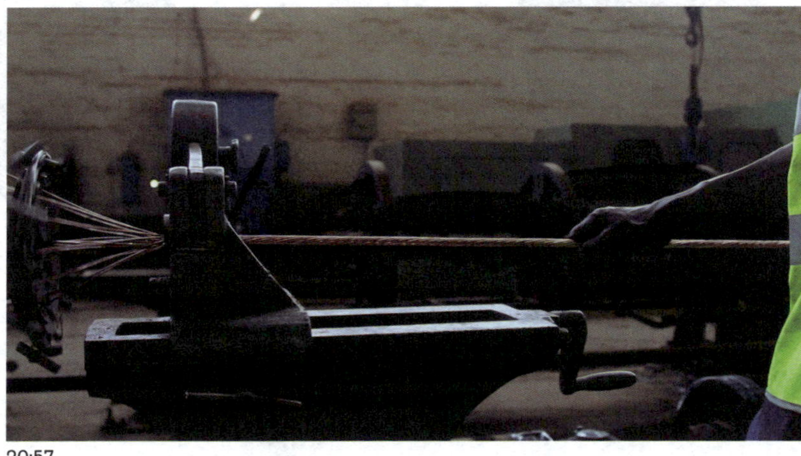
20:57

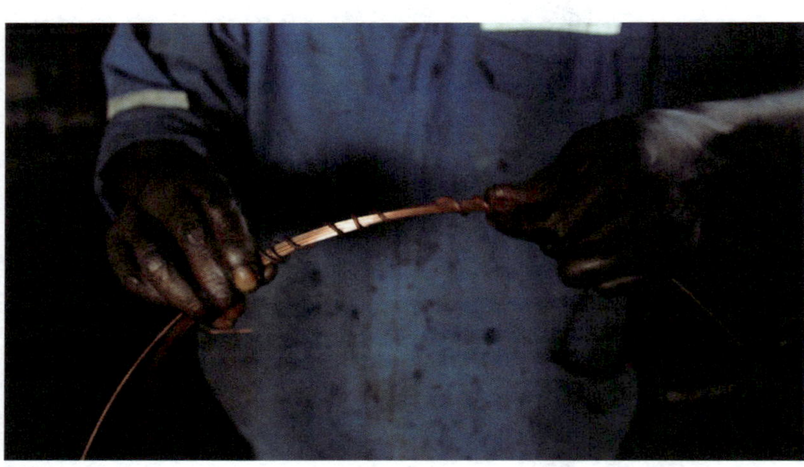
31:06

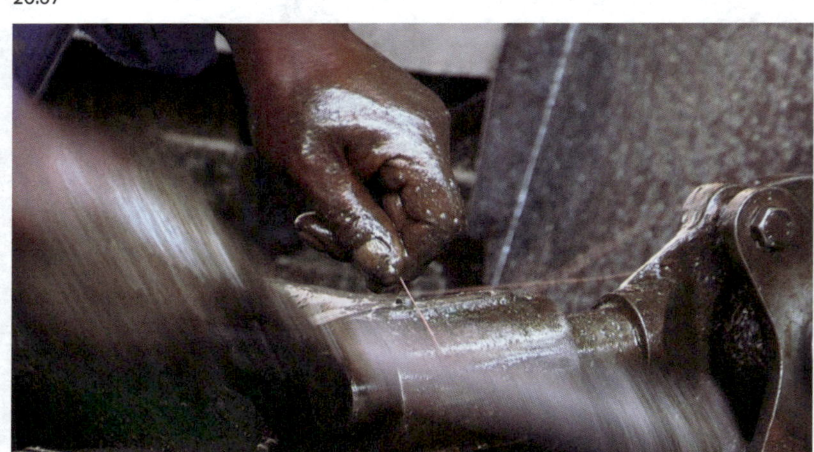
33:42

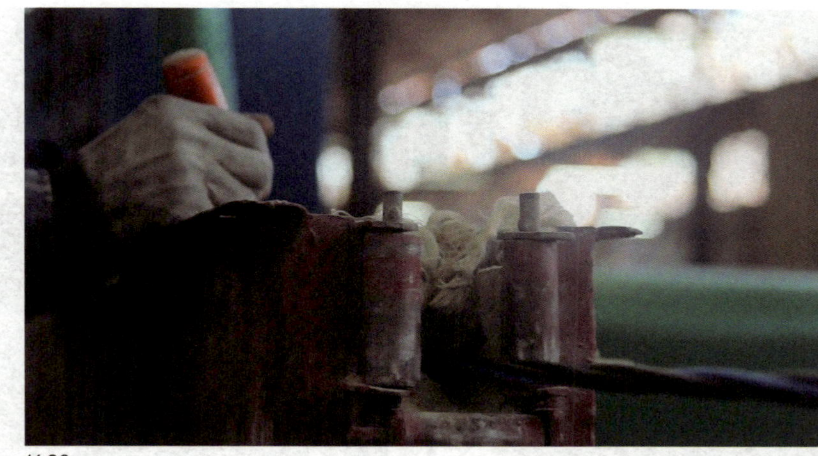

14:36

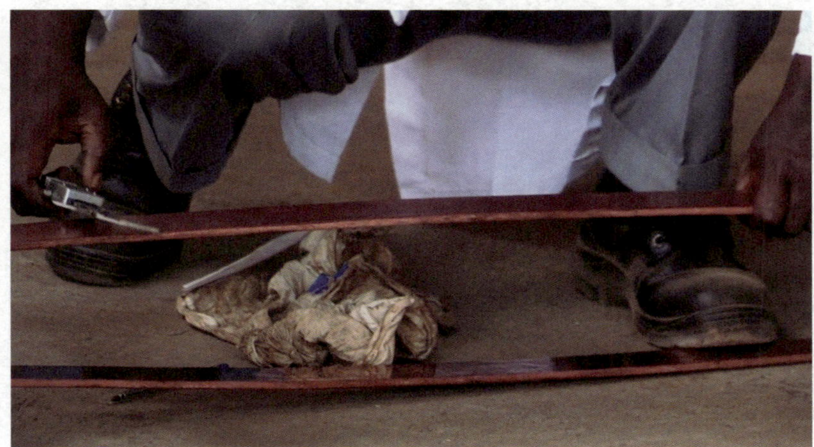

18:17

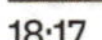

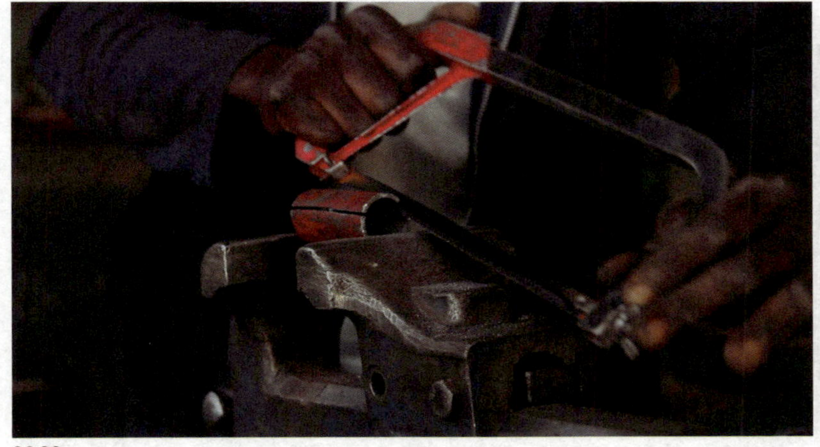

30:33

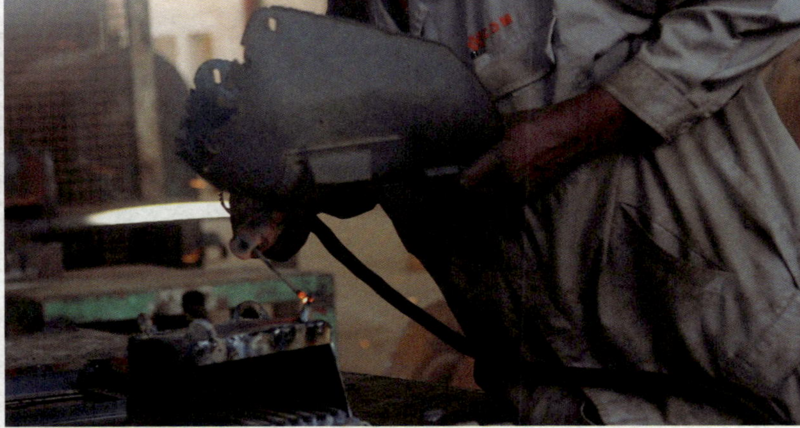

30:40

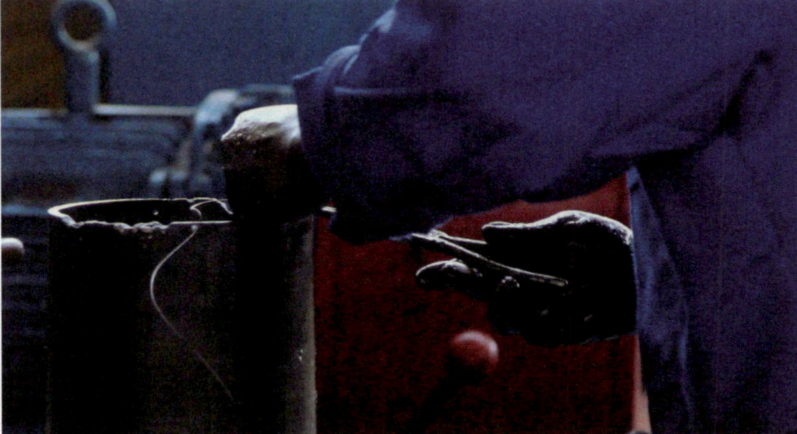

34:32

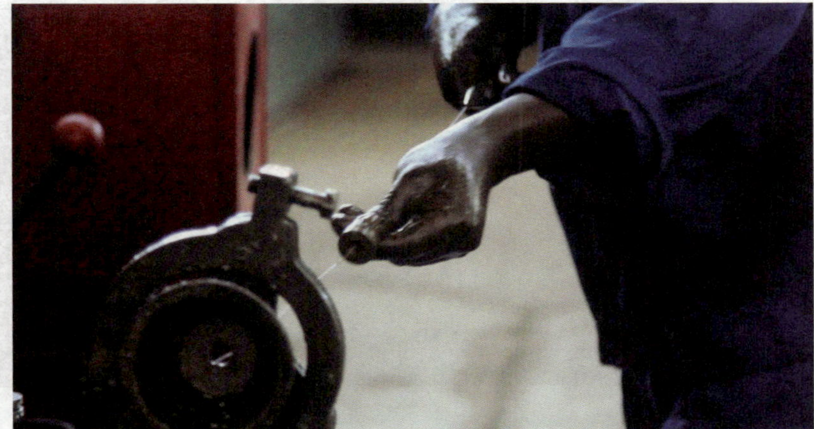

34:40

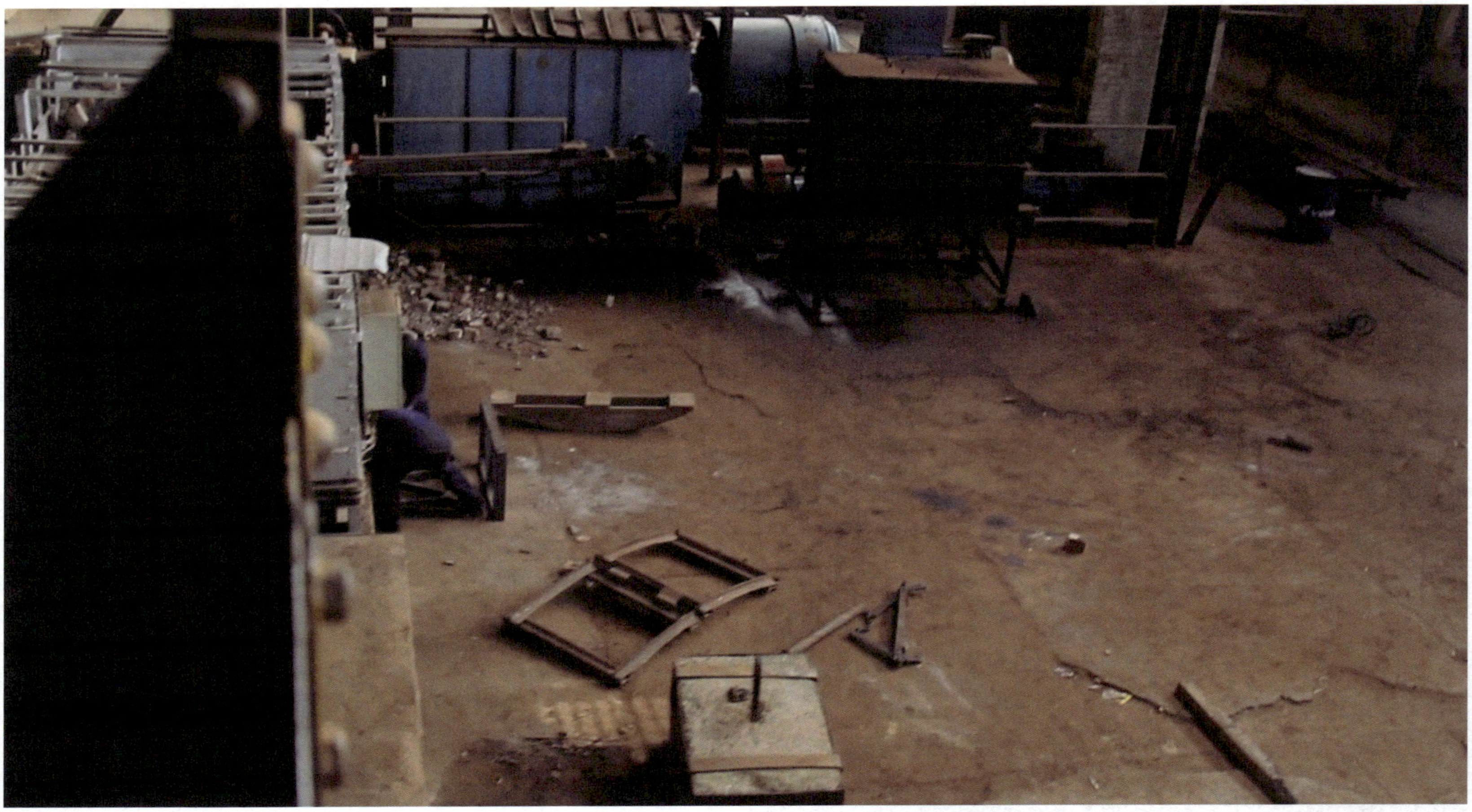

01:56

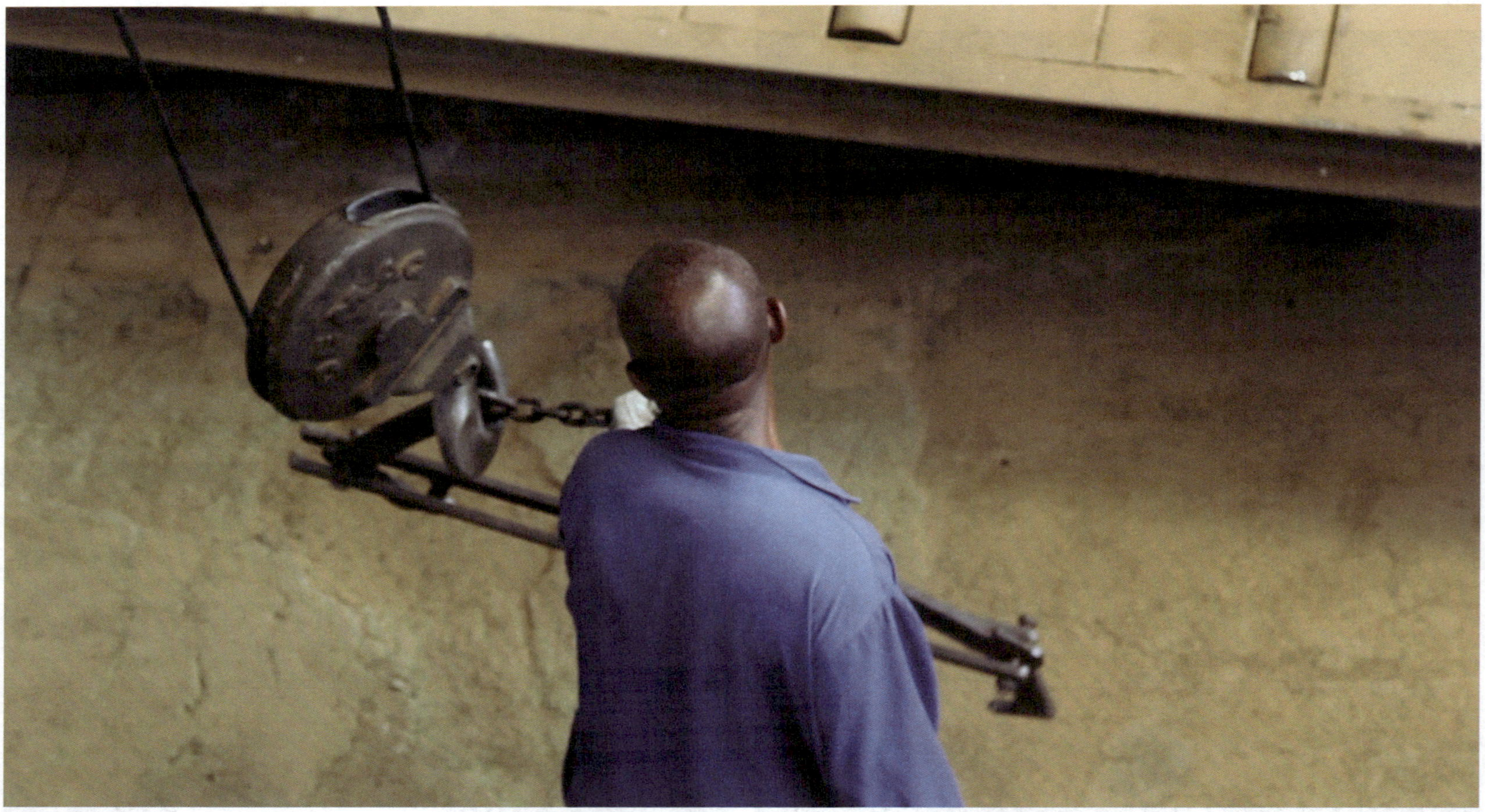

09:06

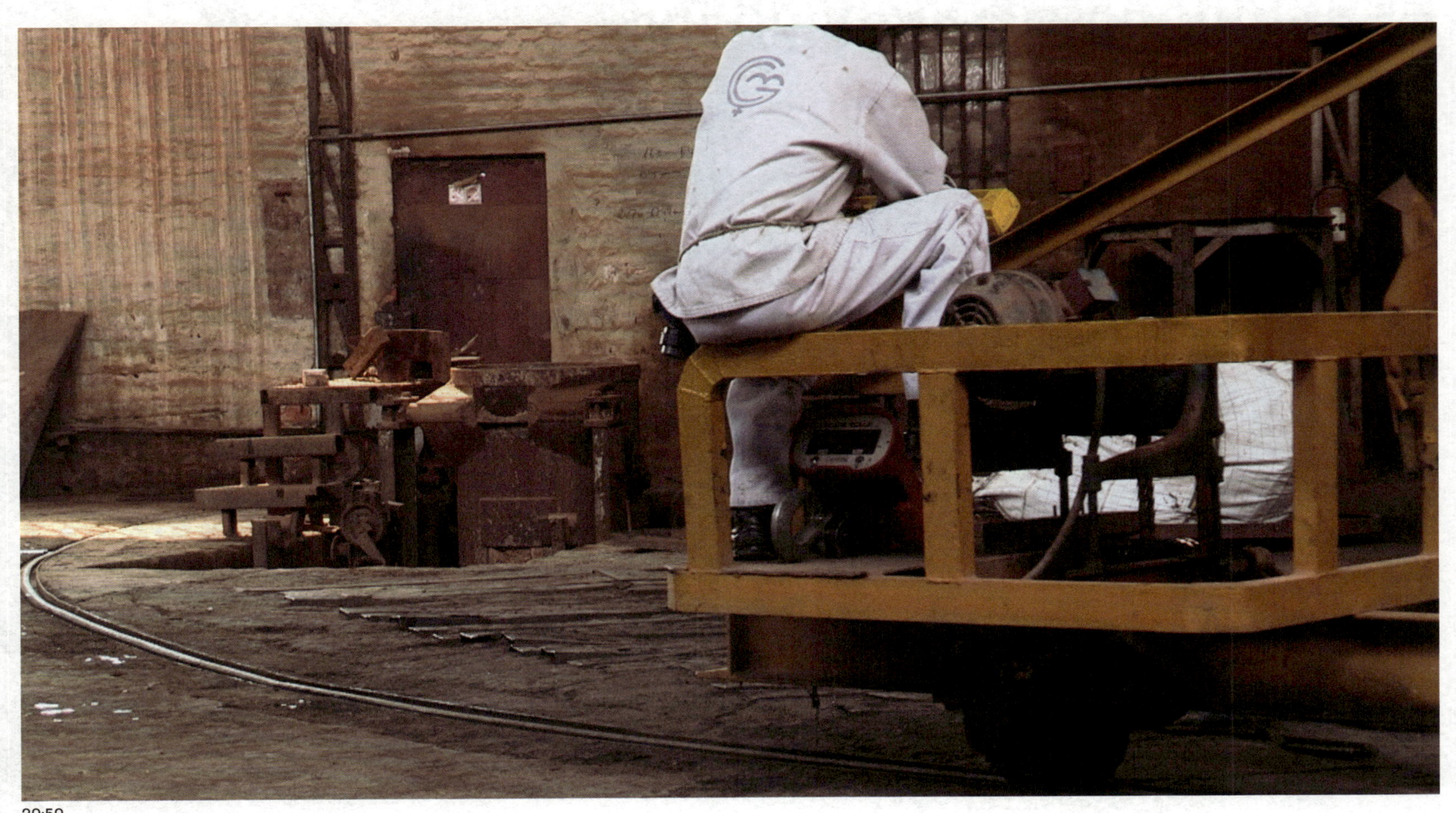

39:59

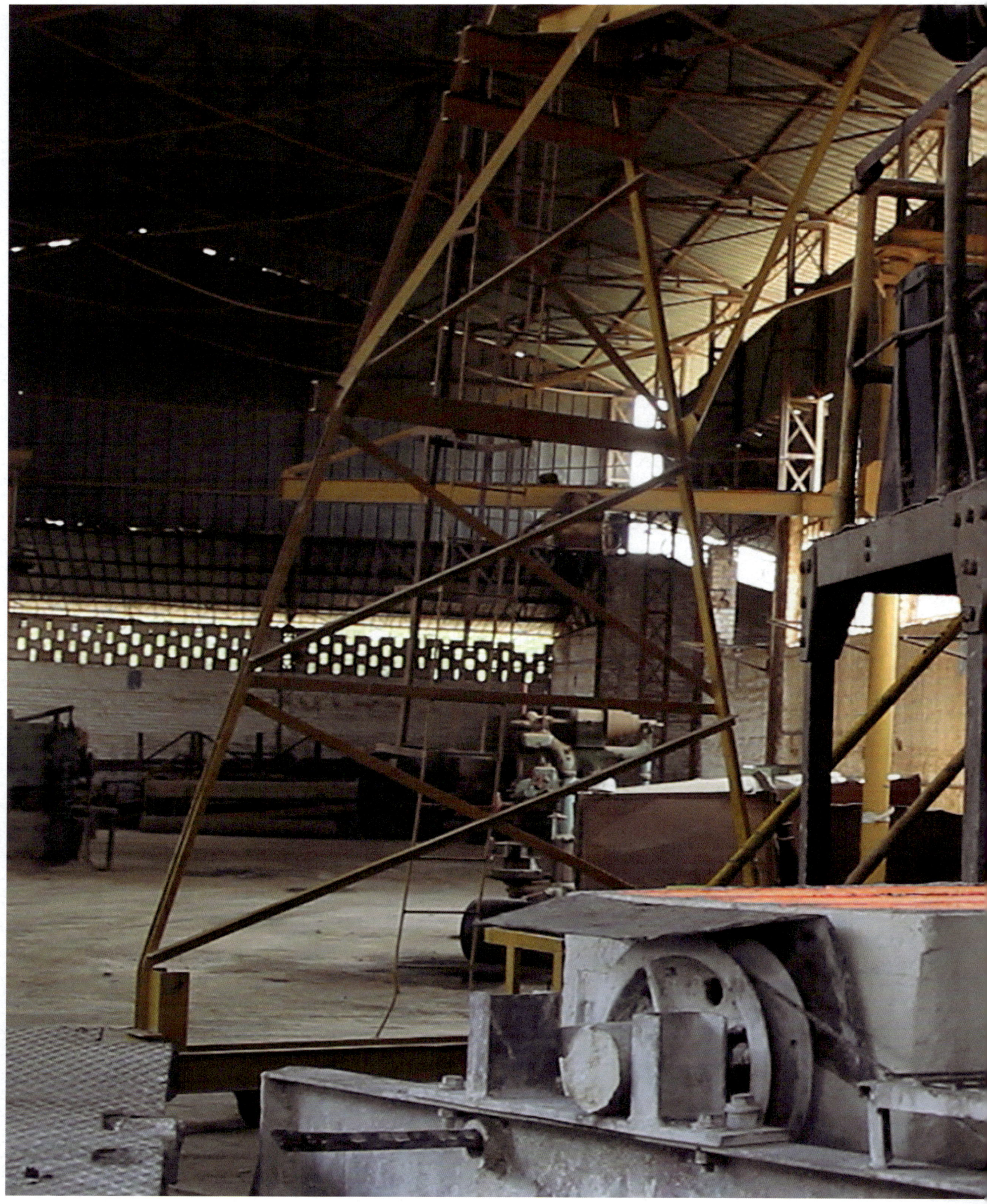

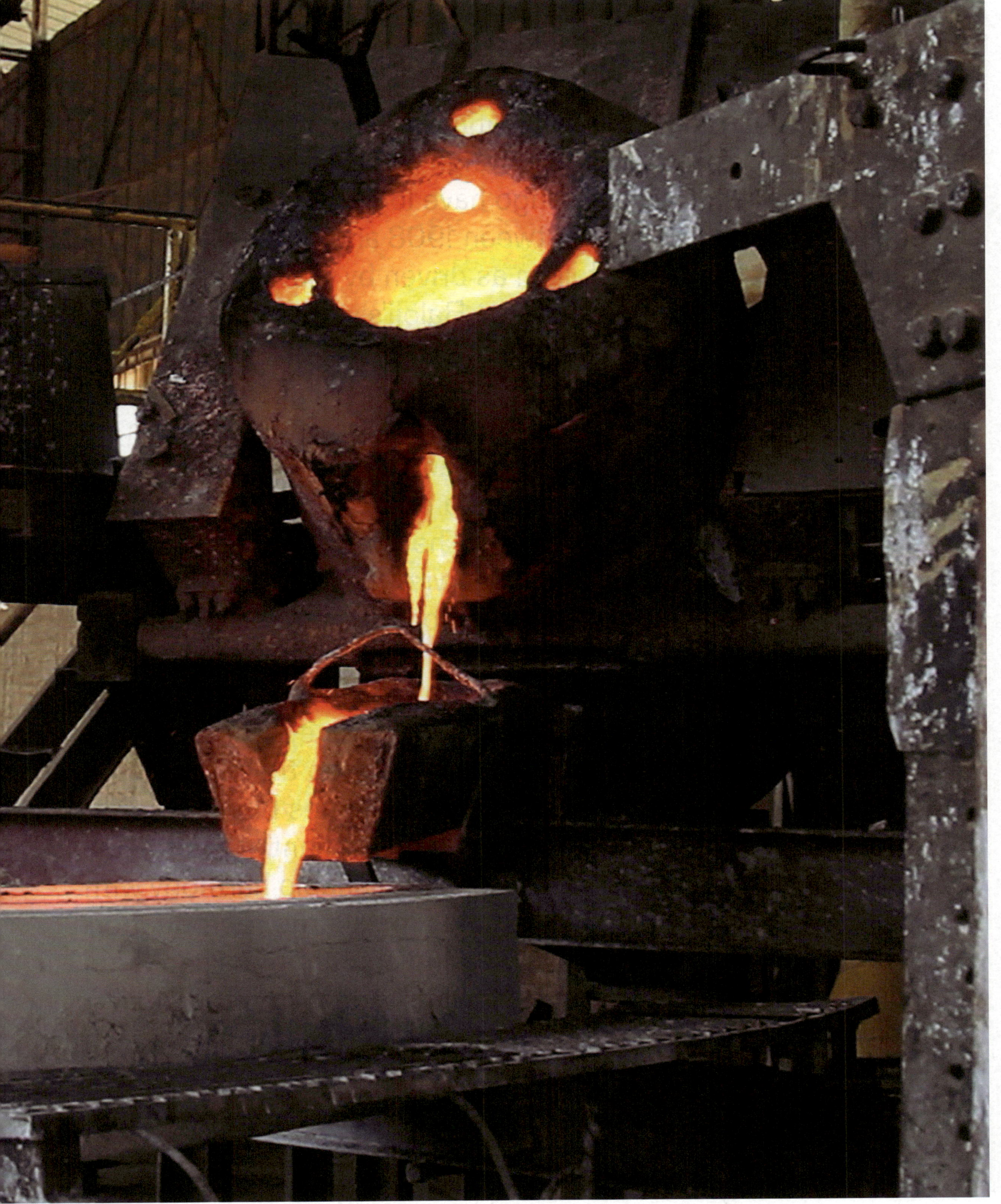

Sammy Baloji's work in photography and film explores the ways in which Congolese culture and history have been erased, altered, or buried throughout the colonial and postcolonial periods. Often looking to his hometown of Lubumbashi, Democratic Republic of the Congo, Baloji centers resource extraction as a through line across historical periods. The mineral-rich lands of the Congo have long been a draw for colonial powers, from Belgian control between 1908 and 1960 to the current neocolonial influence of capitalism as driven by the United States. Based on extensive archival research, Baloji's works bring to light the human element of resource extraction.

*Tales of the Copper Cross Garden: Episode 1* (2017), an installation created for Documenta 14, explores the role of copper in the Congo. The valuable metal, which was and continues to be a major export of the region, made the Congo a prime candidate for resource extraction under Belgian colonial rule. The central film juxtaposes the current industrial fabrication of copper wire with a historical recording of the Singers of the Copper Cross, a boys' choir in Elizabethville (now Lubumbashi). The recording, produced in 1937, is hailed in an inscription pictured at the start of the film as "one of the most human, one of the most beautiful" artistic works ever created in Africa. The scuffed and age-worn vinyl plays atop the repetitive mechanical sounds of the copper foundry, at times blending with the whirring machinery until the ecclesiastical chant of the Kyrie and other elements of the mass are in indistinguishable harmony with the sounds of production. Opposite the film, a large reproduction of a photograph shows choirboys wearing church robes and large Katanga crosses: copper crosses of Saint Andrew, utilized historically both ceremonially and as currency.[1]

This juxtaposition of modern industry with historical references is central to Baloji's work; his practice spans centuries, collapsing the colonial past into the current day. At its heart is a desire to uncover histories not told by the mainstream, pieced together from dissociated scraps held in colonial archives.[2] By reshaping a history first told through a colonial lens, Baloji creates space for the nuances of local histories to form over and around it. (LRL)

1 "Tales of the Copper Cross Garden: Episode I," Twenty Nine, http://twentyninestudio.net/research/tales-of-the-copper-cross-garden-episode-i.

2 Léopold Lambert and Caroline Honorien, "Colonial Extractivism and Epistemic Geologies in the Congo: A Conversation with Sammy Baloji," *The Funambulist*, no. 35 (May–June 2021): 28–35.

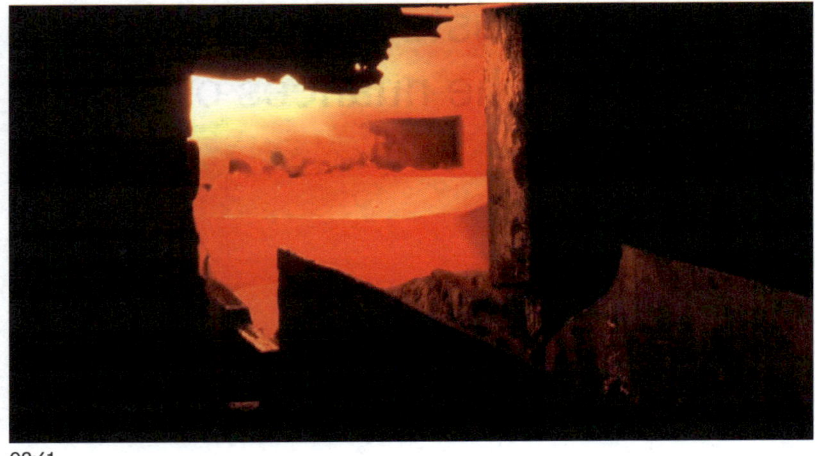
02:41

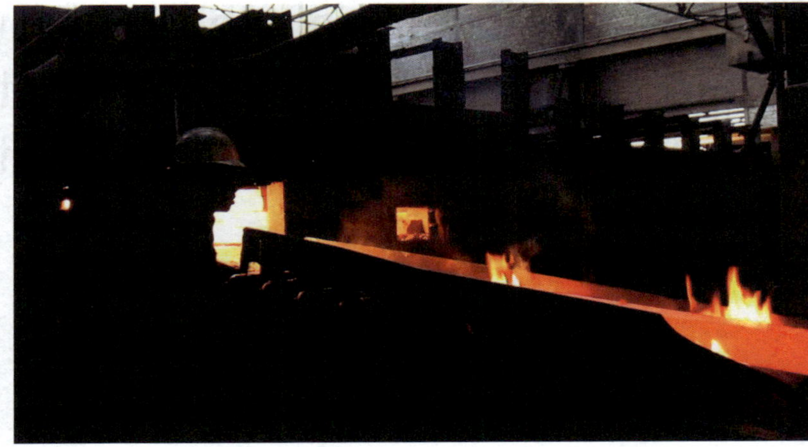
03:10

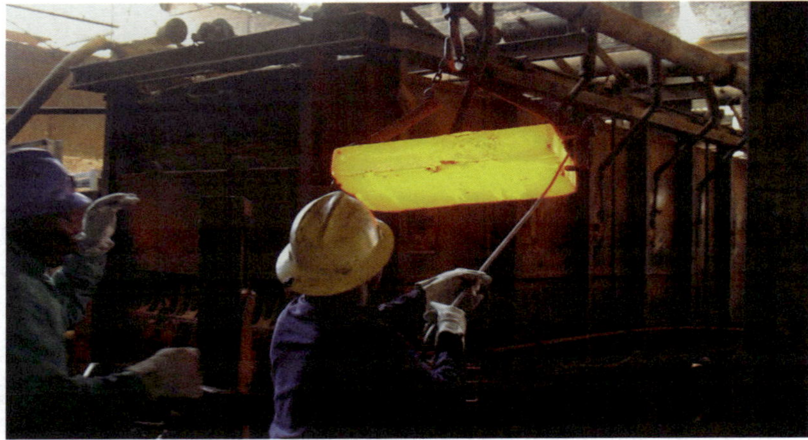
06:24

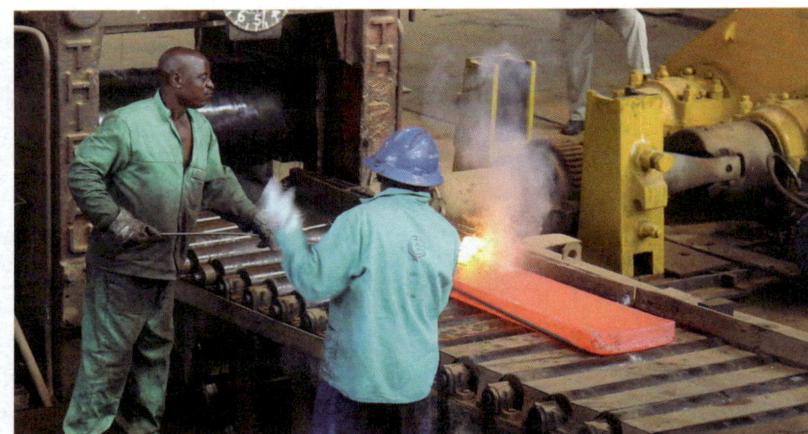
08:05

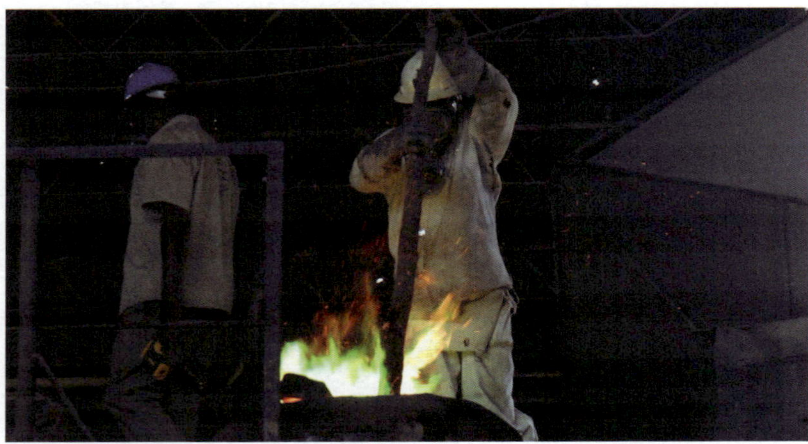
36:05

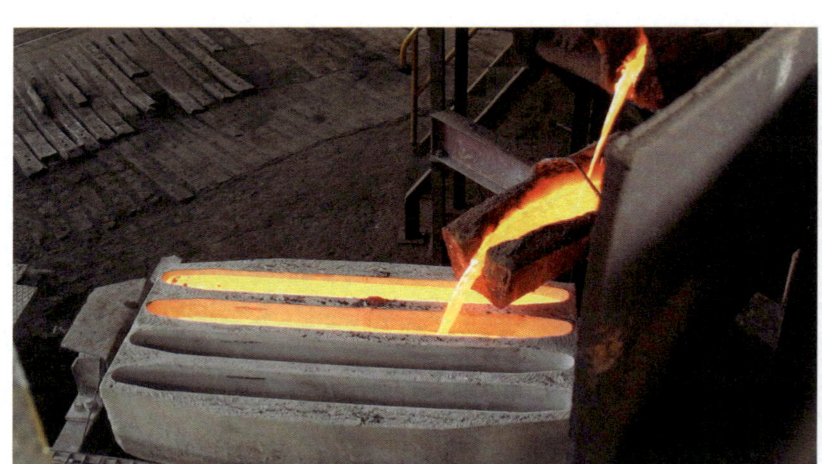
37:18

ROUNDTABLE Claire Bishop, Nicolás Guagnini, Rosario Güiraldes, and Cuauhtémoc Medina

A conversation between
Claire Bishop (CB)
Nicolás Guagnini (NG)
Rosario Güiraldes (RG)
Cuauhtémoc Medina (CM)

This roundtable took place via videoconference on April 1, 2024.

RG I wanted to give each of you an opportunity to talk about how the main ideas of this exhibition intersect with your work. Claire, I'd like to start with you. Your essay "Information Overload," published in the April 2023 issue of *Artforum*, was important to the conception of this exhibition.

CB Most of my art critical writing derives from a disconnect between my experience of art and its supporting discourse. In the case of the essay you mention, which I began writing around 2016, I was seeing research-based art in biennials, nonprofits, even Chelsea galleries. I was aware of a formal language being deployed: an aggregative structure with material in vitrines—ephemera, documents, texts, labeled images—and a preference for outmoded media. Much of it had an earnest, intellectual tone. Yet the discourse around this work tended to focus on the *subject matter* of each installation (its research topic), not on the visual strategies of display. At the same time, I became aware that my capacity to take in this kind of art was decreasing. Was my own capacity for attention reaching a limit, or was this a broader cultural condition?

I remembered experiencing research-driven, fragmented installation art in the 1990s and how excited and stimulated I was to piece together all the different elements. Twenty years later, I was primarily experiencing unease, even panic. Why was this? I understood that this change in visual literacy had to be connected to shifts in the attention economy over the last thirty years: the proliferation of the internet and digital media, the interminable streams of social media, the effort of having to visually block out ads and pop-ups, and the transformation of our news consumption from punctual to perpetual (the very word *feed* implies saturation and bloating). In short, the way in which we were reading outside the gallery was affecting how we came to read art inside the gallery. And this wasn't just in the art—it was the curatorial wall texts too.

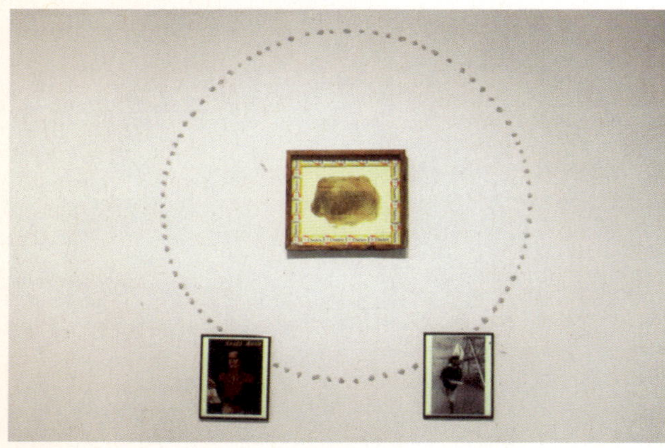

10.1

NG When I started making art in 1977, I was eleven, and the requirement for being an artist was to learn how to draw. When I started teaching art in the early aughts at Barnard College at Columbia University, the college's requirement was to be able to write a statement.

There has been a discursive shift. Artists must be able either to express what they want to do in an articulate manner or to clearly represent an identity that will replace that discourse and be easily discoursed by a third party in turn. So this is what brought me to both an understanding and a critique of the proposition implicit in the exhibition title *Ways of Knowing*.

In addition, my generation and the generations that preceded mine in Argentina were all modeled on the figure of Jorge Luis Borges, who was first and foremost a literary critic. I've grown up—like the Argentine artist Roberto Jacoby, like

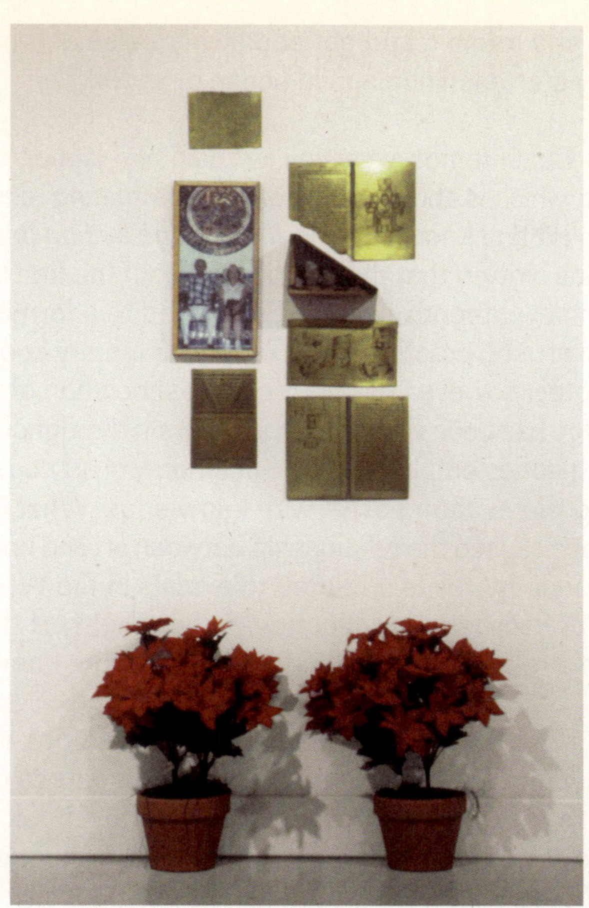

10.2

Dan Graham, and like many of the people who are my real or imaginary mentors—with the idea that galleries are not good. You have to open your own gallery. Criticism is not good. You have to write your own criticism. Pedagogy is not good. You have to make your own pedagogy. Perhaps because of Dan Graham's mentorship and his always-negative relationship to sociology, in the past decade or so, I've been increasingly more interested in anthropology as a discipline that has to deal with the entwined problem of otherness and knowledge.

CM The way I became a curator included my total surprise when I started working with Luis Camnitzer (figs. 10.1, 10.2) and learned that artists could actually get involved in extremely detailed research. Being an outsider to the art world and learning that artworks like Francis Alÿs's *Fabiola Project* (fig. 10.3) could involve even rudimentary research not only convinced me to continue in this field but also made me understand that I could be useful. It was the fact that there was a certain proper production of knowledge and a challenging of stereotypes and a questioning of myths that convinced me to stay in this field. And it really had to do with the potential of installation art as a space of study and examining and viewing.

I still understand the exhibition space as a space of thinking and reading, a part of seeing and feeling. In a certain way, I am absolutely culpable of having an intellectualized bias toward what I work on as a curator. I've been working for a decade for a contemporary art museum that is also part of the Universidad Nacional Autónoma in Mexico City. Maybe that bias of trying to connect with practices that have a possibility of interaction with an academic community is also something that solidifies the tie between art and research.

I am totally guilty of what Claire is denouncing, but I'm going to try to introduce an alibi. I was recently reading a book by Xavier Nueno called *El arte del saber ligero: Una breve historia del exceso de información*.[1] The author demonstrates convincingly that the concern about the excess of information has existed since classical Roman times. There were real concerns about the proliferation of commentary that was part of the process of editing texts in the Renaissance in order to produce the canon of classical writing. Nueno demonstrates the ambivalence of the Enlightenment toward producing encyclopedias and dictionaries; scholars wanted to avoid creating an unending number of books. So it's a theme of Western thinking that there is a moment when we are not able to deal with the horrible weight of history. I agree with Claire that the fact that this particular daughter of conceptualism has become the most prevalent suggests either that it has to produce

Figs. 10.1, 10.2
Luis Camnitzer, *Los San Patricios*, 1992, photoetchings on brass, mixed media

1 Xavier Nueno, *El arte del saber ligero: Una breve historia del exceso de información* (Madrid: Siruela, 2023).

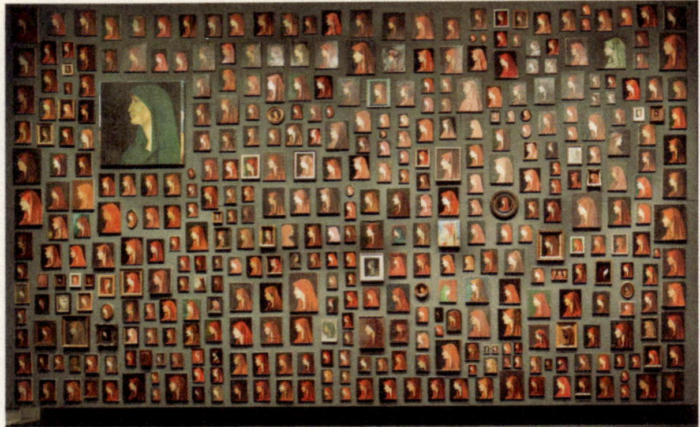

10.3

a canon and refine it and get somewhere else or that it will probably start instilling a mild sense of terror.

RG Cuauhtémoc, what you just said brings me to my next question, which is about the historically fluctuating relationship between art and knowledge. In *Knowledge beside Itself*, Tom Holert has written that the establishment of the first art academies in seventeenth-century Europe led to a formalization between artistic practice and scientific or literary knowledge.[2] As he notes, however, an overly close association of art with knowledge has been viewed with skepticism throughout history, with art theories emphasizing the autonomy of art consistently rejecting the equating of art with knowledge. What factors might have caused the relationship between art and knowledge to shift once more? Is it related to a crisis in the Western system of knowledge production? What might art teach us about this relationship and more broadly about knowledge?

NG That is the question. The big critical book on the futility and accumulation of knowledge is of course Gustave Flaubert's *Bouvard et Pécuchet* [1881]. In this book two middle-class clerks purport to synthesize all of human knowledge. They fail and come to ridiculous conclusions.

Claire's critique is unquestionable. It is impossible to absorb the quantity of information in much of today's research-based art. Cuauhtémoc proposes that it is a Western problem. He says that the very structure and nature of information itself is to be excessive and unknowable, but to Claire's point, there is a separation between knowledge and information. There is a threshold between these two fuzzy categories. There is a balance between what is valued as knowledge and what is not. How does that apply to an artwork? Is that the criteria for deciding what is a good artwork?

CB You can go around in circles trying to differentiate knowledge and information, and it's very tempting to do that. But I don't find it a useful exercise, because both terms are linchpins of a neoliberal knowledge economy. But I just want to pause and say that I'm worried that my essay reads like a denunciation, because I prefer it to be seen as a problematization!

I see the essay asking questions: How do spectators engage with the artistic presentation of information? What has happened to attention as a result of ubiquitous digitalization? How can artworks be mapped onto broader intellectual shifts, like the relationship to truth (which has done a U-turn from the 1990s, when it was denigrated by poststructuralism, to the 2010s, when it has been fully redeemed by the left in response to right-wing disinformation)? I'm less interested in denouncing contemporary art than in charting how artists' relationship to knowledge and information reflects intellectual shifts that show the entanglement of digital technology and capitalism more broadly.

Fig. 10.3
*Francis Alÿs: The Fabiola Project*, installation view, The Menil Collection, Houston, 2016–2018. Originally exhibited at Dia at the Hispanic Society of America, 2007–2008

One of the many post-COVID phenomena noticeable in contemporary art is an explosion of interest in alternative epistemologies. This has arisen in tandem with the rise of decolonization discourse and the perceived failures of Western enlightenment rationality. We see any number of exhibitions and performances fascinated with non-Western spirituality, with shamanism, with the ceremonial, the ritual, the esoteric, with healing and care, and many other "ways of knowing." Importantly, these practices prioritize embodiment and entrainment, rather than the verbal and the textual. All of which is to say that this decade is seeing yet another shift in the artistic relation to knowledge. This kind of neo-ancestralism signals the end of a certain phase of research-based art, which means that it's an interesting moment to be holding this exhibition and thinking about what lies ahead.

CM Contemporary art in institutional settings is currently providing space for a number of practices performed or produced by artists that would have been described as culture in a previous era rather than being artistic in a classical sense. That transformation relates to the fact that we have a change of participants in the art world. Aside from what Claire is describing quite accurately as a fascination with the idea of another epistemology outside of Western rationality, there is also the fact that we have different accounts of history coming from different minoritarian identities. These include participants from Native nations and gender-nonconforming identities, and these and many other voices are in conversation. The connection to the internet is key. A lot of artworks are processing contemporary anxieties. The complete crisis of the nation-state is a very important one. Others include the transformation of modern capitalism and the impact of technology on our ways of living, which is extreme. We cannot even pretend to underscore sufficiently how much and how quickly that's changing everything.

So what we have, borrowing from a concept I learned about from Adam Lerner, is a new salon. Adam was thinking about and activating through practice the idea that we are now doing something like the gatherings that French aristocrats would organize in the evening. You have people actually performing, talking, discussing, a formalized space for the circulation of ideas, images, and power. So rather than having the traditional viewer, the viewer of modernism, we have returned to a situation in which we are trying to evoke something like a society with participants carrying political positions and their own specific knowledges. There's a sense in which I feel that the art world or the art museum is akin to a refugee camp for forms of academic thinking that are not entirely legitimate in the university world. The art museum in particular is now occupying what used to be the space of the fine arts for these other interactions.

And in that sense it doesn't seem extravagant that forms of artistic practice characterized by trying to process information find accommodation in the museum as well. A lot of what artists do is to give an experiential character to these arid, sometimes hard-to-find speculative or blatantly unbelievable accounts. There is an attempt to produce a concrete experience on the basis of a history of art.

RG Claire, I wanted to ask you about installation art and how "Information Overload" and your thinking and previous writing are connected. In the essay you describe research-based art as an accumulation of materials—documents, ephemera, images, and especially large volumes of text—distributed spatially. And in this exhibition there are many discrete artworks and individual bodies of work in traditional mediums. There are series of photographs or drawings; there are moving-image works and large-scale installations. How did your writing on installation art inform your thinking about research-based art? Are they in fact one and the same? And then, following from that, do you think that works in traditional mediums are at odds with how you define research-based art?

CB My definition of installation art is quite simple: any gathering in a space of dispersed objects that come together as a single work. But the question of what constitutes an installation was already falling apart when I published my book in 2005.[3] The unity of installation art had been put under pressure by relational aesthetics and its openness to different temporalities and socialities. None of those artists were using the word *installation* to describe their work—everything was a *project*. Form was delayed and postponed rather than definitive and finalized.

You're right that I privilege installation as a mode of research-based art. Of course, there are more concise examples that have more discrete and unitary forms. But I wanted to underscore this genre's aggregative quality, its tendency toward modular repetition and excess, in order to more clearly elaborate the type of attention it elicits (skimming and sampling).

I ignore other types of research-based art too. I decided not to deal with the film essay, which is a significant avenue of this practice. One reason is because it already has a huge literature; another is because it's linear. By contrast, my argument about the historical emergence of research-based art centers on the shift from linearity (as seen in conceptual art and other serial modes, like photodocumentary) to the *rhizome*: the spatialization of visual materials for the viewer, which mirrors the rise of hyperlinking. One of my key examples is Renée Green's project *Import/Export Funk Office* (1992–1993; fig. 10.4).

2 Tom Holert, *Knowledge beside Itself: Contemporary Art's Epistemic Politics* (Berlin: Sternberg, 2020), 8.
3 Claire Bishop, *Installation Art: A Critical History* (New York: Routledge, 2005).

Fig. 10.4
Renée Green, *Import/ Export Funk Office*, 1992–1993, installation with audio, video, and reading materials

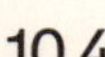

10.4

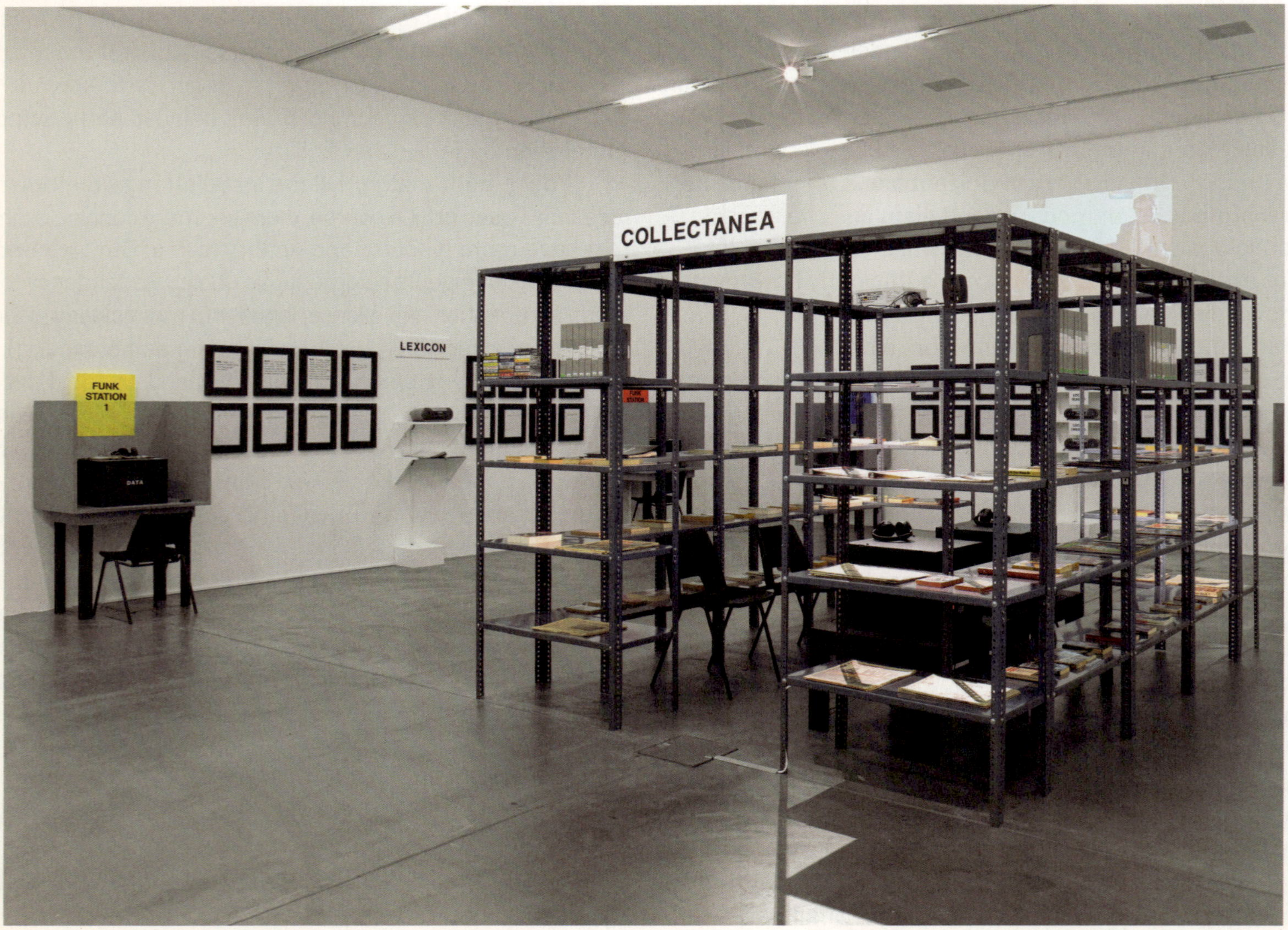

NG Cuauhtémoc did an incredible job of diagnosing how the public sphere and the counterpublic sphere have collapsed. He mentions the crisis of the nation-state, the destruction of the attention span, and the impact of technology. I would like to point out the existence of three fantasies that are linked to both the crisis of the nation-state and the crisis of democracy itself as a place where the public sphere will function in a way that we suppose the legacy institutions in which we exist—for example, the Walker Art Center, academia, or the gallery system—do.

The first thing I see is that the demand on freedom of expression is not viable in society because the salon that Cuauhtémoc mentions is a kaleidoscopic fractal salon. In the eighteenth-century salon, there were limited numbers of participants belonging to the aristocracy in a room. In the contemporary salon there are echo chambers that are global. That in turn creates a demand that the university realize democratic freedom of speech, and there's a demand that the museum realize the question of authentic experience.

Those two demands are fantasies. We have seen in the crisis of museums and universities that these demands made a concrete limit. And then there's the third fantasy, which is the fantasy of the Other outside the West, the fantasy of the original. The fantasy of otherness would be that there are original things and original peoples and original epistemologies that are completely outside the West and that we are going to find them and present them and that they have a level of truth that will provide us with an experience.

And thirty or forty years after Néstor García Canclini's notion of hybridity or Kenneth Frampton's ideas on architecture, we have Rosario's exhibition, in which perhaps the organizing principle for presenting this way of knowledge happens to be primarily a grid. I don't know that any form of knowledge consumption, distribution, and classification represents the West more than the grid. This is to point out that conversations will be a lot more fruitful if we don't think that there is an absolute other, that there will be an authentic experience, and that the university will actually provide freedom of expression. We should work perhaps with the reality of this collapse of the public sphere and the counterpublic sphere.

CM The difference between the public sphere and the salon is that in the salon freedom of speech is not applied in the same way. What is interesting about the salon is that there's a general rule that is beginning to fail in precisely dogmatic conversations, which is the idea of curiosity. So curiosity animates a lot of the works that are being considered, in the sense that they tend not to be so partisan or argumentative as others that Rosario could have chosen.

Another aspect that is interesting is that, I would argue, this exhibition is not a collection of identities; there's nothing of the fantasy of absolute otherness. There are moments of not even knowledge or specific knowledge coming through some of the works, but in reality there's no arguing outside of certain strategies or rules of art. Those are the elements of that modulated encounter. But my main point probably has to do with the feeling that the standards of these spaces are not to be defined by the ideas of liberal democracy. Because in the end the space of argumentation is not expected to lead to decision-making.

Our world is being reformed by the progressive demands coming from inclusivity and the #MeToo movement. The museum world, particularly in the United States, feels very advanced in relation to other institutions. Until now, beyond the demands for fairness and representation, for changing the outlook of institutions and their staffs, there isn't a clear idea of where you want to get. Independent of that, I would argue that there is a sense in which the institution's change of outlook is moving a certain political sphere of representation. And there has been an effect in that regard. So maybe I'm basically saying, yes, there's no total freedom of representation, of speech, but nonetheless there's a certain attempt not to rule in a partisan sense.

RG As you were talking, Cuauhtémoc, I was thinking two things. The first relates to representation. In the script of the work of Cabello/Carceller, there's a moment when one of the characters talks about this moment of overrepresentation and whether we need to overrepresent ourselves within institutions, because we're talking about how, as you were just saying, our world, and specifically our arts institutions, are being reconfigured.

Of course, starting to think about this emphasis on research as a methodology of artistic practice led me to think about its roots as a practice that was so entangled with the colonial project and with colonial expansion and imperialism. The Maori educator Linda Tuhiwai Smith wrote a seminal book in which she discusses a shared sentiment among Indigenous communities that *research* is the dirtiest word there has ever been.[4] And so that needs somehow to be wrestled with. What does it mean and how does that history inform our discussion?

The artists whose work is included in the show hail from all over the world, and they aren't exclusively Western artists. Nevertheless, the concept of research consistently came up as a method or practice, even as their approaches to research differ. I'm interested in what it means in relation to reclaiming a term that is burdened with colonial historical baggage. So I wanted to think about this question of counterresearch. How might a notion of counterresearch help us think about some of the artworks or practices represented in the exhibition?

4 Linda Tuhiwai Smith, *Decolonizing Methodologies: Research and Indigenous Peoples* (London: Zed; Dunedin, New Zealand: University of Otago Press, 1999), 1.

CM Cabello/Carceller's video about Erauso (pp. 184–197) is in my view a masterpiece of a certain genre. The work has two screens, which create a diptych. This form addresses the question of the grid. They are alluding to the idea of a polyptych. And then they are also suggesting the duplicity of the narrative that goes from the past to the present and then to the future. If we are going to talk about the demand of research in art, this will involve challenging academic knowledge and other established forms of knowledge. In Cabello/Carceller's work, the viewer is challenged to learn through modes of historical thinking that are extremely innovative and demanding. The artists raise these questions: What is the relationship between gender and postcolonial histories? What is the condition of gender history? What does it mean to bring research outside the expectations of academia, of distance?

Smith's book is extremely important, and there is a serious concern with research and its relationship to colonialism and imperialism and capitalism. It is true that research is power, but it's also a modality of the powers to be. She's not advocating for the elimination of research; she's trying to open Indigenous research or bicultural research or at least research that is made in relation to the needs and the positions of Indigenous communities. As a Maori, she's right in bringing up the question of the necessary bias of research.

10.5

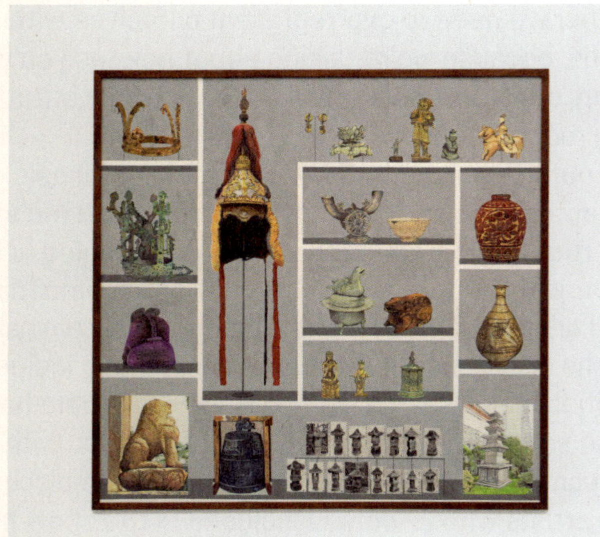

Many of the works in the show touch on something that I would call supplementary research. In the case of Gala Porras-Kim, there is a certain body of knowledge and a tradition of scientific archaeology, and she develops methodologies that are parasitic and that extend and disarm those archaeological arguments and modes of representation and produce a different set of representations (figs. 10.5–10.7). So the production of that second narrative is the actual knowledge product. She's not content to just be critical in the sense of looking at the possible failures of existing research. She adds something that actually goes in the line of Bouvard and Pécuchet's useless effort. There's a certain idea that the accumulation of knowledge can be supplemented so as to turn it in a different direction. And that is probably a way to address the idea of information overload.

10.6

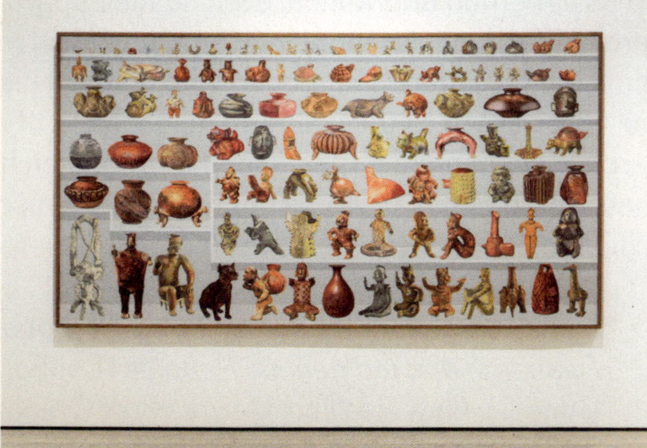

NG To taxonomize, again, Cuauhtémoc's discourse: he speaks of the "supplementary" and the "parasitic." Those are both cousins and functions of hybridity. Without the hybrid, those two ideas wouldn't exist. I think that work like Porras-Kim's is post-Western art. The work is predicated not only on a grid but also on the mastery of realistic representation in Western terms. As Cuauhtémoc said, these are politically oriented toward a notion of inclusion and—this is a forbidden Hegelian term—*progress*. Art can provide a model for things, and what you're describing—supplementary, parasitic—implies an absorption, a reabsorption, regurgitation, or, if you will, a digestion of the West.

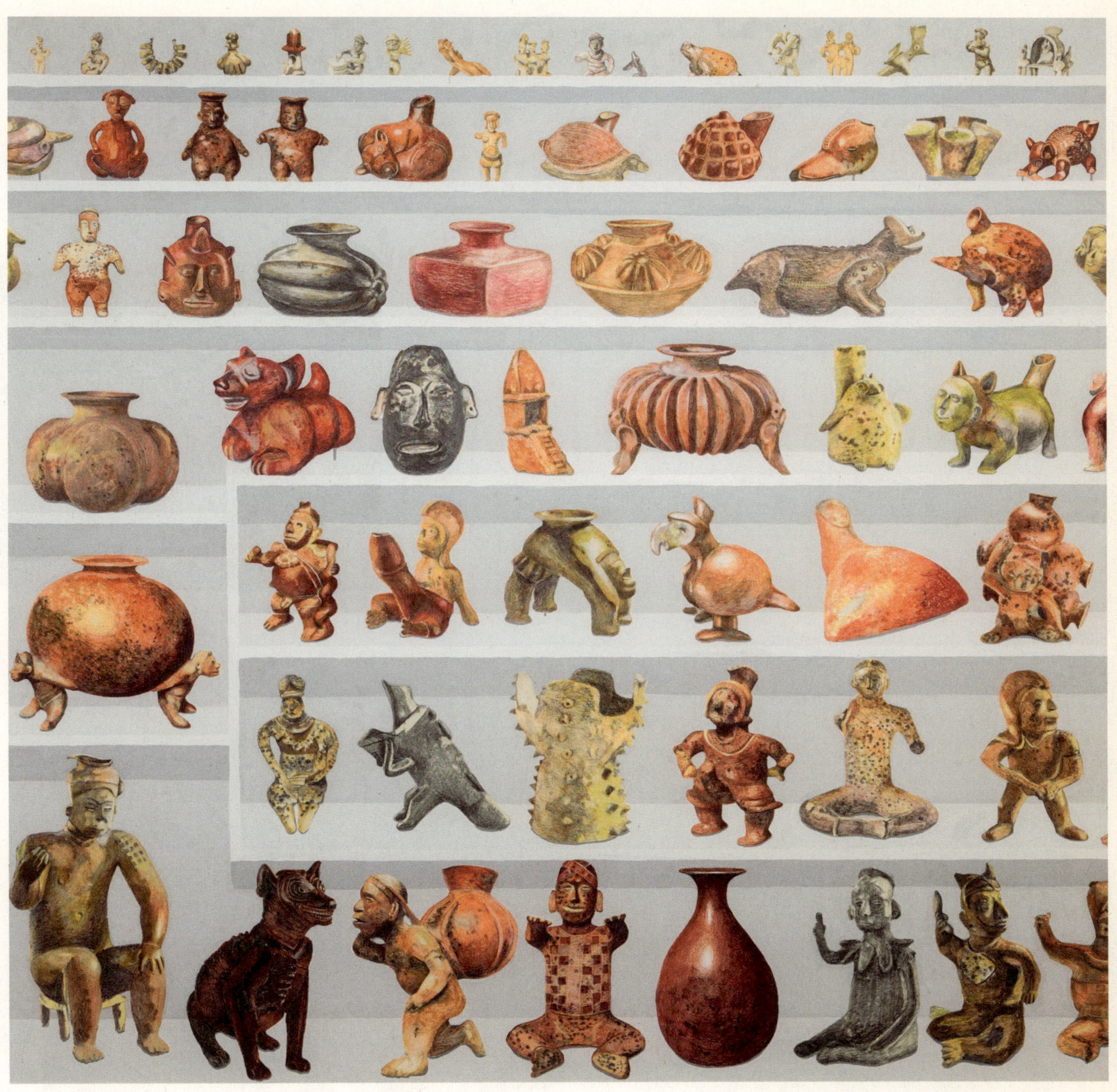

10.7

Fig. 10.5
Gala Porras-Kim, *37 Uprooted Artifacts*, 2023, colored pencil and Flashe on paper

Figs. 10.6, 10.7 (detail)
Gala Porras-Kim, *109 west Mexico ceramics from the LACMA collection: Colima Index*, 2017, graphite, colored pencil, and ink on paper mounted on canvas with mahogany artist's frame

Figs. 10.8, 10.9
Walid Raad, *Two Drops per Heartbeat*, 2021, performance at Museo Nacional Thyssen-Bornemisza, Madrid

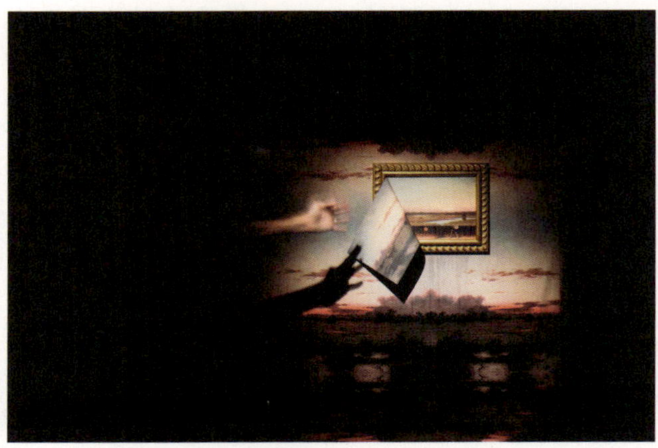

10.8

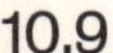

10.9

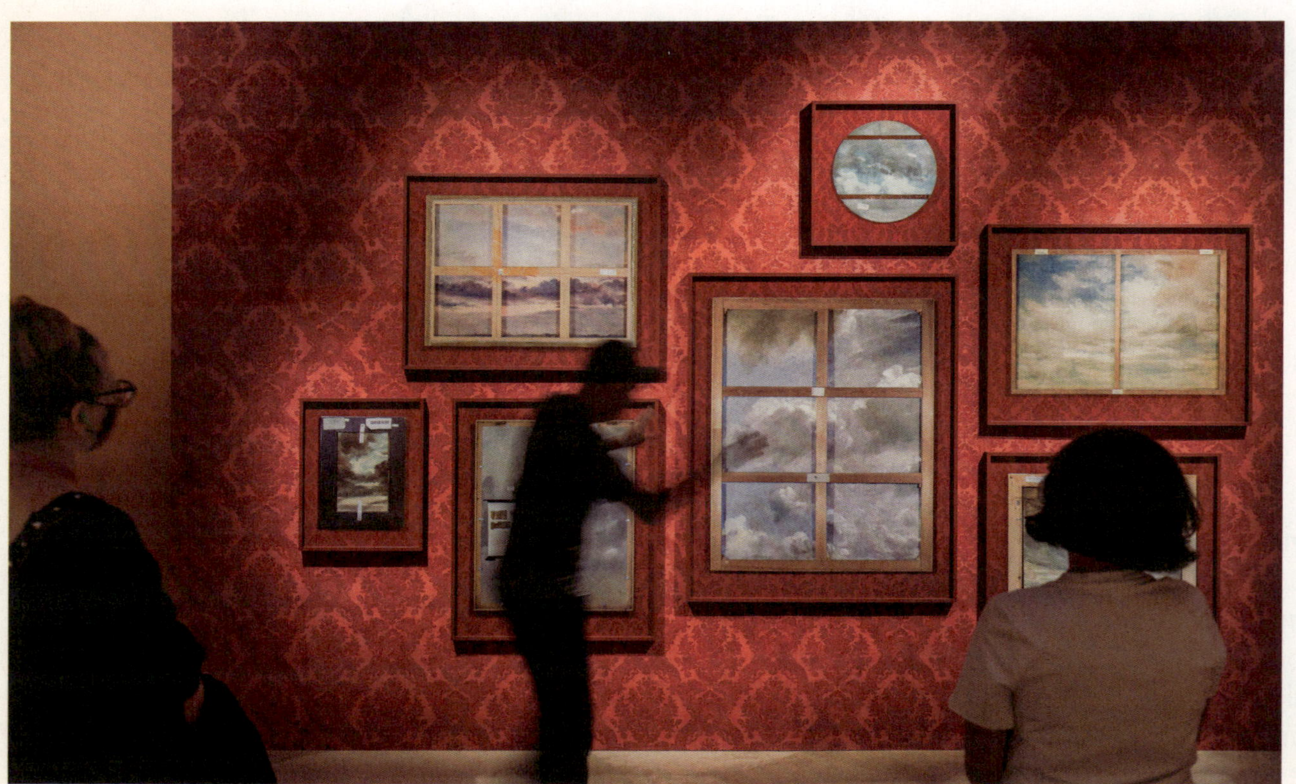

I think what Rosario has identified, in the way curators do, is maybe a repurposing of the absurdity that Claire identified in research-based art. In many ways Claire opens a discussion and says, "Well, this is good for nothing." Your essay is critical, Claire, let's make no mistake about it. Rosario's exhibition argues in response, "Wait, there's research-based art that actually does something or tries to do something."

RG I was excited to think of the show as a way to try to answer that call, to wrestle with those arguments. And that led me to necessarily be kind of partial in the kind of work I decided to look at. To me it also represented a departure from interventionist work, like that of Forensic Architecture (figs. 10.12–10.14). I was interested in thinking about that other kind of work that is embedded and that results from a variable relationship of the artist to a subject matter or a territory or a history but that was not necessarily trying to intervene. But I wanted to continue with a question about evaluation and quality. I think that becomes important because in a way, Claire, I've taken your essay as sort of arguing for what's good research-based art and what isn't and how we ground that kind of evaluation. It's probably a question that doesn't have an answer. But do we have a more or less objective way of judging? And what kind of criteria do we have to judge research-based art?

CB I would say I'm no longer in the business of providing criteria and allocating value judgments. I'm more interested in asking questions: Why has this kind of work taken the forms that it has taken? What do these developments tell us about culture more broadly? In what ways are they symptomatic? Of course, at the end of the essay I gesture toward some practices that I find more interesting or that run counter to the norm. This is because diagnosis alone can be unsatisfying and it's helpful to rise to the challenge of redemption! My own personal gauge, which I don't expect to apply to anybody else, is whether the work moves me. Can it move beyond the cerebral and the intellectual and connect me to something larger than myself? I also appreciate metabolization: research that has gone through lived experience rather than being cut-and-pasted into a vitrine or a shelf of further reading.

Last summer I saw Walid Raad's lecture-performance at Hamburger Kunsthalle, which on paper didn't sound promising: an investigation of the Thyssen-Bornemisza collection and its relationship to the Hamburg museum (figs. 10.8, 10.9).[5] But by the end I was in tears. Walid managed to take a dry research topic and turn it into a metaphysics of seeing and believing, combining the preposterous with the political: self-restoring angels, the financialization of weather data, gremlins in Hudson River School paintings, insects that swarm around goblets, shady art collectors controlling US foreign policy.

I try to write from a position of fidelity to my response while in the work, even if I don't understand it immediately. Everyone has different criteria and will be affected by different things, but I think there's a value in articulating these differences.

When Nic mentioned the prevalence of the grid, it does make me wonder if artists are just making minor variations on well-established moves. It makes me think of artists who value the embodied as a counterpoint to the virtual. I recently attended a sound bath by Guadalupe Maravilla that offered a physiological, vibroacoustic way of knowing—entirely bypassing cerebral taxonomies and the optical (figs. 10.10, 10.11).

RG On the question of the grid and taxonomy and the structured way of organizing information, the process led me to ask, OK, if we want to realize an exhibition about research-based art, what is a more universally accepted common ground around the representation and organization of knowledge and artifacts? I was interested in the idea that some artists are sort of reappropriating established conventions of categorization like taxonomies. And I felt that this would be a way into trying to find some common ground also with viewers and with an audience that is coming to this without necessarily being immersed in these ideas.

But with what you're touching upon with Guadalupe Maravilla, that is where, for instance, I come back to the ideas of Linda Tuhiwai Smith and the sense that there are ways of knowing that haven't been universally accepted, especially by the Western world. What is that experience? It cannot be canonized academic knowledge. It's something else. And there's a unique way in which artists can make that point come across, move you to tears, give you a different kind of experience in your body with a sound bath. And I think that I've simply tried to organize some of those different modalities. And some of them perhaps necessarily had to have this more legible, formal way of presenting themselves.

CM One thing that we need to keep affirming is the idea that there are mileposts, there are certain works or certain moments that redefined the root entirely, that actually made it very difficult to just reestablish the same arguments that we used before. And I tend to believe that Forensic Architecture has done that. What was impressive when we made the project on Ayotzinapa (fig. 10.12) is that because it was made entirely with a device that was foreign to the aesthetics of empathy, the impact was huge.[6] And I mean

5 Walid Raad, *Cotton under My Feet: The Hamburg Chapter*, Hamburger Kunsthalle, August 10–November 12, 2023, https://www.hamburger-kunsthalle.de/en/exhibitions/walid-raad.

Figs. 10.10, 10.11
Healing sound bath performance as part of *Guadalupe Maravilla: Luz y fuerza*, Museum of Modern Art, New York, 2021

Figs. 10.12–10.14
*Forensic Architecture: Towards an Investigative Aesthetics*, installation views, Museo Universitario Arte Contemporáneo (MUAC), Mexico City, 2017

10.10
10.11

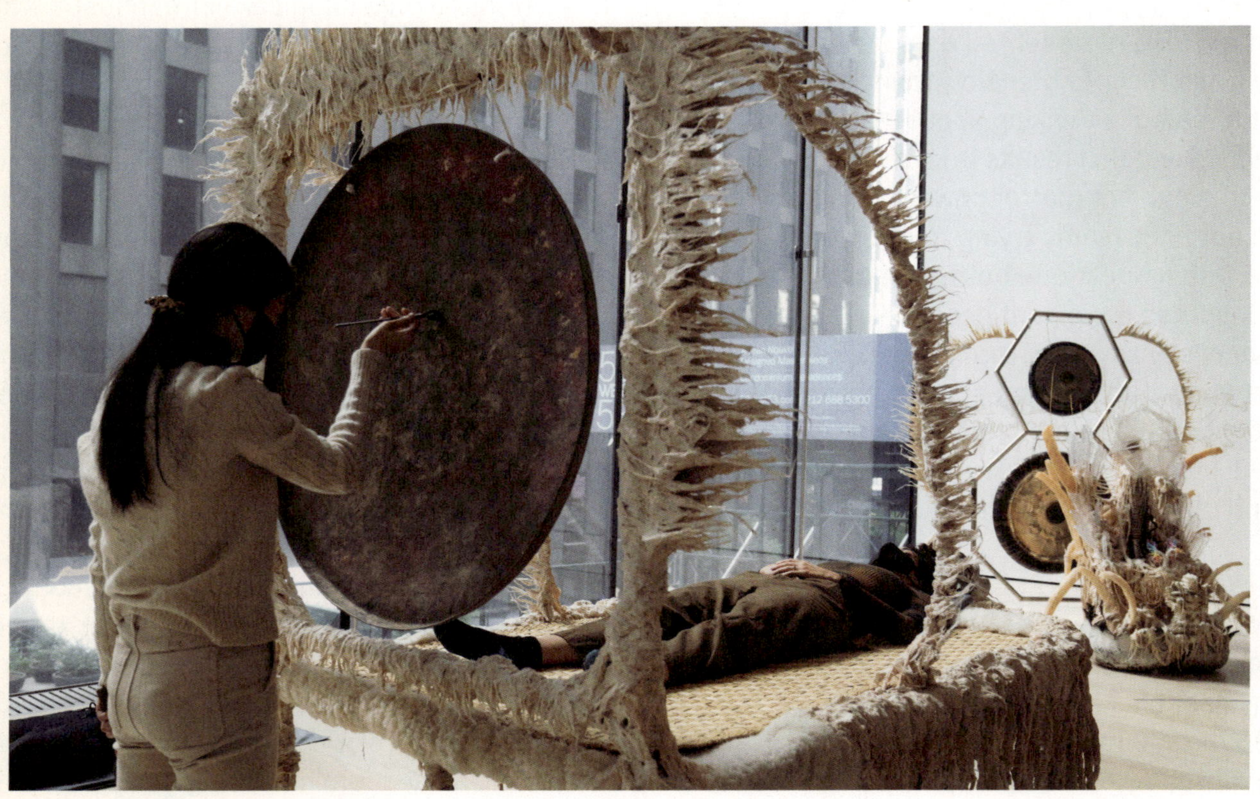

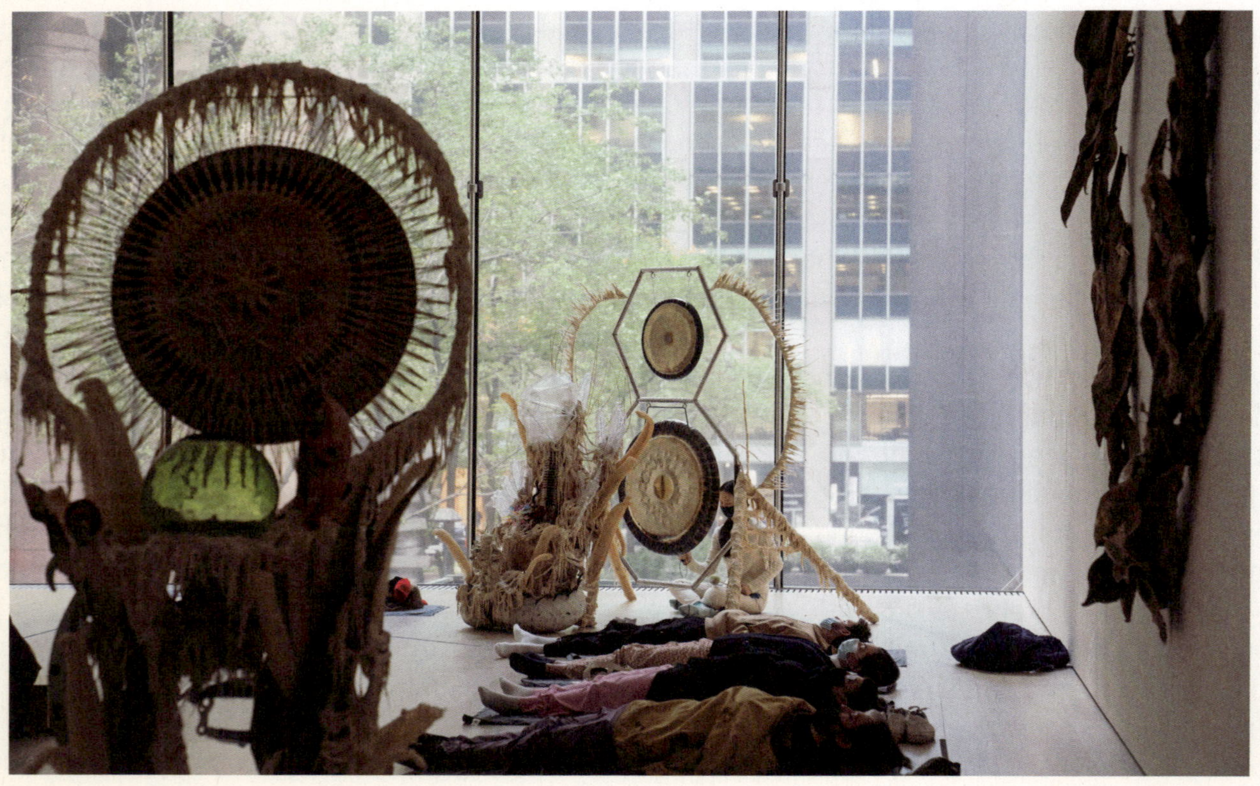

that the criteria here are not so much about the social impact but just the idea that you would challenge the aesthetics in a specific field. And suddenly something that was alien—like this very dry, scientific order of exposition—lent it not only authority but also a certain immediate utility that most of the other works that have tried to engage with the spectator couldn't make any longer, like an argument that was beyond any avoidance. In this case—let me be very specific—Forensic Architecture demonstrated convincingly that the Mexican army was informed and participated in the events step by step.

Forensic Architecture has really changed our notion of what we expect from media. They've been copied formally by the corporate media. So that confronts us with a very peculiar situation because I understand that it is possible that occasionally artworks will become effective in the general information sphere.

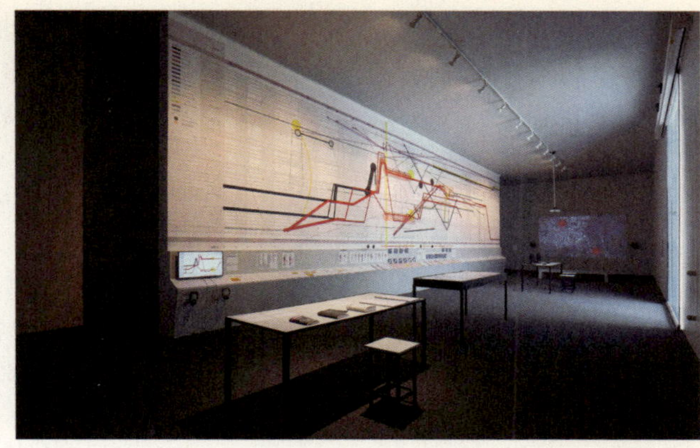

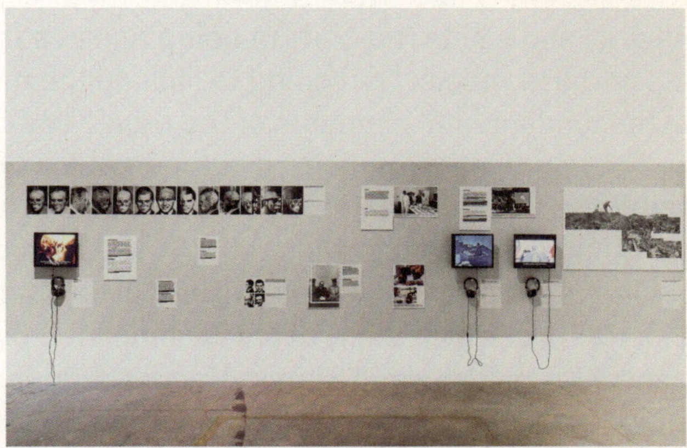

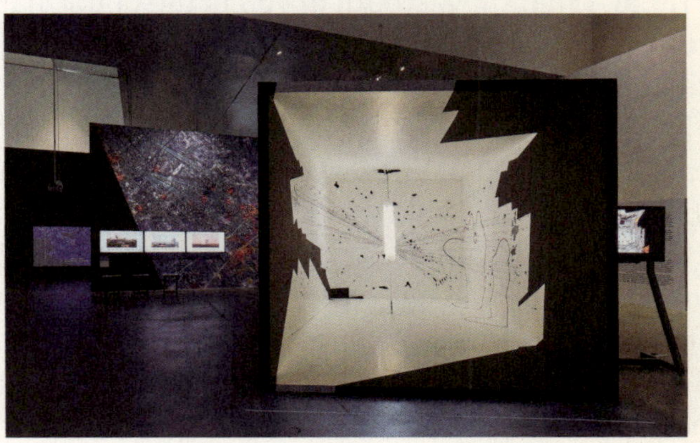

RG What you're saying is leading me to want to follow up with a question about spectatorship. I think you and Claire come from different understandings of who is the subject and the viewer of art. So can each of you talk about your conceptions of spectatorship and how they inform your perspectives?

CM Claire will be better at this, but when I read Claire or other people, it's not that I feel that they have a conception of spectatorship; they're reporting on concepts of spectatorship that are in the works. We need to go back to reread Brian O'Doherty because he is in a sense the author of the concept of the difference between the viewer and the spectator in that regard.[7] And I believe it is entirely logical that when the installation art moment became central, these
spectators that O'Doherty had dealt with in Minimalism also 10.12
became knowing spectators. But I guess that we all agree 10.13
that occasionally what we have is not the spectator or the 10.14
viewer but a combination of the citizen, the policeman, the victims, and the lawyers.

CB OK, I do not have a theory of spectatorship beyond saying that I think spectators are always human. I'm not a posthumanist or animist who imagines various nonhuman actors to be the spectators of art—at least, not yet. As Cuauhtémoc says, each work of art generates a model of spectatorship. Each work assumes a spectator who will

6 Forensic Architecture, *The Enforced Disappearance of the Ayotzinapa Students*, https://forensic-architecture.org/investigation/the-enforced-disappearance-of-the-ayotzinapa-students.

7 Brian O'Doherty, "The Eye and the Spectator," part 2 of *Inside the White Cube: The Ideology of the Gallery Space* (Santa Monica, CA: Lapis Press, 1986), 35–64.

attend to it in some way. Each work sets up a relationship to its audience. In my latest book, I've shifted from thinking about the "spectator," which is always a model of the *subject* gazing at an *object*, to thinking about attention, which is more relational, in the space between viewers and the work.[8]

NG Claire, I'm going to go back to this question of the ritual and your experience in the Guadalupe Maravilla sound bath. We could talk about this, for instance, in relation to the development of Latin American modernism. When Joaquín Torres-García comes back from Europe and says: "OK, we have the grid, and inside the grid I'm going to place the elements of these rituals. I am going to include the man, the sun, the fundamental elements of the ritual." We can talk about the production of modern autonomous artworks under the pressure of those knowledges and those rituals, particularly and especially synthesized in Neo-Concretism, in Lygia Clark's *Objetos sensoriais* (Sensorial objects; figs. 10.15, 10.16), in which the artwork is completed by the participant. We could describe Latin American modernism as the autonomous object developed under the pressure of the ritual. What moves both of you is the confirmation of a truth. For Cuauhtémoc, the reason why this Forensic Architecture piece is moving is that we all know that the army did it. Nobody doubts that the army did it. In general terms, Mexican society kind of knows that the army did it. But if somebody comes and tells you, "It is the truth; it was the army," we can confirm that it is the truth. And if you, Claire, can go to the ritual and say, "Yes, it is my body; I need the healing," it is there.

There is a connection between the need for the truth and the experience, that the experience relieves us from seeking the truth in information. It's the one moment when we can find that we don't have to make the enormous effort to decide whether it is this or that or that or that or that. But I see that we are today in an inverse trajectory in which we don't need to derive a set of theories and objects from the ritual and the experience. Rather we're trying to get rid of those objects and theories to get back to the direct experience. I'm not sure that's inherently good.

CM I wouldn't necessarily characterize the drive of the artists and their spectators as a search for the truth. I would say that they are all on journeys that need to be accounted for. One that is important in the sense of this spatial display is the notion of a need for evidence, material evidence. I guess one important element of the way in which we experience the museum today is precisely that it is not the internet. It's not something that can just be fabricated with artificial intelligence. And that's going to pose a significant challenge in the future because again we are going to live in a world of images that are going to be entirely made up. And so the index is over. Welcome to whatever construction you want to make. And the second issue is not so much the journey of truth but the possibility of a reversal of the account.

And again some of the issues here are about when it is possible to actually grasp a certain complicated or dirty reality. And that has an importance in questions of coloniality, that you are never facing something clear. Everything is dirty. There's no argument that comes out without having to pay a certain lip service to violence.

And I would say that another thing that is still very important is that you should be able to step out from the official account. Now those are the same elements that produce the mentality of conspiratorial, paranoiac theories and narratives. I would argue that the fact that a lot of this work is very similar to fiction is something to be discussed. Much of what is wrong in the political sphere is coming from, again, the notion of expertise, the idea that citizens want to know, and the fact that they are able to enjoy the most complicated narratives without any limit or any need for proof. I take it for granted that there's a new narrative order. I imagine that Claire is also a little bit concerned about the fact that we are entering a twenty-first century made of a lot of narratives.

NG Cuauhtémoc, you have an incredible insight regarding the flip side of *Ways of Knowing* and Rosario's exhibition. The works have an analogous structure to conspiracy theories. I think that's a fundamental insight. And the reason why I say that is because we spent years and years talking to students and saying, "Read McLuhan, the medium is the message. Read Walter Benjamin." And then Donald Trump comes along and applies all these lessons masterfully with a phone, with a new medium. And I don't think it can be argued that the mastery of this new medium-as-message is in the hands of progressives in any way, shape, or form. I have yet to see a progressive gaining power tweeting or governing by Twitter. The replacement of reason by affect is one of the effects of the use of technology, and I think the far right has a monopoly on the use of media for that right now. Hopefully this changes, but I think Cuauhtémoc has an insight that truly transcends our field.

CB Right. But also it's not only the new medium that is being exploited but an appeal to the past and to the spiritual and the religious. Trump is now ending rallies with prayer, in a direct appeal to evangelical Christians. He is weaponizing the same kind of trans-individual fervor that is mobilizing artists to look to ritual and ceremony—albeit for quite different ends.

NG At the iconographic level—Celtic iconography, Masonic iconography, Viking iconography, alchemical

8 Claire Bishop, *Disordered Attention: How We Look at Art and Performance Today* (London: Verso, 2024).

Fig. 10.15
Lygia Clark, *Diálogo: Óculos* (Dialogue: Goggles), 1968, custom goggles

Fig. 10.16
Lygia Clark, *O eu e o tu* (The I and the you), 1967, cloth, body

10.15

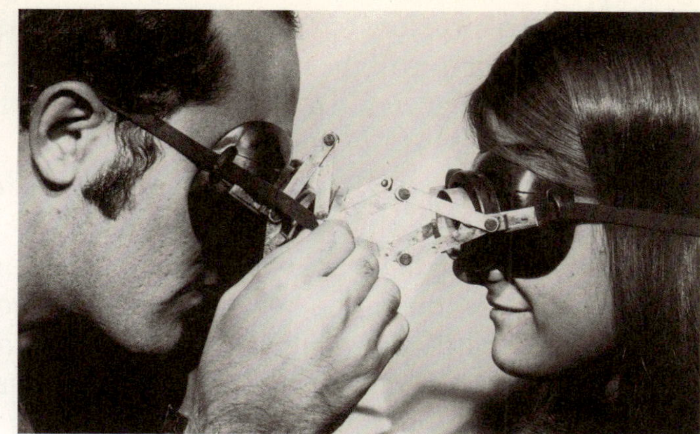

10.16

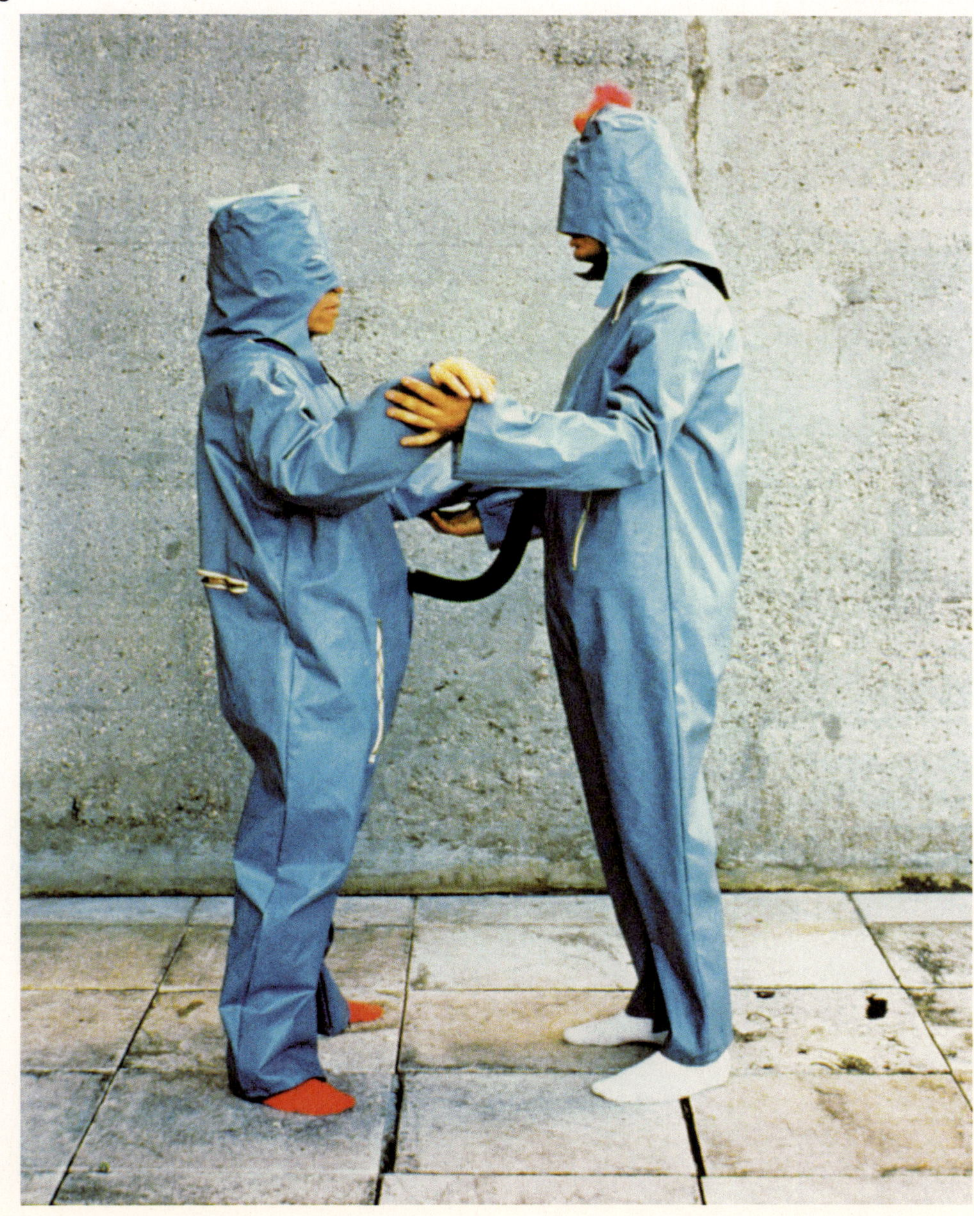

iconography—all this has been taken over by the far right. So the idea that the structure of the conspiracy theory is analogous to the structure of the work of some forward-thinking contemporary artists is a very important insight.

CM I guess I should quote my favorite saying by the late Carlos Monsiváis, which was, "Either I don't understand what is happening or what I understand has already happened." Yeah, welcome to the new world. And I guess that one important thing we need to say is that we are going to have to walk through it without any map. I learned that maps haven't gotten us too far. And yeah, it's scary, it's exciting. Luckily the most important problems are not going to be addressed by our generation.

CB Yes, there is also AI, which I see as the big threat on the horizon. The informatization of daily life—be this through data and metrics or tips and hacks—all of this is going to be upended by the dubious truth value of AI-generated images and text. It's going to throw another wrench into the itinerary of truth, knowledge, and research (which I see as intertwined terms). AI will be the problem of our decade, and perhaps many decades to come. We will see how artists react. At best, perhaps, we can hope for new modes of sensory, embodied, and nonvirtual work or an emphasis on haptic, material spaces and social relations. But we can't really predict what artistic backlashes to AI-generated images and knowledge will be.

NG For the time being, it's text-based. Whoever can write the best prompt will end up with the best image for now. It still depends on the text, but this will change tonight probably.

CB And Duchamp wrote good texts.

CABELLO/CARCELLER *Una voz para Erauso. Epílogo para un tiempo trans* (A voice for Erauso. Epilogue for a trans time), 2021–2022, two-channel 4K video transferred to HD video (color, sound), 28:15 min., courtesy the artists, Madrid

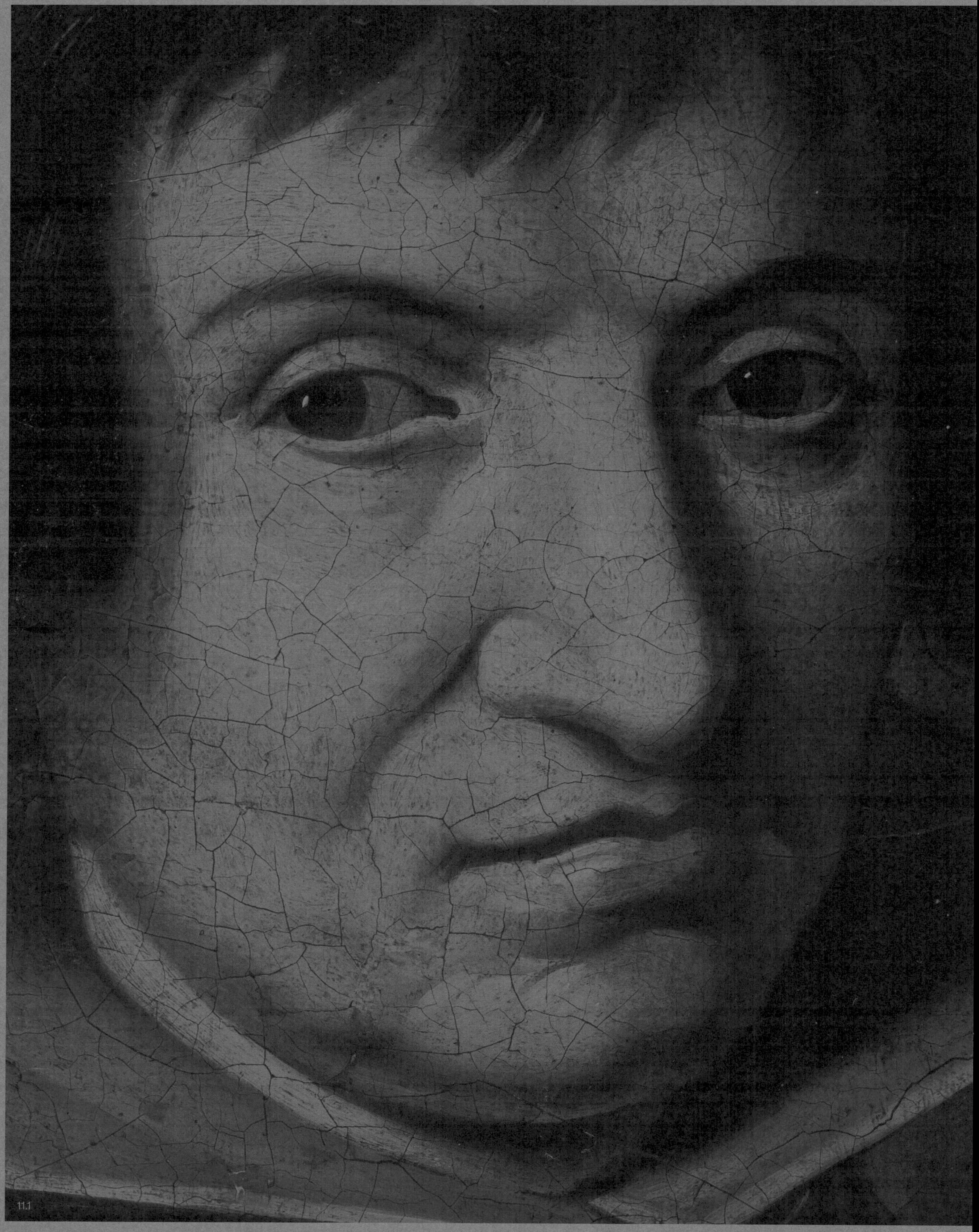

11.1

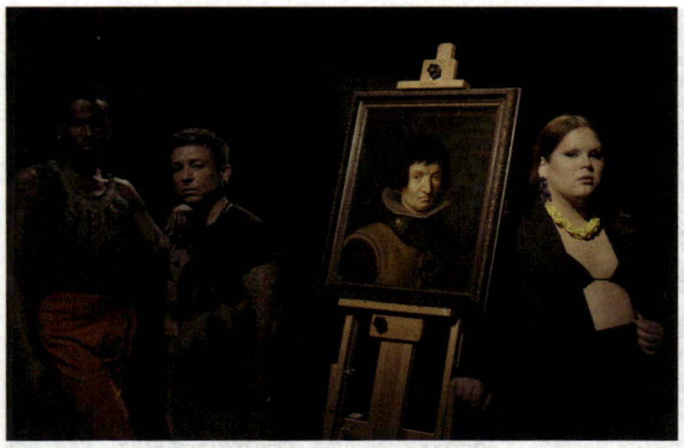

23:46

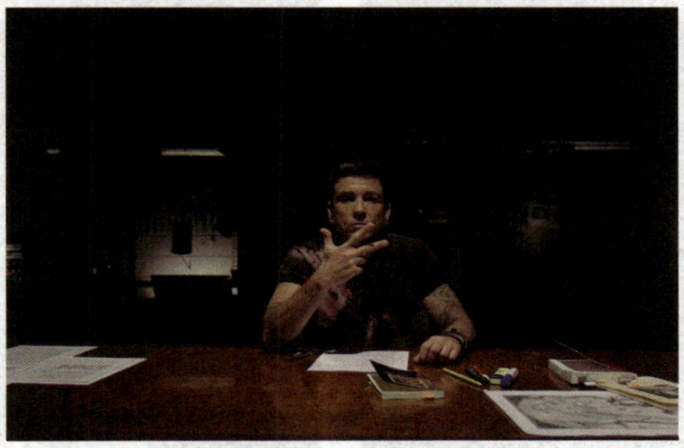

01:56

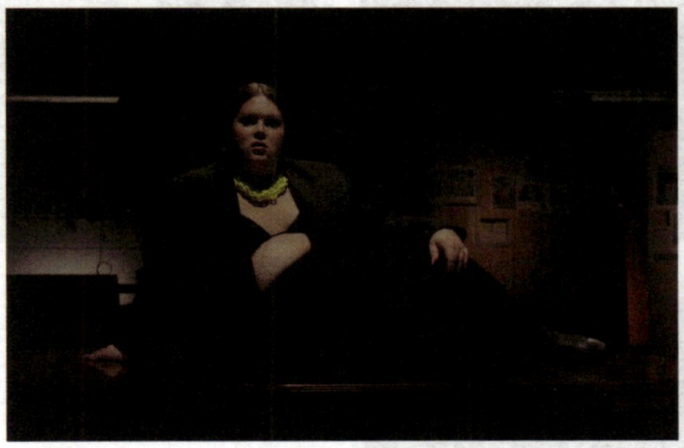

20:22

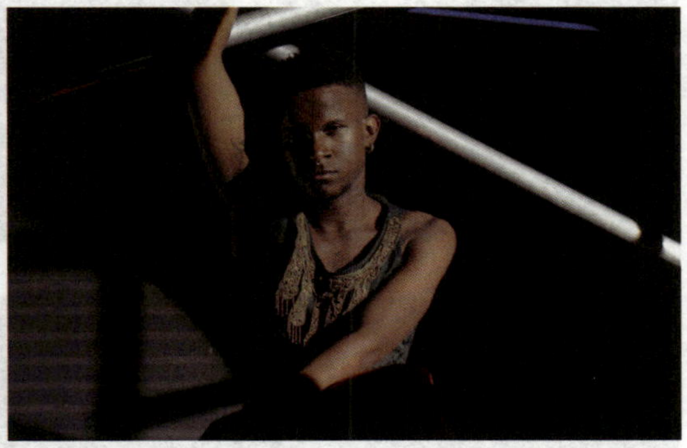

11:05

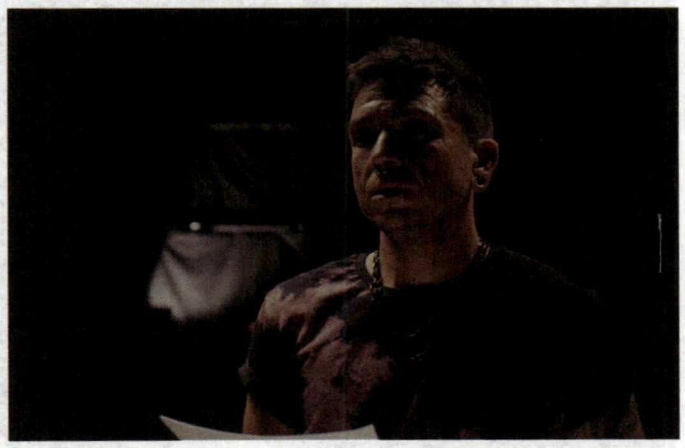

03:10

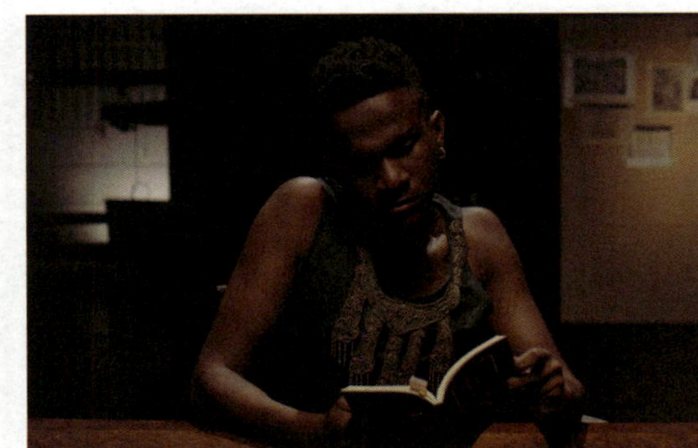

13:09

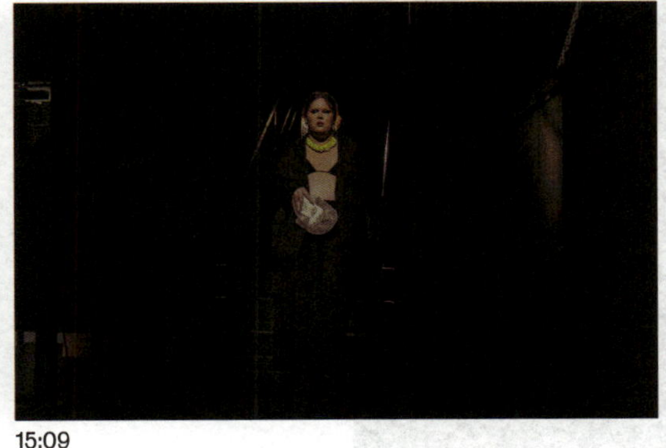

15:09

Stills from *Una voz para Erauso. Epilogo para un tiempo trans*, 2021–2022 11.2

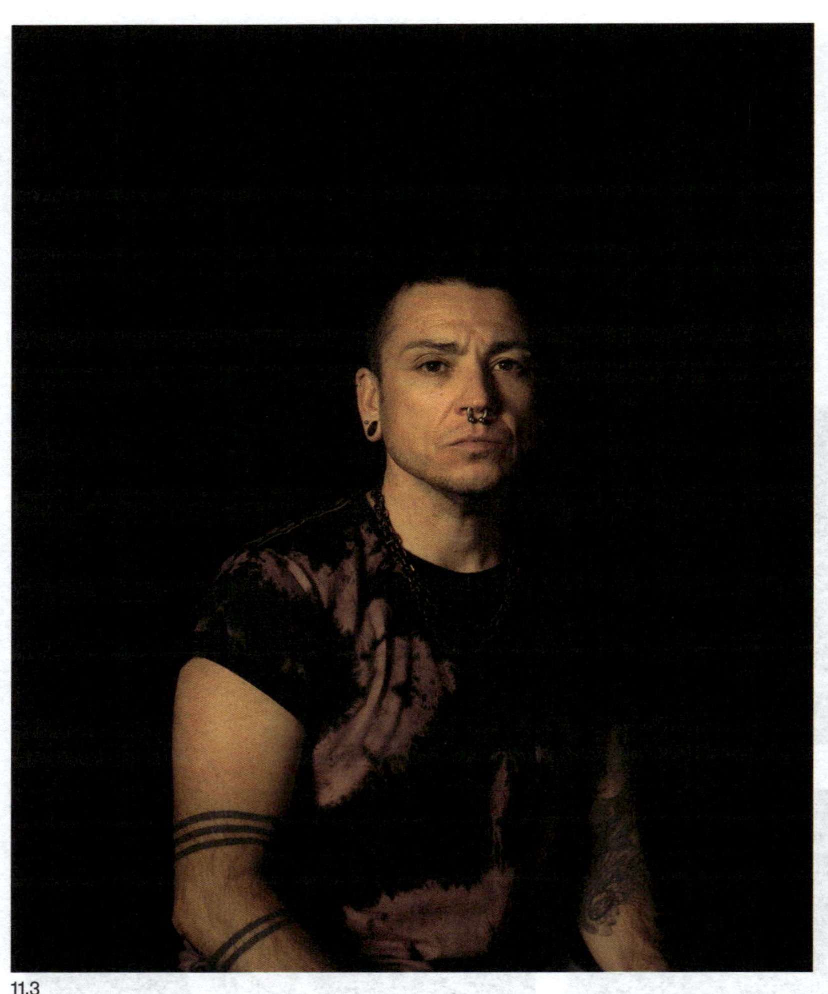

11.3

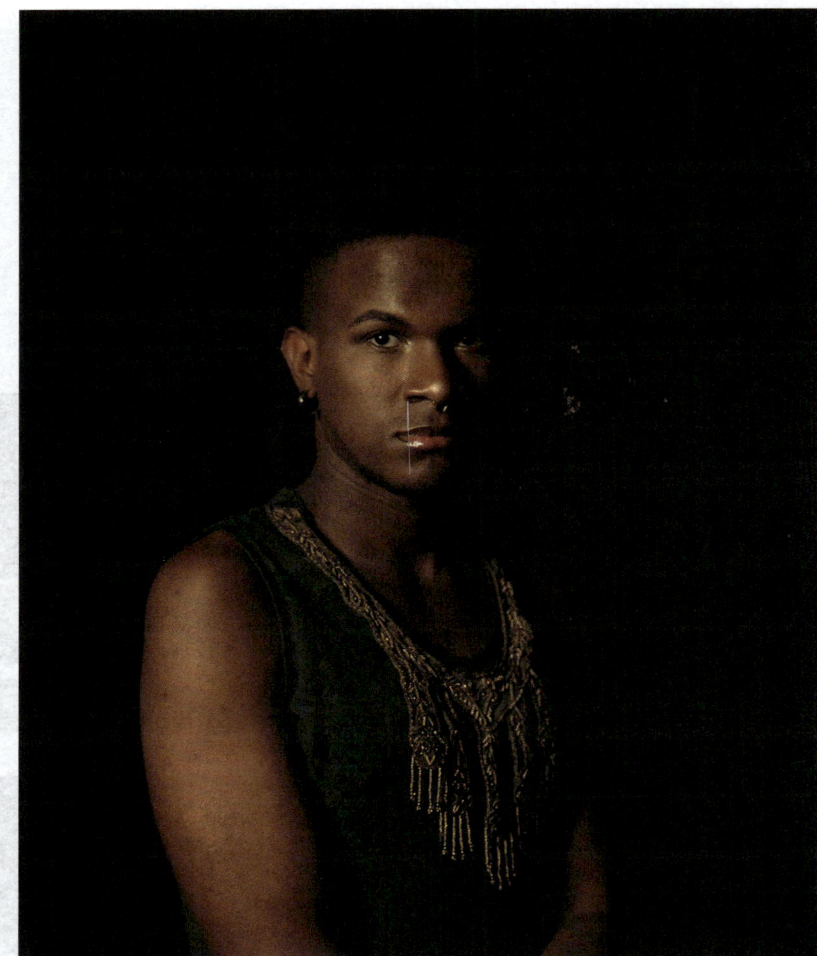

11.4

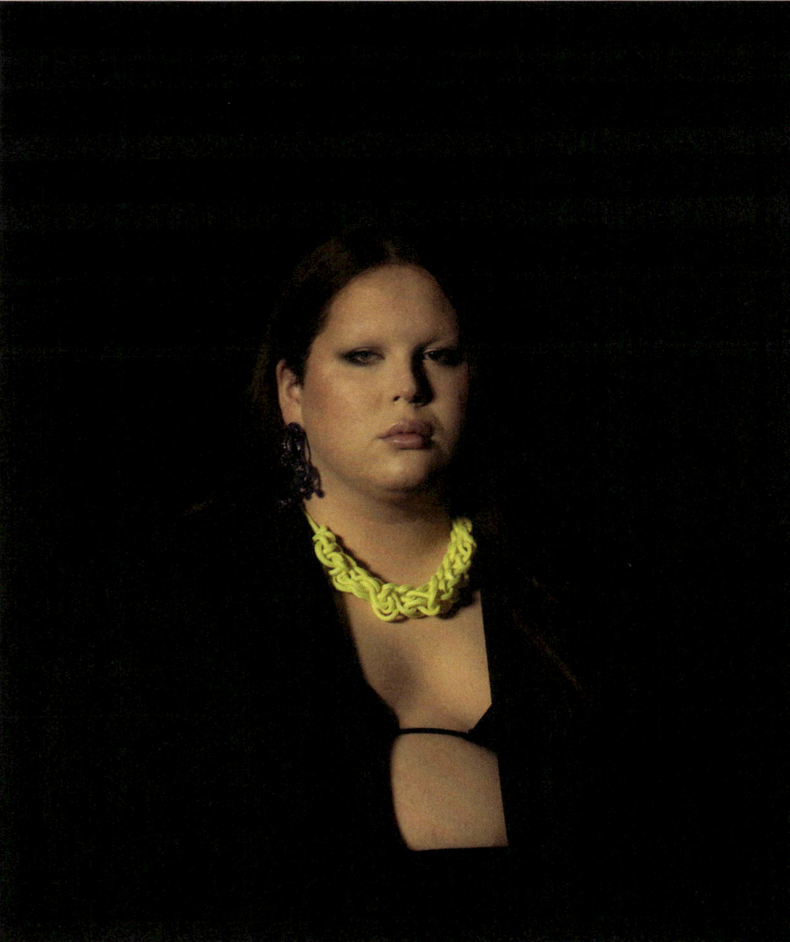

11.5

Clockwise from top left: *Personaje 1 (Tino)*, 2022; *Personaje 2 (Lewin)*, 2022; *Personaje 3 (Bambi)*, 2022

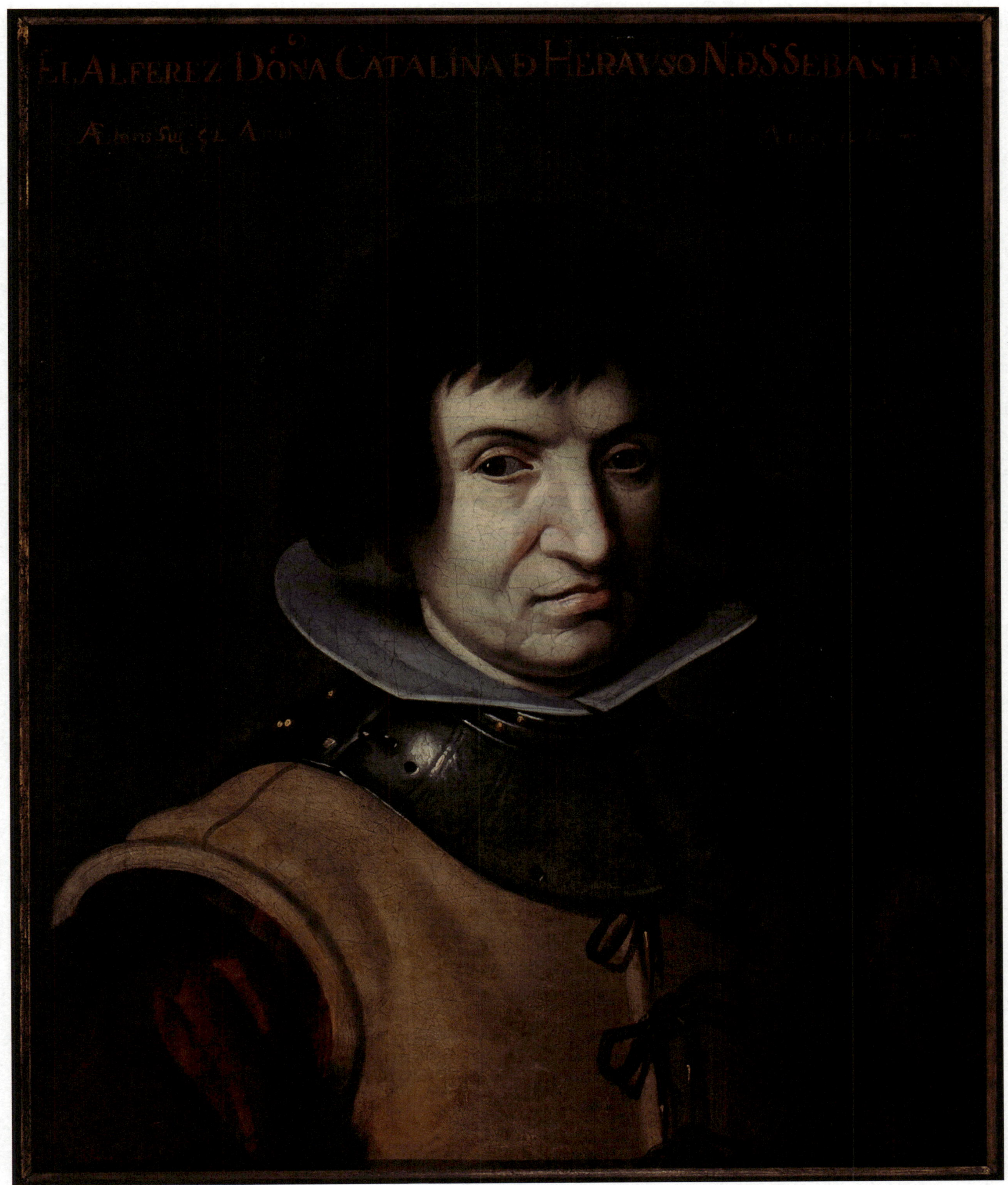


11.6

Juan van der Hamen y León. *Retrato de Doña Catalina de Erauso. La monja alférez*, c. 1630

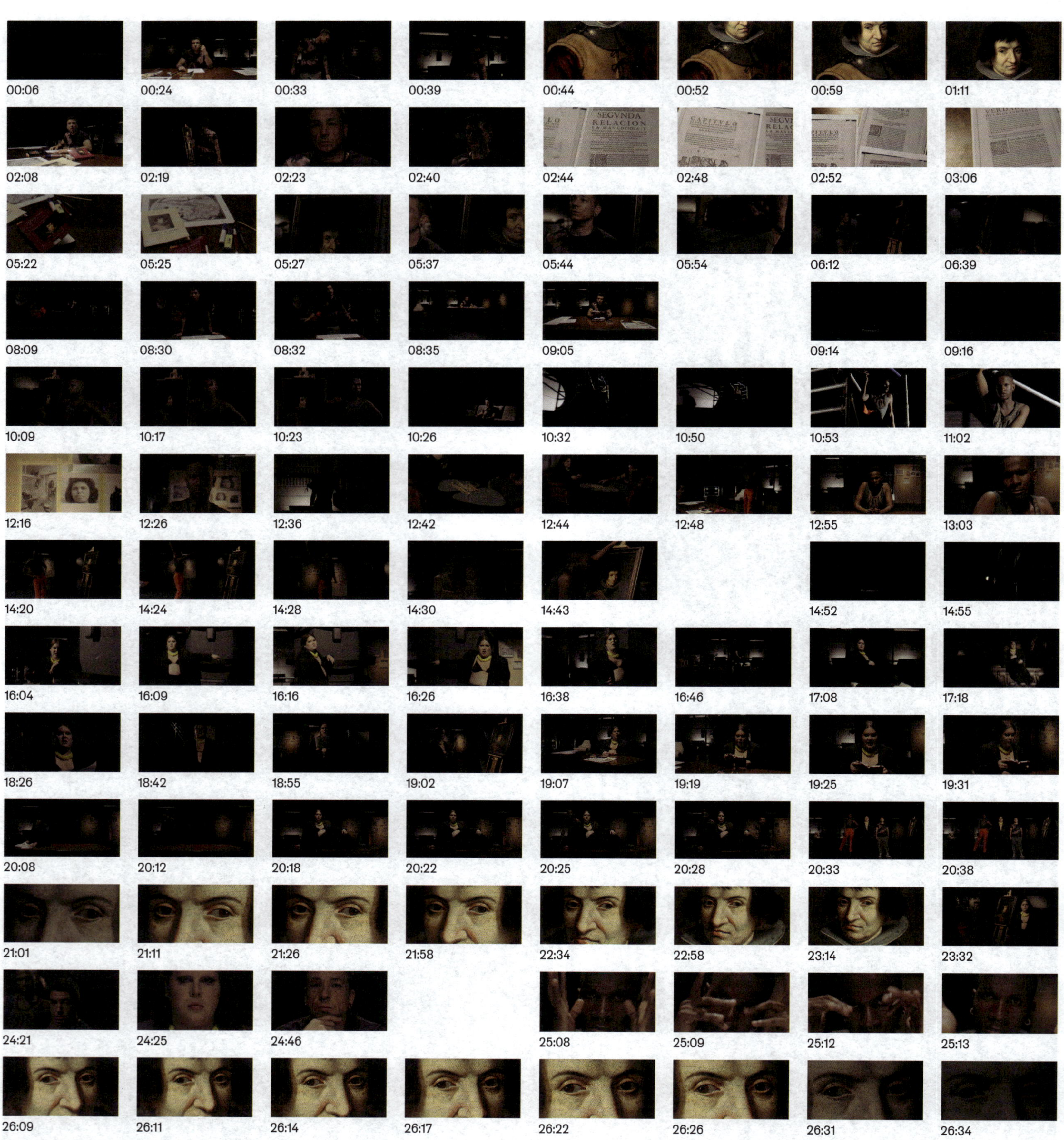
00:06
00:24
00:33
00:39
00:44
00:52
00:59
01:11
02:08
02:19
02:23
02:40
02:44
02:48
02:52
03:06
05:22
05:25
05:27
05:37
05:44
05:54
06:12
06:39
08:09
08:30
08:32
08:35
09:05
09:14
09:16
10:09
10:17
10:23
10:26
10:32
10:50
10:53
11:02
12:16
12:26
12:36
12:42
12:44
12:48
12:55
13:03
14:20
14:24
14:28
14:30
14:43
14:52
14:55
16:04
16:09
16:16
16:26
16:38
16:46
17:08
17:18
18:26
18:42
18:55
19:02
19:07
19:19
19:25
19:31
20:08
20:12
20:18
20:22
20:25
20:28
20:33
20:38
21:01
21:11
21:26
21:58
22:34
22:58
23:14
23:32
24:21
24:25
24:46
25:08
25:09
25:12
25:13
26:09
26:11
26:14
26:17
26:22
26:26
26:31
26:34

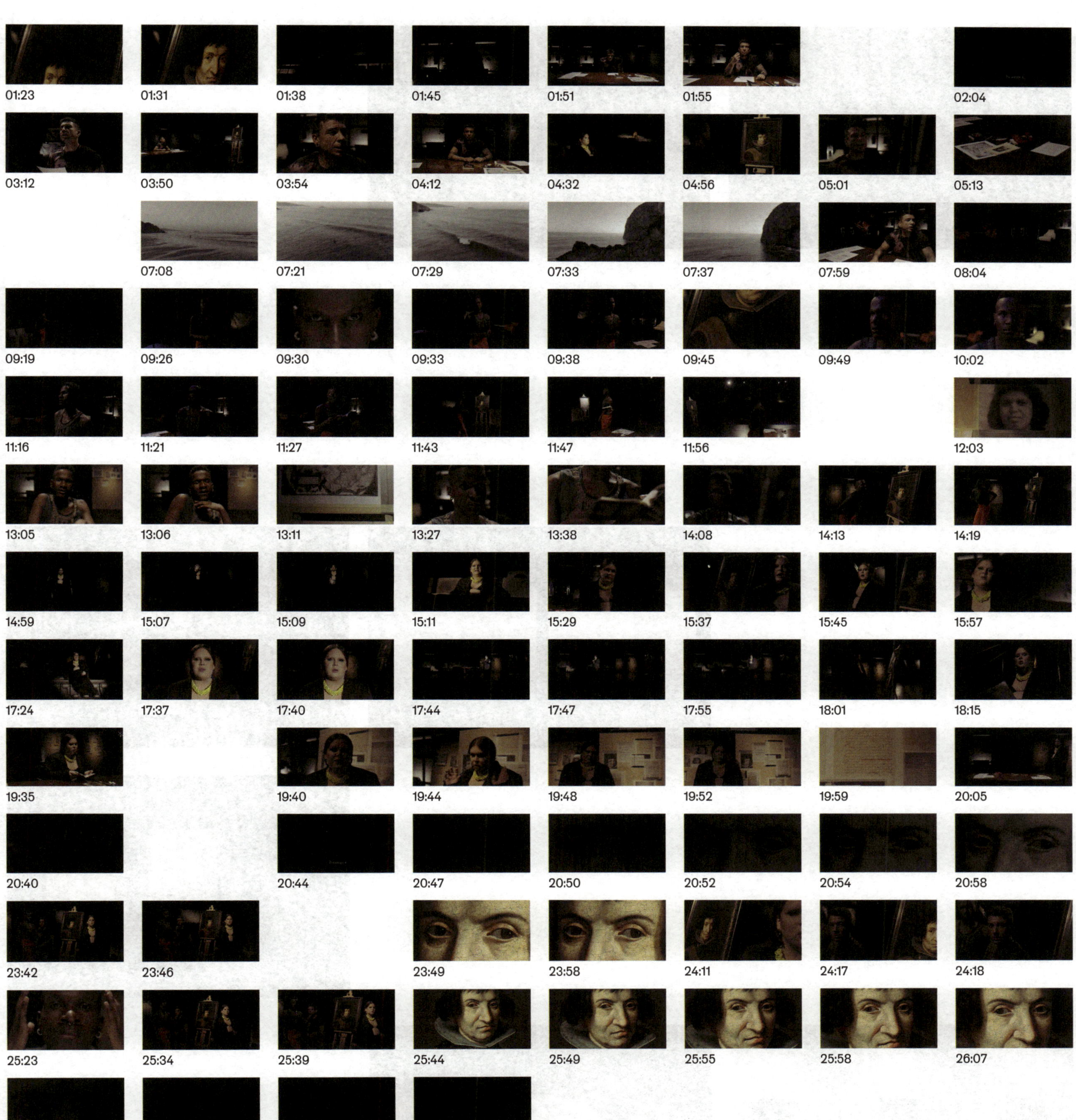
01:23 01:31 01:38 01:45 01:51 01:55 02:04
03:12 03:50 03:54 04:12 04:32 04:56 05:01 05:13
07:08 07:21 07:29 07:33 07:37 07:59 08:04
09:19 09:26 09:30 09:33 09:38 09:45 09:49 10:02
11:16 11:21 11:27 11:43 11:47 11:56 12:03
13:05 13:06 13:11 13:27 13:38 14:08 14:13 14:19
14:59 15:07 15:09 15:11 15:29 15:37 15:45 15:57
17:24 17:37 17:40 17:44 17:47 17:55 18:01 18:15
19:35 19:40 19:44 19:48 19:52 19:59 20:05
20:40 20:44 20:47 20:50 20:52 20:54 20:58
23:42 23:46 23:49 23:58 24:11 24:17 24:18
25:23 25:34 25:39 25:44 25:49 25:55 25:58 26:07
26:35 26:37 26:42 26:46

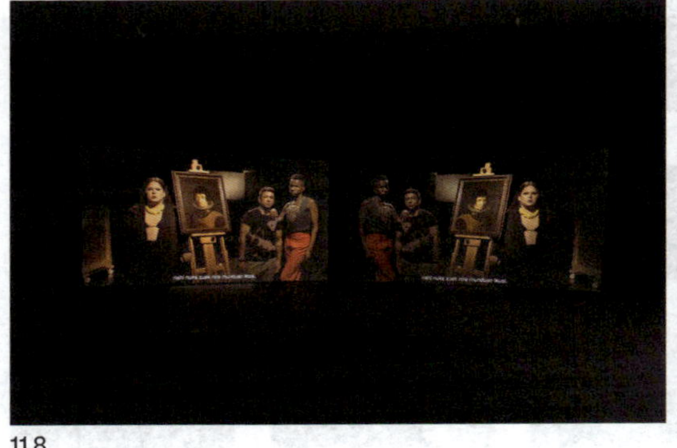
11.8

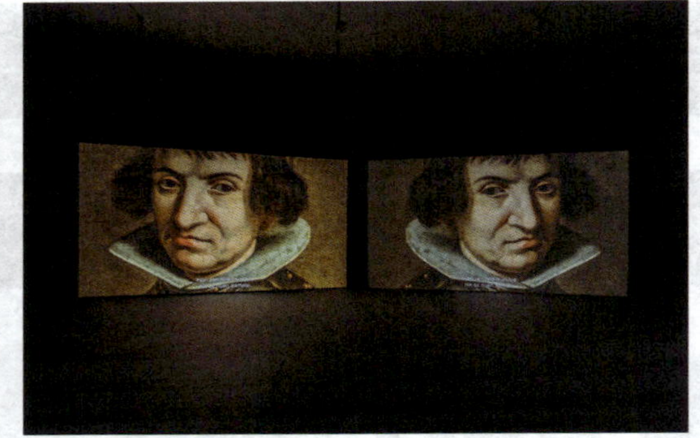
11.9

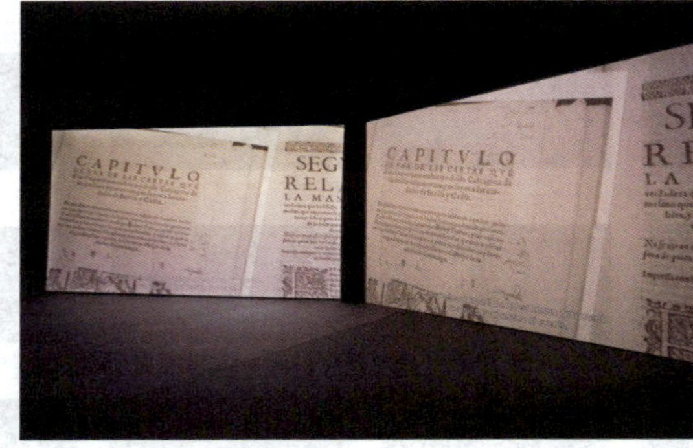
11.10

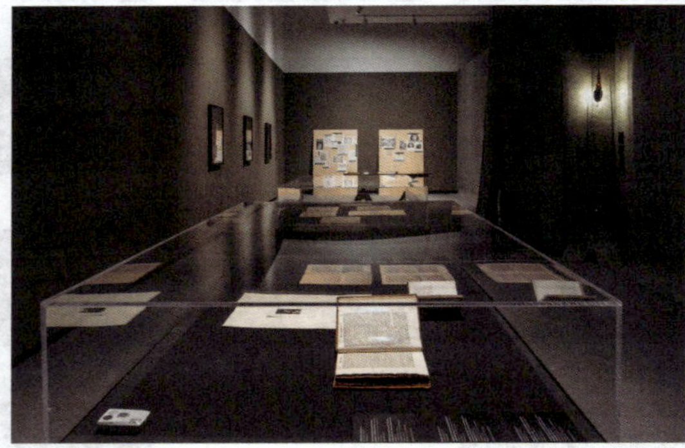
11.11

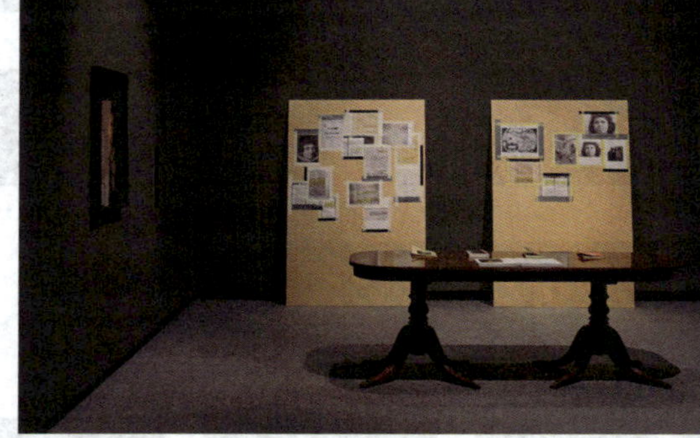
11.12

11.13

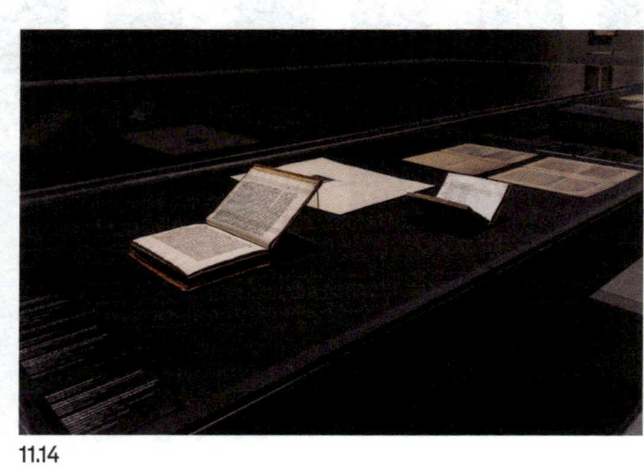
11.14

Installation views of *Cabello/Carceller: A Voice for Erauso. Epilogue for a Trans Time*, 2022

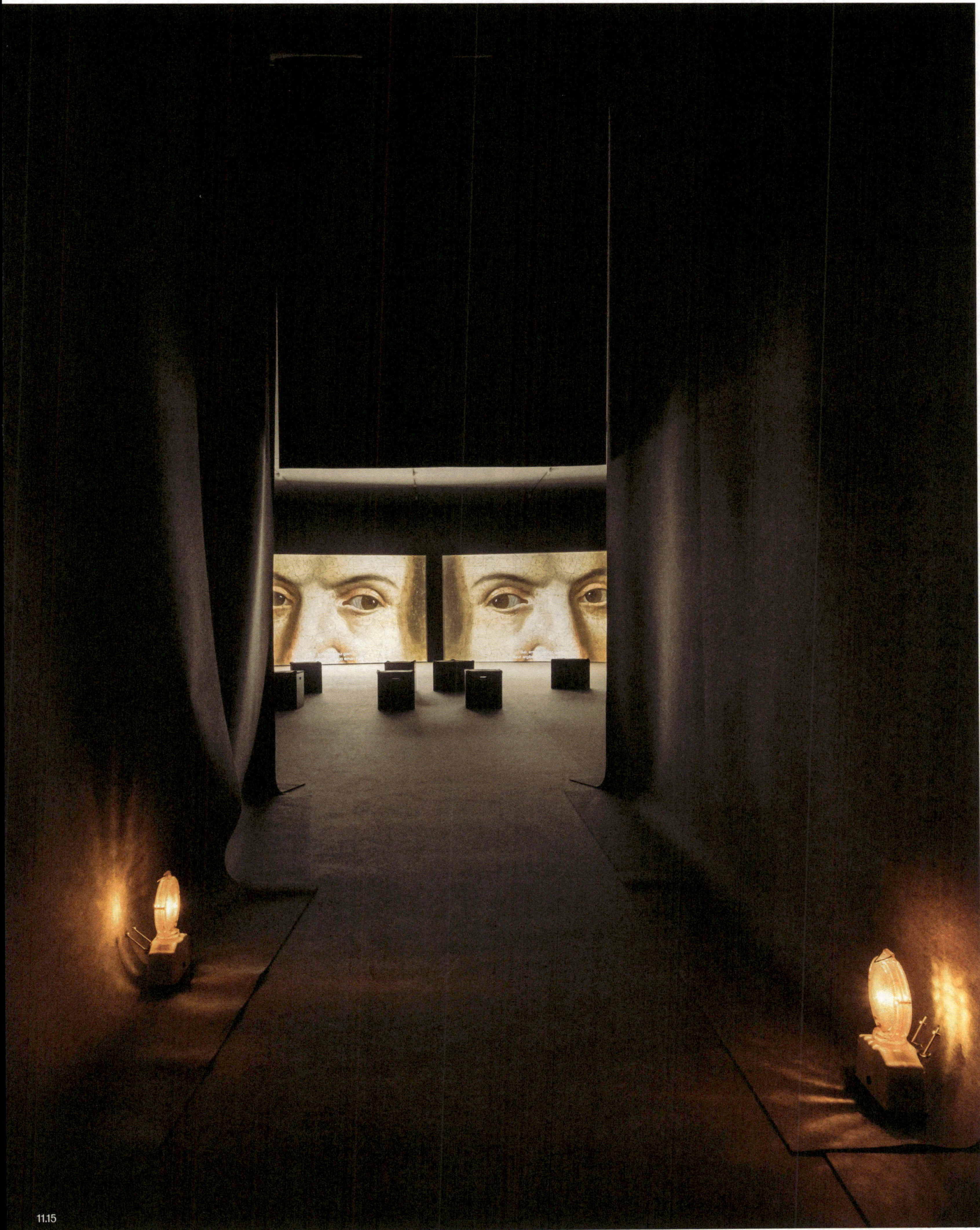

11.15

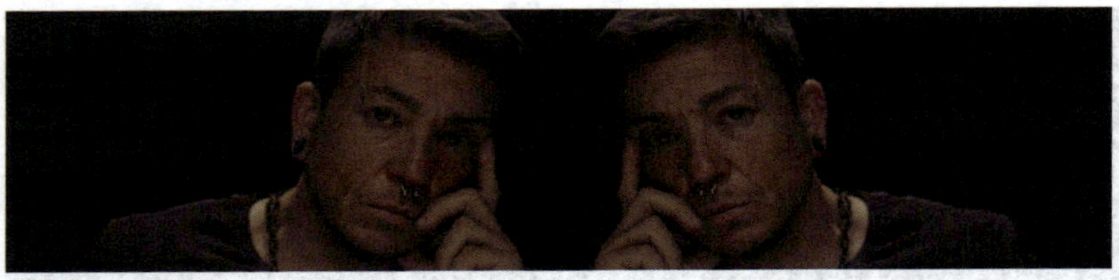

24:55

09:35

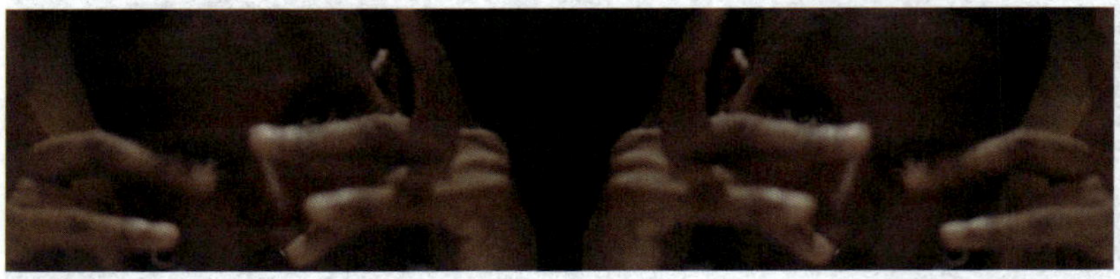

24:43

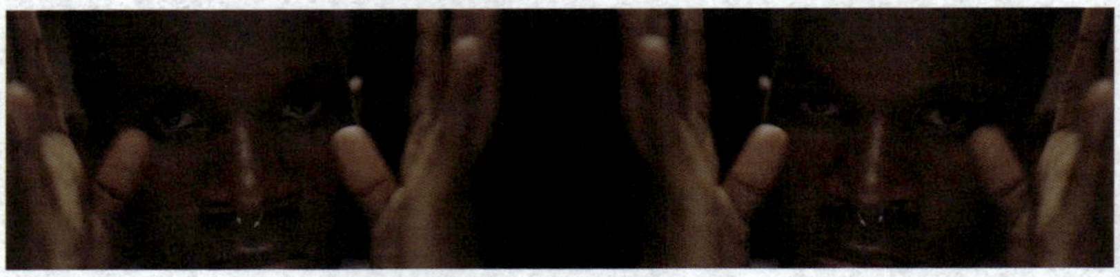

25:11

25:06

24:26

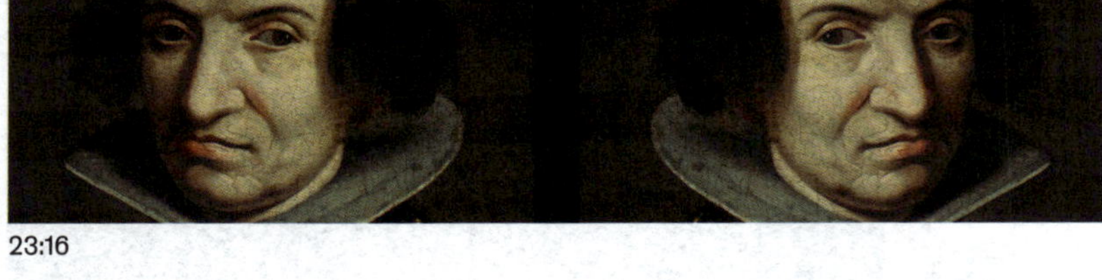

23:16

24:36

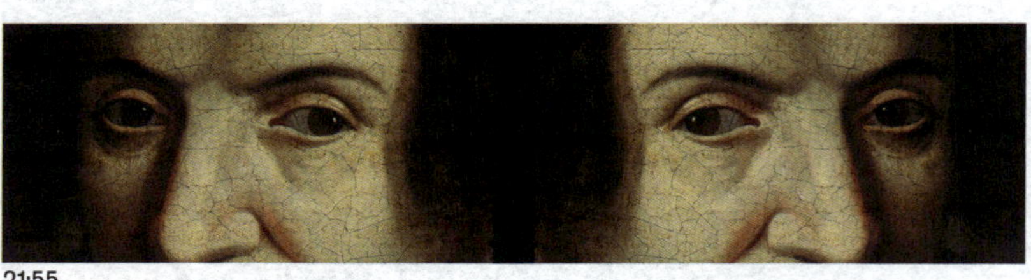

21:55

Orain ez naiz ni.
Orain ez naiz ni.

11.17

Denen kontra bizi izan nintzen.
Denen kontra bizi izan nintzen.

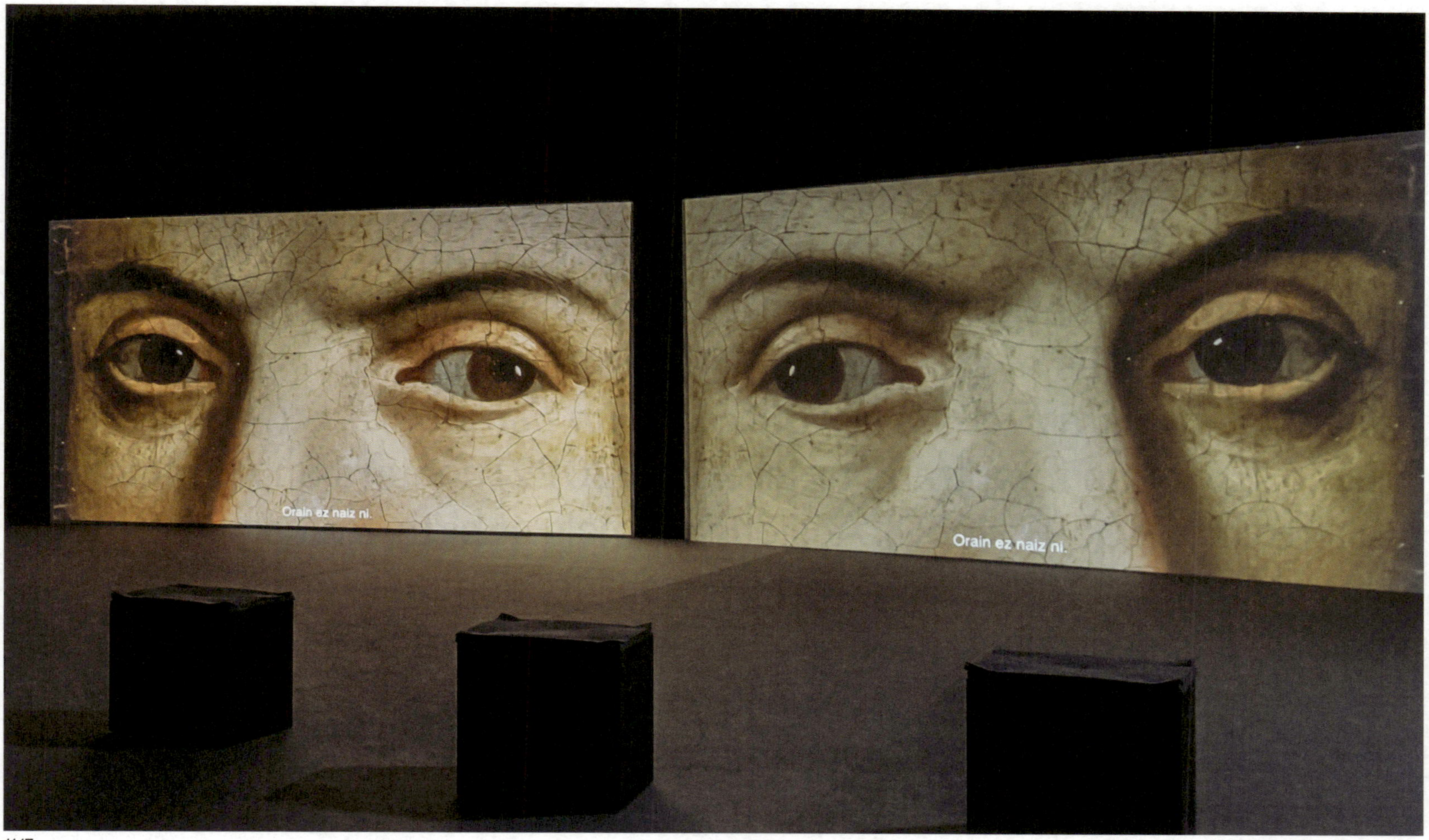

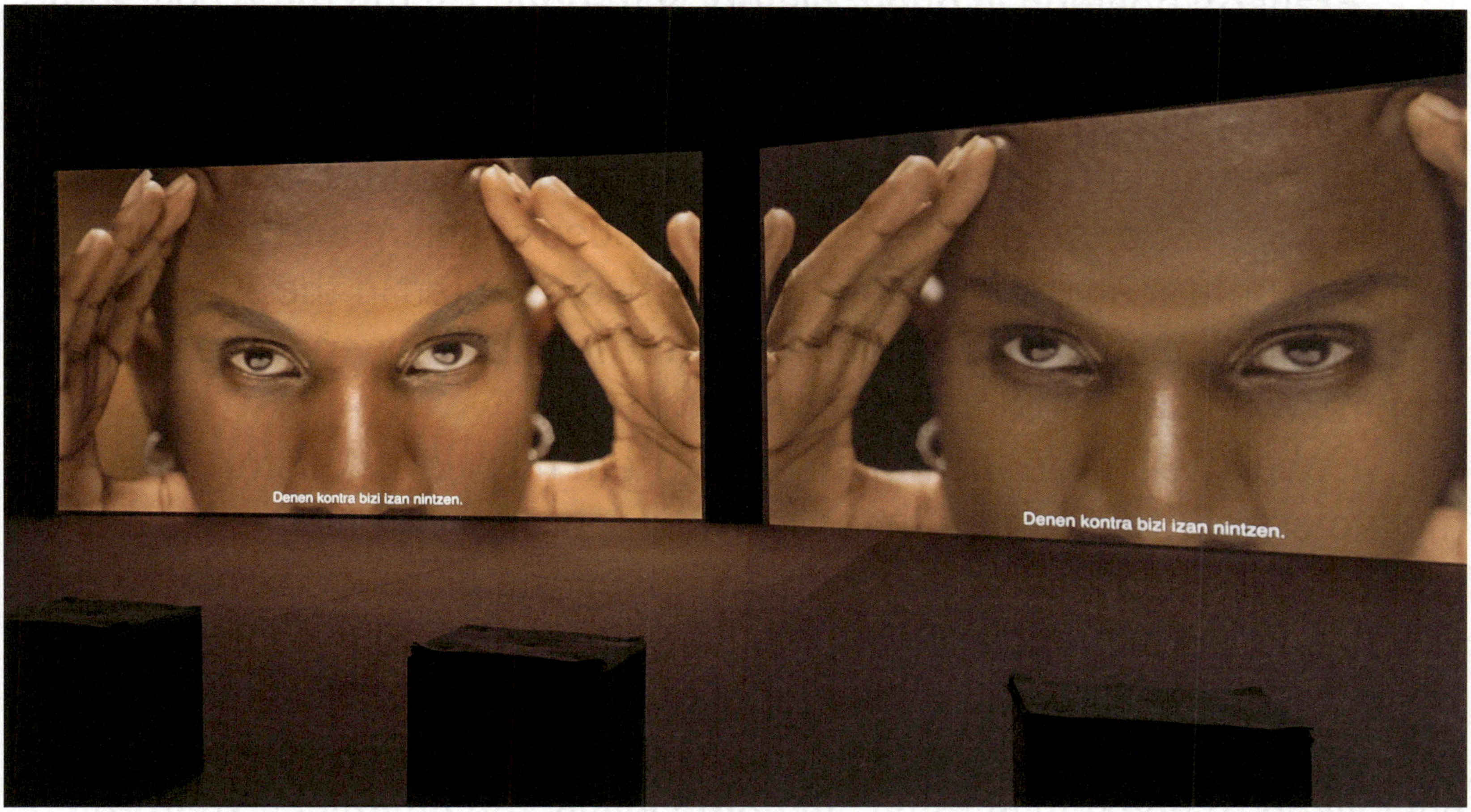

11.18

Cabello/Carceller examine the means of representation through their multidisciplinary practice, utilizing appropriation and fiction to interrogate hegemonic narratives of identity. Their work creates collaborative structures through which minority voices are centered and disrupts the normative means by which political and social relationships are built. Queer theory and experience form the basis of many works, utilized to create new modes of storytelling and narrative.

*Una voz para Erauso. Epílogo para un tiempo trans* (A voice for Erauso. Epilogue for a trans time, 2021–2022) centers on Antonio de Erauso (c. 1585/1592–1650). Assigned female at birth, Erauso lived most of his life as a man, adopting many masculine identities, including that of a soldier. The central image of the film is a portrait of Erauso in which he is dressed in military garb, face sallow and hair short. Inscribed later with the name Catalina, the portrait captures a clearly male presentation and so renders one of the earliest portrayals of trans identity.[1]

Erauso's position in queer history is fraught. As the three characters, all portrayed by trans actors, address Erauso's portrait, they acknowledge the futility of assigning modern terminology to a historical figure, at once placing Erauso into a trans lineage and understanding that to do so is anachronistic. So too do they confront Erauso's racism and participation in the slaughter and enslavement of Native peoples in the Americas. By claiming masculinity, Erauso was granted the power of the colonial empire, which he wielded to bloody ends.[2]

Cabello/Carceller do not shy away from this violent history; instead, the "voice" of Erauso, modulated into song, proudly proclaims his deeds. By giving Erauso a voice, the film collapses the distance between the viewer and the subject, allowing the historical to respond to the ways in which modern examination has highlighted contentious deeds. "Now you're…bringing me into your world, your time," Erauso sings. "I would have liked to see you in mine." In some ways, the colonial structure afforded Erauso more power than many trans people have today. The contradictions central to Cabello/Carceller's Erauso evade a sanitizing, heroizing view, reminding us that queer history is just as entangled with colonial power as any other.

The trans lineage created by the film is not an unequivocal truth. The "trans time" referenced in the title demands the recognition of incomplete or obscure historical narratives; it requires an understanding not limited to the discourse of the present. It invites the contemplation of alternative genealogies shaped by concepts that either have been lost to time or have not yet been conceived. (LRL)

1 Paul B. Preciado, "Una voz para Erauso. Epílogo para un tiempo trans," exhibition brochure, Azkuna Zentroa Alhóndiga Bilbao, March 2022, https://issuu.com/azkunazentroa/docs/folleto-una-voz-para-erauso.

2 Preciado, "Una voz para Erauso."

PETRIT HALILAJ *Very volcanic over this green feather*, 2021, UV-printed felt, spray-painted ink, thread, metal pipe, variable selection of up to 46 hanging elements, installed dimensions variable, courtesy the artist; ChertLüdde, Berlin; Mennour, Paris; kurimanzutto, Mexico City/New York

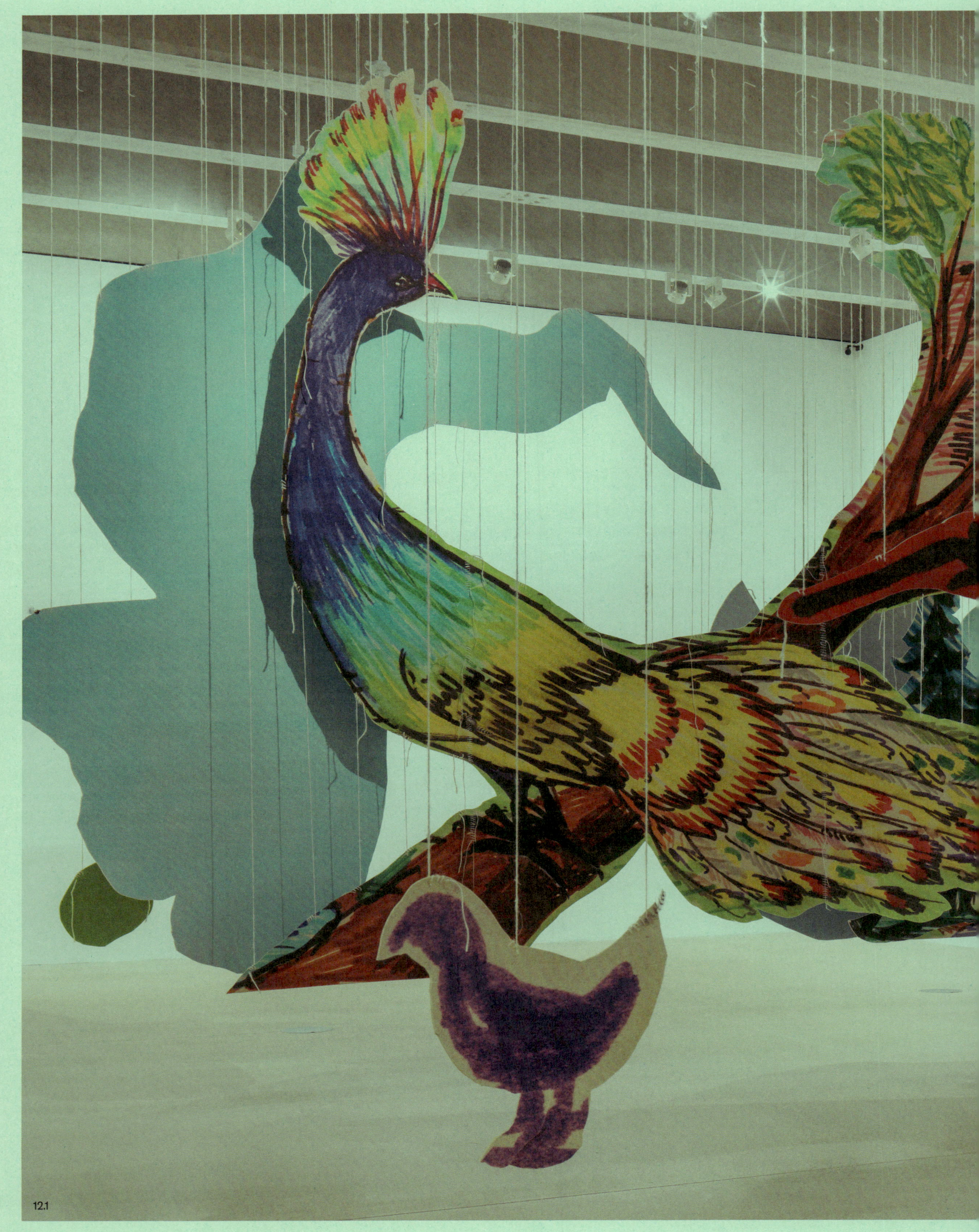

12.1

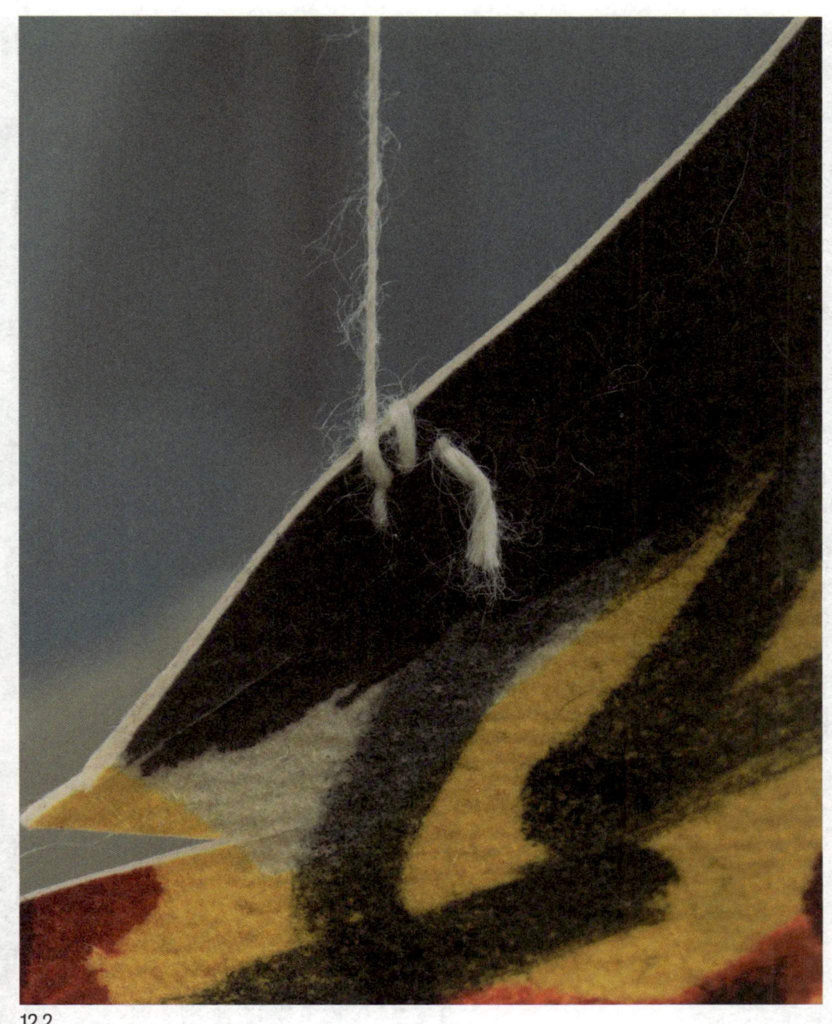
12.2

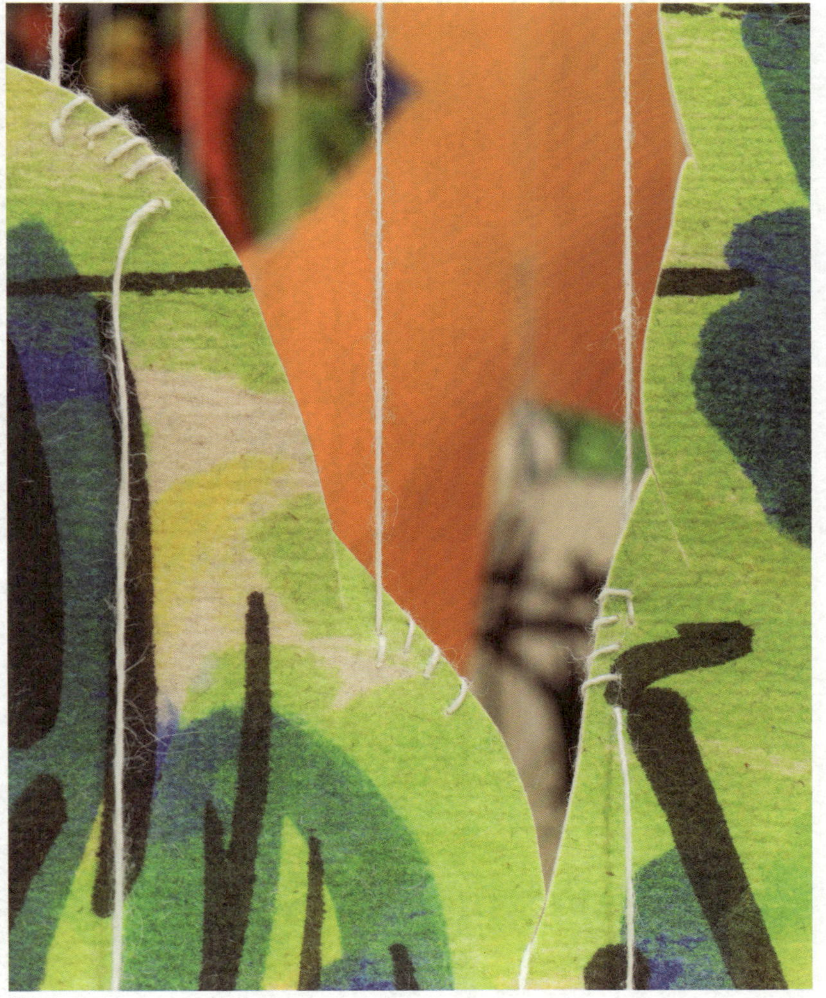
12.3

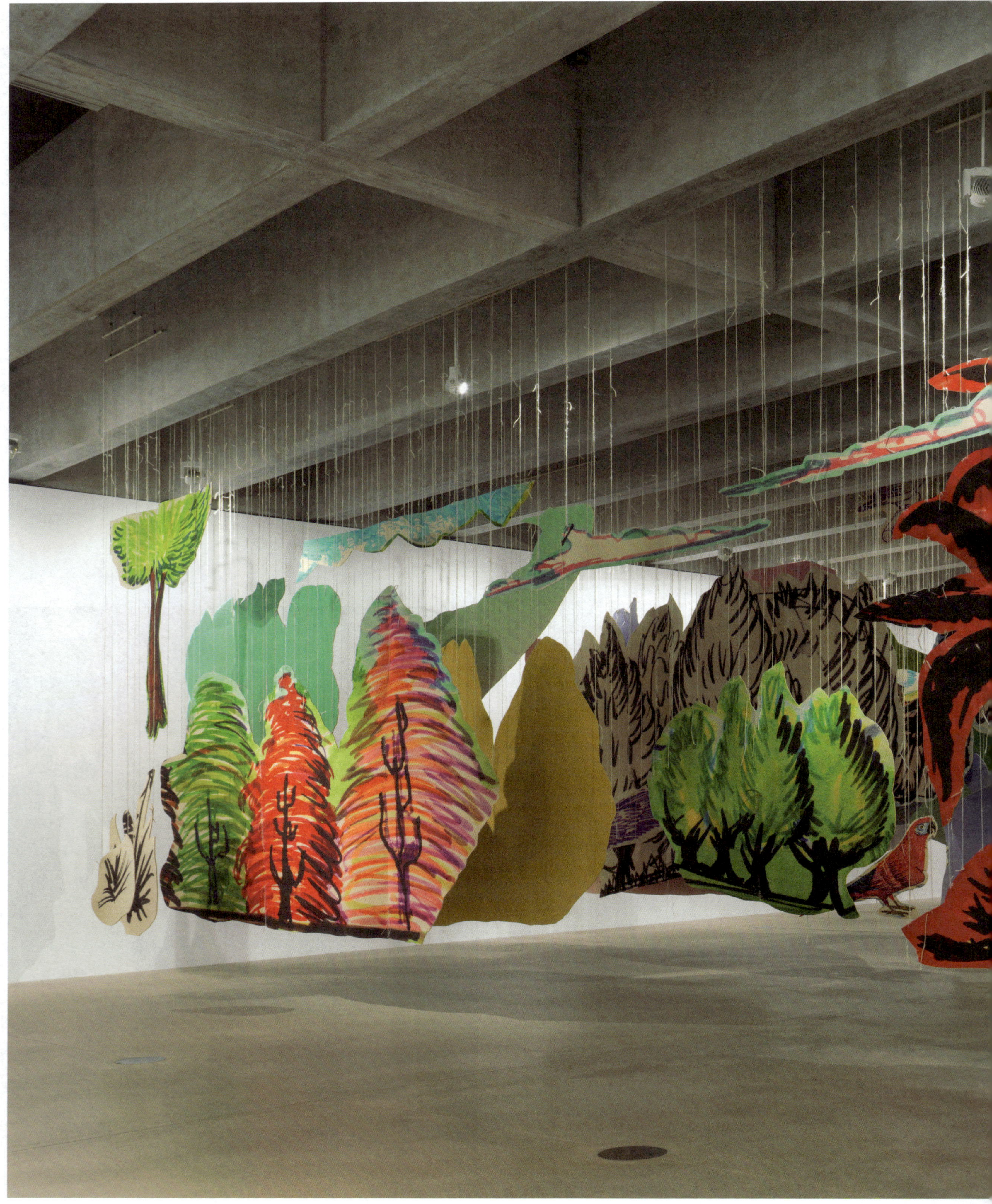

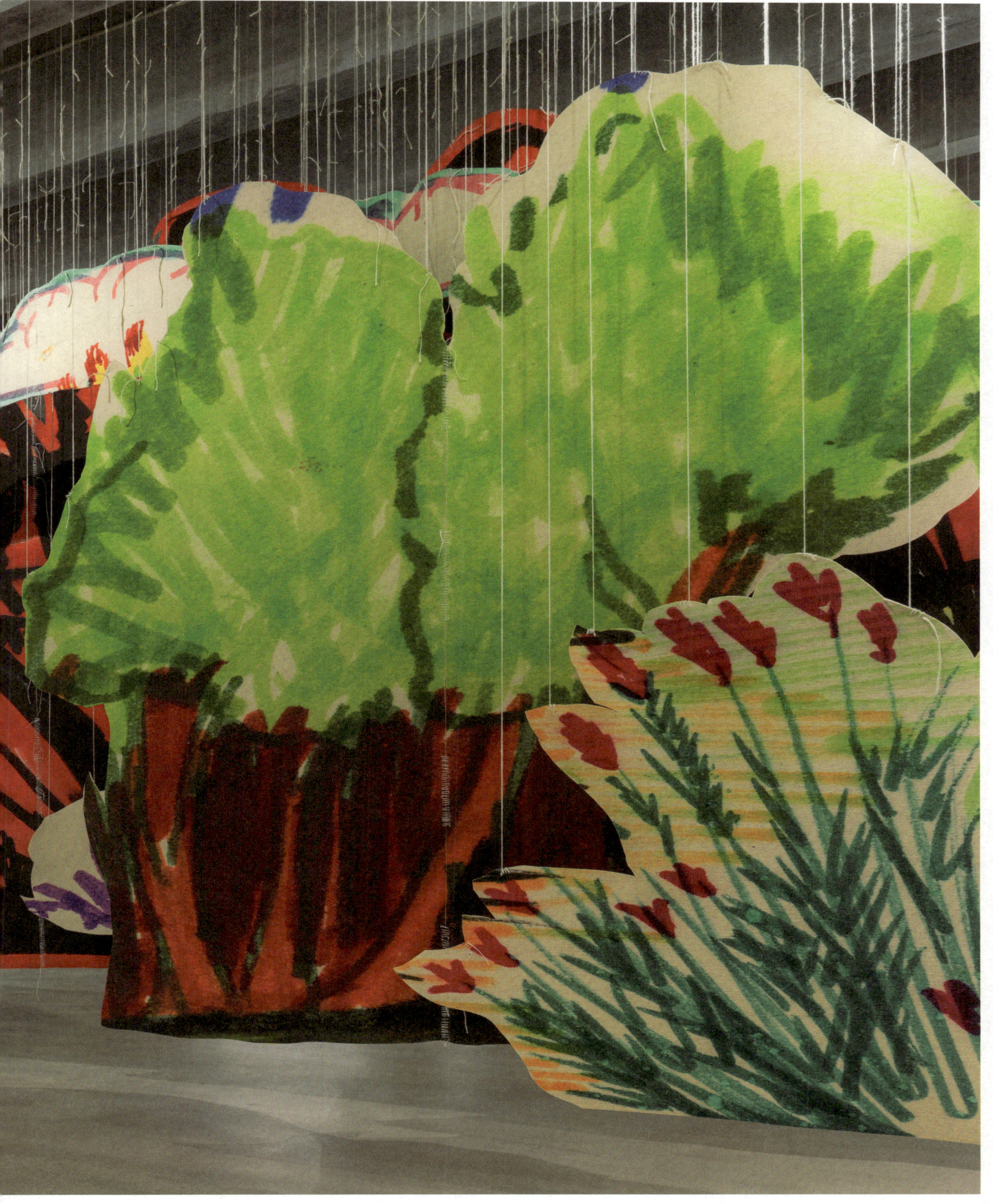

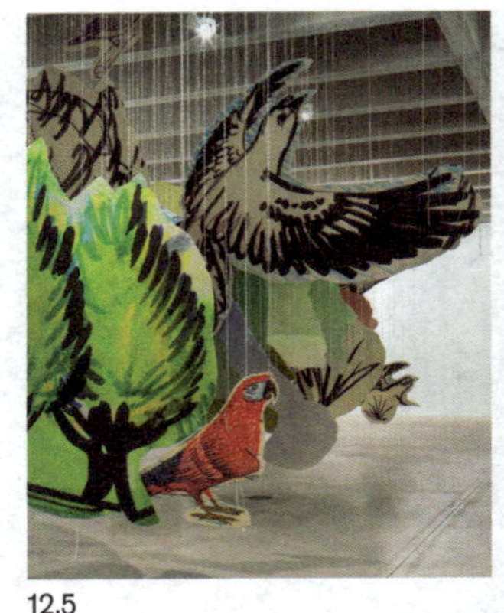
12.5

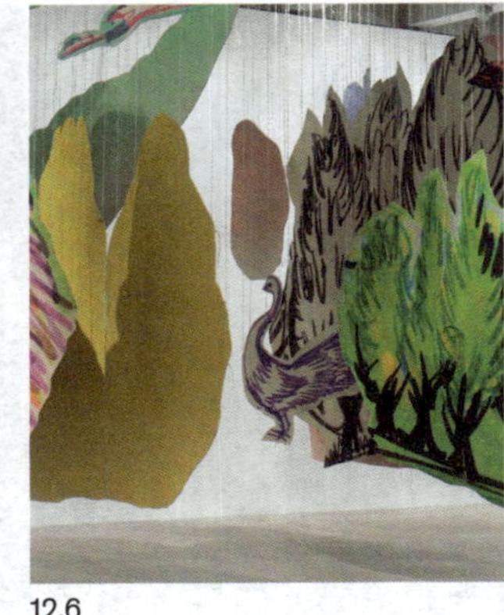
12.6

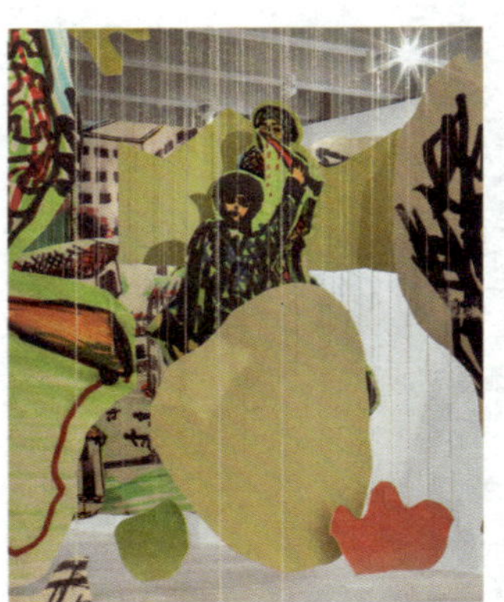
12.7

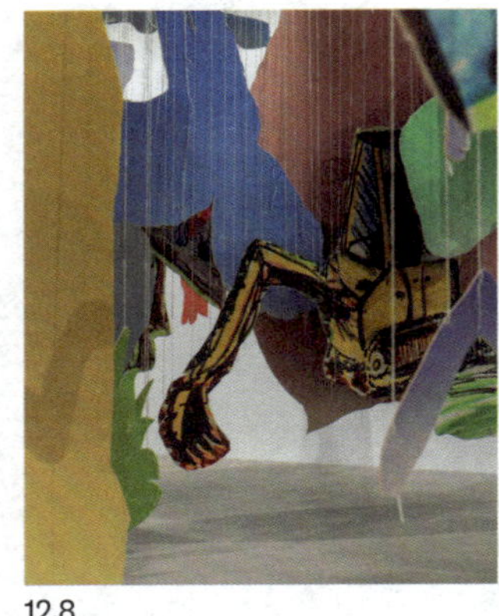
12.8

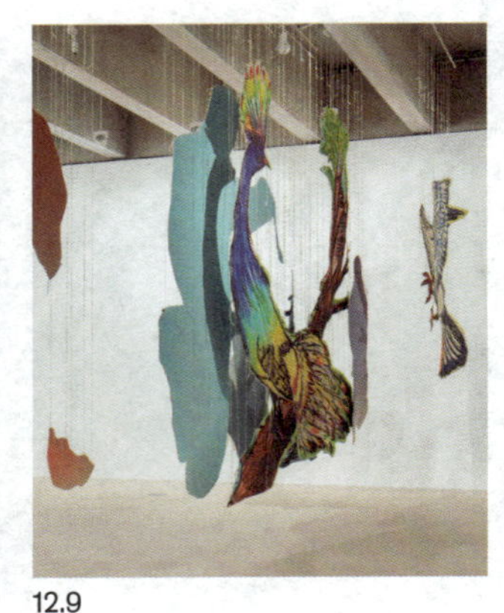
12.9

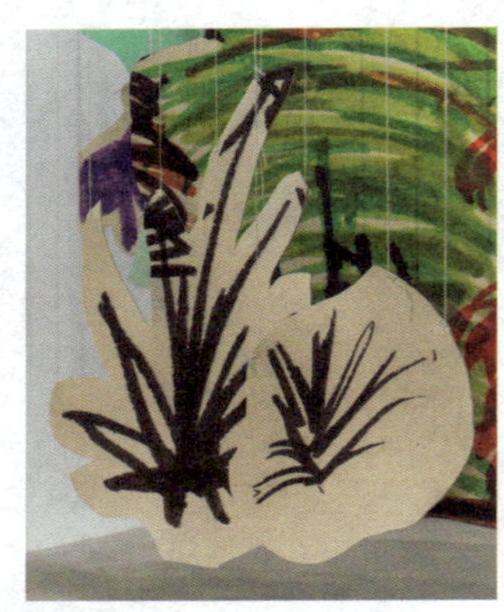
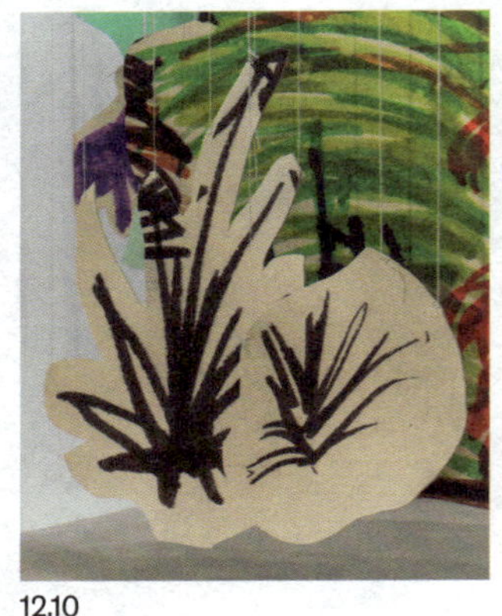
12.10

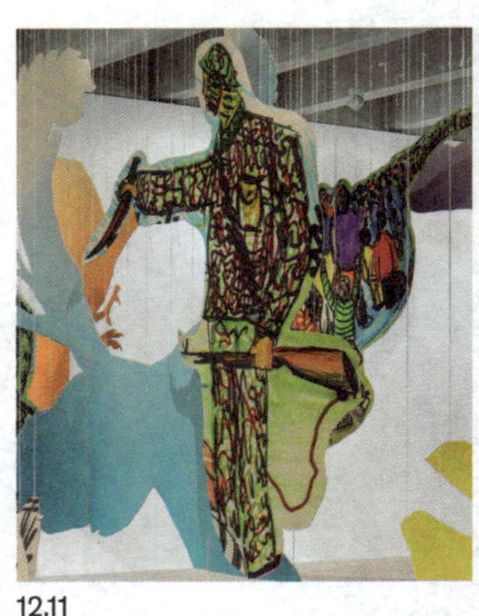
12.11

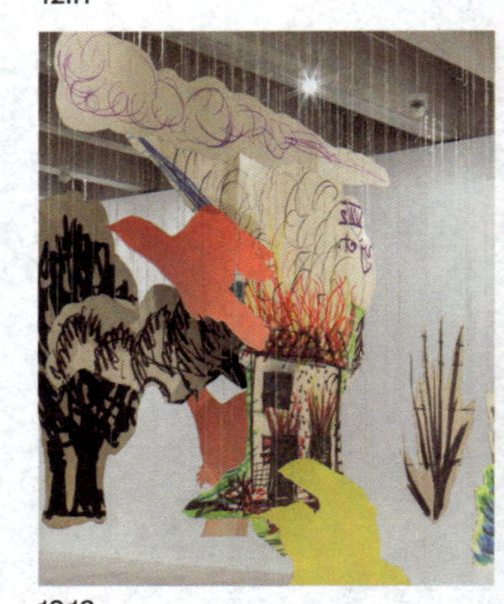
12.12

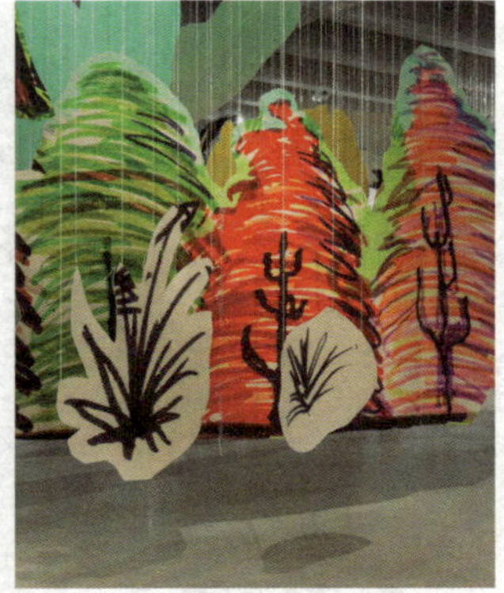
12.13

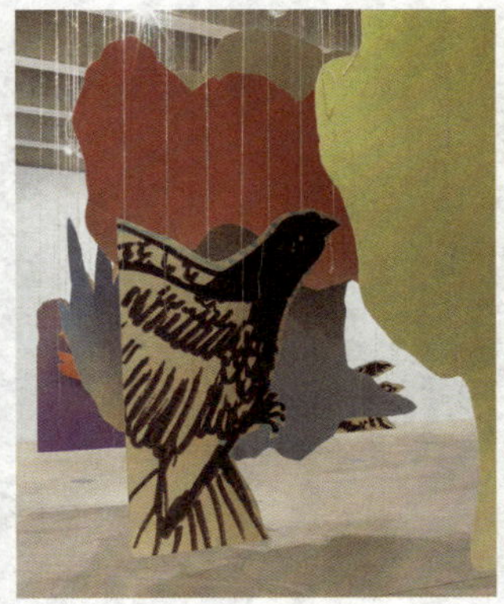
12.14

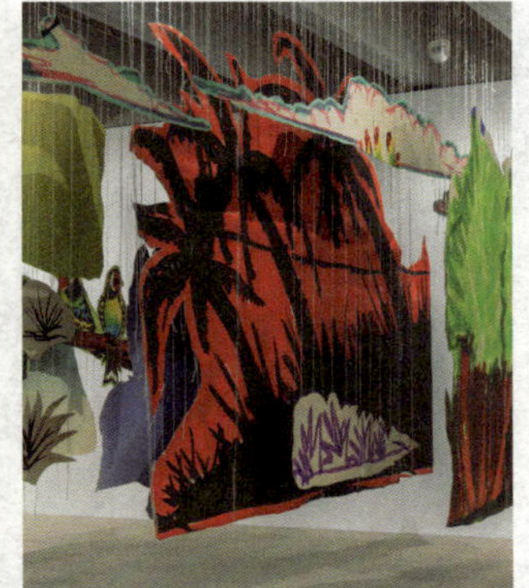
12.15

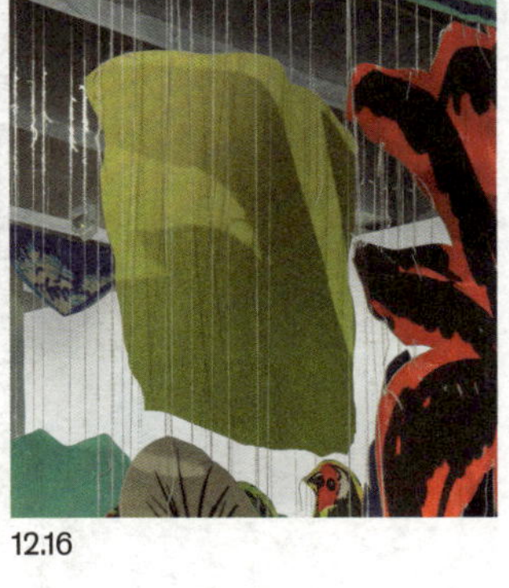
12.16

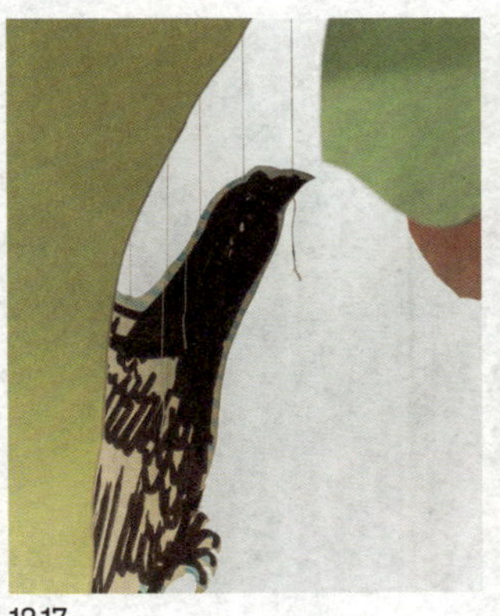
12.17

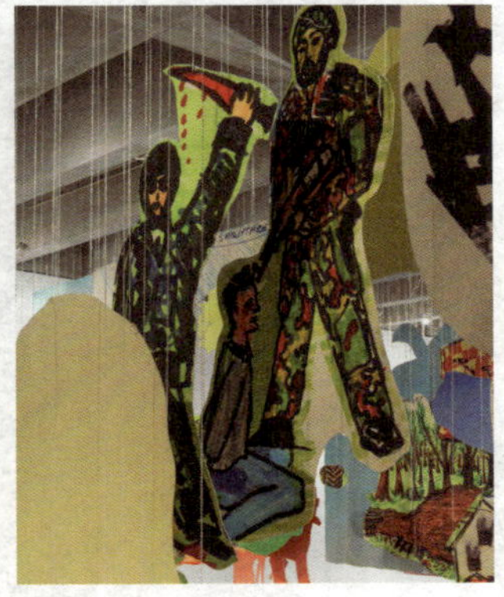
12.18

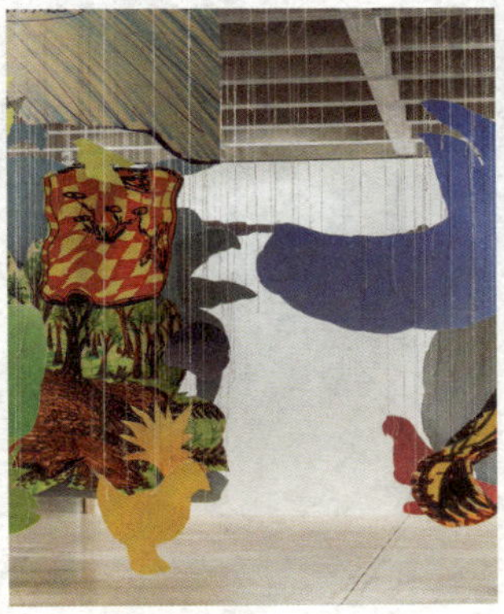

12.19

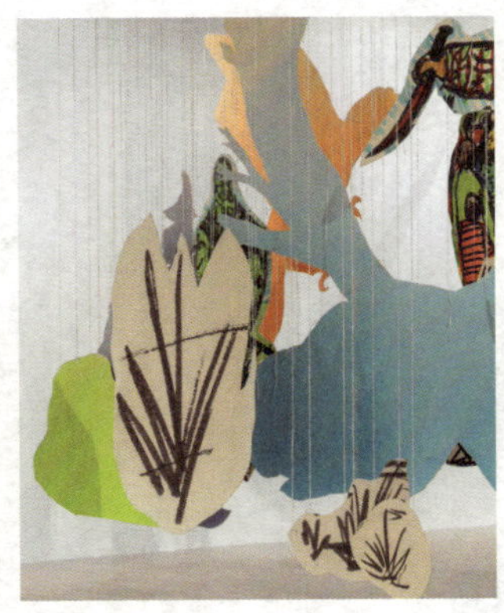
12.20

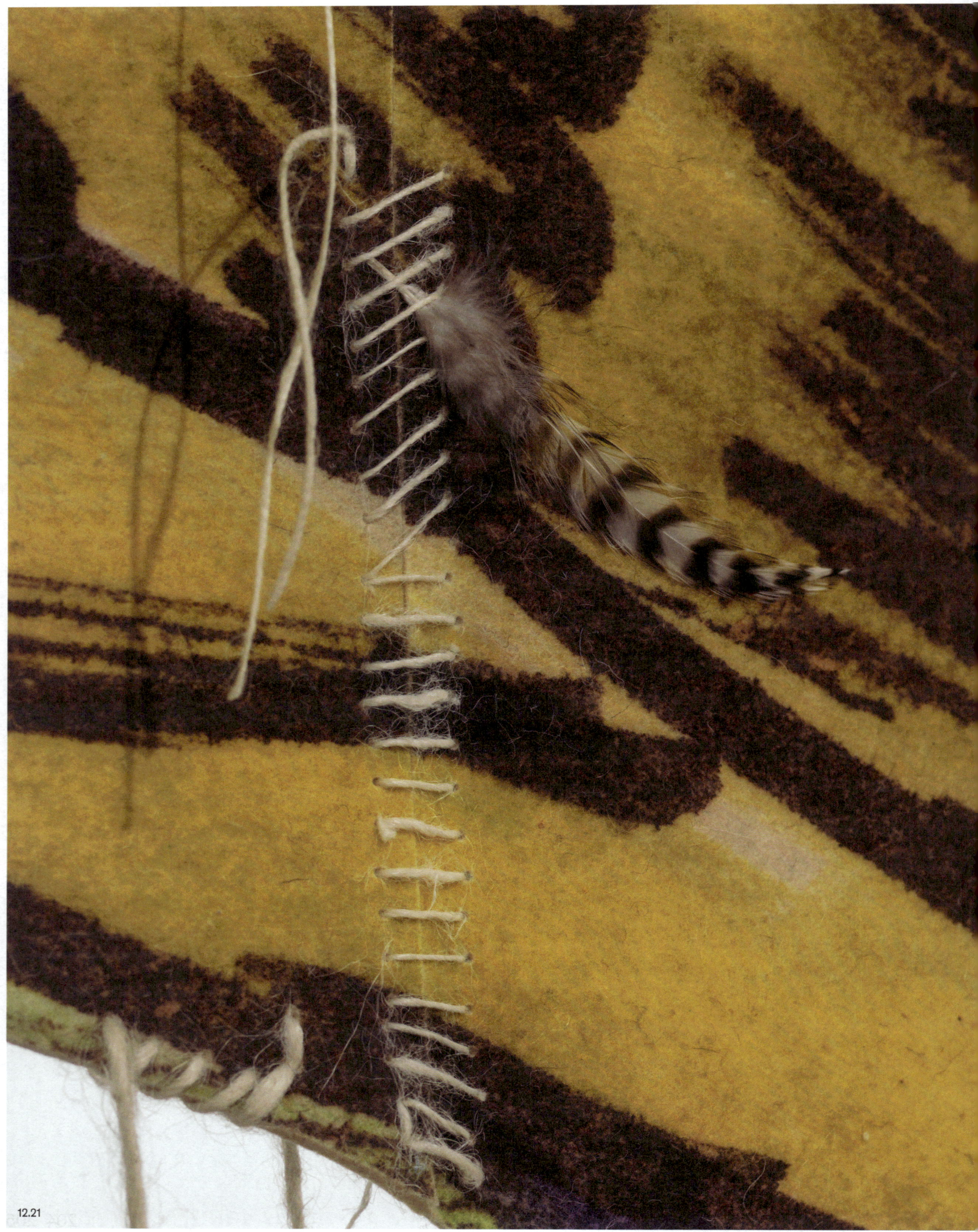

12.21

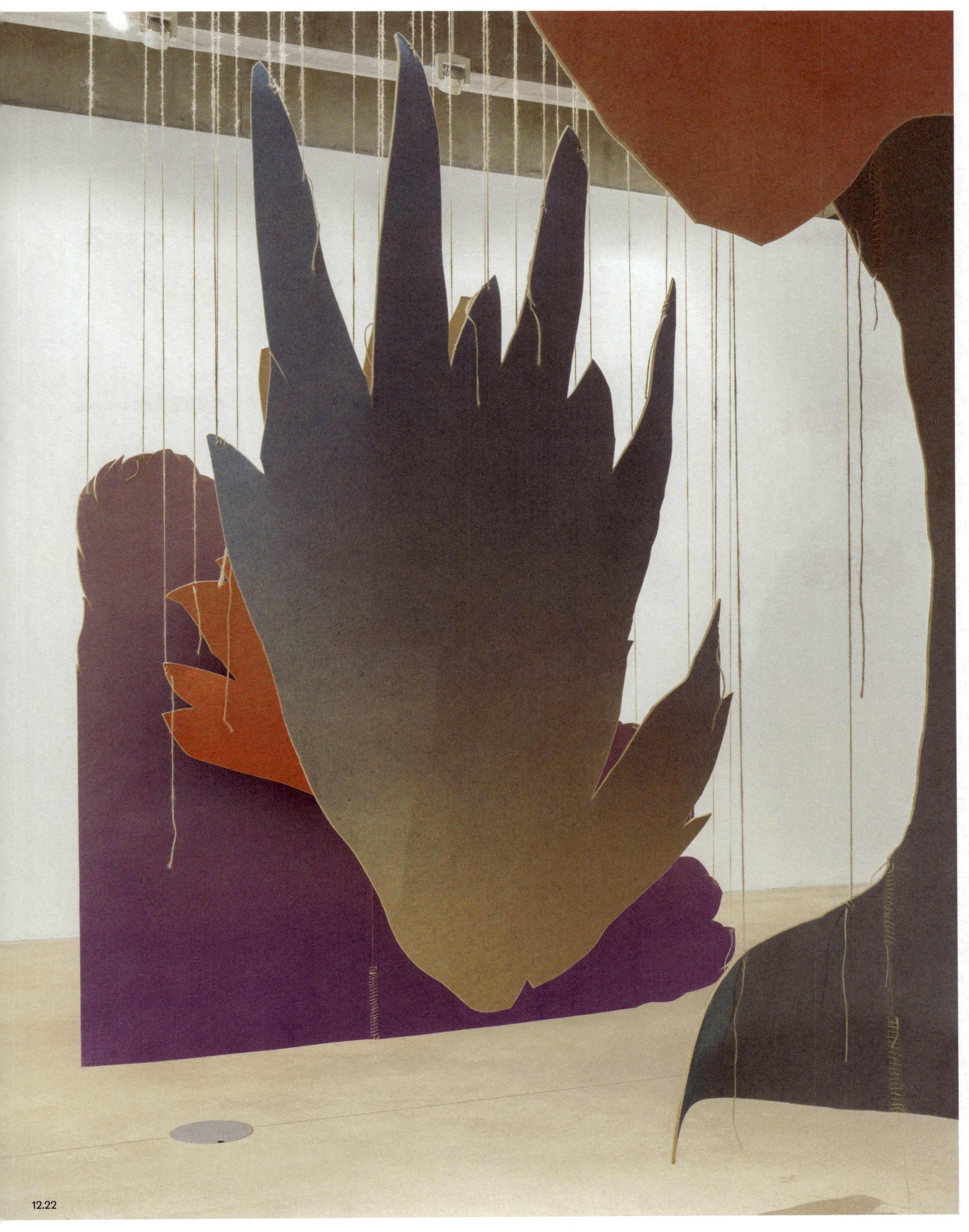

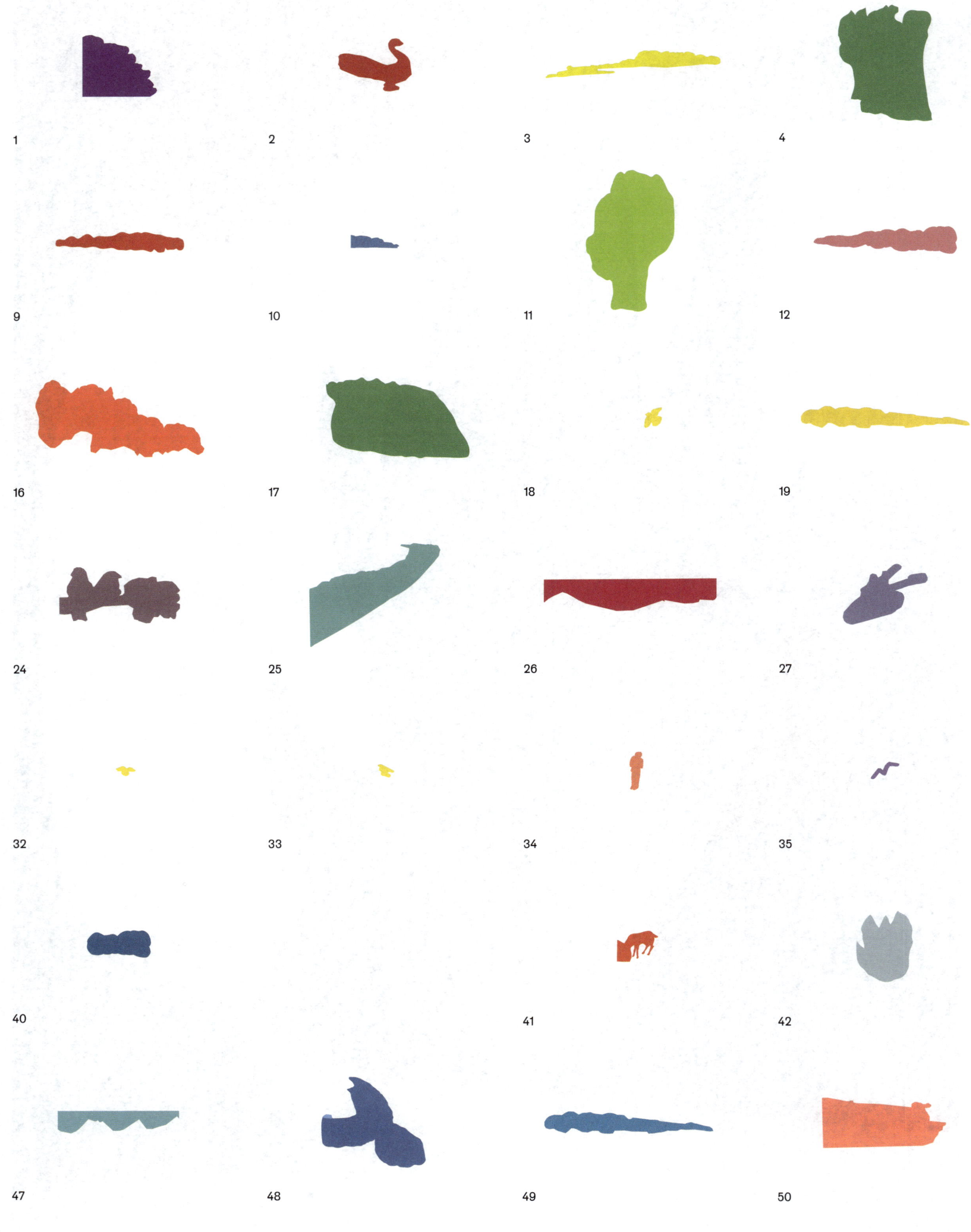
1
2
3
4
9
10
11
12
16
17
18
19
24
25
26
27
32
33
34
35
40
41
42
47
48
49
50

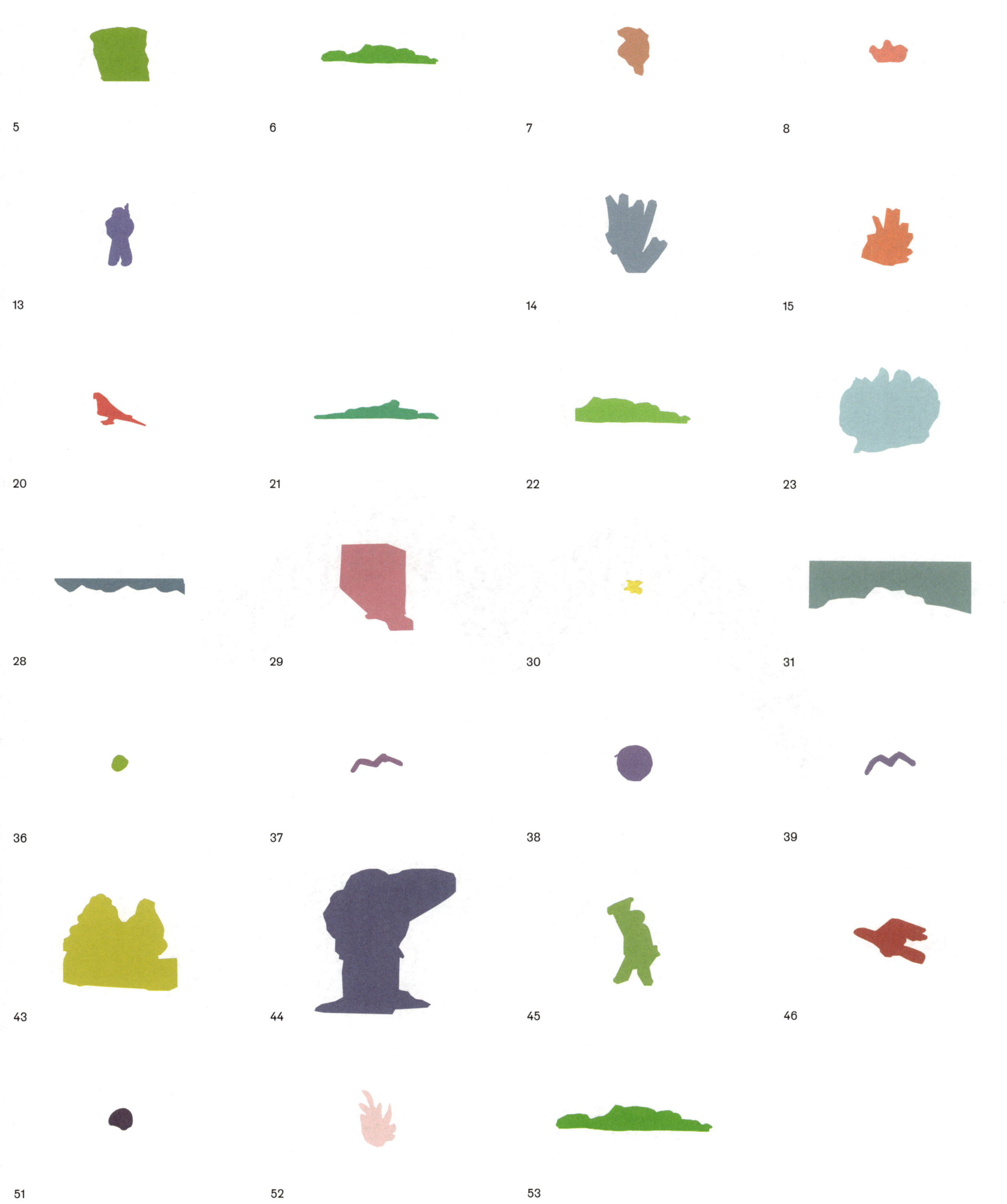
5
6
7
8
13
14
15
20
21
22
23
28
29
30
31
36
37
38
39
43
44
45
46
51
52
53

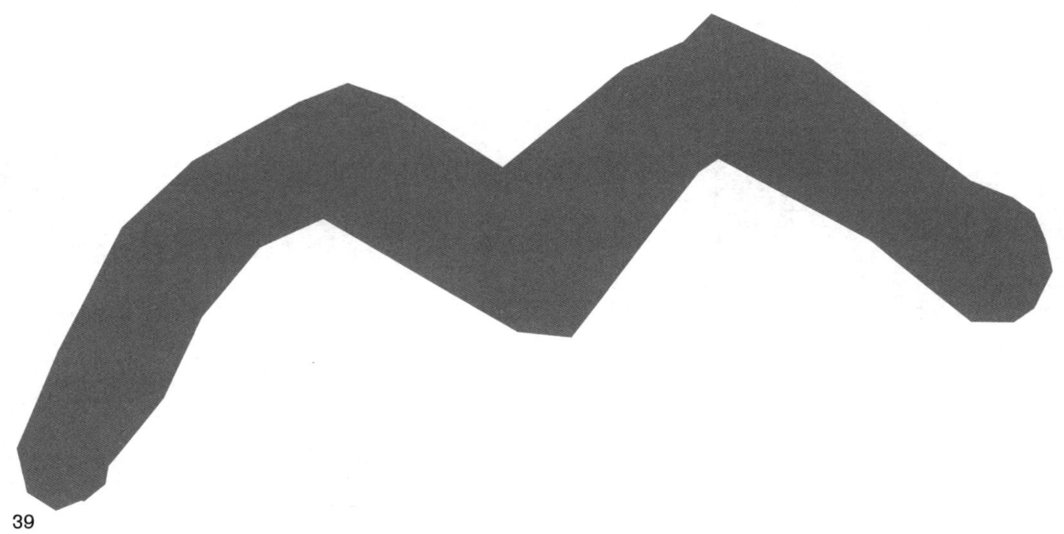

39

29

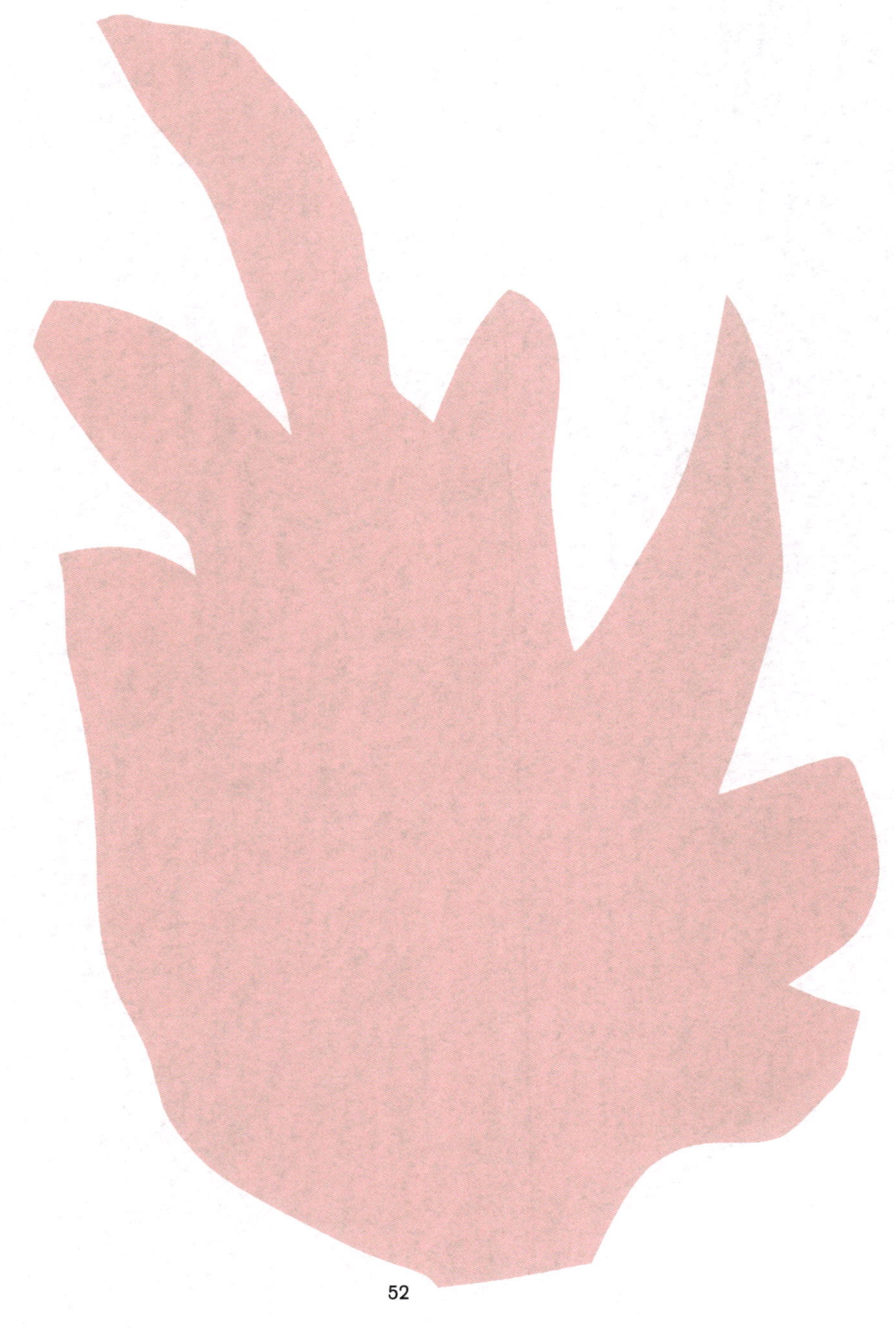

52

18

In April 1999 the Italian psychologist Giacomo Poli visited children at the Kukës II refugee camp—one of several near the Yugoslav-Albanian border that hosted Kosovar Albanians fleeing persecution in the Kosovo War. Among the children he met was thirteen-year-old Petrit Halilaj, who went on to create a series of thirty-eight drawings. Some drawings recorded violence he had seen firsthand, while others depicted scenes of the war that he had encountered in the media. Still others were speculative or imaginary. In one drawing Halilaj depicted his family home in the town of Runik; at the time he had heard that the house had burned, but he had not visited the site himself. He showed the small, two-story structure on a rolling green hill below mountains. The roof is on fire, and smoke rises from the windows. Another drawing, titled *Fantastic Landscape*, shows no trace of war or conflict. A large peacock on a tree branch poses in front of a background of candy-colored trees and a small yellow house under a teal sky. In addition to these thirty-eight drawings, Halilaj created another drawing that depicted scenes of the war, which he presented to Kofi Annan, who was then secretary-general of the United Nations, during his visit to Kukës II. The drawings were held by Poli (with whom Halilaj remains close) in Italy with the exception of the work created for Annan, which remained in Albania. Halilaj began to revisit these early works after the curator Amy Zion included several in a presentation of children's drawings organized for the Queens Museum in New York.[1]

The artist selected elements from his drawings and began to experiment with enlarging and printing them, eventually settling on felt panels. The resulting installation, *Very volcanic over this green feather*, was commissioned and presented in the United Kingdom at Tate St Ives in 2021–2022.[2] It included eighty-seven elements printed onto shaped felt and hung from the ceiling with string, arranged in parallel vertical planes throughout the room. As visitors entered the space, they saw pink-tinged clouds, bright trees and houses, and Halilaj's menagerie: a peacock, doves, parakeets, and parrots. The lone hint of discord was the image of a small boy crying, hung close to the floor. As visitors reached the back of the room and turned around, they were confronted with burning buildings, tent encampments, and a soldier wielding a knife and a gun. The viewer is dwarfed by the beauty and horror of a child's perspective on history.

Since its initial presentation in the UK, *Very volcanic over this green feather* has been exhibited in galleries and museums in Paris, Geneva, Mexico City, and Melbourne. The work's success and itinerant life enact what Mark Godfrey describes (with reference to the titles of works by David Hammons) as Halilaj's "flight fantasies" and the capacity for birds to "fly wherever they wish, borders notwithstanding."[3] The installation shifts in response to the size and shape of different exhibition spaces, and at each venue Halilaj and his studio embark on a new process of laying out the individual elements. Each time it is revisited, it is reworked to create new relationships, new narrative pathways, and new meanings. In this way *Very volcanic over this green feather* holds the fluidity of memory itself. **(BE)**

1 *The Conference of the Animals (An Exhibition of Children's Drawings)*, Queens Museum, NY, September 16, 2020–January 31, 2021.

2 *Petrit Halilaj: Very volcanic over this green feather*, Tate St Ives, UK, October 16, 2021–January 16, 2022.

3 Mark Godfrey, "Flight Fantasies: Mark Godfrey on the Art of Petrit Halilaj," *Artforum* 60, no. 3 (November 2021), https://www.artforum.com/features/mark-godfrey-on-the-art-of-petrit-halilaj-250832.

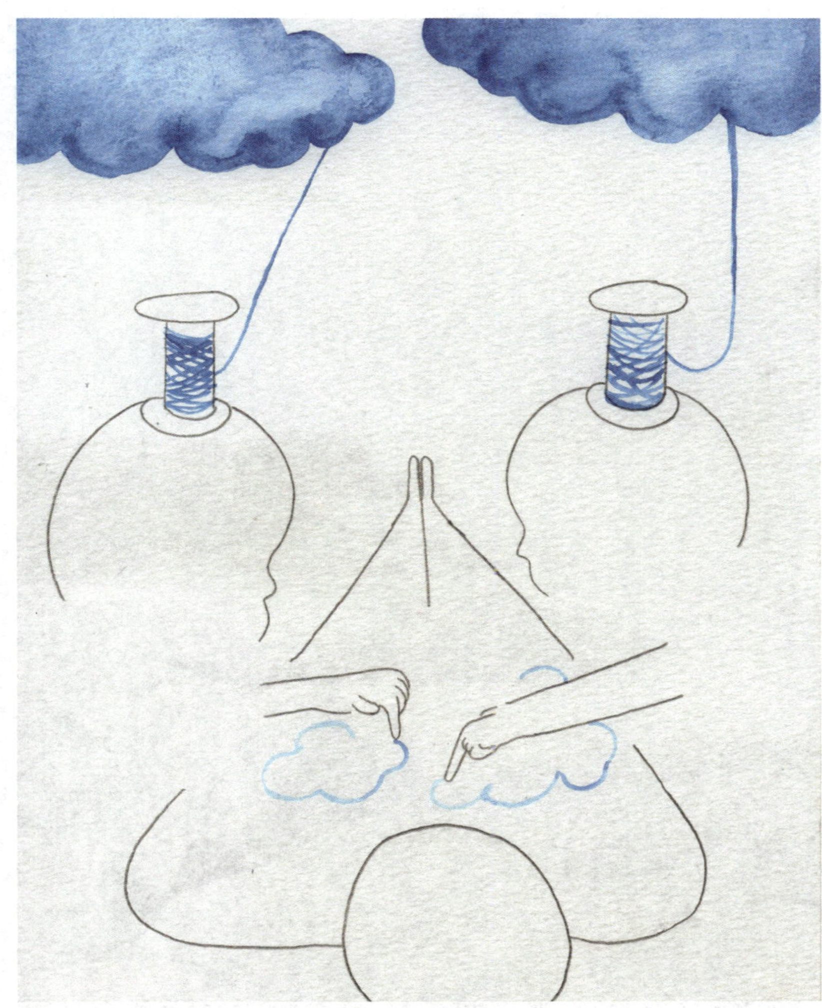

13.2

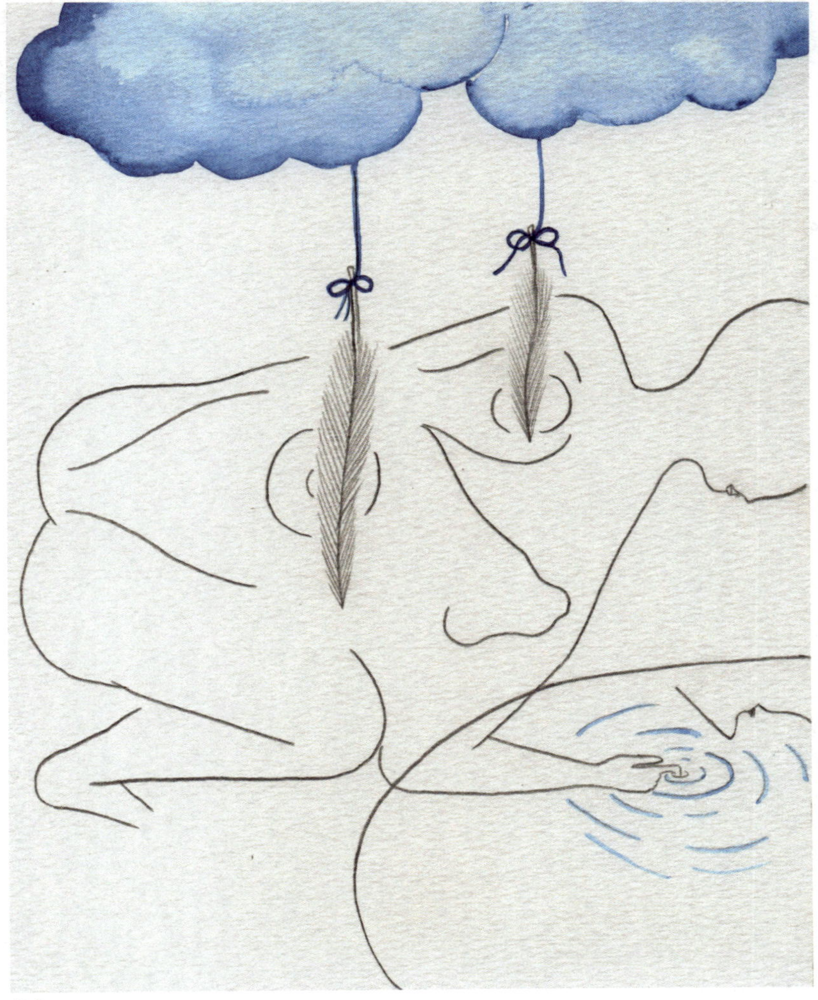

13.3

*Inner sky sketches for Cloud Museum*, 2024

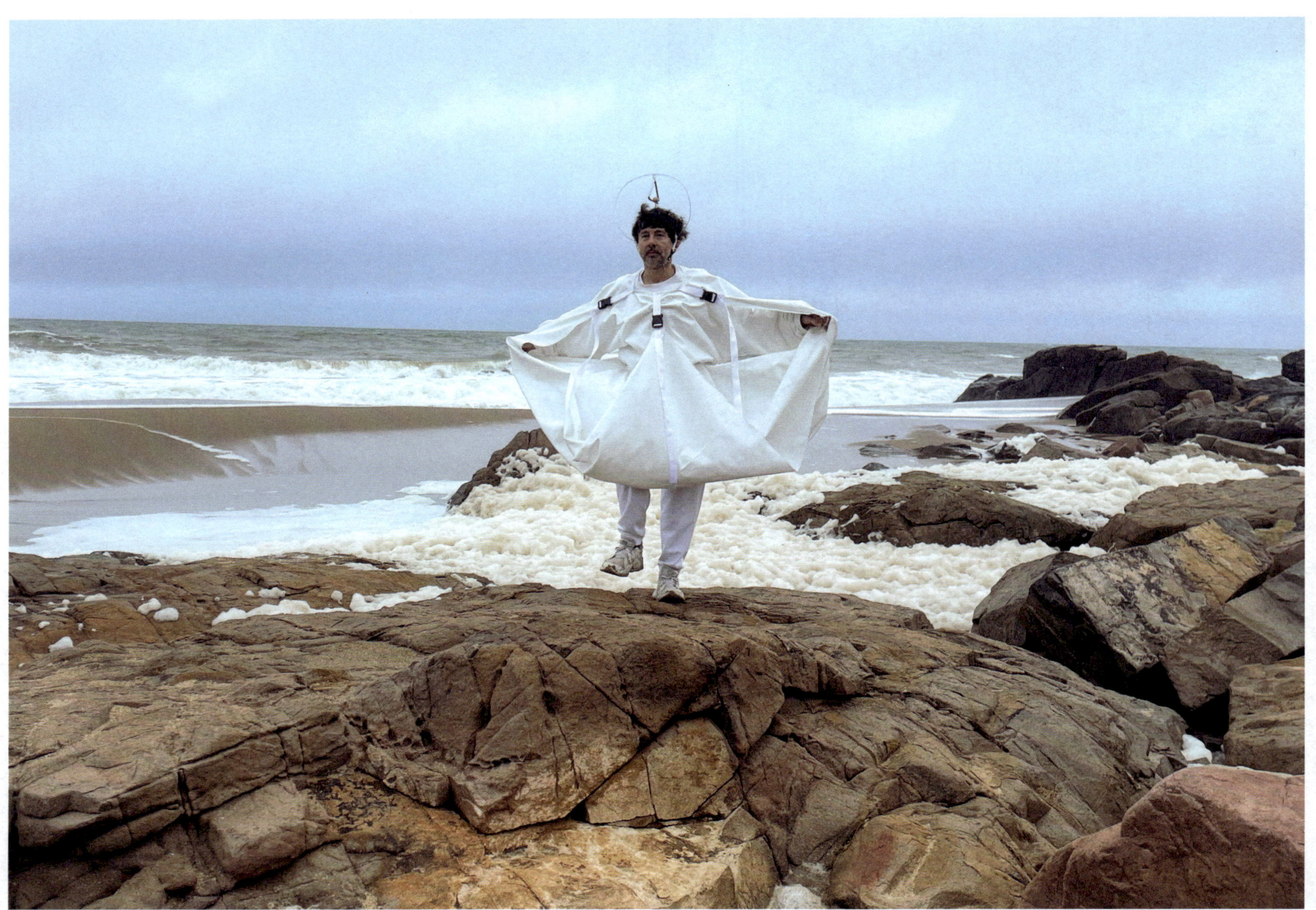

13.4

Invocation for *Cloud Museum*, 2024

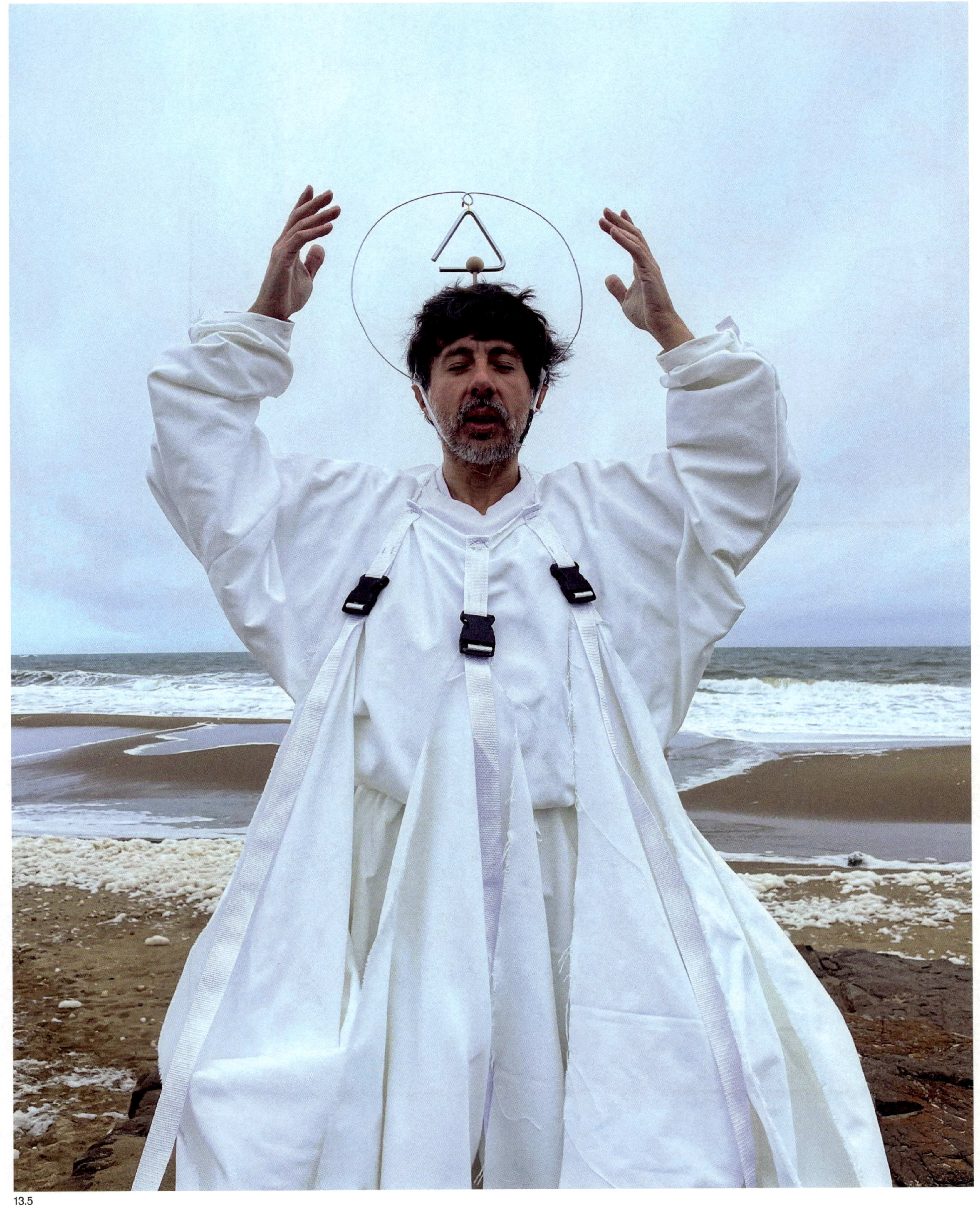

13.5

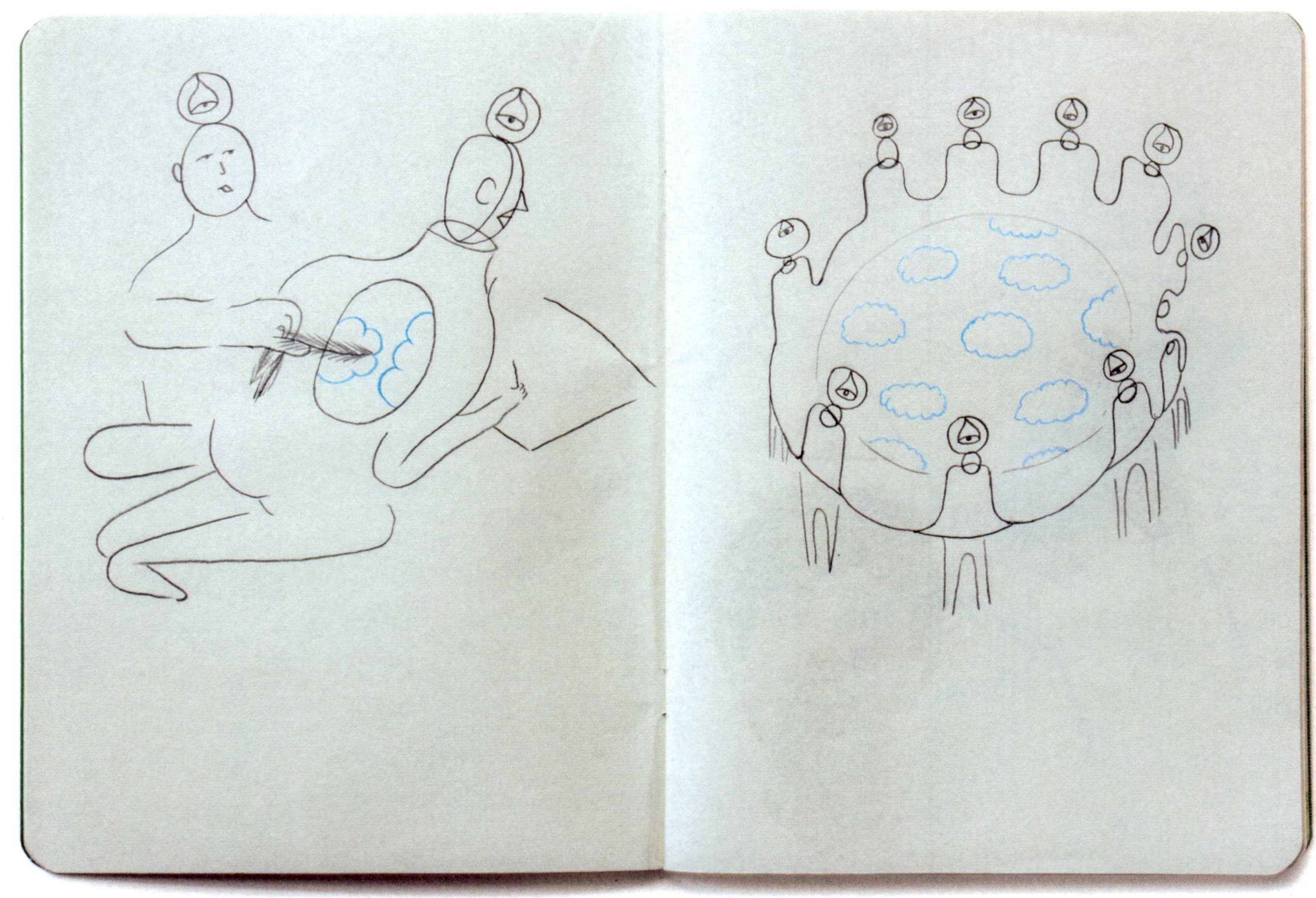

13.6

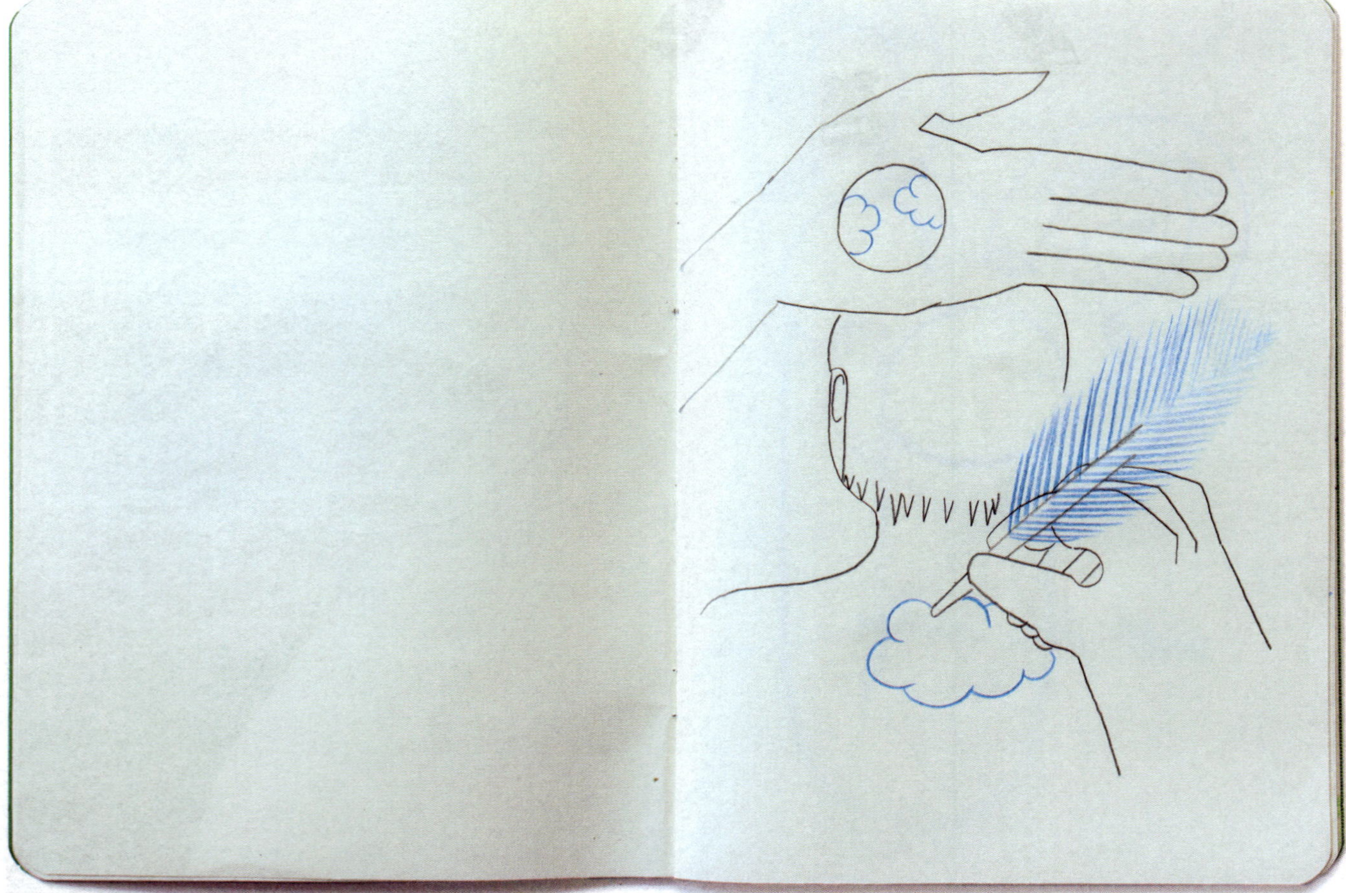

13.7

*Inner sky sketches for Cloud Museum*, 2024

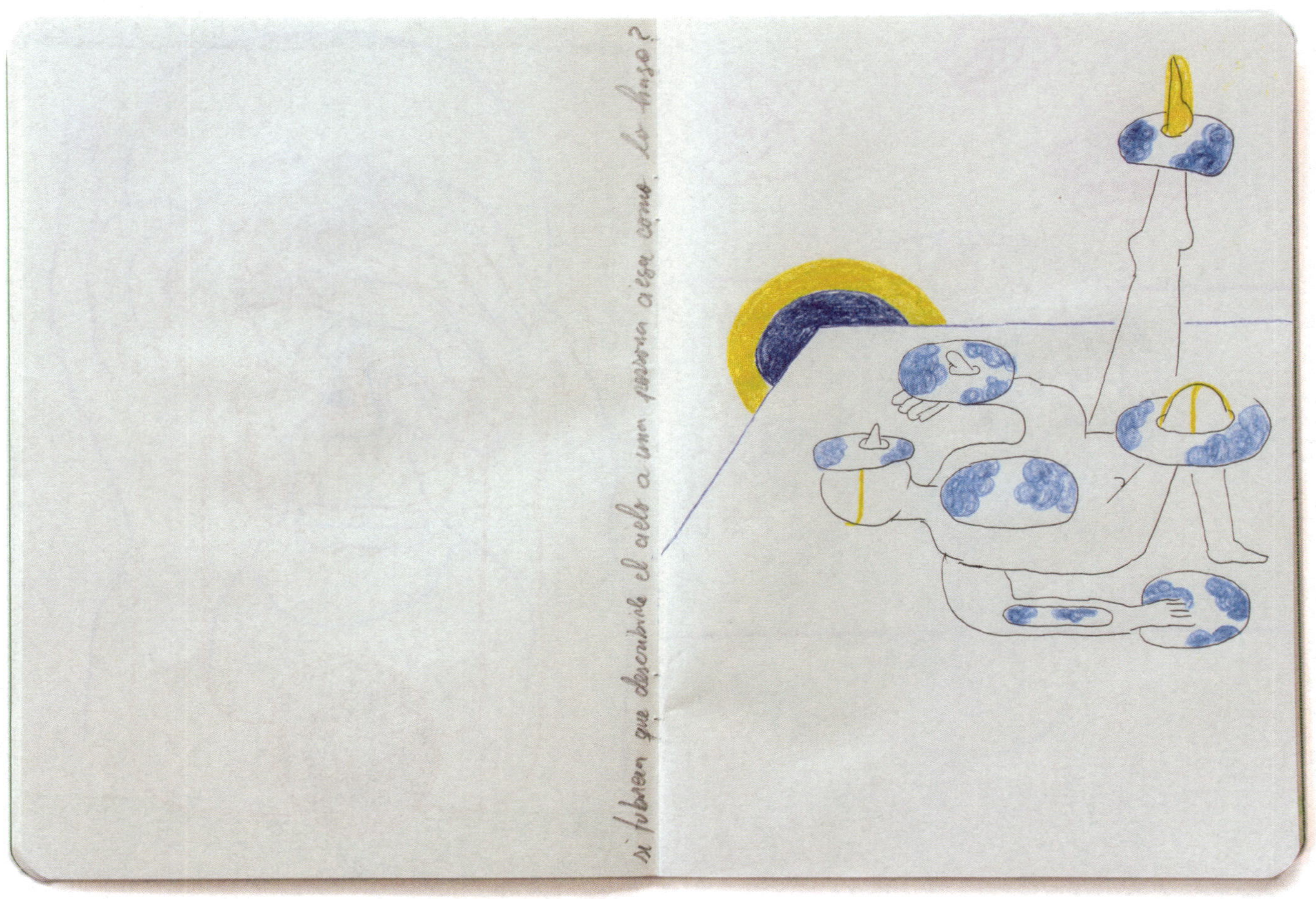

13.8

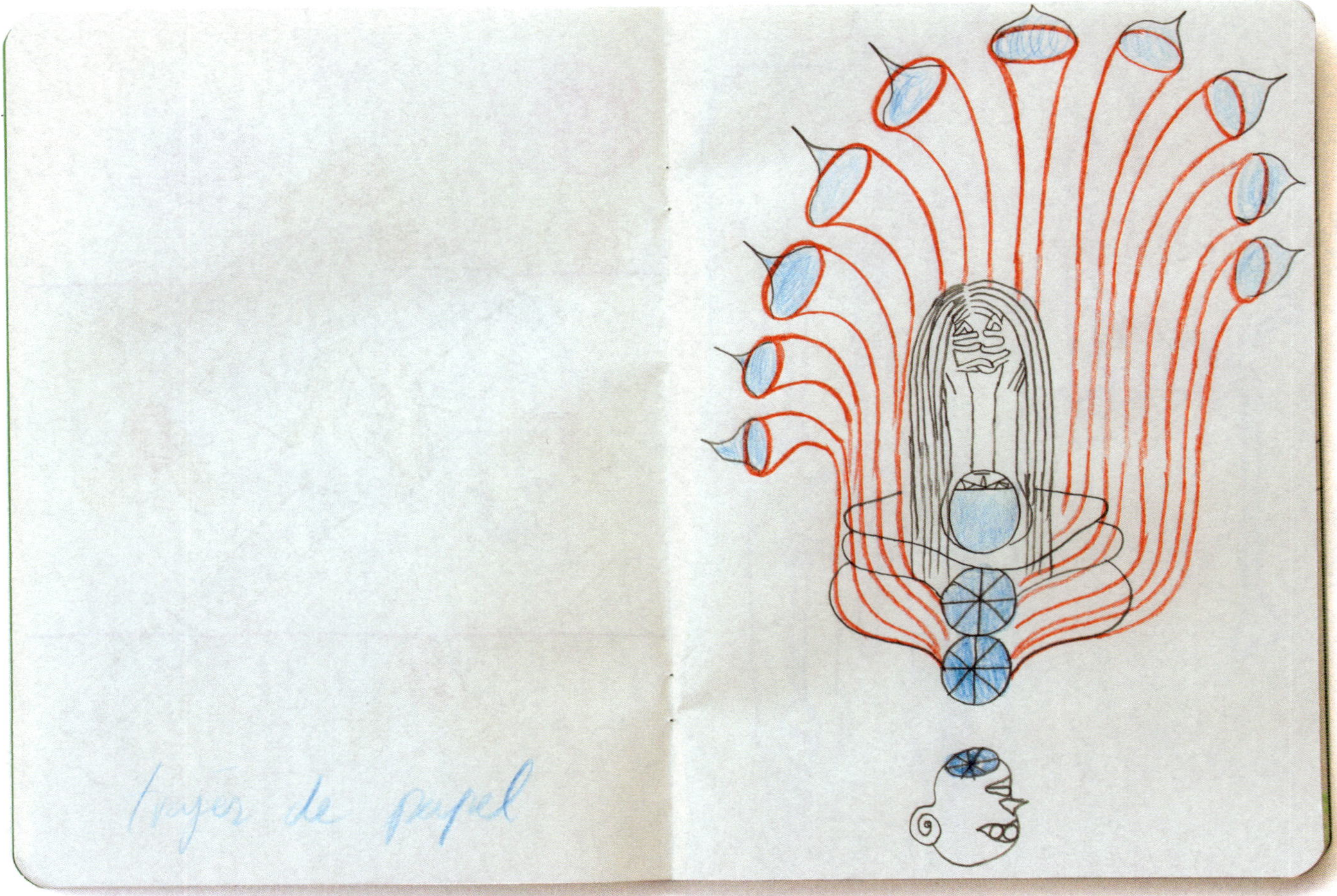

13.9

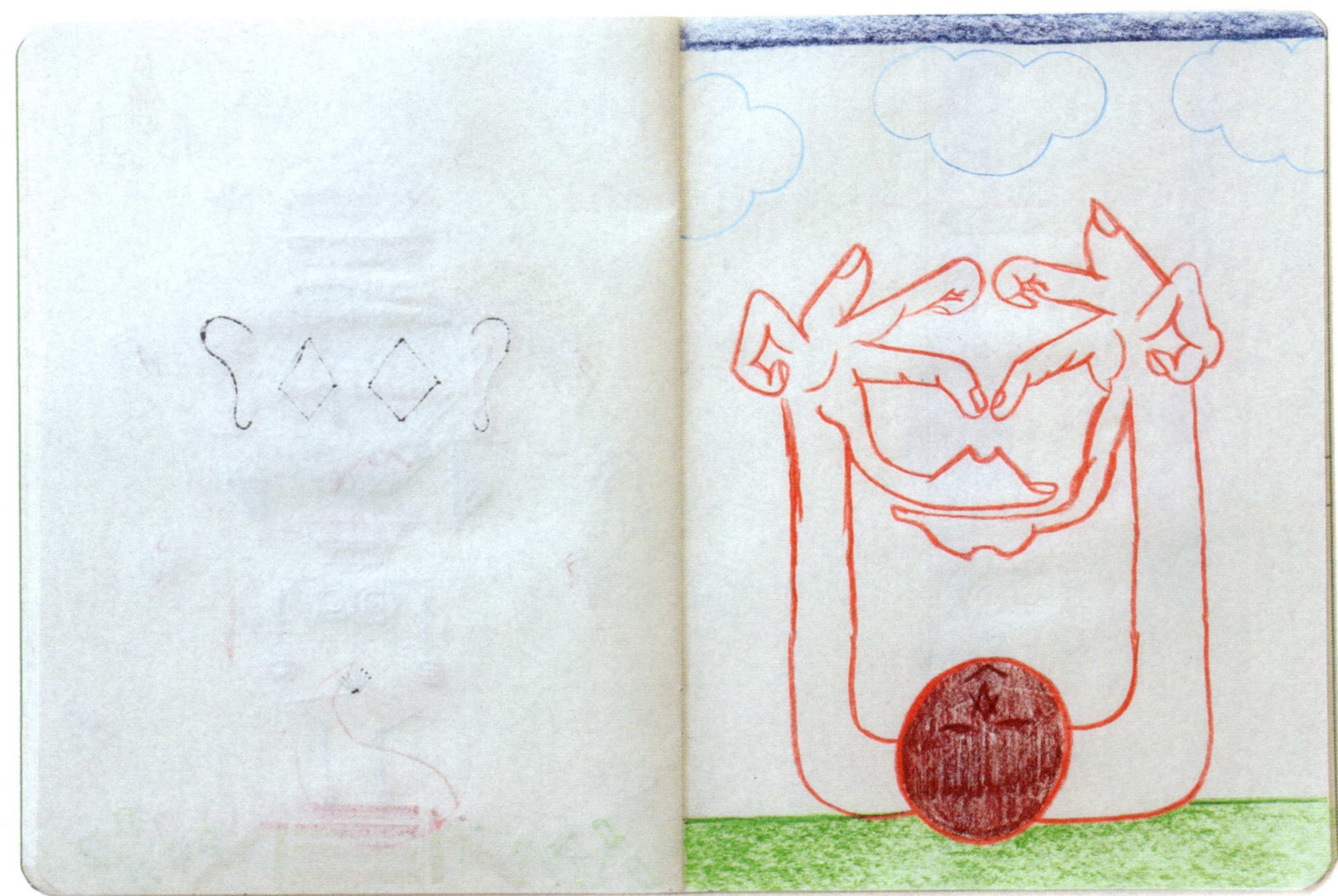

13.10

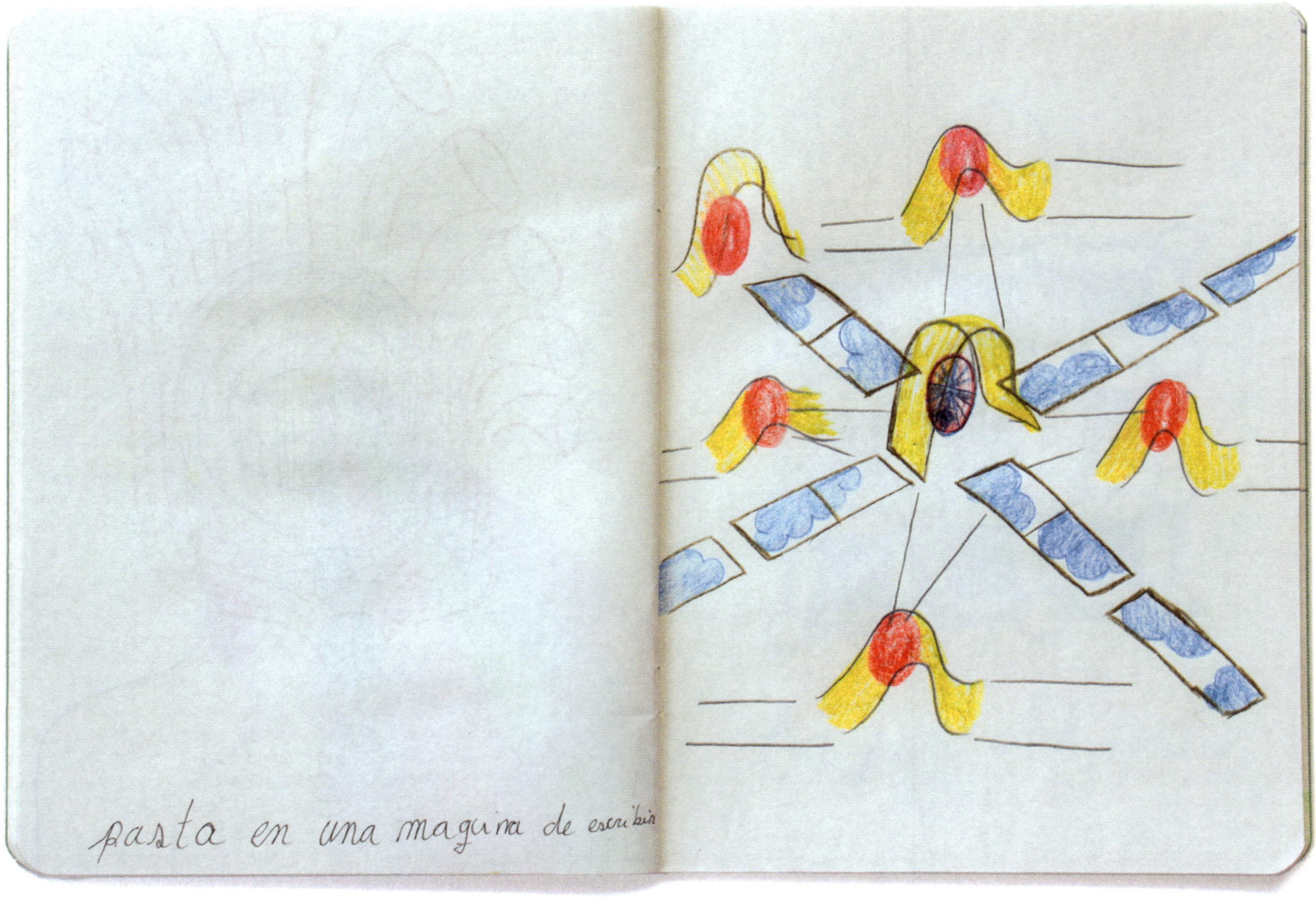


13.11

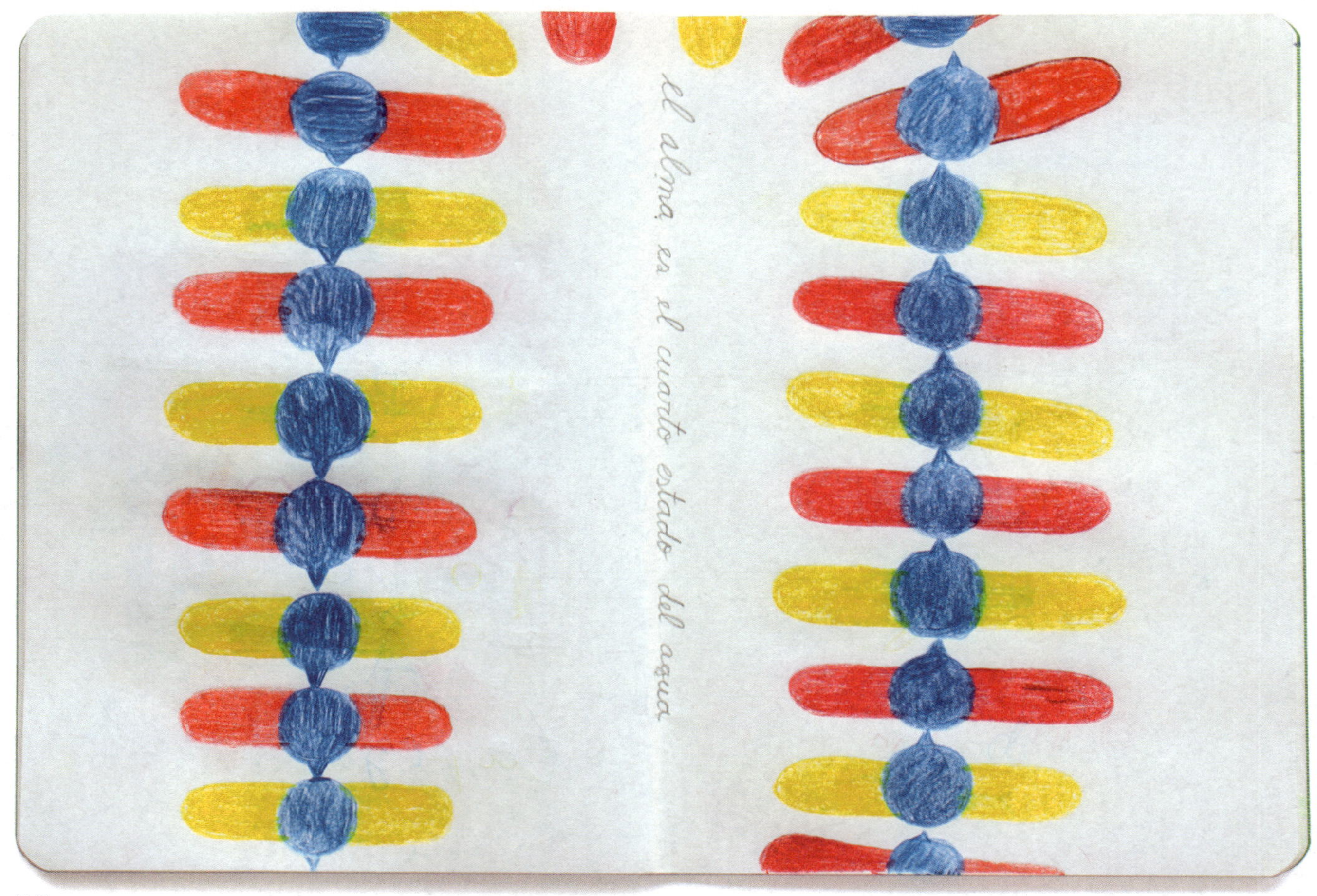


13.12

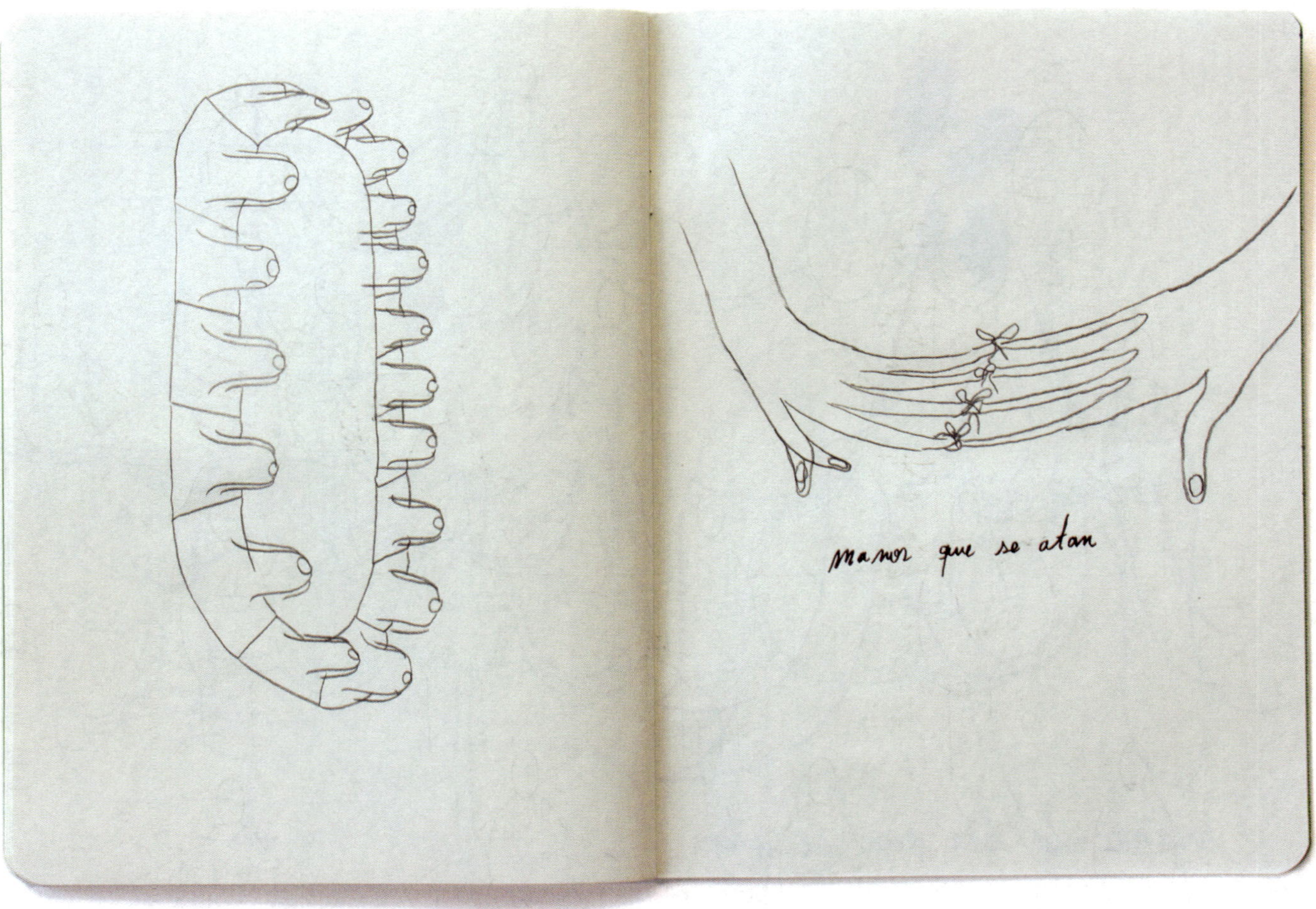


13.13

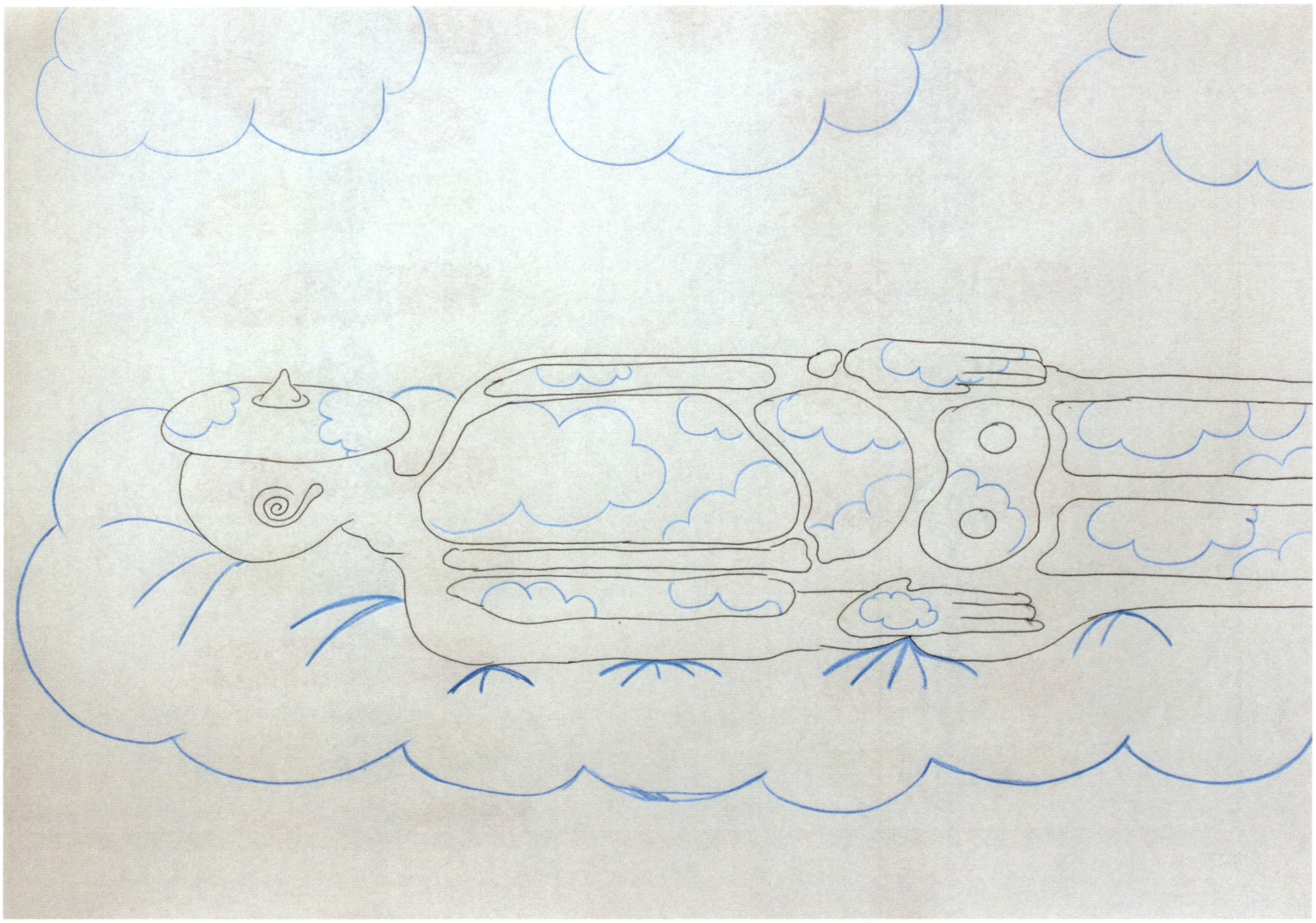

13.14

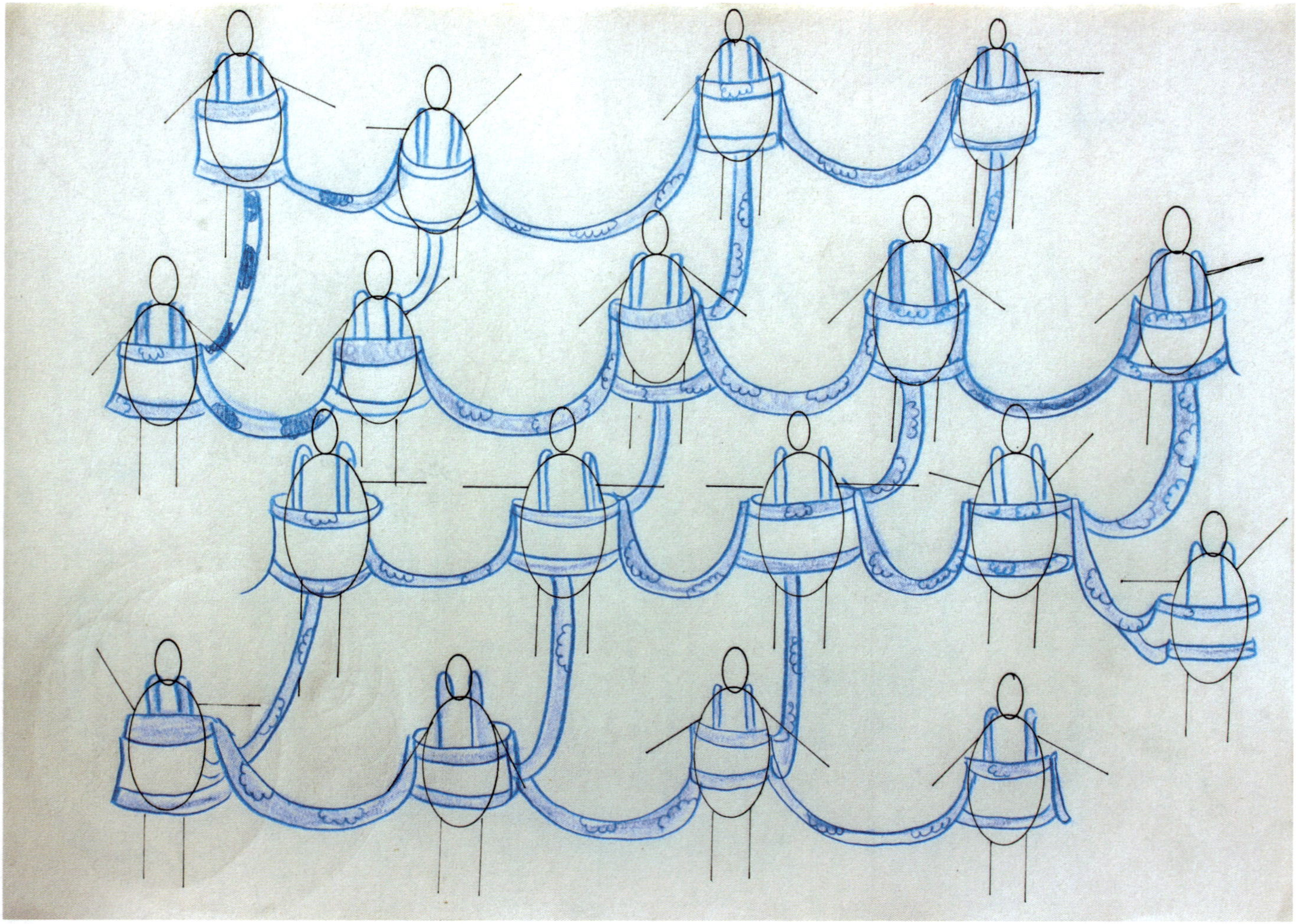

13.15

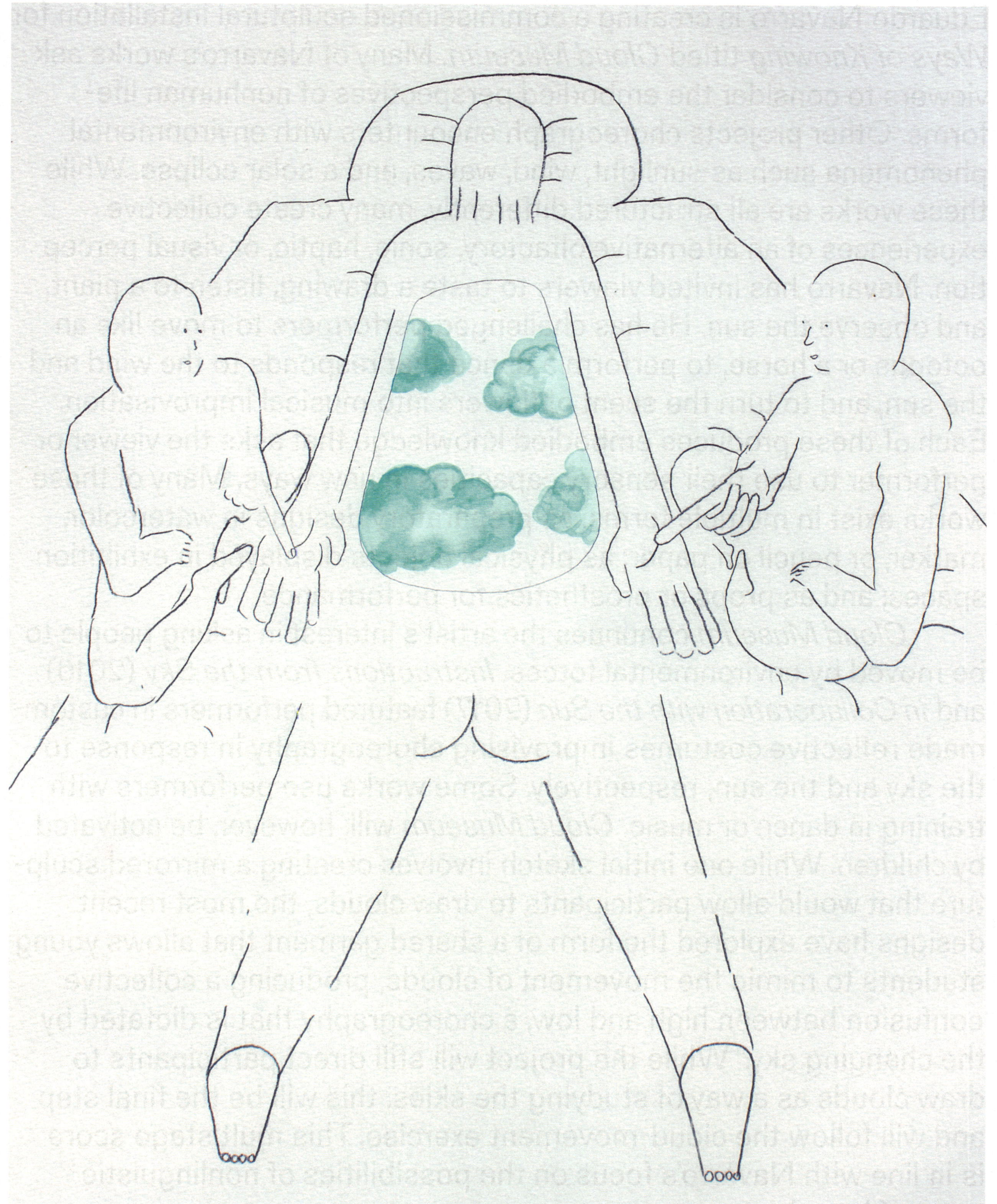

13.16

Eduardo Navarro is creating a commissioned sculptural installation for *Ways of Knowing* titled *Cloud Museum*. Many of Navarro's works ask viewers to consider the embodied perspectives of nonhuman life-forms. Other projects choreograph encounters with environmental phenomena such as sunlight, wind, waves, and a solar eclipse. While these works are all structured differently, many create collective experiences of an alternative olfactory, sonic, haptic, or visual perception. Navarro has invited viewers to taste a drawing, listen to a plant, and observe the sun. He has challenged performers to move like an octopus or a horse, to perform a dance that responds to the wind and the sun, and to turn the scent of flowers into musical improvisation. Each of these produces embodied knowledge that asks the viewer or performer to use their sensory capacities in new ways. Many of these works exist in multiple forms: as preparatory designs in watercolor, marker, or pencil on paper; as physical objects displayed in exhibition spaces; and as props or prosthetics for performance.

*Cloud Museum* continues the artist's interest in asking people to be moved by environmental forces. *Instructions from the Sky* (2016) and *In Collaboration with the Sun* (2017) featured performers in custom-made reflective costumes improvising choreography in response to the sky and the sun, respectively. Some works use performers with training in dance or music. *Cloud Museum* will, however, be activated by children. While one initial sketch involves creating a mirrored sculpture that would allow participants to draw clouds, the most recent designs have explored the form of a shared garment that allows young students to mimic the movement of clouds, producing a collective "confusion between high and low, a choreography that is dictated by the changing sky." While the project will still direct participants to draw clouds as a way of studying the skies, this will be the final step and will follow the cloud-movement exercise. This multistage score is in line with Navarro's focus on the possibilities of nonlinguistic ways of knowing.

*Cloud Museum* aims to produce shared knowledge, but the work in development will also consider the unevenness of our individual perceptual capacities. Contemplating the inclusion of those who are blind or have low vision, Navarro has produced several sketches that depict two participants sketching clouds with their fingers onto bodies that lie flat between them, asking, "Can we draw with our fingertips a cloud on the palm of a visually impaired person?" In one drawing, the heads of the people sketching are topped by spools of blue thread that connect them to the clouds. In another, feathers with strings drop from the clouds, where they seem to have drawn eyes and a nose on the back of a figure leaning over a mirrored surface. In a third preparatory sketch for the project, the artist outlines eight koan-like phrases, including "bones as ideas," "skin as stories," "thoughts as communion," "aura as result," and "eyes as mirrors." These metaphors point to the artist's deep interest in acts of translation. Drawing clouds requires knowing clouds, and knowing clouds requires an act of transference, a belief in "clouds as muscles" and "wind as those who are moved by it." (BE)

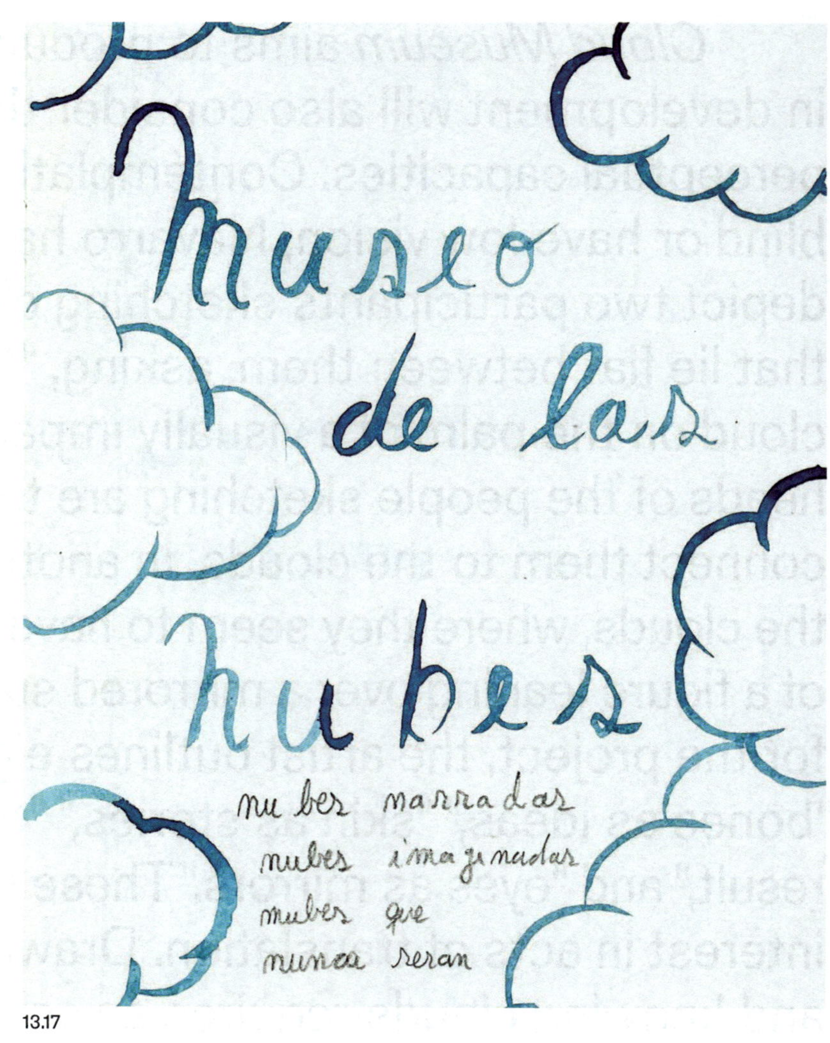


13.17

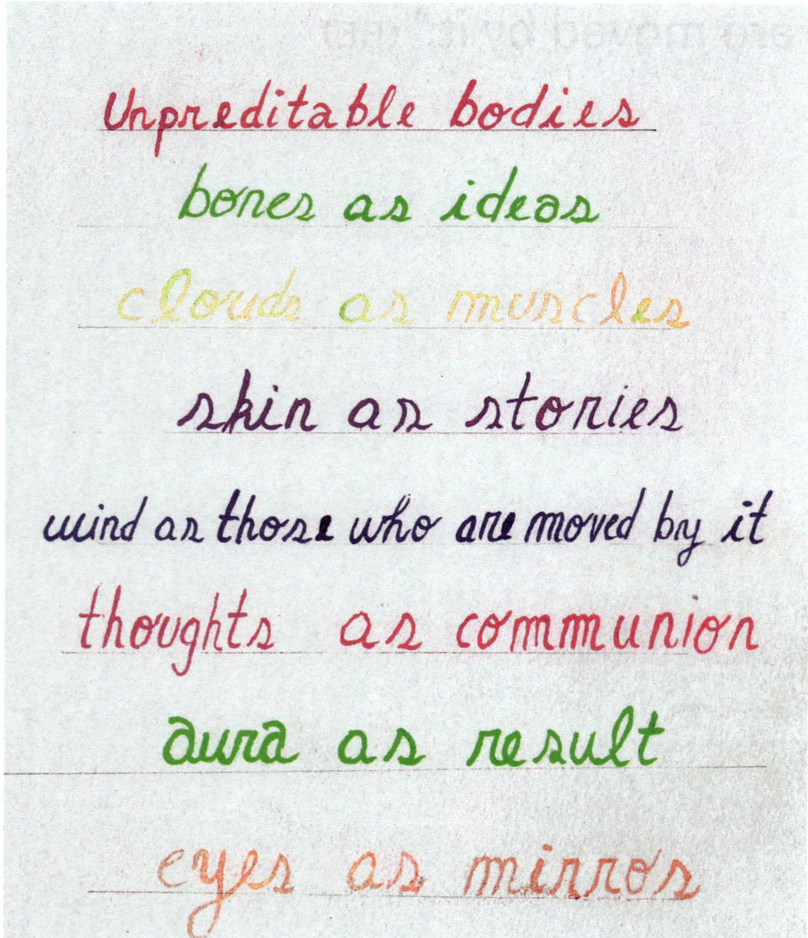

Unpreditable bodies
bones as ideas
clouds as muscles
skin as stories
wind as those who are moved by it
thoughts as communion
aura as result
eyes as mirros

13.18

IOSU ARAMBURU (b. 1986, Lima, Peru) lives and works in Lima. His work has been the subject of institutional solo exhibitions at Sala de Arte Público Siqueiros (SAPS), Mexico City (2024); Q Galería, Universidad San Francisco de Quito, Ecuador (2023); Sala Luis Caballero, Universidad de los Andes, Bogotá (2022); and Museo de Arte de la Universidad San Marcos, Lima (2018), among others. His work has been included in numerous group exhibitions, including those at Museo del Banco Central de Reserva, Lima (2022); Museo Amparo de Puebla, Mexico (2019); Real Academia de Bellas Artes de San Fernando, Madrid (2019); and Museo de Arte de Lima (2017). Aramburu received the Artist Research Fellowship from the Patricia Phelps de Cisneros Research Institute for the Study of Art from Latin America at the Museum of Modern Art, New York (2021), and a residency at Delfina Foundation, London (2021), among other significant awards and fellowships. He studied at the Facultad de Arte y Diseño, Pontificia Universidad Católica del Perú, Lima.

SAMMY BALOJI (b. 1978, Lubumbashi, Democratic Republic of the Congo) lives and works in Lubumbashi and Brussels. His work has been the subject of institutional solo exhibitions at Kunsthalle Mainz, Germany (2023); Lunds Konsthall, Lund, Sweden (2020); and National Museum of African Art, Smithsonian Institution, Washington, DC (2012), among others. He participated in the 35th Bienal de São Paulo (2023); 15th Sharjah Biennial, United Arab Emirates (2023); 12th Berlin Biennale for Contemporary Art (2022); Documenta 14, Athens, Greece, and Kassel, Germany (2017); 11th Shanghai Biennale (2016); and 56th Venice Biennale (2015). His work has appeared in group exhibitions and screenings, including those at Middelheim Museum, Antwerp, Belgium (2022); Centro Atlántico de Arte Moderno, Las Palmas, Spain (2021); Musée du Quai Branly–Jacques Chirac, Paris (2020); Palais de Tokyo, Paris (2020); Museum für Moderne Kunst, Frankfurt (2020); Kadist, Paris (2019); and WIELS Brussels (2017). He has received major awards, including the Chevalier des Artes et des Lettres (2016). His work is in the permanent collections of Mathaf—Arab Museum of Modern Art, Doha, Qatar; Minneapolis Institute of Art; Musée du Quai Branly–Jacques Chirac; Museum für Moderne Kunst, Frankfurt; National Gallery of Canada, Ottawa; National Museum of African Art, Smithsonian Institution, Washington, DC; Tate Modern, London; and Victoria & Albert Museum, London, among others. He studied arts and humanities and computer sciences and communications at the University of Lubumbashi and fine arts at the Haute École des Arts du Rhin, Strasbourg, France. He holds a PhD in artistic research from Sint Lucas Antwerpen, Antwerp.

ANNA BOGHIGUIAN (b. 1946, Cairo) lives and works in Cairo. Her work has been the subject of institutional solo exhibitions at the Power Plant, Toronto (2023); Kunsthaus Bregenz, Austria (2022); Stedelijk Museum voor Actuele Kunst (S.M.A.K.), Ghent, Belgium (2021); Tate Modern, London (2019); Beaux-Arts de Paris (2019); New Museum of Contemporary Art, New York (2018); Museum der Moderne, Salzburg, Austria (2018); Castello di Rivoli Museo d'Arte Contemporaneo, Italy (2017); and Carré d'Art, Nîmes, France (2016), among others. She participated in the the 35th Bienal de São Paulo (2023); 22nd Biennale of Sydney (2020); SITE Sante Fe International Biennial (2016); Armenian Pavilion, 56th Venice Biennale (2015); Istanbul Biennial (2015); Sharjah Biennial, United Arab Emirates (2015, 2011); 31st Bienal de São Paulo (2014); and Documenta 13, Kassel, Germany (2012). Her work has been featured in group exhibitions at Museo Jumex, Mexico City (2019); Museum of Modern Art, New York (2017); Art Institute of Chicago (2013); and ZKM Center for Art and Media, Karlsruhe, Germany (2013), among others. In 2015 her work for the Armenian Pavilion was awarded the Golden Lion for best national participation at the 56th Venice Biennale. Her work is in the permanent collections of the Art Institute of Chicago; Benaki Museum, Athens; Castello di Rivoli Museo d'Arte Contemporaneo, Italy; Guggenheim Abu Dhabi, United Arab Emirates; Kadist, Paris; Museo Jumex, Mexico City; Museum der Moderne, Salzburg, Austria; New Museum of Contemporary Art, New York; Tate Modern, London; and Van Abbe Museum, Eindhoven, Netherlands, among others. She studied economics and political science at the American University in Cairo and later studied art and music at McGill University, Montreal.

CABELLO/CARCELLER (b. 1963, Paris/b. 1964, Madrid) is an artist team formed in 1992. They live and work in Madrid and teach in the Faculty of Fine Arts, Universidad de Castilla–La Mancha, Cuenca, Spain. Their work has been the subject of solo exhibitions at Museo Patio Herreriano, Valladolid, Spain (2023); Azkuna Zentroa–Alhóndiga, Bilbao, Spain (2022); Museo Universitario Arte Contemporáneo (MUAC), Mexico City (2019); and Institut Valencià d'Art Modern (IVAM), Spain (2016), among others. Their work was included in 35th Bienal de São Paulo (2023) and in group exhibitions at the Museo Centro Nacional de Arte Reina Sofía, Madrid (2023); Museu d'Art Contemporani de Barcelona (MACBA) (2020); and Centre Pompidou, Paris (2016), among others. Their work is held in the permanent collections of the Museo Nacional Centro de Arte Reina Sofía; Museu d'Art Contemporani de Barcelona; Colección de Arte Contemporáneo Fundación "la Caixa," Barcelona; and Museo Artium Centro–Museo Vasco de Arte Contemporáneo, Vitoria-Gasteiz, Spain, among others. Cabello/Carceller both hold BFAs from Universidad

Complutense de Madrid and MFAs in aesthetics and art theory from Universidad Autónoma de Madrid. They studied English literature at the University of Glasgow, Scotland, and new genres at San Francisco Art Institute, and they hold a PhD in fine arts from Universidad de Vigo, Spain.

CHANG YUCHEN (b. 1989, Shanxi, China) lives and works in New York. Her work has been included in group exhibitions at Beijing Art Biennale (2023); UCCA Dune, Beidaihe, China (2022, 2021); Power Station of Art, Shanghai (2021); and Para Site, Hong Kong (2019), among others. She has given performance-lectures at Carnegie Museum of Art, Pittsburgh (2024); Amant, Brooklyn (2023); Artists Space (2022), Poetry Project (2022), and Abrons Art Center (2019), all New York; and Tai Kwun Contemporary, Hong Kong (2019), among others. Her work is in many institutional collections, including Asia Art Archive, Hong Kong and Brooklyn; Aspen Art Museum; the library of the Museum of Modern Art and Thomas J. Watson Library at the Metropolitan Museum of Art, both New York; Power Station of Art, Shanghai; Tai Kwun Contemporary Artists' Book Library, Hong Kong; Rosemary Furtak Collection, Walker Art Center Library, Minneapolis; and the Yale University Arts of the Book Collection, New Haven, CT. She holds a BA in photography from Central Academy of Fine Arts, Beijing, and an MFA in print media from School of the Art Institute of Chicago.

PETRIT HALILAJ (b. 1986, Kostërrc [Skenderaj], Kosovo) lives and works in Berlin; Bozzolo, Italy; and Pristina, Kosovo. He teaches at Beaux-Arts de Paris. His work has been the subject of institutional solo exhibitions at the Metropolitan Museum of Art, New York (2024); Museo Tamayo, Mexico City (2023); Fries Museum, Leeuwarden, Netherlands (2022); Tate St Ives, Cornwall, UK (2021); Palacio de Cristal, Madrid (2020); Hammer Museum at UCLA, Los Angeles (2018); Zentrum Paul Klee, Bern, Switzerland (2018); Fondazione Merz, Turin, Italy (2018); New Museum of Contemporary Art, New York (2018); Hangar Bicocca, Milan (2015); Kölnischer Kunstverein, Cologne; (2015); WIELS, Brussels (2013); and the Kosovo Pavilion, 54th Venice Biennale (2013), among others. His work has been included in the National Gallery of Victoria Triennial, Melbourne, Australia (2023); Manifesta 14, Pristina, Kosovo (2022); and the 57th Venice Biennale (2017), as well as in group presentations at the Louisiana Museum of Modern Art, Humlebæk, Denmark (2021, 2019); Fundació Joan Miró, Barcelona (2021); Palais des Beaux-Arts, Paris (2021); Queens Museum, NY (2020); Hamburger Kunsthalle, Hamburg (2017); and Museo Jumex, Mexico City (2016), among others. His work is held in the permanent collections of Centre Pompidou, Paris; Colección Jumex, Mexico City; FRAC Champagne-Ardenne, France; Kölnischer Kunstverein, Cologne; Musée National d'Art Moderne, Paris; and Museum of Contemporary Art Chicago, among others. Since 2014 he has also exhibited collaboratively with his partner, the architect and artist Alvaro Urbano. He studied at the Accademia di Belle Arti di Brera, Milan.

SKY HOPINKA (Ho-Chunk Nation/Pechanga Band of Luiseño Indians, b. 1984, Ferndale, WA) lives and works in Brooklyn and is an assistant professor in the Department of Art, Film, and Visual Studies at Harvard University, Cambridge, MA. His work has been shown at festivals including Sundance, Park City and Salt Lake City, UT; Toronto International Film Festival; and New York Film Festival. His work has been the subject of solo exhibitions and installations at the Memorial Art Gallery, University of Rochester, NY (2022); Museum of Modern Art, New York (2021); Hessel Museum of Art, Center for Curatorial Studies, Bard College, Annandale-on-Hudson, NY (2020); and Saint Louis Art Museum (2020), among others. He has participated in group exhibitions, including the Göteborg International Biennial for Contemporary Art, Sweden (2023); 14th Gwangju Biennial, South Korea (2023); Prospect.5, New Orleans (2021); 2018 FRONT Triennial, Cleveland; and 2017 Whitney Biennial, Whitney Museum of American Art, New York. His work is held in the permanent collections of the Brooklyn Museum; Guggenheim Museum and Museum of Modern Art, both New York; Marielouise Hessel Collection, Hessel Museum of Art, Center for Curatorial Studies, Bard College, Annandale-on-Hudson, NY; Minneapolis Institute of Art; and Walker Art Center, Minneapolis. In 2022 he was named a MacArthur "Genius" Fellow and has also held a Guggenheim Fellowship and a MacDowell Residency, among other major honors. He holds a BA from Portland State University, OR, and an MFA from the University of Wisconsin-Milwaukee.

CHRISTINE HOWARD SANDOVAL (enrolled member of Chalon Nation, Bakersfield, CA, b. 1975, Anaheim, CA) lives and works in the unceded territories of the Squamish, Tsleil-Waututh, and Musqueam First Nations and is an assistant professor of interdisciplinary praxis in the Audain Faculty of Art at Emily Carr University, Vancouver. Howard Sandoval's work has been the subject of solo exhibitions at the Institute of Contemporary Art San Diego (2021); Contemporary Art Gallery, Vancouver (2021); Oregon Contemporary, Portland (2021); and Colorado Springs Fine Arts Center at Colorado College (2019), during which time she was the Mellon Artist in Residence at Colorado College. Her work has been exhibited in the 12th Seoul Mediacity Biennale (2023) and in group exhibitions at Clark Art Institute, Williamstown, MA (2023); Henry Art Gallery, University of Washington, Seattle (2023); Museu de Arte Contemporânea da Universidade de São Paulo (MAC

USP) (2022); Designtransfer, Universität der Künste Berlin (2013); El Museo del Barrio, New York (2013); and Socrates Sculpture Park, Long Island City, NY (2010). Her work is held in the permanent collections of Forge Project, traditional lands of the Moh-He-Con-Nuck; Hammer Museum at UCLA, Los Angeles; and Museum of Contemporary Art San Diego. She holds a BFA from Pratt Institute, Brooklyn, and an MFA from Parsons, the New School for Design, New York.

EDUARDO NAVARRO (b. 1979, Buenos Aires) lives and works in Piriápolis, Uruguay, and Buenos Aires. His work has been the subject of institutional solo exhibitions at Gasworks, London (2020); Museu de Arte Contemporânea de Niterói (MAC), Rio de Janeiro (2019); Drawing Center, New York (2018); Der TANK, Institut Kunst Gender Natur, Hochschule für Gestaltung und Kunst FHNW, Basel, Switzerland (2017); and Museo Tamayo, Mexico City (2016), among others. His work has been included in the Toronto Biennial of Art (2022); SITE Santa Fe Biennial (2018); Seoul Mediacity Biennial (2016); 32nd Bienal de São Paulo (2016); 12th Sharjah Biennial, United Arab Emirates (2015); 9th Mercosul Biennial, Porto Alegre, Brazil (2013); and 29th Bienal de São Paulo (2010) as well as in group exhibitions at the Socrates Sculpture Park, Long Island City, NY (2020); Guggenheim Museum, New York (2020); TBA21, Madrid (2020); Castello di Rivoli Museo d'Arte Contemporaneo, Italy (2018); Sculpture Center, Long Island City, NY (2016); and New Museum of Contemporary Art, New York (2015); among others. His work is in the permanent collections of Castello di Rivoli Museo d'Arte Contemporaneo; Kadist, Paris; Los Angeles County Museum of Art; Museo de Arte Latinoamericano (MALBA), Buenos Aires; Museum of Modern Art, New York; and Sharjah Art Foundation, United Arab Emirates, among others. He studied in the Beca Kuitca, artist Guillermo Kuitca's visual arts residency for Argentine artists, the Universidad de Buenos Aires, and the Centro Cultural Ricardo Rojas, Buenos Aires.

GALA PORRAS-KIM (b. 1984, Bogotá) lives and works in Los Angeles and London. Her work has been the subject of institutional solo exhibitions at Storefront for Art and Architecture, New York (2024); Asia Art Archive, Hong Kong (2024); Museum of Contemporary Art Denver (2024); National Museum of Modern and Contemporary Art, Seoul (2023); Leeum Museum of Art, Seoul (2023); Fowler Museum at UCLA, Los Angeles (2023); Museo Universitario Arte Contemporáneo (MUAC), Mexico City (2023); and Museum of Contemporary Art, Los Angeles (2019), among others. Her work has been included in the Liverpool Biennial (2023); 34th Bienal de São Paulo (2021); and 13th Gwangju Biennale, South Korea (2021), and in group exhibitions at the Los Angeles County Museum of Art (2021, 2017); Museum of Contemporary Art Chicago (2021, 2019); Hammer Museum at UCLA, Los Angeles (2019, 2016); PinchukArtCentre, Kyiv, Ukraine (2019); Whitney Museum of American Art, New York (2019, 2017); Para Site, Hong Kong (2019); and Seoul Museum of Art (2017), among others. She has held residencies at the Getty Research Institute, Los Angeles (2021–2022); Delfina Foundation, London (2021); Radcliffe Institute for Advanced Study, Harvard University, Cambridge, MA (2020); and Skowhegan School of Painting and Sculpture, ME (2010), among others. Her work is included in the permanent collections of the Brooklyn Museum; Museum of Modern Art and Whitney Museum of American Art, both New York; Dallas Museum; Museum of Contemporary Art Chicago; Los Angeles County Museum of Art; Hammer Museum at UCLA and Museum of Contemporary Art, both Los Angeles; Kadist, San Francisco; Pérez Art Museum, Miami; Seoul Museum of Art; and Leeum Museum of Art, Seoul. She holds a BA from the University of California, Los Angeles, and an MA in Latin American studies from the University of California, Los Angeles, as well as an MFA from California Institute of the Arts, Valencia.

ROSE SALANE (b. 1992, New York) lives and works in New York. Her work has been the subject of institutional solo exhibitions at TANK, Shanghai (2024); Hessel Museum of Art, Center for Curatorial Studies, Bard College, Annandale-on-Hudson, NY (2021); and MIT List Visual Arts Center, Cambridge, MA (2019). Her work has been included in group exhibitions at the Massachusetts Museum of Contemporary Art (MASS MoCA), North Adams (2023); and Renaissance Society, University of Chicago (2022), among others. She participated in the 2022 Whitney Biennial, Whitney Museum of American Art, New York, and the 2021 Triennial, New Museum of Contemporary Art, New York. Her work is in the permanent collections of the Santa Barbara Museum of Art, CA; the Whitney Museum of American Art; and the Walker Art Center, Minneapolis. She holds a BFA in fine arts from Cooper Union, New York, and an MA in urban planning from the Bernard and Anne Spitzer School of Architecture, City University of New York.

## WORKS IN THE EXHIBITION

IOSU ARAMBURU
*Atlas of Andean Modernism*
2022–
printed paper, taped to the wall; number of pages variable
8½ × 11 in. (21.6 × 27.9 cm) each sheet; wall: 93 in. (236.2 cm) high
Courtesy the artist and 80m2 Livia Benavides Gallery, Lima, Peru

SAMMY BALOJI
*Tales of the Copper Cross Garden: Episode 1*
2017
HD video (color, sound); 42 min., wall vinyl (size variable)
Courtesy the artist and Galerie Imane Farès, Paris

ANNA BOGHIGUIAN
*Time of Change*
2022
mixed media on paper
96 drawings: 18⅞ × 24 7/16 in. (48 × 62 cm) each
Courtesy the artist and Milani Gallery, Brisbane, Australia

CABELLO/CARCELLER
*Una voz para Erauso. Epílogo para un tiempo trans* (A voice for Erauso. Epilogue for a trans time)
2021–2022
two-channel 4K video transferred to HD video (color, sound); 28:15 min.
Courtesy the artists, Madrid

*Una voz para Erauso. Personaje 1 (Tino)* (A voice for Erauso. Character 1 [Tino])
2022
color photograph mounted on Dibond
31½ × 25 9/16 in. (80 × 65 cm)
Courtesy the artists, Madrid

*Una voz para Erauso. Personaje 2 (Lewin)* (A voice for Erauso. Character 2 [Lewin])
2022
color photograph mounted on Dibond
31½ × 25 9/16 in. (80 × 65 cm)
Courtesy the artists, Madrid

*Una voz para Erauso. Personaje 3 (Bambi)* (A voice for Erauso. Character 3 [Bambi])
2022
color photograph mounted on Dibond
31½ × 25 9/16 in. (80 × 65 cm)
Courtesy the artists, Madrid

Juan van der Hamen y León
Spain, 1596–1631
*Retrato de Doña Catalina de Erauso. La monja alférez* (Portrait of Doña Catalina de Erauso. The lieutenant nun)
c. 1630
oil on canvas
29½ × 25⅜ × 3⅛ in. (75 × 64.4 × 8 cm) framed
Kutxa Fundazioa Bilduma, Donostia/San Sebastián

CHANG YUCHEN
*Coral Dictionary (Sentences)*
2019–
pencil on paper
selection of up to 76 drawings: 17 × 14 in. (43.2 × 35.6 cm) each unframed
Courtesy the artist, New York, and Beijing Commune

*Coral Dictionary Vol. 1: 2019–2022 (Accordion)*
printed 2022 by Gong Press
accordion-fold book, clamshell box
edition 23/30
3⅜ × 5 13/16 × 2⅝ in. (8.6 × 14.7 × 6.6 cm)
Rosemary Furtak Collection, Walker Art Center Library

*Coral Dictionary (words)*
date unknown
found coral fragments
dimensions variable
Courtesy the artist and Dinawan Island

PETRIT HALILAJ
*Very volcanic over this green feather*
2021
UV-printed felt, spray-painted ink, thread, metal pipe
variable selection of up to 46 hanging elements
installed dimensions variable
Courtesy the artist; ChertLüdde, Berlin; Mennour, Paris; kurimanzutto, Mexico City/New York

SKY HOPINKA
*Visions of an Island*
2016
HD video (color, sound); 15:03 min.
Walker Art Center, Minneapolis, Ruben/Bentson Moving Image Collection

CHRISTINE HOWARD SANDOVAL
*Arch—A Passage Formed By A Curve*
2020
adobe mud and graphite on paper
60 × 96 in. (152.4 × 243.8 cm)
Forge Project Collection, traditional lands of the Moh-He-Con-Nuck

*A Wall Is A Shadow On The Land*
2020–
adobe mud and graphite on paper
60 × 96 in. (152.4 × 243.8 cm)
Courtesy the artist, Vancouver

*Pillars—An Act of Decompression*
2020
adobe mud and graphite on paper
60 × 96 in. (152.4 × 243.8 cm)
Forge Project Collection, traditional lands of the Moh-He-Con-Nuck

*Surface of Emergence*
2023
adobe mud and graphite on paper
2 drawings: 60 × 96 in. (152.4 × 243.8 cm) each
Courtesy the artist, Vancouver

EDUARDO NAVARRO
*Cloud Museum*
2025
Collectively becoming a cloud with the use of emotional energy and inviting the weather to be the choreographer
The dimensions of the work are relative to the sky on the day of the activation, the location of the activation, and the perception of the observer
Courtesy the artist, Piriápolis, Uruguay

GALA PORRAS-KIM
*National Treasures*
2015
ink on paper
161½ × 7⅜ in. (410.2 × 18.7 cm)
Courtesy the artist

*530 National Treasures*
2023
colored pencil and Flashe on paper
4 panels: 71¼ × 118 in. (181 × 300 cm) each
Leeum Museum of Art, Seoul

ROSE SALANE
*Confession 1*
2023
chromogenic print
edition 3/3 + 2 AP
30⅝ × 42¾ × 1⅞ in. (77.8 × 108.6 × 4.8 cm) framed
Returned fragment from Pompeii courtesy the Archaeological Park of Pompeii
Walker Art Center, Minneapolis, Butler Family Fund, 2024

*Confession 2*
2023
chromogenic print
edition 3/3 + 2 AP
30⅝ × 42¾ × 1⅞ in. (77.8 × 108.6 × 4.8 cm) framed
Returned fragment from Pompeii courtesy the Archaeological Park of Pompeii
Walker Art Center, Minneapolis, Butler Family Fund, 2024

*Confession 3*
2023
chromogenic print
edition 2/3 + 2 AP
30⅝ × 42¾ × 1⅞ in. (77.8 × 108.6 × 4.8 cm) framed
Returned fragment from Pompeii courtesy the Archaeological Park of Pompeii
Private collection, New York

*Confession 4*
2023
chromogenic print
edition 2/3 + 2 AP
30⅝ × 42¾ × 1⅞ in. (77.8 × 108.6 × 4.8 cm) framed
Returned fragment from Pompeii courtesy the Archaeological Park of Pompeii
Private collection

*Confession 5*
2023
chromogenic print
AP 1 from an edition of 3 + 2 AP
30⅝ × 42¾ × 1⅞ in. (77.8 × 108.6 × 4.8 cm) framed
Returned fragment from Pompeii courtesy the Archaeological Park of Pompeii
Private collection

*Confession 6*
2023
chromogenic print
AP 2 from an edition of 3 + 2 AP
30⅝ × 42¾ × 1⅞ in. (77.8 × 108.6 × 4.8 cm) framed
Returned fragment from Pompeii courtesy the Archaeological Park of Pompeii
Walker Art Center, Minneapolis, Butler Family Fund, 2024

*Confession 7*
2023
chromogenic print
edition 1/3 + 2 AP
30⅝ × 42¾ × 1⅞ in. (77.8 × 108.6 × 4.8 cm) framed
Returned fragment from Pompeii courtesy the Archaeological Park of Pompeii
Collection Leopold Oetker, New York

*Confession 8*
2023
chromogenic print
edition 2/3 + 2 AP
30⅝ × 42¾ × 1⅞ in. (77.8 × 108.6 × 4.8 cm) framed
Returned fragment from Pompeii courtesy the Archaeological Park of Pompeii
Private collection

*Confession 9*
2023
chromogenic print
edition 2/3 + 2 AP
30⅝ × 42¾ × 1⅞ in. (77.8 × 108.6 × 4.8 cm) framed
Returned fragment from Pompeii courtesy the Archaeological Park of Pompeii
Private collection

*Confession 10*
2023
chromogenic print
edition 2/3 + 2 AP
30⅝ × 42¾ × 1⅞ in. (77.8 × 108.6 × 4.8 cm) framed
Returned fragment from Pompeii courtesy the Archaeological Park of Pompeii
Private collection

*Confession 11*
2023
chromogenic print
edition 2/3 + 2 AP
30⅝ × 42¾ × 1⅞ in. (77.8 × 108.6 × 4.8 cm) framed
Returned fragment from Pompeii courtesy the Archaeological Park of Pompeii
Collection Michael Hershaft, Arlington, Virginia

*Confession 12*
2023
chromogenic print
edition 2/3 + 2 AP
30⅝ × 42¾ × 1⅞ in. (77.8 × 108.6 × 4.8 cm) framed
Returned fragment from Pompeii courtesy the Archaeological Park of Pompeii
Walker Art Center, Minneapolis, Butler Family Fund, 2024

# LIST OF ILLUSTRATIONS

## IOSU ARAMBURU
pp. 13–25

Fig. 1.1

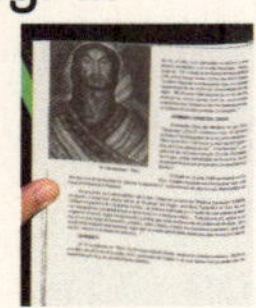

*Atlas of Andean Modernism*
2022–
Page 1939-C7 (detail)
printed paper, taped to the wall; number of pages variable

Fig. 1.2

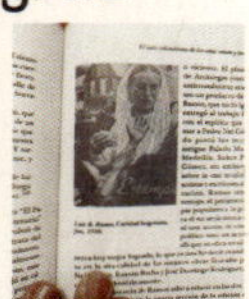

*Atlas of Andean Modernism*
2022–
Page 1939-A6 (detail)
printed paper, taped to the wall; number of pages variable

Fig. 1.3

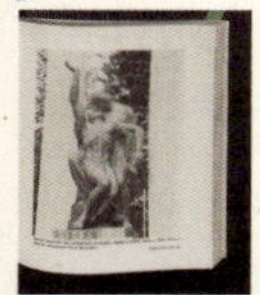

*Atlas of Andean Modernism*
2022–
Page 1939-D5 (detail)
printed paper, taped to the wall; number of pages variable

Fig. 1.4

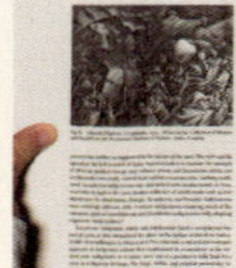

*Atlas of Andean Modernism*
2022–
Page 1939-D11 (detail)
printed paper, taped to the wall; number of pages variable

Fig. 1.5

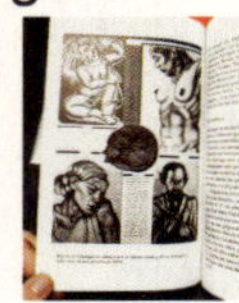

*Atlas of Andean Modernism*
2022–
Page 1939-B6 (detail)
printed paper, taped to the wall; number of pages variable

Fig. 1.6

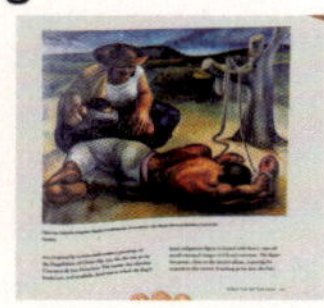

*Atlas of Andean Modernism*
2022–
Page 1939-D7 (detail)
printed paper, taped to the wall; number of pages variable

Fig. 1.7

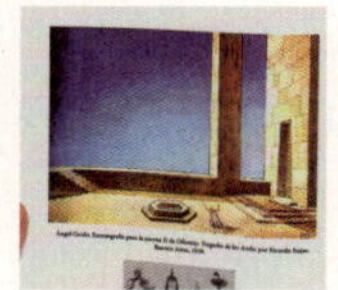

*Atlas of Andean Modernism*
2022–
Page 1939-D8 (detail)
printed paper, taped to the wall; number of pages variable

Figs. 1.8–1.10

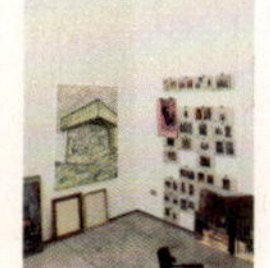

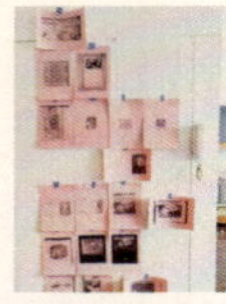

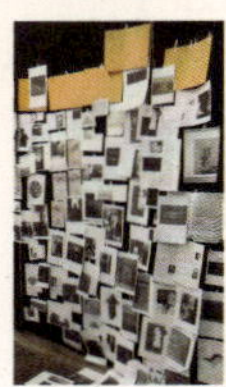

Installation tests for *Atlas of Andean Modernism*
2022–

Fig. 1.11

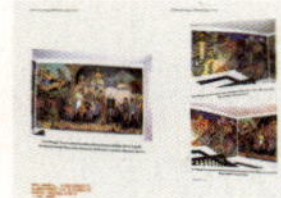

*Atlas of Andean Modernism*
2022–
Page 1939-A8
printed paper, taped to the wall; number of pages variable

Fig. 1.12

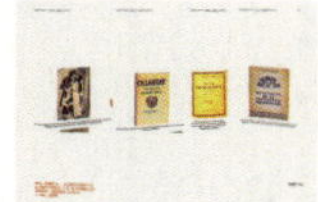

*Atlas of Andean Modernism*
2022–
Page 1939-A9
printed paper, taped to the wall; number of pages variable

Fig. 1.13

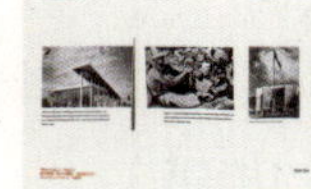

*Atlas of Andean Modernism*
2022–
Page 1939-B8
printed paper, taped to the wall; number of pages variable

Fig. 1.14

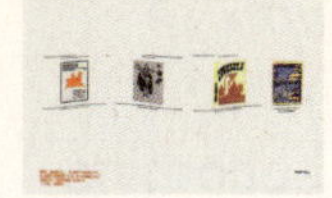

*Atlas of Andean Modernism*
2022–
Page 1939-B9
printed paper, taped to the wall; number of pages variable

Fig. 1.15

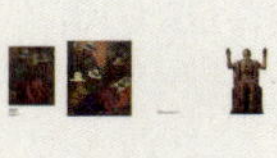

*Atlas of Andean Modernism*
2022–
Page 1939-C10
printed paper, taped to the wall; number of pages variable

Fig. 1.16

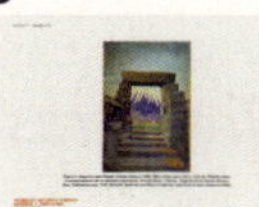

*Atlas of Andean Modernism*
2022–
Page 1939-C11
printed paper, taped to the wall; number of pages variable

Fig. 1.17

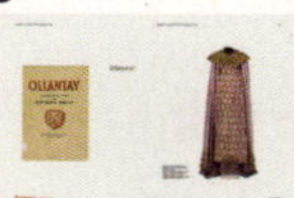

*Atlas of Andean Modernism*
2022–
Page 1939-D10
printed paper, taped to the wall; number of pages variable

Fig. 1.18
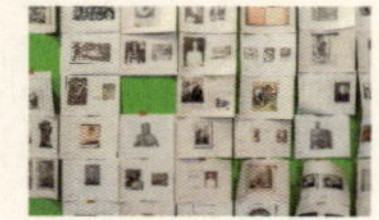
Installation view of
*Atlas of Andean Modernism*
2022–
Part of *La revolución se bajó del caballo y el caballo del muro*, Sala de Arte Público Siqueiros, Mexico City, November 2023–March 2024

Figs. 1.19, 1.20
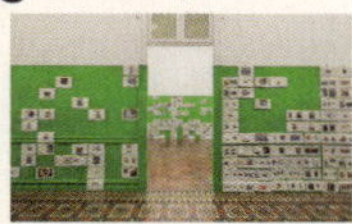
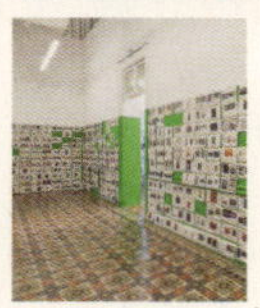
Installation views of
*Atlas of Andean Modernism*
2022–
Part of *Atlas subterráneo [1933 [1810-1983] 2020]*, 80m2 Livia Benavides, Lima, Peru, June–August 2022

GALA PORRAS-KIM
pp. 27–39

Fig. 2.1
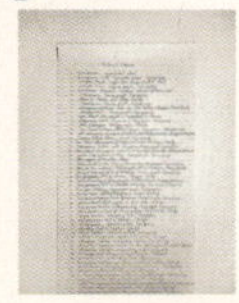
*National Treasures*
(detail)
2015
ink on paper

Figs. 2.2, 2.3
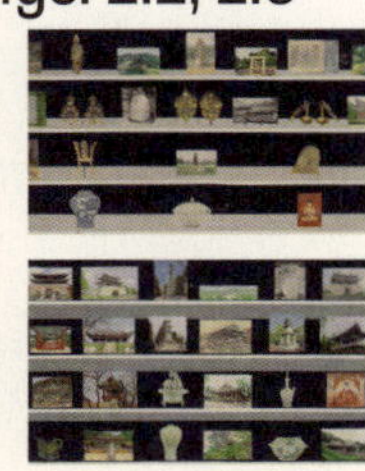
Panel 1 of 4 (details)
*530 National Treasures*
2023
colored pencil and Flashe on paper

Fig. 2.4
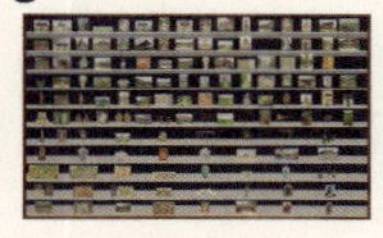
Panel 1 of 4
*530 National Treasures*
2023
colored pencil and Flashe on paper

Fig. 2.5
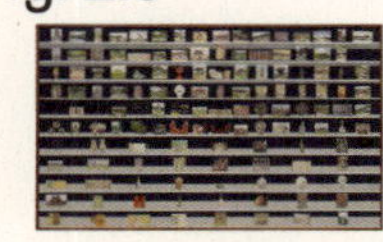
Panel 2 of 4
*530 National Treasures*
2023
colored pencil and Flashe on paper

Fig. 2.6
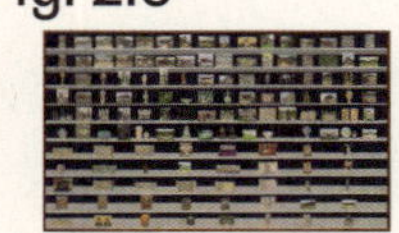
Panel 3 of 4
*530 National Treasures*
2023
colored pencil and Flashe on paper

Fig. 2.7
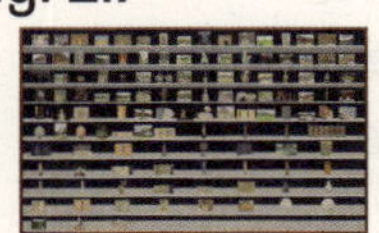
Panel 4 of 4
*530 National Treasures*
2023
colored pencil and Flashe on paper

Fig. 2.8
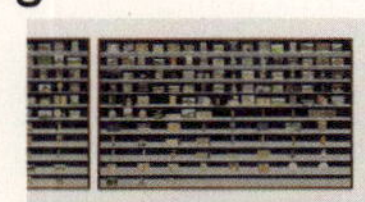
*530 National Treasures*
2023
(detail)
colored pencil and Flashe on paper

Figs. 2.9–2.11
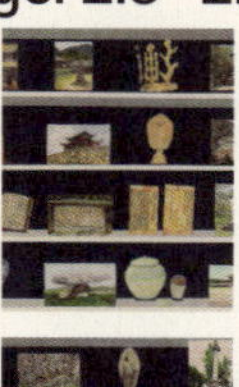
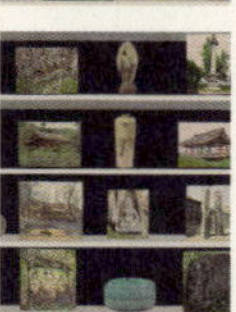
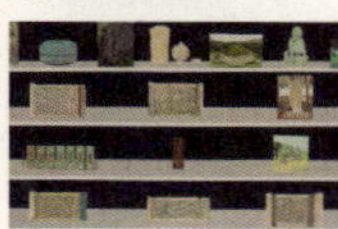
Panel 3 (details)
*530 National Treasures*
2023
colored pencil and Flashe on paper

ROSE SALANE
pp. 41–53

Fig. 3.1
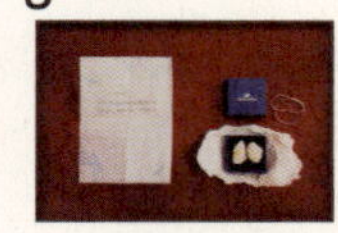
*Confession 1*
2023
chromogenic print

Fig. 3.2
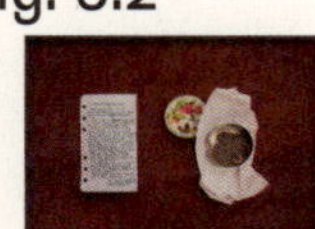
*Confession 2*
2023
chromogenic print

Fig. 3.3
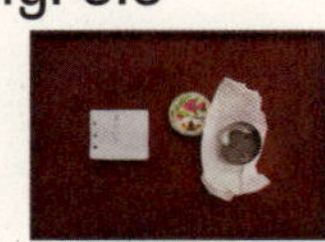
*Confession 3*
2023
chromogenic print

Fig. 3.4
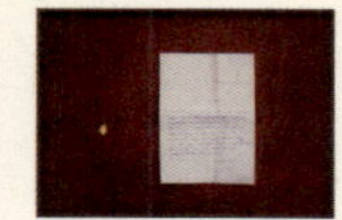
*Confession 9*
2023
chromogenic print

Fig. 3.5
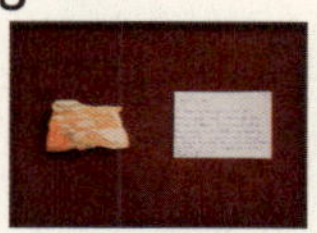
*Confession 8*
2023
chromogenic print

Fig. 3.6
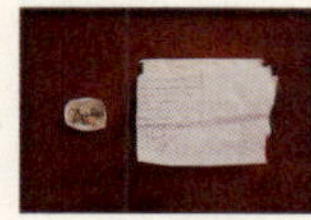
*Confession 7*
2023
chromogenic print

Fig. 3.7
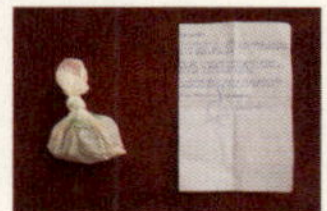
*Confession 12*
2023
(detail)
chromogenic print

Fig. 3.8
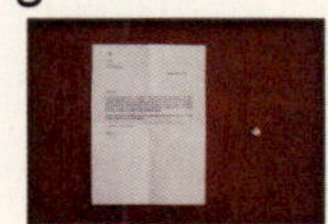
*Confession 6*
2023
chromogenic print

Fig. 3.9
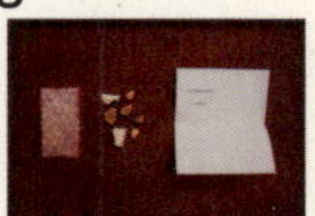
*Confession 11*
2023
chromogenic print

Fig. 3.10

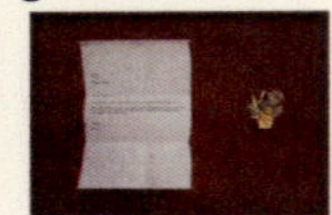

*Confession 10*
2023
chromogenic print

Fig. 3.11

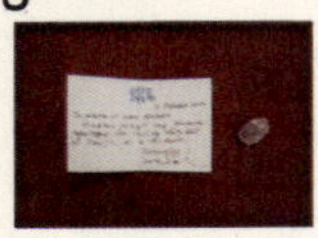

*Confession 4*
2023
chromogenic print

Fig. 3.12

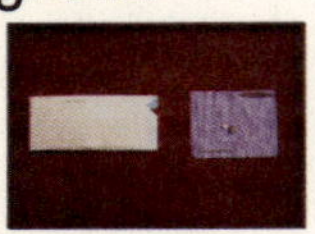

*Confession 5*
2023
chromogenic print

Fig. 3.13

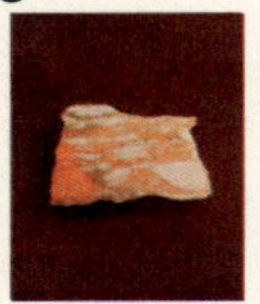

*Confession 8*
2023
(detail)
chromogenic print

Fig. 3.14

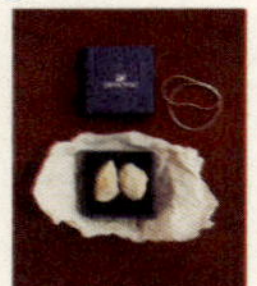

*Confession 1*
2023
(detail)
chromogenic print

Fig. 3.15

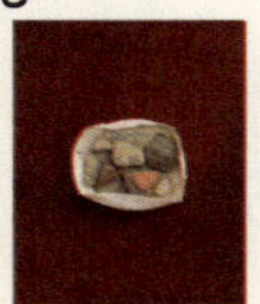

*Confession 7*
2023
(detail)
chromogenic print

Fig. 3.16

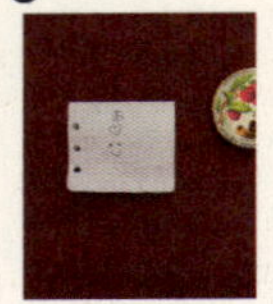

*Confession 2*
2023
(detail)
chromogenic print

CHANG YUCHEN
pp. 55–80

Fig. 4.1

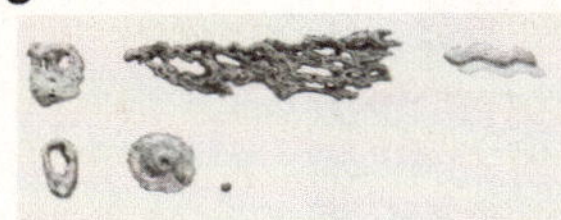

*Coral Dictionary (The surface of the sea waves in the morning.)*
2019
(detail)
pencil on paper

Fig. 4.2

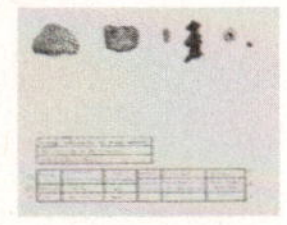

*Coral Dictionary (The vastness of the sky is unbound.)*
2022
pencil on paper

Fig. 4.3

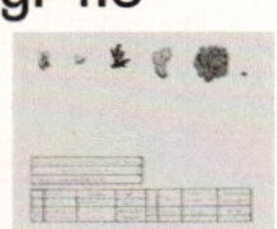

*Coral Dictionary (Cicadas' buzzing is really noisy.)*
2021
pencil on paper

Fig. 4.4

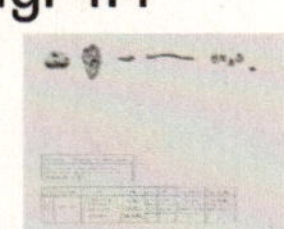

*Coral Dictionary (The sun sets in the west horizon.)*
2021
pencil on paper

Fig. 4.5

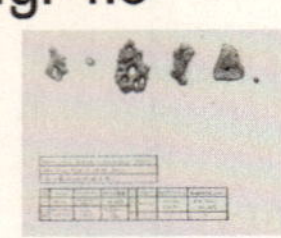

*Coral Dictionary (The dewy leaf is utterly fresh.)*
2022
pencil on paper

Fig. 4.6

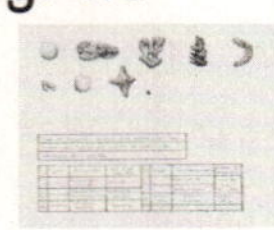

*Coral Dictionary (Natural rubber is facing serious competition from synthetic rubber.)*
2019
pencil on paper

Fig. 4.7

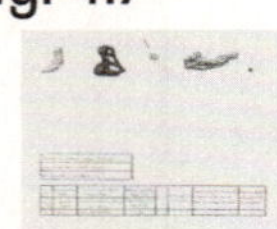

*Coral Dictionary (Put aside the dated theories.)*
2019
pencil on paper

Fig. 4.8

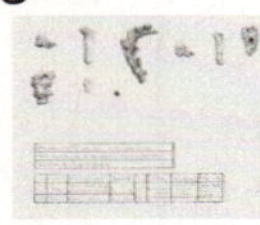

*Coral Dictionary (There are people against that proposal, there are people for it.)*
2019
pencil on paper

Fig. 4.9

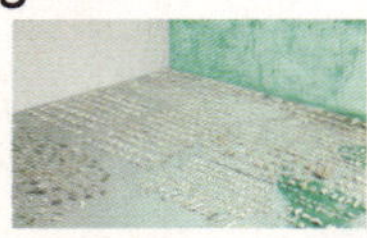

*Coral Dictionary (words)*
date unknown
found coral fragments

Fig. 4.10

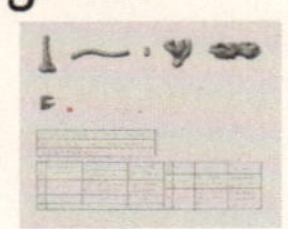

*Coral Dictionary (The end of this road is still very far.)*
2023
pencil on paper

Fig. 4.11

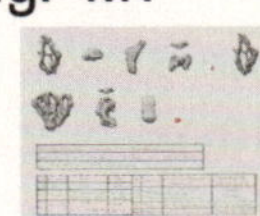

*Coral Dictionary (Debt of gold can be paid off, debt of kindness is carried over death.)*
2024
pencil on paper

Fig. 4.12

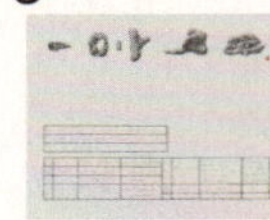

*Coral Dictionary (It's the movement of the air that causes wind.)*
2021
pencil on paper

Figs. 4.13–4.20

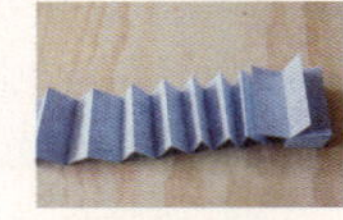

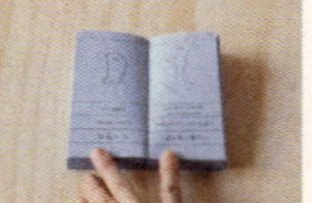

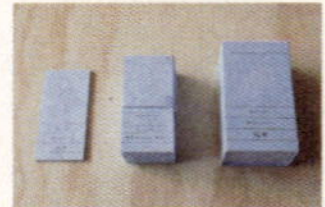

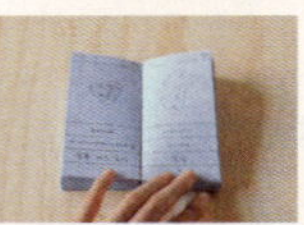

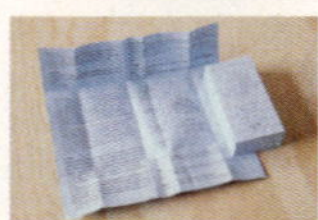

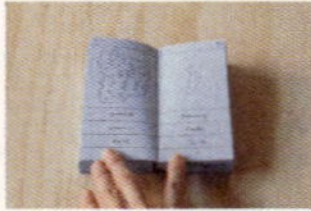

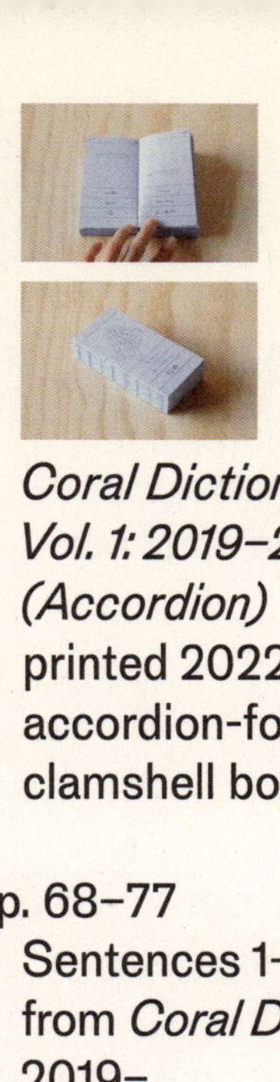

*Coral Dictionary*
*Vol. 1: 2019–2022*
*(Accordion)*
printed 2022
accordion-fold book,
clamshell box

pp. 68–77
Sentences 1–76
from *Coral Dictionary*
2019–

Fig. 4.21

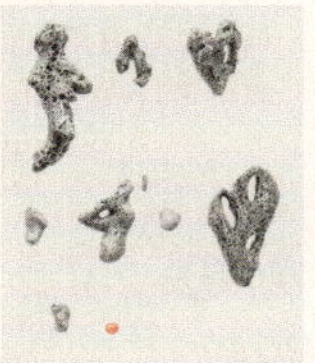

*Coral Dictionary*
*(Princess misses*
*the lost mouse deer*
*very much.)*
2022
(detail)
pencil on paper

SKY HOPINKA
pp. 105–121
Stills from
*Visions of an Island*
2016
HD video (color, sound);
15:03 min.

Fig. 6.1

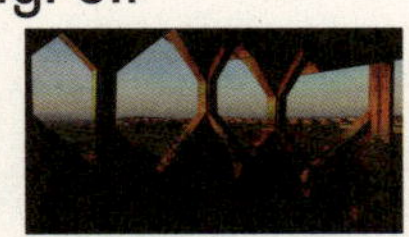

01:05

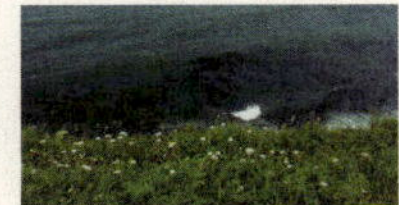

03:38

04:42

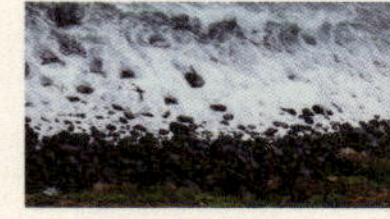

04:04

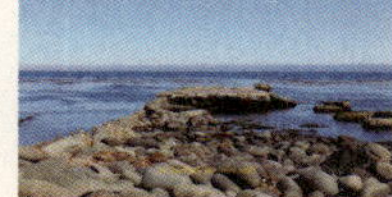

06:31

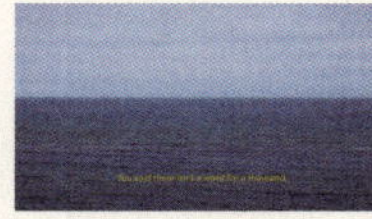

07:16

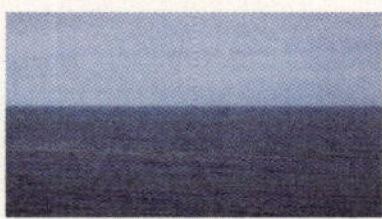

07:30

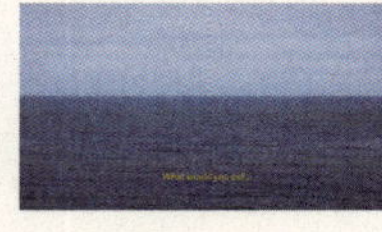

07:23

Fig. 6.2

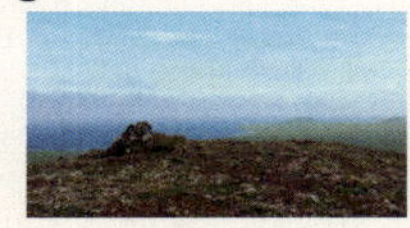

02:50

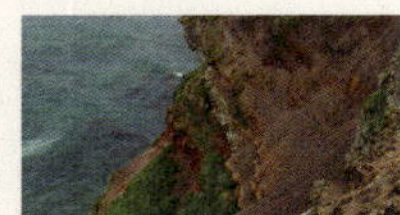

04:30

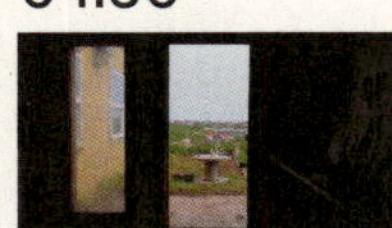

10:43

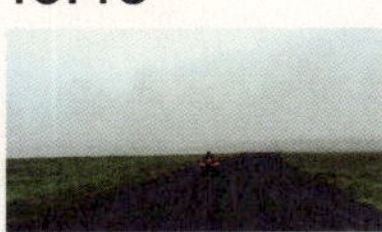

09:27

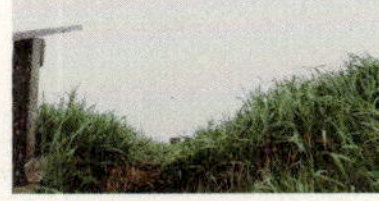

05:05

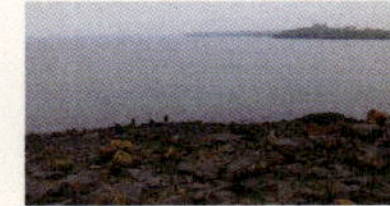

12:56

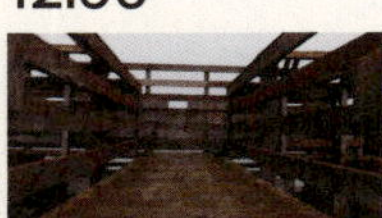

13:14

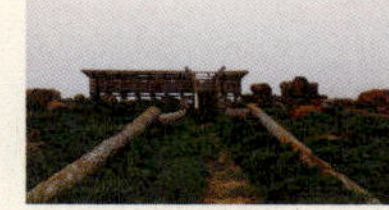

13:35

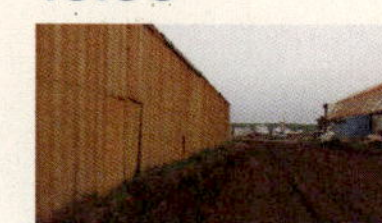

11:01

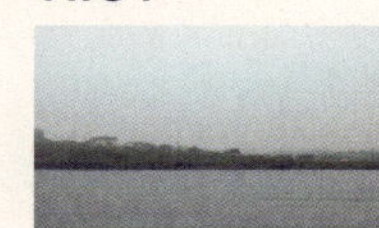

11:12

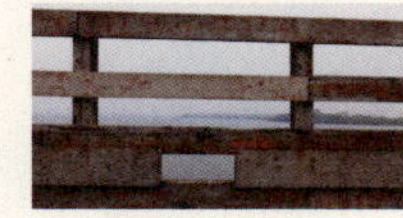

13:06

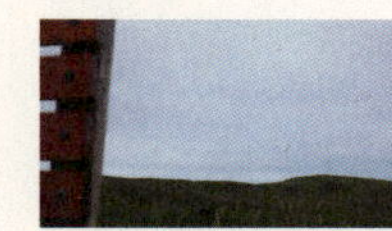

09:02

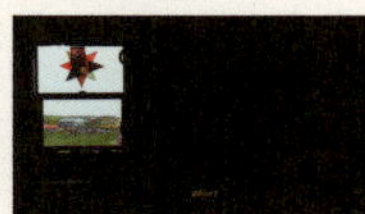

06:27

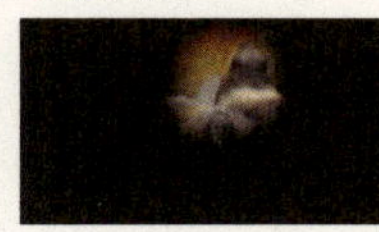

01:44

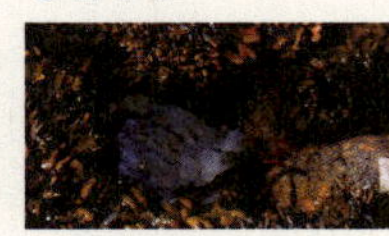

06:42

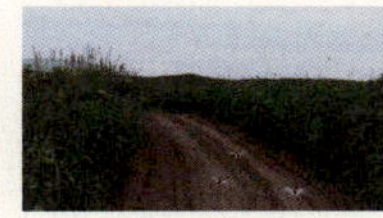

04:54

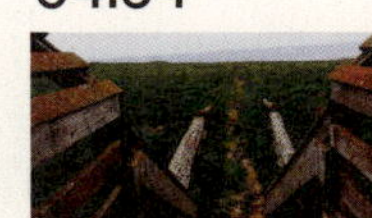

07:06

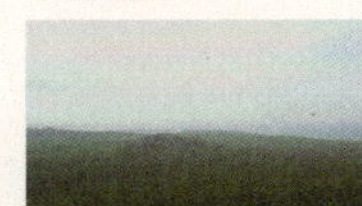

04:37

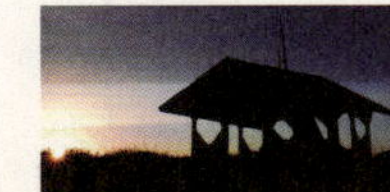

14:16

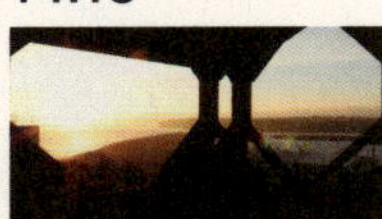

01:25

Fig. 6.3

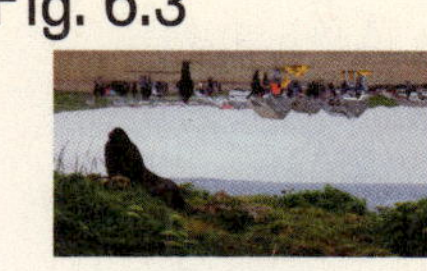

09:54

Fig. 6.4

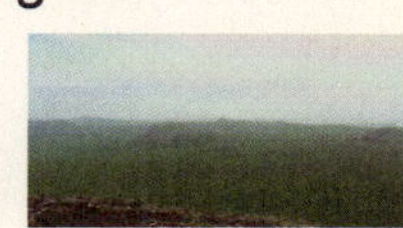

03:13

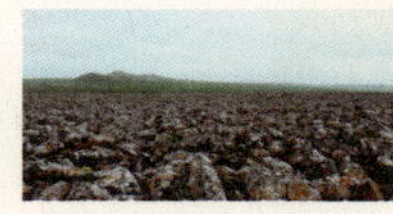

10:41

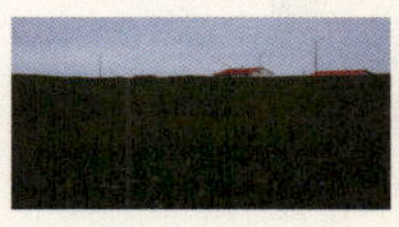

08:06

Fig. 6.5

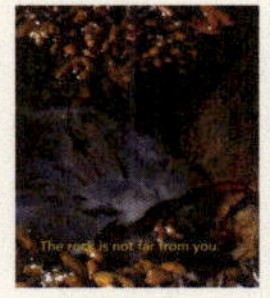

06:39 (detail)

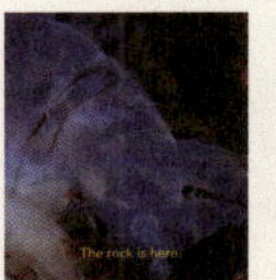

06:57 (detail)

Fig. 6.6

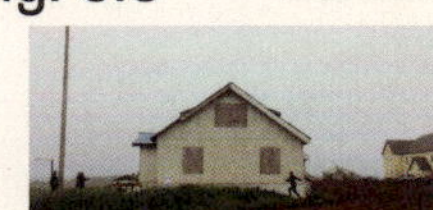

11:37

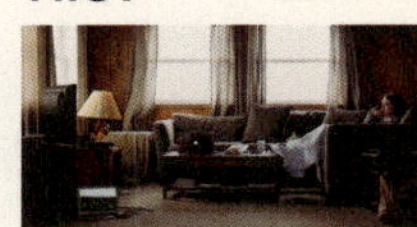

05:16

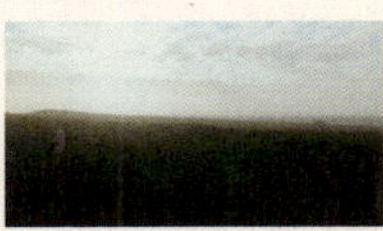

12:14

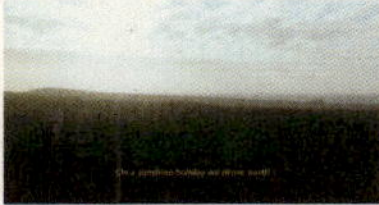

12:17

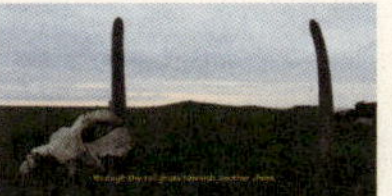

12:26

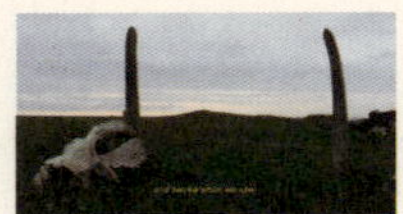

12:30

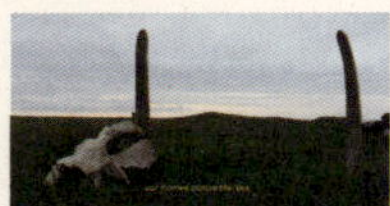

12:37

Fig. 6.7

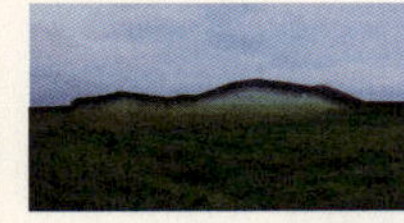

03:32 (detail)

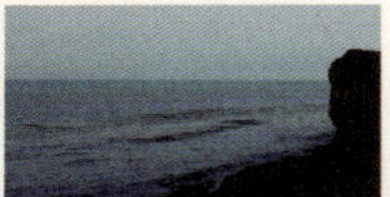

04:21

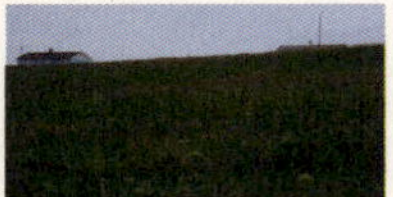

08:17

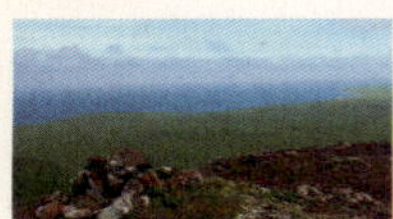

02:55

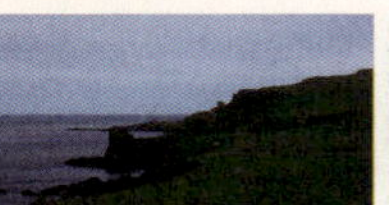

07:49

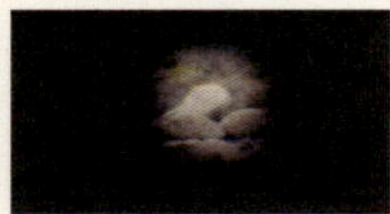

01:49

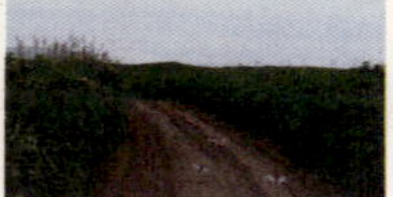

04:48

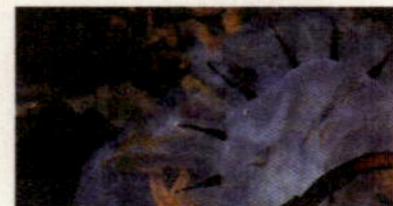

07:05

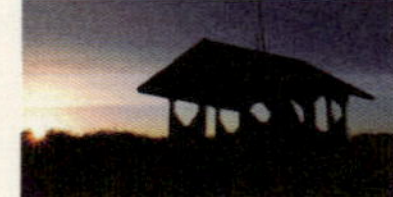

14:11

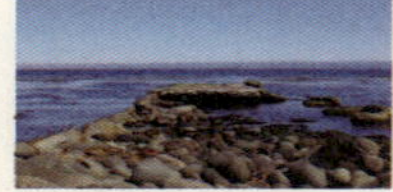

06:35

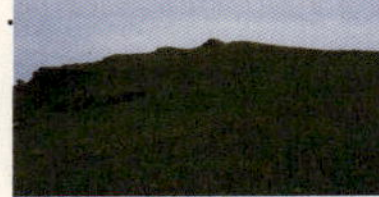

07:56

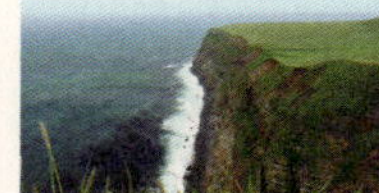

03:57

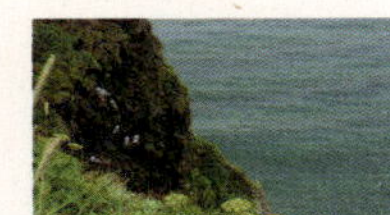

04:27

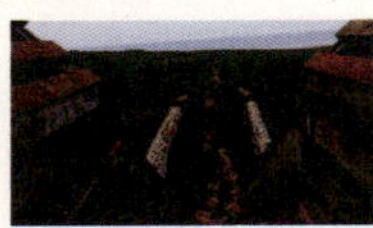

07:06

02:34

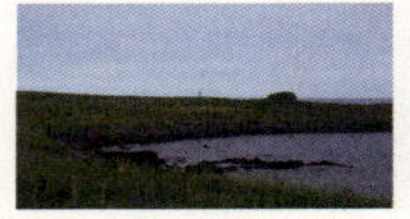

09:19

ANNA BOGHIGUIAN
pp. 123–135

Fig. 7.1

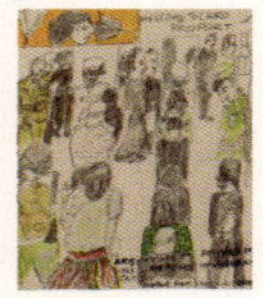

Drawing 83 (detail)
from *Time of Change*
2022
mixed media on paper

Fig. 7.2

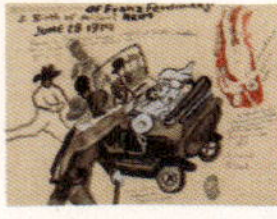

Drawing 48 from
*Time of Change*
2022
mixed media on paper

Fig. 7.3

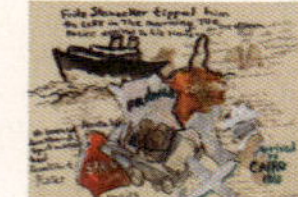

Drawing 63 from
*Time of Change*
2022
mixed media on paper

Fig. 7.4

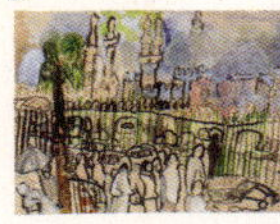

Drawing 90 from
*Time of Change*
2022
mixed media on paper

Fig. 7.5

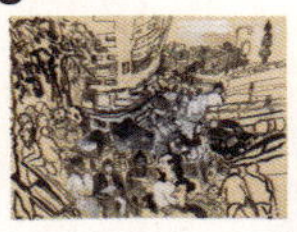

Drawing 45 from
*Time of Change*
2022
mixed media on paper

Fig. 7.6

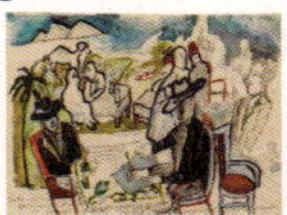

Drawing 65 from
*Time of Change*
2022
mixed media on paper

Fig. 7.7

Drawing 19 from
*Time of Change*
2022
mixed media on paper

Fig. 7.8

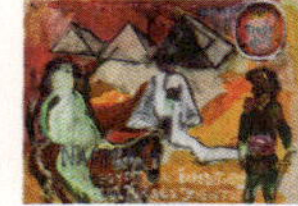

Drawing 29 from
*Time of Change*
2022
mixed media on paper

Fig. 7.9

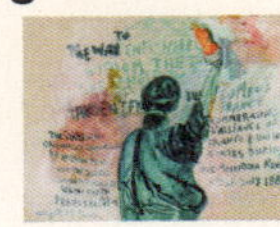

Drawing 33 from
*Time of Change*
2022
mixed media on paper

Fig. 7.10

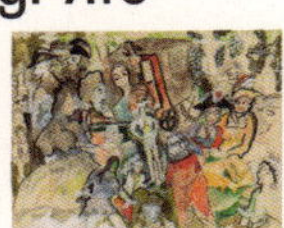

Drawing 4 from
*Time of Change*
2022
mixed media on paper

Fig. 7.11

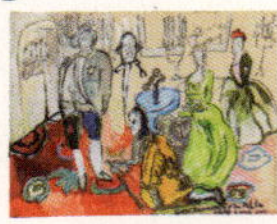

Drawing 23 from
*Time of Change*
2022
mixed media on paper

Fig. 7.12

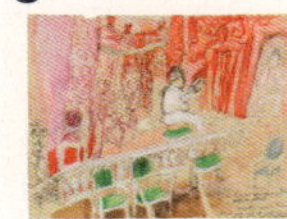

Drawing 11 from
*Time of Change*
2022
mixed media on paper

Fig. 7.13

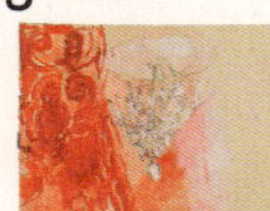

Drawing 15 from
*Time of Change*
2022
mixed media on paper

Fig. 7.14

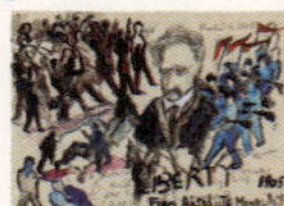

Drawing 42 from
*Time of Change*
2022
mixed media on paper

Fig. 7.15

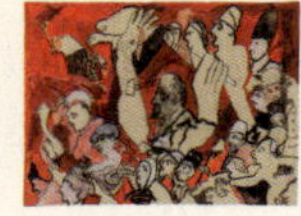

Drawing 36 from
*Time of Change*
2022
mixed media on paper

CHRISTINE HOWARD SANDOVAL
pp. 137–149

Fig. 8.1

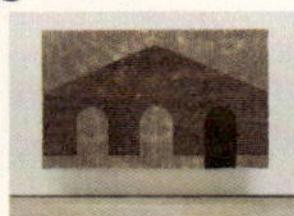

*Arch—A Passage Formed By A Curve*
2020
adobe mud and graphite on paper

Fig. 8.2

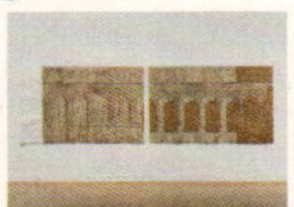

*Surface of Emergence*
2023
adobe mud and graphite on paper

Fig. 8.3

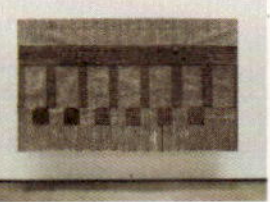

*Pillars—An Act of Decompression*
2020
adobe mud and graphite on paper

Fig. 8.4

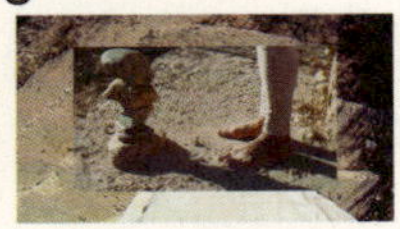

02:48 (Channel 2)

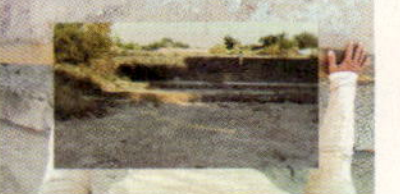

03:46 (Channel 1)

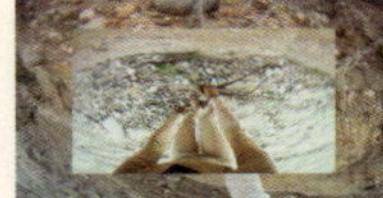

01:31 (Channel 3)

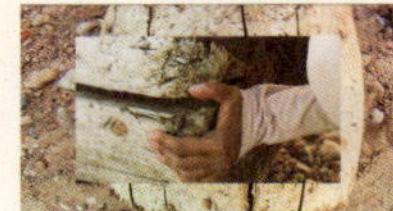

05:37 (Channel 1)

Stills from *CHANNEL*, 2017, three-channel HD video (color, sound); 07:43 min.

Figs. 8.5, 8.8, 8.9, 8.11, 8.13, 8.14

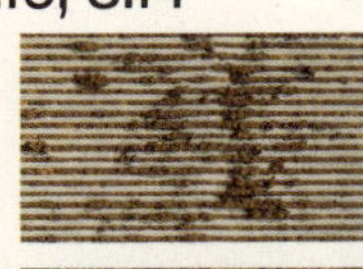

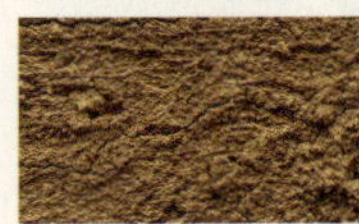

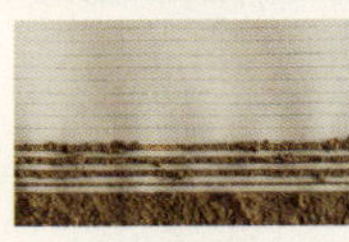

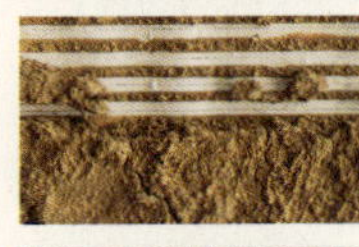

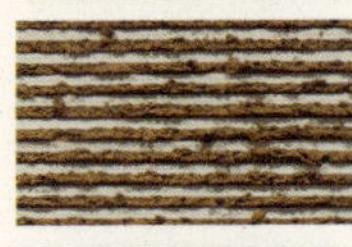

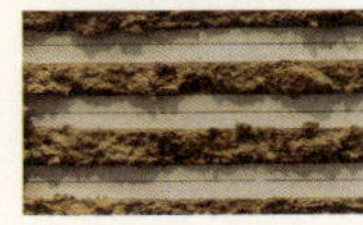

*Surface of Emergence*
2023
(details)
adobe mud and graphite on paper

Figs. 8.6, 8.7

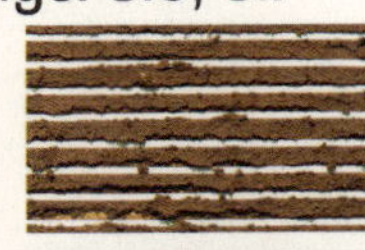

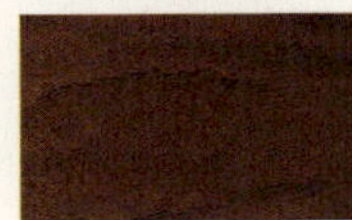

*A Wall Is A Shadow On The Land*
2020
(details)
adobe mud and graphite on paper

Figs. 8.10, 8.12

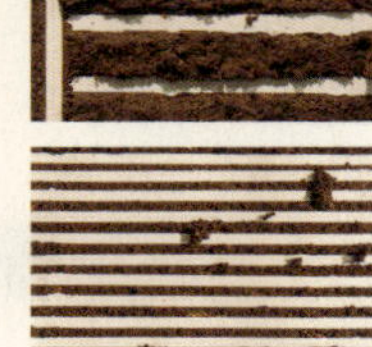

*Pillars—An Act of Decompression*
2020
(details)
adobe mud and graphite on paper

Fig. 8.15

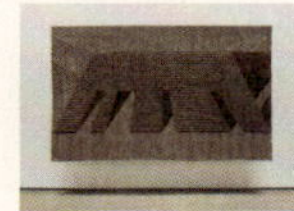

*A Wall Is A Shadow On The Land*
2020
adobe mud and graphite on paper

Fig. 8.16

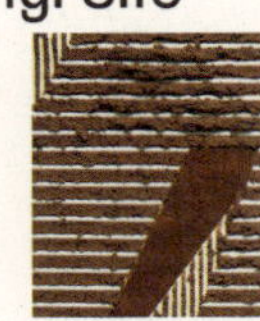

*A Wall Is A Shadow On The Land*
2020
(detail)
adobe mud and graphite on paper

SAMMY BALOJI
pp. 151–168

Stills from
*Tales of the Copper Cross Garden: Episode 1*
2017
HD video (color, sound); 42 min.

Fig. 9.1

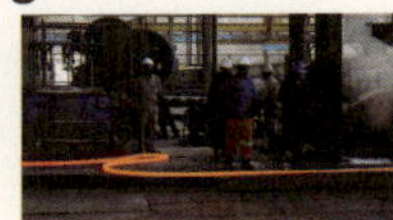

04:05

Fig. 9.2
(thumbnail gallery)
*Tales of the Copper Cross Garden: Episode 1*
2017
HD video (color, sound); 42 min.

Fig. 9.3

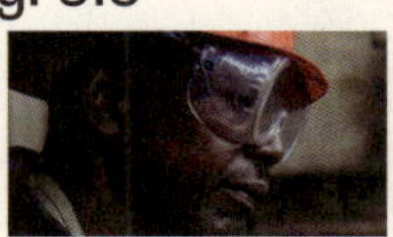

29:59

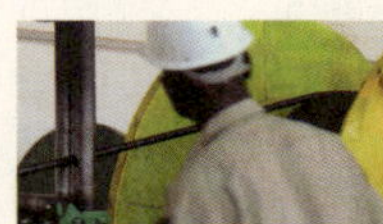

16:52

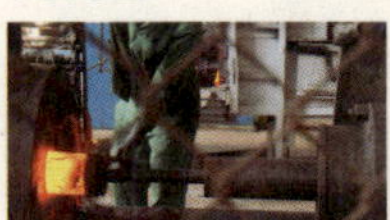

25:06

Fig. 9.4

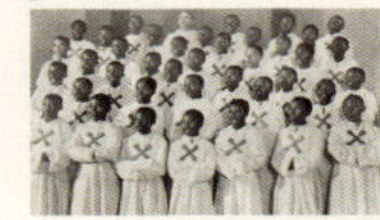

*Les petits Chanteurs à la Croix de Cuivre*
(black-and-white archival photograph)
1960
Courtesy the Royal Museum for Central Africa

Fig. 9.5

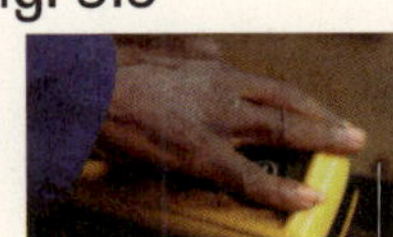

01:47

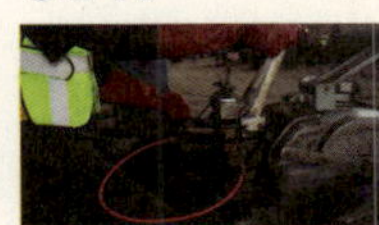

12:29

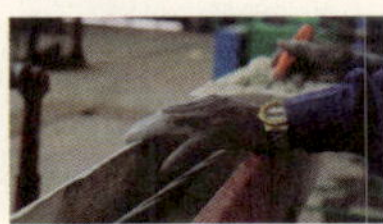

14:49

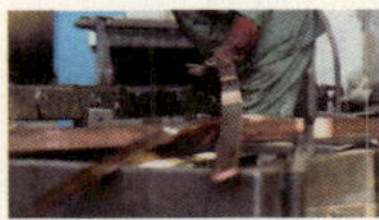

17:15

Fig. 11.7
(thumbnail gallery)
*Una voz para Erauso. Epílogo para un tiempo trans* (A voice for Erauso. Epilogue for a trans time)
2021–2022
two-channel 4K video transferred to HD video (color, sound); 28:15 min.

Figs. 11.8–11.15

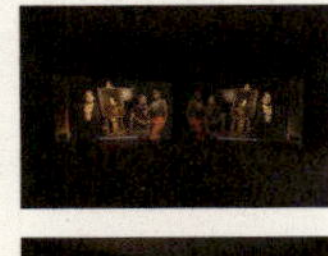

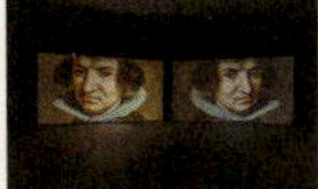

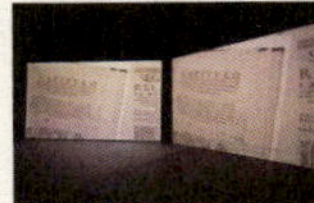

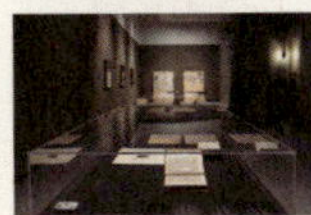

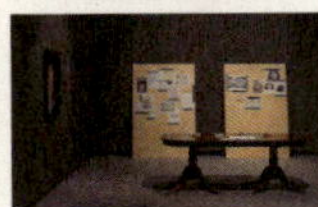

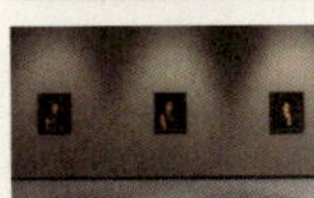

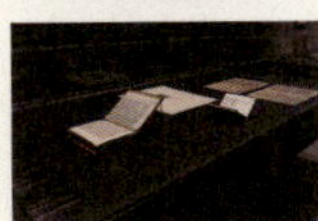

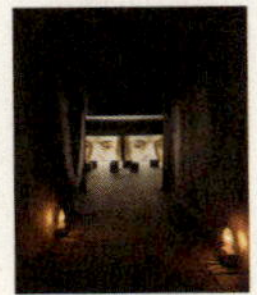

Installation views of *Cabello/Carceller: A Voice for Erauso. Epilogue for a Trans Time*
Azkuna Zentroa–Alhóndiga Bilbao, Spain
March 10–September 25, 2022

Fig. 11.16

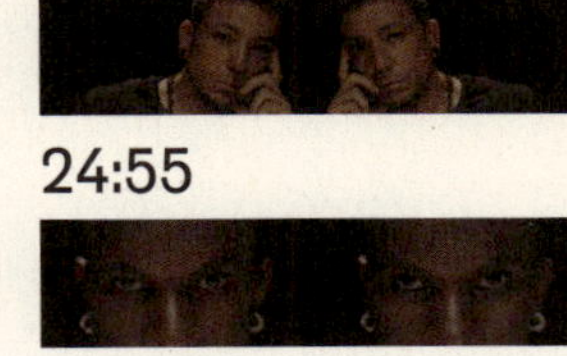

24:55

09:35

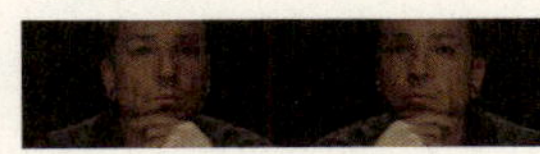

24:43

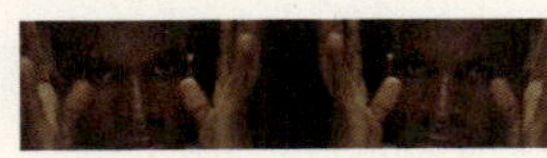

25:11

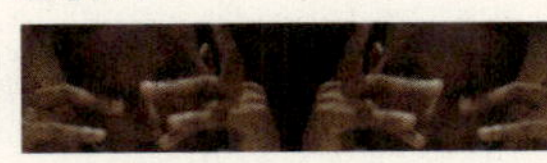

25:06

24:26

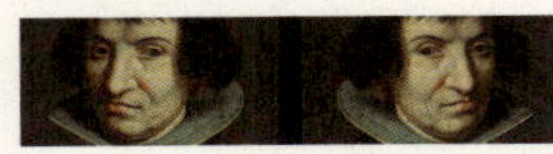

23:16

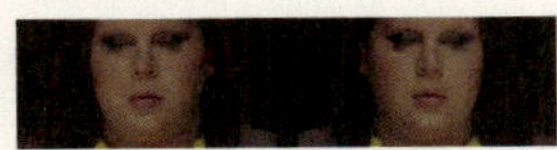

24:36

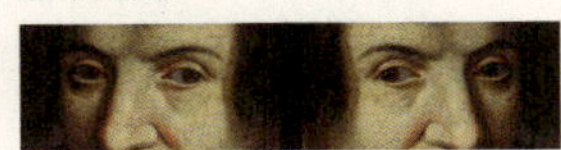

21:55

Stills from *Una voz para Erauso. Epílogo para un tiempo trans* (A voice for Erauso. Epilogue for a trans time)
2021–2022
two-channel 4K video transferred to HD video (color, sound); 28:15 min.

Figs. 11.17, 11.18

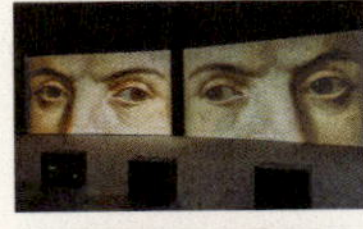

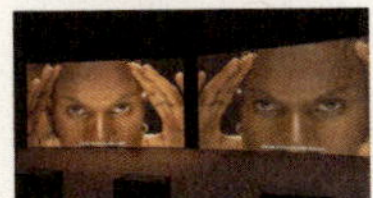

Installation views of *Cabello/Carceller: A Voice for Erauso. Epilogue for a Trans Time*
Azkuna Zentroa–Alhóndiga Bilbao, Spain
March 10–September 25, 2022

PETRIT HALILAJ
pp. 199–215

Figs. 12.1–12.3

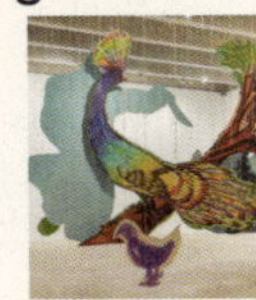

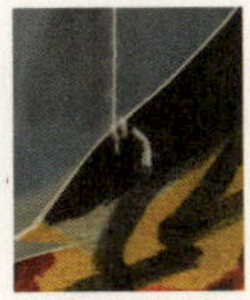

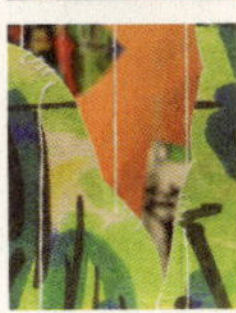

*Very volcanic over this green feather*
2021
(details)
UV-printed felt, spray-painted ink, thread, metal pipe, variable selection of up to 46 hanging elements

Fig. 12.4

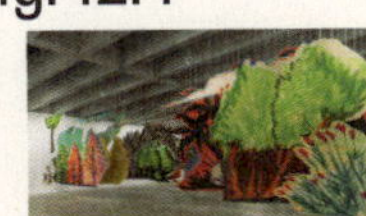

*Very volcanic over this green feather*
2021
UV-printed felt, spray-painted ink, thread, metal pipe, variable selection of up to 46 hanging elements

Figs. 12.5–12.22

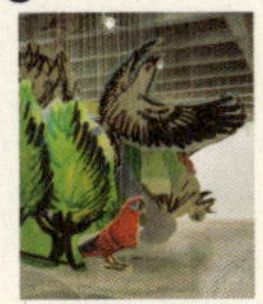

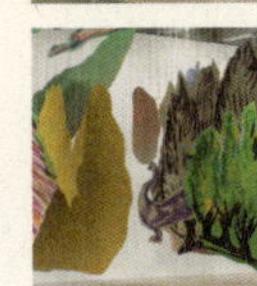

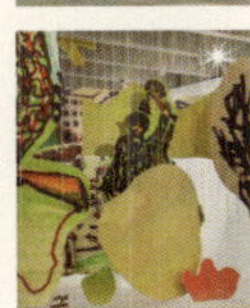

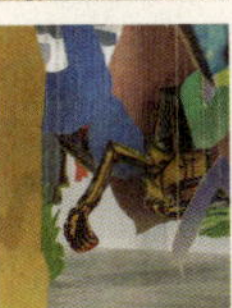

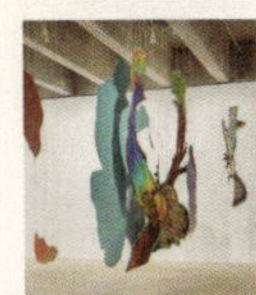

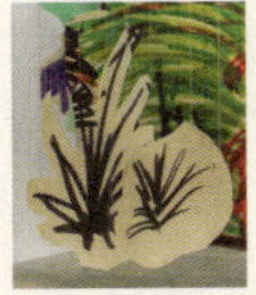

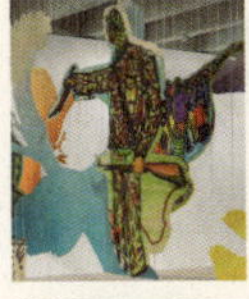

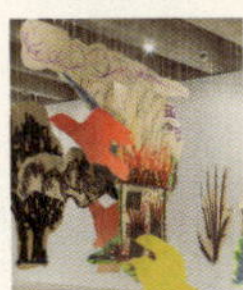

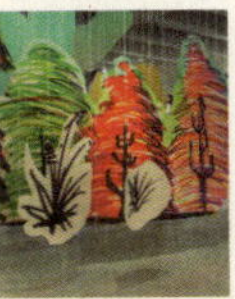

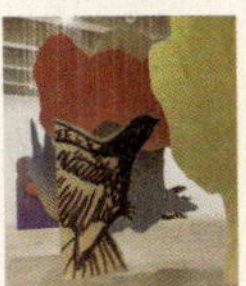

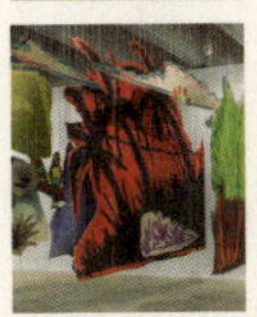

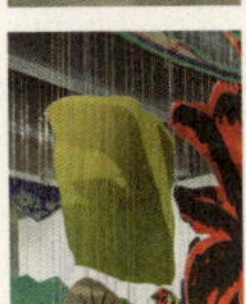

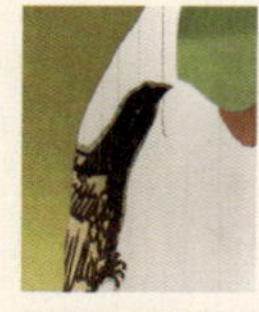
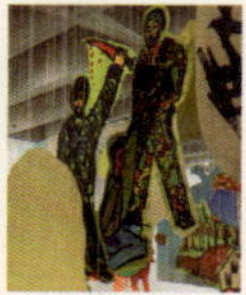
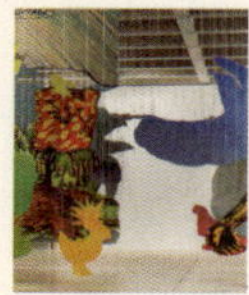
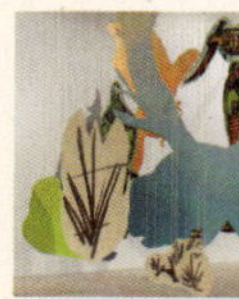
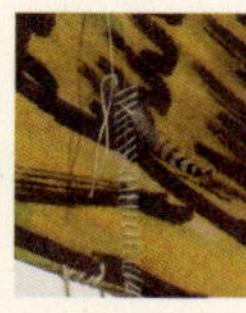
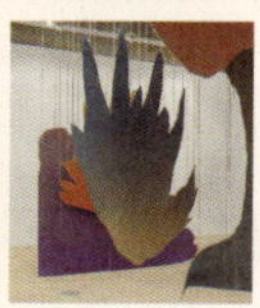

*Very volcanic over this green feather*
2021
(details)
UV-printed felt, spray-painted ink, thread, metal pipe, variable selection of up to 46 hanging elements

Figs. 12.23–12.25
Silhouettes extrapolated from the technical drawings and color sampling for the verso of Petrit Halilaj's *Very volcanic over this green feather*
2021

EDUARDO NAVARRO
pp. 217–230

Fig. 13.1
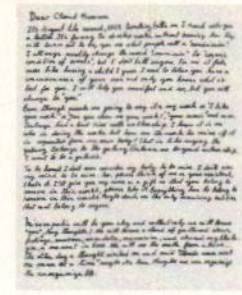
*Dear Cloud Museum (Letter to My Work)*
2024
ink on paper

Fig. 13.2
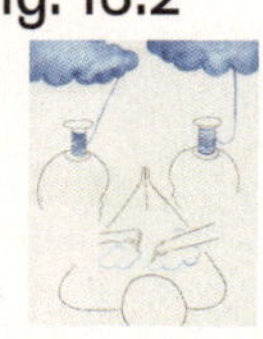
*Inner sky sketches for Cloud Museum I*
2024
watercolor and graphite on watercolor paper

Fig. 13.3
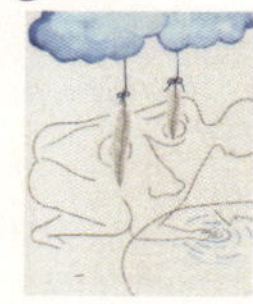
*Inner sky sketches for Cloud Museum II*
2024
watercolor and graphite on watercolor paper

Figs. 13.4, 13.5
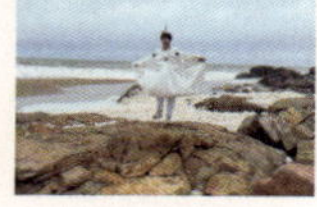
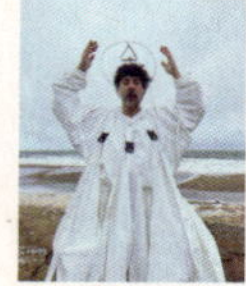
Invocation for *Cloud Museum*: visualizing an artwork that has not been done yet
August 2024
Punta Colorada, Maldonado, Uruguay

Fig. 13.6
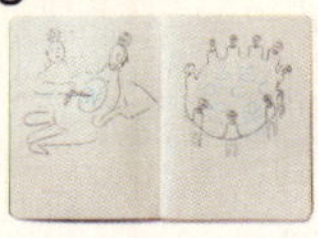
*Inner sky sketches for Cloud Museum VI and VII*
2024
colored pencil and graphite on paper

Fig. 13.7
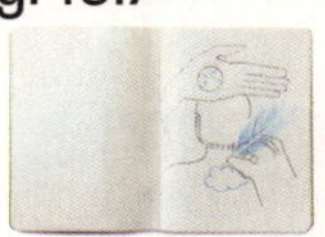
*Inner sky sketches for Cloud Museum VIII*
2024
colored pencil and graphite on paper

Fig. 13.8
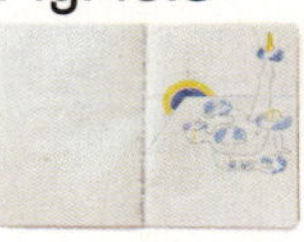
*Inner sky sketches for Cloud Museum V*
2024
colored pencil and graphite on paper

Fig. 13.9
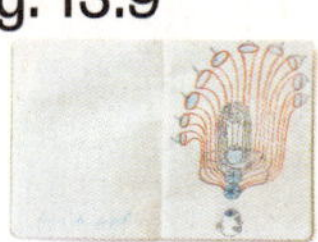
*Inner sky sketches for Cloud Museum XI*
2024
colored pencil and graphite on paper

Fig. 13.10
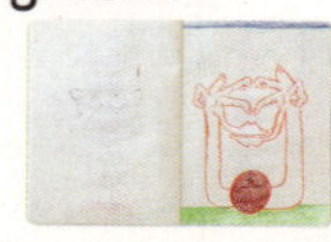
*Inner sky sketches for Cloud Museum XIII*
2024
colored pencil and graphite on paper

Fig. 13.11
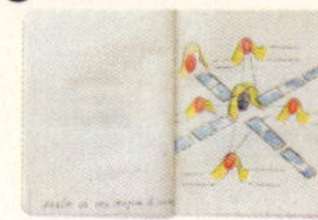
*Inner sky sketches for Cloud Museum XVII*
2024
colored pencil and graphite on paper

Fig. 13.12
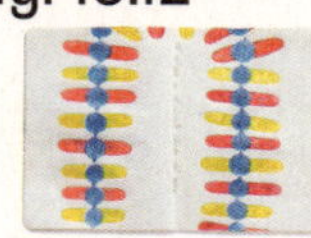
*Inner sky sketches for Cloud Museum IX*
2024
colored pencil and graphite on paper

Fig. 13.13
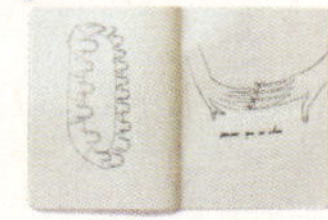
*Inner sky sketches for Cloud Museum X*
2024
colored pencil and graphite on paper

Fig. 13.14
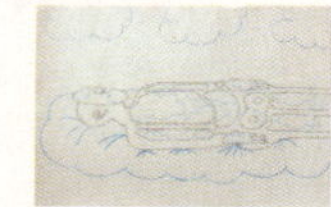
*Inner sky sketches for Cloud Museum III*
2024
colored pencil and graphite on paper

Fig. 13.15
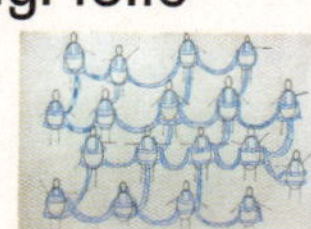
*Inner sky sketches for Cloud Museum IV*
2024
colored pencil and graphite on paper

Fig. 13.16

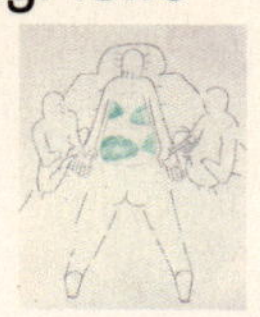

*Inner sky sketches for Cloud Museum XV*
2024
watercolor and graphite on watercolor paper

Fig. 13.17

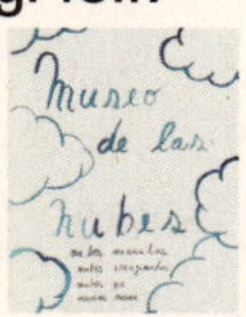


*Inner sky sketches for Cloud Museum XXI*
2024
watercolor and graphite on watercolor paper

Fig. 13.18

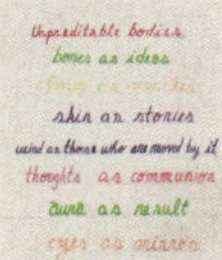


*Inner sky sketches for Cloud Museum XXII*
2024
watercolor and graphite on watercolor paper

## CONTRIBUTORS

Claire Bishop
is an art critic and Presidential Professor in the PhD Program in Art History at the Graduate Center, City University of New York.

Brandon Eng
is curatorial assistant, visual arts, at the Walker Art Center.

Nicolás Guagnini
is an artist and writer living in New York.

Rosario Güiraldes
is curator, visual arts, at the Walker Art Center.

Cuauhtémoc Medina
is an art critic, curator, and historian and former chief curator at the Museo Universitario Arte Contemporáneo in Mexico City.

Laurel Rand-Lewis
is curatorial fellow, visual arts, at the Walker Art Center.

## LENDERS TO THE EXHIBITION

Iosu Aramburu
Lima

Sammy Baloji
Lubumbashi and Brussels

Cabello/Carceller
Madrid

Chang Yuchen
New York

Forge Project Collection
traditional lands of the Moh-He-Con-Nuck

Michael Hershaft
Arlington, Virginia

Christine Howard Sandoval
Vancouver

Kutxa Fundazioa
Bilduma, Donostia/San Sebastián

Leeum Museum of Art
Seoul

Milani Gallery
Brisbane

Leopold Oetker
New York

Gala Porras-Kim
Los Angeles

Walker Art Center
Minneapolis

Private collections

## REPRODUCTION CREDITS



Page 22 (top)
Courtesy of Iosu Aramburu, 80m2 Livia Benavides, and Sala de Arte Público Siqueiros, Mexico City. Photograph by David Zamorano

Pages 22 (bottom), 23
Courtesy of Iosu Aramburu and 80m2 Livia Benavides. Photographs by Juan Pablo Murrugarra

Pages 29–37, 87 (figs. 5.6, 5.7)
Courtesy Gala Porras-Kim and Commonwealth and Council; ©Gala Porras-Kim

Pages 42–51
Images ©Rose Salane 2024, courtesy the artist, Carlos/Ishikawa, London, and the Archaeological Park of Pompeii, in the context of Pompeii Commitment: Archaeological Matters

Pages 56–67, 80, 89 (fig. 5.12)
Courtesy Chang Yuchen and Beijing Commune

Page 83 (fig. 5.1)
Courtesy Mary Kelly and Hammer Museum, Los Angeles. Gift of Eileen Norton Harris

Page 83 (fig. 5.2)
Courtesy Thomas Hirschhorn and DRAC Provence-Alpes-Côte d'Azur, Aix-en-Provence. Exhibited as part of *La Beauté* at DRAC Provence-Alpes-Côte d'Azur, Aix-en-Provence, Avignon, France

Page 83 (fig. 5.3)
Artwork ©Hans Haacke/Artists Rights Society (ARS), New York/VG Bild-Kunst, Bonn. Digital image ©Whitney Museum of American Art/Licensed by SCALA/Art Resource, NY. Purchased jointly by the Whitney Museum of American Art, New York, with funds from the Director's Discretionary Fund and the Painting and Sculpture Committee, and the Fundació Museu d'Art Contemporani de Barcelona. Inv. 2007.148x.

Page 84 (figs. 5.4, 5.5)
Courtesy the Warburg Institute

Page 87 (figs. 5.8, 5.9)
Courtesy of Iosu Aramburu and 80m2 Livia Benavides

Page 88 (fig. 5.10)
Courtesy Rose Salane and the Archaeological Park of Pompeii

Page 89 (fig. 5.11)
Courtesy Rose Salane and Carlos/Ishikawa, London ©Rose Salane

Page 91 (figs. 5.15, 5.16)
Courtesy Chang Yuchen, and Amant, New York. Photographs by Lucas Brito

Pages 94 (figs. 5.21–5.23), 124–133
Courtesy of Anna Boghiguian and Milani Gallery, Brisbane, Australia. Photographs by Markus Tretter

Page 95 (fig. 5.24)
Courtesy of Anna Boghiguian and Kunsthaus Bregenz, Austria. Photograph by Markus Tretter

Pages 95 (figs. 5.25, 5.26), 138–147
Courtesy Christine Howard Sandoval and parrasch heijnen gallery, Los Angeles

Page 97 (fig. 5.27)
Courtesy Christine Howard Sandoval. Photograph by Rachel Topham

Pages 96–97 (figs. 5.28–5.30), 152–165, 168
Courtesy Sammy Baloji and Galerie Imane Farès, Paris/Mu.ZEE, Ostend

Pages 98 (fig. 5.33), 200–207
Courtesy Petrit Halilaj; ChertLüdde, Berlin; Mennour, Paris; kurimanzutto, Mexico City/New York. Artwork ©Petrit Halilaj. Photographs ©Tate (Matt Greenwood)

Page 100 (figs. 5.34, 5.35)
Courtesy and ©Petrit Halilaj

Page 101 (figs. 5.36–5.38)
Courtesy Eduardo Navarro and Museu de Arte Contemporânea de Niterói–MAC, Rio de Janeiro. Photographs by Manoela Marini

Page 102 (fig. 5.39)
Courtesy Eduardo Navarro and Pivô, São Paulo. Photograph by Erika Mayumi

Page 102 (fig. 5.40)
Courtesy Eduardo Navarro and Frieze Art Fair. Photograph by Timothy Schenck

Page 103 (fig. 5.41)
Courtesy Forensic Architecture. More information about this investigation can be found at https://forensic-architecture.org/investigation/the-bombing-of-rafah#resources

Pages 170–171 (figs. 10.1, 10.2)
Installation views, *Encounters/Displacements: Luis Camnitzer, Alfredo Jaar, Cildo Meireles*, Archer Huntington Gallery, University of Texas, Austin, 1992. Courtesy Alexander Gray Associates, New York, ©2024 Luis Camnitzer/Artists Rights Society (ARS), New York

Page 172 (fig. 10.3)
Courtesy Menil Archives, The Menil Collection, Houston

Page 174 (fig. 10.4)
Courtesy Renée Green and Bortolami Gallery

Page 176 (fig. 10.5)
Courtesy the artist and Commonwealth and Council, ©Gala Porras-Kim. Photograph by Paul Salveson

Pages 176–177 (figs. 10.6, 10.7)
Courtesy the artist and Commonwealth and Council; ©Gala Porras-Kim. Photographs ©Museum Associates/LACMA

Page 178 (figs. 10.8, 10.9)
Courtesy TBA21 at Museo Nacional Thyssen-Bornemisza. Photographs ©Moritz Bernoully

Page 180 (figs. 10.10, 10.11)
Images of the event "Guadalupe Maravilla: Luz y fuerza Healing Sound Baths" in conjunction with the exhibition *Guadalupe Maravilla: Luz y fuerza* [MoMA Exh. #2479], November 3, 2021. MoMA Archives. Digital Image ©The Museum of Modern Art/Licensed by SCALA /Art Resource, NY. Photographs by Julieta Cervantes

Page 181 (figs. 10.12–10.14)
Courtesy Forensic Architecture and Museo Universitario Arte Contemporáneo, MUAC, 2017. Photographs by Oliver Santana

Page 183 (fig. 10.15)
Courtesy The World of Lygia Clark Cultural Association. Reference Number 21900. Photograph by Eduardo Clark

Page 183 (fig. 10.16)
Courtesy The World of Lygia Clark Cultural Association. Reference Number 20056. Photographer unknown

Pages 192 (left two columns), 193, 194
Courtesy Cabello/Carceller and Azkuna Zentroa. Photographs by Elssie Ansareo

Page 192 (right column)
Courtesy Cabello/Carceller and Azkuna Zentroa. Photographs by José Hevia

Pages 208–213
Original images courtesy Studio Petrit Halilaj

Pages 218–219, 222–227, 230
Courtesy Eduardo Navarro

Pages 220–221
Courtesy Eduardo Navarro. Photographs by Patricia Domínguez

Doug Livesay
Cuba Lopeztegui
Kaya Lovestrand
John Lyon

M
Elizabeth MacNally
Julie Magnuson
Jaidyn Martin
Michelle Maser
Dita Masters
Becca Mayo
Kirk McCall
Erin McNeil
Kyle Meerkins
Lena Menefee-Cook
Cortney Mentzos
Deborah Meyer
Aloe Miller
Laura Moran
Kaya Morris
Jeff Morrison
Chelsea Moskal
Michael Muenchow
Diane Mullen
Peter Murphy

N
Kayla Nordlund
Nastja Nykaza

O
Sherisa Oie
Mark Owens

P
Shivani Pargal
Keith Parker
YunYun Patten
Ashani Peissigma
Tim Piotrowski
Michelle Poss
Matthew Prediger
Barthollomew Presby
Sarah Purgett
Pavel Pyś

R
Laurel Rand-Lewis
Sophia Reed
Evan Reiter
Wallace Rice
Jennifer Riestenberg Pepin
Aaron Robinson
Jessica Rolland
Mark Rusch
Aster Ryan

S
Crystal Sander
Annie Schmidt
Tracy Schultz
Joel Schwarz
Morgan Seemann
Jeffrey Sherman
Gordon Silva
Tammy Smith-Foyt
Diana Soderholm
Ashley Solem
Robert Somers
Tonette Sowell
Marla Stack
Christopher Stevens
Glen Straight
Sara Suppan

T
Kim Hollingsworth Taylor

V
Jesstine Voeltz
Julie Voigt
Krista Vosper
Jill Vuchetich

W
Kazjmire Wagner
Kova Walker-Lečić
Leia Wambach
Lydia Wilkie
La'Kayla Williams
Fletcher Wolfe

Y
Ivonne Yañez
Jake Yuzna

WAYS OF KNOWING ©2025
Walker Art Center, 725 Vineland Pl.,
Minneapolis, MN 55403

WAYS OF KNOWING
Published on the occasion of the exhibition *Ways of Knowing*, curated by Rosario Güiraldes, Curator, Visual Arts, with Brandon Eng, Curatorial Assistant, Visual Arts, and organized by the Walker Art Center, Minneapolis.

Walker Art Center
March 8–September 7, 2025

*Ways of Knowing* is organized by the Walker Art Center, with major support from the KHR McNeely Family Fund, thanks to Kevin, Rosemary, and Hannah Rose McNeely; and the Martin and Brown Foundation.

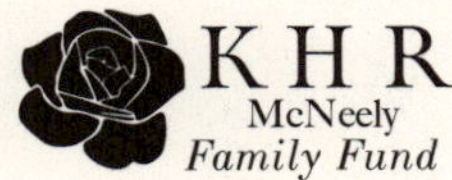


Additional support is provided by Lewis Baskerville.

The exhibition catalogue is supported by Rosina Lee Yue and a grant from the Andrew W. Mellon Foundation in support of Walker Art Center publications.



Available through D.A.P./Distributed Art Publishers, 75 Broad Street, Suite 630, New York, NY 10004
www.artbook.com

LIBRARY OF CONGRESS CATALOGING-IN-PUBLICATION DATA
Names: Güiraldes, Rosario, editor. | Bishop, Claire, contributor. | Guagnini, Nicolás, contributor. | Medina, Cuauhtémoc, contributor. | Walker Art Center, organizer, host institution.
Title: Ways of knowing/ edited by Rosario Güiraldes; contributions by Claire Bishop, Nicolás Guagnini, Cuauhtémoc Medina, Brandon Eng, and Laurel Rand-Lewis.
Other titles: Ways of knowing (Walker Art Center)
Description: First edition. | Minneapolis, MN : Walker Art Center, [2025] | Includes bibliographical references. | Summary: "Featuring works by 11 artists from 9 different countries, the exhibition Ways of Knowing highlights different ways that artists give form to complex ideas. This accompanying catalog to the exhibition highlights how some of today's most compelling artists resist conventional assumptions about how information should be gathered, documented, and shared. Bringing their own perspectives to cultural artifacts and histories, they find new narratives and possibilities within them. Some focus on the ethics of research or the connections between culture, place, and language, while others examine the impacts of colonialism across continents or the historical formation of gender identity, among other themes"—Provided by publisher.
Identifiers: LCCN 2024034110 | ISBN 9781935963325 (cloth)
Subjects: LCSH: Art, Modern—21st century —Exhibitions.
Classification: LCC N6496.M56 W359 2025 | DDC 709.05—dc23/eng/20240815
LC record available at https://lccn.loc.gov /2024034110

Head of Design, Content, and Communications
Aslı Altay

Director of Design
Mark Owens

Publications Manager
Jake Yuzna

Designer
Brian Huddleston

Editor
Karen Jacobson

Proofreader
Jennifer Boynton

Image Specialist
Sebastiaan Hanekroot
Colour and Books

Printer
Musumeci S.p.A.
Valle d'Aosta

Typeface
Ways Grotesk
Typeface designed by Brian Huddleston

Papers
Holmen Book
Munken Polar White

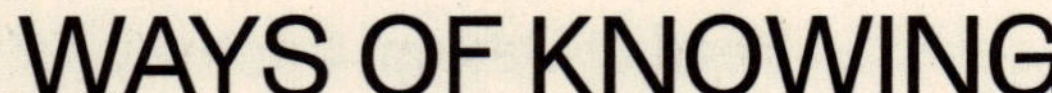
WAYS OF KNOWING

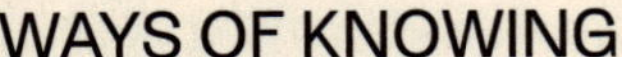